Is Rational Choice Theory All of Social Science?

Is Rational Choice Theory All of Social Science?

Mark I. Lichbach

The University of Michigan Press

Ann Arbor

Copyright © by the University of Michigan 2003
All rights reserved
Published in the United States of America by
The University of Michigan Press
Manufactured in the United States of America
♾ Printed on acid-free paper

2006   2005   2004   2003   4   3   2   1

A CIP catalog record for this book is available from the British Library.

Library of Congress Cataloging-in-Publication Data

Lichbach, Mark Irving, 1951–
    Is rational choice theory all of social science? / Mark I.
Lichbach.
        p.   cm.
    Includes bibliographical references and index.
    ISBN 0-472-09819-5 (Cloth : alk. paper) — ISBN 0-472-06819-9
    (Paper : alk. paper)
    1. Rational choice theory.   I. Title.
HM495 .L53   2003
301'.01—dc21   2002011937

For Faye, Sammi Jo, and Yossi

Most books have a foil as well as a model. They are written to criticize some books and emulate others.

—Guenther Roth

The experience of this study has certainly been that it is always helpful to attempt to understand a writer in terms of the polemical oppositions of the thought of his time.

—Talcott Parsons

Interesting philosophy is rarely an examination of the pros and cons of a thesis. Usually it is, implicitly or explicitly, a contest between an entrenched vocabulary which has become a nuisance and a half-formed new vocabulary which vaguely promises great things.

—Richard Rorty

Any cultural field involves a struggle; people with different and incompatible views contend, criticize, and condemn each other.

—Charles Taylor

It is through conflict and sometimes only through conflict that we learn what our ends and purposes are.

—Alasdair MacIntyre

True thinking is not a silent dialogue of the soul with itself, but a discussion between thinkers.

—Emmanuel Lévinas

Unanimity of opinion may be fitting for a church, for the friend or greedy victims of some (ancient, or modern) myth, or for the weak and willing followers of some tyrant. Variety of opinion is necessary for objective knowledge. And a method that encourages variety is also the only method that is compatible with a humanitarian outlook.

—Paul Feyerabend

Unanimity of opinion is a very ominous phenomenon, and one characteristic of our modern mass age.

—Hannah Arendt

And academic prophecy, finally, will create only fanatical sects but never a genuine community.

—Max Weber

Contents

Preface   xiii

Acknowledgments   xix

Part I. Foils and Stories

1. Three Approaches to Foils   3
   1.1. Rational Choice Theory and Its Foils   3
   1.2. Social Scientific Theories and Their Foils   4
   1.3. Foils in the Academy   7
   1.4. My Hope for This Book   9

2. Three Types of Stories   11
   2.1. Deep Stories   11
   2.2. Exemplar Theorists   14
   2.3. Ideal Types   16
   2.4. The Rational Reconstruction of Research Programs   18
   2.5. The Trouble with Stories: Thin and Thick
        Research Communities   19
   2.6. Typologies and Genealogies   23

Part II. The Rationalist Challenge

3. Rational/Social Choice Theory   29
   3.1. Thin and Thick Rationalists   29
   3.2. Rationalist Ontology   32
   3.3. Rationalist Methodology   33

4. Rationalism and Hegemony   41
   4.1. Why Rationalist Social Science Tends
        toward Hegemony   41

4.2. The Result: Theoretical Synthesis and Empirical
   Conciliation   48
4.3. Countertendencies: How Rationalist Social Science
   Defines Its Baselines and Boundaries   55
4.4. Countertendencies: Why Rationalist Social
   Science Lowers Its Positivistic Pretensions   64
4.5. Modest Rational Choice Theory   69

Part III. The Alternatives to Rationalist Hegemony

5. Cultural/Interpretive Theory   73
   5.1. Thin and Thick Culturalists   73
   5.2. Culturalist Ontology   78
   5.3. Culturalist Methodology   88
   5.4. Culturalist Lacunae   90

6. Structural/Institutional Theory   99
   6.1. Thin and Thick Structuralists   99
   6.2. Structuralist Ontology   102
   6.3. Structuralist Methodology   105
   6.4. Structuralist Lacunae   111

Part IV. The Debate about the Debate

7. The Need for Synthesis: Structure and Action   115
   7.1. For Synthesis   115
   7.2. Types of Syntheses   117
   7.3. Structure/Institution and Action/Process   125
   7.4. Methodological Synthesis: The Causal and
      the Interpretive   129
   7.5. The Importance of Synthesis   131

8. The Need for Analysis: Models and Foils   133
   8.1. For Models and Foils   133
   8.2. Against Synthesis   141
   8.3. Conclusion: Synthesis and Analysis   147

Part V. The Philosophy of Science

9. The General and the Particular   151
   9.1. The Research Programs   152

9.2. Weber's Approach   161
9.3. The General and the Particular in the Social Sciences   166

10. Models and Foils: A Modest Philosophy of Science for
    Social Science   168
    10.1. Theory   170
    10.2. Evidence   173
    10.3. Theory and Evidence   182
    10.4. Evaluation   194
    10.5. How a Modest Rationalist Evaluates Theory
          and Evidence   210

Notes   215

References   281

Index   313

Preface

Some years ago, the *National Interest* published an attack on rational choice theory in political science (Johnson and Keehn 1994). The rationalist bid for intellectual hegemony in contemporary social science has more recently made the pages of the *New York Times* (February 26, 2000) and the *New Republic* (October 7, 1999). And after a group of over two hundred political scientists, self-identified as Perestroika, protested the dominance of rational choice theory and quantitative methods in their discipline's flagship journal, the *American Political Science Review* (*APSR*), yet another *New York Times* article appeared on November 4, 2000.

Within the confines of the academy, the rationalists' drive for hegemony has occasioned several disciplinary crises and paradigm wars. The managing editor of *APSR* responded to Perestroika in the December 2000 issue, and the controversy filled the December issue of *PS*, a journal devoted to disciplinary matters. A hard-hitting debate occurred between rational choice theorists and area specialists (Johnson 1997; Bates 1996, 1997a). Green and Shapiro's (1994) attack on rational choice theory begot a dozen responses and a rejoinder (Friedman 1996). A review symposium (Elster 2000; Bates et al. 2000) on a rationalist treatise, *Analytical Narratives,* appeared in the *American Political Science Review.* In security studies a critique of rational choice theory by Stephen Walt begot five responses and a rejoinder (Brown et al. 2000). And in comparative politics my analysis of the rationalist challenge began a number of years ago with a co-edited book, *Interests, Identities, and Institutions in Comparative Politics,* that evolved into a series at the University of Michigan Press.

The would-be hegemons[1] make one wonder: Is rational choice theory all of social science?

I answer this question by exploring three perspectives on foils in the social sciences—*competitors* evaluate alternative research traditions, *pragmatists* do normal science in their own tradition, and *synthesizers* develop a monopolistic center encompassing all traditions—and three types of social theorists—*rationalists* explain interests, *culturalists* understand identities, and *structuralists* typologize institutions. My first theme is that the rationalist bid for hegemony and synthesis is rooted in the weaknesses not the strengths of rationalist thought. Rationalist lacunae, in other words, lead rationalists to incorporate competing paradigms—culture and structure—in a subordinate fashion. My second theme is that the rationalist attempt to subsume its opponents is based on an individualistic reduction of culture and structure. Since culturalists conceive of culture as intersubjective and structuralists conceive of structure as configurational, culturalists and structuralists will forever reject the rationalists' bid for hegemony. My final theme is that this opposition is good because social science needs multiple perspectives—competitors who advance models and foils rather than synthesizers who seek rationalist hegemony. In sum, the three research traditions studied here provide the models and foils needed by social science.

The book is organized into five parts consisting of two chapters each. Part I, "Foils and Stories," begins the discussion. Chapter 1 explores how rational choice theorists approach their opposition. Rationalists have moved, generally speaking, in the wrong direction: from competing with their opponents, to pragmatically ignoring them, and finally to synthesizing those who steadfastly refuse to yield to their hegemony. While urging a disputationalist position, the chapter also shows how these three alternatives characterize all theorists in the social sciences and in the academy.

Chapter 2 offers a preliminary exploration of the three ideal-type research communities[2] in contemporary social science, especially in sociology/historical sociology and political science/comparative politics. Rationalists, culturalists, and structuralists, for example, Robert Bates, James Scott, and Theda Skocpol, offer *deep stories.* Since such parables try to penetrate appearances and uncover the hidden secrets and invisible truths of the human condition, they justify claims to unique historical traditions, and they legitimate beliefs about doing something different from and better than one's opponents. The heterogeneous nature of research programs, however, weakens such claims and beliefs.

Part II, "The Rationalist Challenge," further explores the rationalist tradition. Chapter 3 dissects rationalist ontology and methodology. While rationalist ontology depicts a world populated by rational individuals and often irrational collectivities, rationalist methodology involves positivist comparative-static experiments that link structure to action. The chapter also argues that the rationalist research program in comparative politics and historical sociology has developed from one centered on human nature to one centered on social situations.

Chapter 4 is about rationality and hegemony. It first shows how the flaws of rationality—at the microlevel the insufficiency of reason and at the macrolevel the inadequacy of microfoundations—are the source of the rationalist drive for hegemony. The chapter then presents the synthesis that rationalist hegemons appear to want: the Coleman-Boudon microfoundation/macrostructure diagram buttressed by the socially embedded unit act. After showing why culturalists and structuralists reject such rationalist imperialism, the chapter isolates rational choice theory's more pluralistic countertendencies. Modest rational choice theorists move cautiously from thin to thick rationality, synthesizing cultural and structural alternatives into an individualistic decision calculus as they attempt to establish baselines and boundaries. And modest rational choice theorists lower their positivistic pretensions. Social science needs this modest rational choice theory, albeit one that recognizes how its opponents differ.

Part III, "The Alternatives to Rationalist Hegemony," discusses the rationalists' challengers. Culturalists (chap. 5) approach social theory differently than rationalists do because they assume that collective rules and norms constitute individual behavior. Culturalist thought comes in two versions. A subjectivist approach is closer to rational choice theory than structural theory in that it employs survey research to explore individual preferences, beliefs, and actions. *Culturalist* in this book, however, means *intersubjective culturalist.* Since my goal is to show that rational choice theory is not all of social science, I develop the latter approach to culture as the ideal-type culturalist thought; it is closer to structural theory in that it engages people and texts to explore culture in a holistic manner. Culturalist ontology thus depicts a world dominated by intersubjective meaning. Culturalist methodology consists partly of interpretive studies of meaning in which analysts try to discover the rules of social order. Culturalists, moreover, take an idiographic approach to comparison.

Structuralists (chap. 6) offer a third approach to social theory. They also have ontologies and methodologies that cannot be incorporated into rational choice theory. Structuralist ontology depicts a world dominated by relationships. Structuralist methodology consists of positivist studies of how conditions produce action and realist studies of structural dynamics. Structuralists, moreover, take a typological approach to comparison.

Part IV, "The Debate about the Debate," explores the rationalists' different perspectives on their foils. This part discusses the reasons why some rationalists compete with their opponents, why others pragmatically ignore their opponents, and why still others attempt to synthesize their opposition. But, most important, by deepening the debate about the rationalist bid for hegemony to a debate about intellectual imperialism and hegemony throughout the social sciences, it raises important issues in the philosophy of social science.

Chapter 7 draws on discussions of structure and action to explain what leads some rationalists, culturalists, and structuralists to synthesis, or to lump the alternative research traditions into one meta-approach that aims to monopolize a discipline or field. It also examines the combinations of structure and action that social scientists typically adopt: the structure-action (interests-identities, interests-institutions) and structure-structure (institutions-identities) consortia. Finally, it explores the grand structure-action coalition—interests-identities-institutions—and the structure-action and structure-structure problems of institutions and processes.

Chapter 8 draws on debates about transparadigmatic testing and evaluation to explore how some rationalists, culturalists, and structuralists are led to what I earlier called analysis, or to split research alternatives. While pragmatists work with a favorite model, do normal-science problem solving, and seek Whiggish progress within a research tradition, competitors work with competing models and foils and seek to evaluate the alternatives.

Chapters 7 and 8 thus show how the issues confronting rationalists when they face their intellectual adversaries are no different than the issues confronting other social scientists when they face their own antagonists. In order to understand the rationalist drive for hegemony, one therefore must understand that rationalists, culturalists, and structuralists face structure-action and model-foil problems.

Part V, "The Philosophy of Science," continues to deepen the debate about rationalist hegemony by exploring how contemporary philosophy of science can make sense of the paradigm debates. Chapter 9 explores the split among the three types of social theorists over the nature of generalizations in the social sciences. Rationalists are positivists who conduct comparative static exercises in which structural and cultural conditions drive general action processes. They employ a deductive-nomological or covering-law framework to demonstrate the universality of explanation: each case is understood as a particular manifestation of general laws. Structuralists are realists who study how real types of structures contain causal processes and dynamics. They employ a typological framework of explanation that classifies all cases into a set of mutually exclusive and exhaustive social kinds: each case is understood as part of a general classificatory system. Intersubjective culturalists are interpretivists who study idiosyncratic developments. They employ a highly path-dependent mode of understanding in which processes interact with one another and with particular structures, both statically and dynamically, in highly individualistic ways: each case is therefore different and unique. In sum, rationalists are universalists, culturalists are particularists, and structuralists are typologists. How, then, can the three traditions peacefully and fruitfully coexist? Weber, one sees, shows that all three perspectives are valued parts of social science. His work thus encourages multiple perspectives about the nature of generalizations in the social sciences.

Chapter 10 reinforces the Weberian exemplar by going beyond the traditional positivist philosophy of science favored by rationalist hegemons. It advances a philosophy of science for social science based on three principles. First, it argues against the positivist search for covering laws and suggests that theory is based on the conceptual nuts and bolts and causal mechanisms available in research programs. Second, it argues against the positivist search for falsification and suggests that evidence is oriented toward the applicability of concepts and laws and hence that the scope of a theory is delimited in the elaboration of the theory. Third, given that the first two principles could lead to self-serving confirmations and nonfalsifiable arguments, social scientists must evaluate their efforts. The Nazis and their supporters in German academia told a story, after all, and we need to be able to adjudicate among stories.

Different evaluative criteria apply to the three perspectives on alternative social theories. Lakatos's "additional and true" standard holds for pragmatists who wish to develop thin versions of rationality that focus on the core of rational actor theorizing. Popper's "different and better" standard holds for competitors who wish to compare baseline models of thin rationality with culturalist and structuralist alternatives. And "nested models" that combine Lakatos's and Popper's standards hold for synthesizers who wish to develop thick versions of rationality that incorporate culture and structure into an individualistic decision calculus. The different types of theorists and the different types of theories can thus compete in ways that benefit everyone.

Modest rational choice theory, in sum, abandons some of its positivistic pretensions and tries to establish its limits by moving cautiously from thin to thick rationality. Such a modest rational choice theory then concerns itself with important foils: plausible rival hypotheses against which to compare its baseline predictions and further establish its boundaries.

This is therefore a book about rational choice theory and its foils. It is also about models and foils more generally in the social sciences. It takes the rationalist bid for hegemony as an opportunity to rethink important issues in social theory and the philosophy of science. And it assumes that exploring the foundations of inquiry promotes scholarly discourse, facilitates theoretical progress, and enhances empirical work.

Acknowledgments

For many years I have been arguing a certain perspective on rational choice theory and social theory to political scientists, sociologists, economists, and anyone else who was willing to listen. While my message is the virtues of a healthy pluralism, my experience confirms the old adage "The person who stands in the middle of the road gets hit by cars going both ways."

Evaluations of a discipline do tend to be more contentious—perhaps because they involve judgment and taste about fundamentals—than evaluations of substantive work in problem domains. Books like mine are also controversial because almost every social scientist carries one in his or her heads.

I hope my readers bring the books they carry in their heads to the book that I ultimately put down on paper. Several already have. I wish to thank Robert Bates, Jeffrey Kopstein, Peter Lange, David Mapel, Michael McGinnis, James Scarritt, James C. Scott, Adam Seligman, Sven Steinmo, Nina Tannenwald, and Alex Wendt; the participants in the May 1996 Brown University conference "Interests, Identities, and Institutions in Comparative Politics"—Samuel Barnes, Peter Hall, Ira Katznelson, Margaret Levi, Joel S. Migdal, Marc Howard Ross, Sidney Tarrow, and Alan Zuckerman; Barbara Geddes and the audience at the two panels on Theory in Comparative Politics at the 1996 Annual Meetings of the American Political Science Association, San Francisco; the participants in the May 2000 Mershon Center conference on Theories and Evidence—Steven Bernstein, Stephen Hanson, Rick Hermann, Ted Hopf, Jack Levy, Ned Lebow, Brian Pollins, Burt Rockman, Janice Stein, and Steve Weber; and the University of Colorado graduate students in my 5075 course, Introduction to Political Science, for their lively and provocative comments on earlier versions of this material.

I especially wish to thank Jeremy Shine, my wonderful editor at the University of Michigan Press. He solicited extremely insightful and valuable referee reports and then offered excellent advice about a response. I therefore wish to thank Kurt Weyland, Herbert Kitschelt, and an anonymous reviewer for their help in improving this work. My copy editor, Ilene Cohen, improved my prose considerably.

Part of this material appeared in my essay "Social Theory and Comparative Politics," in *Comparative Politics: Rationality, Culture, and Structure,* edited by Mark Irving Lichbach and Alan S. Zuckerman (Cambridge: Cambridge University Press, 1997) and is reprinted here with the permission of Cambridge University Press. Other material is taken from my books *The Rebel's Dilemma* (Ann Arbor: University of Michigan Press, 1995) and *The Cooperator's Dilemma* (Ann Arbor: University of Michigan Press, 1996). I also borrowed some material from my work with Adam Seligman, *Market and Community: Social Order, Revolution, and Relegitimation* (University Park: Penn State University Press, 2000). Matching wits with Adam, my culturalist interlocutor, has been one of the delights of my academic career.

Part I

Foils and Stories

Chapter I

Three Approaches to Foils

Chapter 1 offers a new way to understand intellectual opponents. I explore rational choice theory and its foils (sect. 1.1), social science theories and their foils (sect. 1.2), and foils in the academy (sect. 1.3). I then elaborate my hopes for this book (sect. 1.4).

1.1. Rational Choice Theory and Its Foils

Rational choice theorists in political science have passed through three phases in approaching their opposition—the culturalists who study values and the structuralists who explore institutions.

In the beginning, when their paradigm was underdeveloped, rationalists viewed their opposition as worthy foils, serious alternatives for explaining the world. Anthony Downs (1957) and Mancur Olson (1971), the key developers of the spatial theory of voting and of collective action theory, respectively, sought to win a seat for rational choice theory at the political science table. Brian Barry (1978), for another example, argued that rationalist theories were different from and better than the hegemonic culturalist alternatives. In the middle phase, when the power of such nuts and bolts as the Prisoner's Dilemma and spatial games became clear, rationalists came to view their foils pragmatically as irrelevant and thus not worth engaging. Rationalists were only interested in getting important results and running with them. Thus Downs's (1957) followers McKelvey (1976) and Shepsle (1979) elaborated spatial theory, and Olson's (1971) followers Taylor (1976) and Axelrod (1984) elaborated collective action theory. And rational choice institutionalists North and Weingast (1989) analyzed the Glorious Revolution without exploring such competing historiographic claims as Skocpol's (1979) structuralism.

Nonetheless, even as rational choice theory now reaches the peak of its intellectual dominance in political science, it has not vanquished its opponents. Indeed, Green and Shapiro (1994) and others have mounted stinging counterattacks. Militant antipositivists marching under the banners of interpretivism, constructivism, and postmod-

3

ernism have created a conflict dynamic of movement-countermovement in which the sides dig in their heels. Unable to kill off its opponents, a third perspective has thus emerged within rational choice theory—that its foils are companions to be synthesized. Bates, de Figueiredo, and Weingast thus "explore the possibilities for theoretical integration by suggesting how some of the fundamental concepts used by interpretivists can be incorporated into rational choice theory" (1998, 606). Levi, Ostrom, and Alt predict success: "We expect the next century to witness a major flowering of scientific achievement across the social sciences similar to the neo-Darwinian synthesis of this past century in biology" (1999, 337).

Having accommodated culturalists by incorporating social norms and structuralists by incorporating institutions into an individualistic decision calculus, rationalists appear to be claiming that rational choice theory now constitutes the entirety of social science. If rational choice theory can indeed provide the microfoundations for a new intellectual center in political science, what need is there for other types of theories? Wallerstein, for example, writes that "the only theory in comparative politics today that is sufficiently powerful and general to be a serious contender for the unified theory is rational choice" (2001, 1). And if rational choice theory is all of social science (a generalization of Stinchcombe 1980), what need is there for other types of social scientists? Coleman (1990), a prominent sociologist, attempts to show that rational choice theory can explain just about everything in economics, sociology, political science, anthropology, psychology, and history. Sociologist Collins thus poses the question: "Can rational action theory unify social science?" (1996, 329).

How rationalists approach their opponents—whether in terms of competition, pragmatism, or synthesis—affects the extent to which peace and progress prevail in the social sciences. In exploring these alternative approaches to intellectual foils, this book seeks to evaluate how rationalists grapple with academic opponents who stubbornly refuse to submit to their hegemony.

1.2. Social Scientific Theories and Their Foils

Although I write from the perspective of a rational choice theorist, I develop the important subtheme that culturalists and structuralists relate to other research communities just as rationalists do. That is, social scientific communities of all stripes—not just rationalists—have their competitors who pick fights with their opponents, their pragmatists who ignore other approaches, and their imperialists who claim that their approach is the totality of social science.

More generally, as table 1.1 shows, the intellectual history of social science can be said to begin and end either with one or with multiple theories, and hence three metanarratives are possible (Levine 1995). Pragmatists are Whigs who believe that social science progresses from one theory to a better version of that theory. Synthesizers are lumpers who believe that social science progresses from many starting points to one higher end point, from pluralism to monopoly. Competitors reject the idea of unilinear progress and emphasize pluralism, dialogue, and diversity. They argue that internal factors (e.g., specialization and the division of labor) and external forces (e.g., trends, cycles, and shocks) move disciplines and fields from one or many starting points to several end points. Competitors come in two varieties: splitters believe that inquiry moves from one theory to many theories, and relativists argue that social science is in eternal unresolvable flux.

Most social scientists are myopic pragmatists concerned only with their own research community. They work with one model paradigm and ignore their foils. For MacIntyre (1990), the use of models as a form of theory is "tradition"—a community's conversation, a debate with the past that is oriented toward the future to produce an understanding of a community's successes and failures, achievements and frustrations, and ultimately its scope and limitations. Pragmatists strive for "normal"—liberal or Whiggish—scientific progress within their particular research tradition.

Parsons (1937), by contrast, was the visionary lumper who attempted to move sociology beyond Durkheim, Weber, Pareto, and Marshall and toward a single synthetic paradigm—his own. As Eckstein's (1963) classic survey revealed, many comparativists followed his attempt to create a single voluntaristic theory of action out of theoret-

TABLE 1.1.   Social Science Metanarratives

		End	
		One Theory	Many Theories
Begin	One Theory	Whiggish progress (Pragmatists)	Competition (Competitors—Splitters)
	Many Theories	Synthetic monopoly (Lumpers)	Competition (Competitors—Relativists)

ical chaos.[1] Synthesizers believe that rationalists, culturalists, and structuralists hold important assumptions that are consistent with one another and that the different models can be complementary or part of a more general model. They thus emphasize the interpenetration of rationality, culture, and structure; the convergence among research communities toward a single center; and hence the accumulation of knowledge that culminates in tests of a single explanation of some domain, problem, or puzzle. MacIntyre (1990) aptly calls this form of theory "encyclopedia." It aims to provide a single unified framework that is objectively true and hence uniting and universal. Sometimes the synthesis comes from a consortium of different research communities and sometimes from what amounts to the same thing: a very thick version of one hegemonic community.

A recent symposium on theory in comparative politics (*World Politics* 1995) also stressed the value of synthesis toward a disciplinary center. Comparativists were told that they should work toward "the eclectic messy center that has constituted the traditional core of the study of comparative politics." Indeed, the consensus among the symposium's participants was that it is good to be part of the consensus: most should practice "theoretically informed empirical political analysis" and adopt "diverse conceptual lenses" and "eclectic combinations." Since "comparative politics is very much a problem-driven field of study" concerned with solving "real-world puzzles," comparativists should be interested in "questions" and "empirical puzzles" (2, 5, 46, 10). Most comparativists today indeed stress the virtues of what Almond refers to as "the great cafeteria of the center" and emphasize the dangers of "separate tables" (1990, 16).

Structuralist theories continue to dominate the field of comparative politics. Yet the rationalists, like the barbarians at the gate, are coming, and the postmodern culturalists are not far behind. The participants in the *World Politics* symposium apparently feared the struggle that might ensue. Perhaps some feared rationalist and culturalist challenges to their intellectual hegemony.

Lying outside this consensus, at least at one point in the past, was Harry Eckstein, who stressed the alternative of working with models from a strong research community. Along with Gurr (Eckstein and Gurr 1975) he developed a framework of "authority patterns" that was intended to train graduate students in comparative politics. Eckstein (1980) also recognized the value of foils, or crucial confrontations between distinct research traditions, especially between rationalist and culturalist theories. He advanced, for example, an "explanation sketch" or "ideal type" approach to competing theories of protest and rebellion.

Dahrendorf (1958) was also a splitter or even a relativist who saw Marxist and functionalist theories locked in a fundamental struggle. One may say that today's reemergence of multiple perspectives in social theory—rationalist, culturalist, and structuralist—represents the failure of the Parsonian synthesis and the return to the issues raised by Dahrendorf. The competitors' approach to social theory maintains that different perspectives hold fundamentally incompatible assumptions that are, in the economic sense, substitutes and not complements. Splitters thus emphasize the differentiation of rationality, culture, and structure; the divergence among research communities; and hence the contrast that culminates in competitive evaluations and even crucial experiments. MacIntyre (1990) calls the use of foils a form of theory "genealogy," which involves acknowledging multiple perspectives on truth.[2]

In sum, in social science today one finds three alternative perspectives on foils: competitors (splitters or relativists) probing the rationalist, culturalist, and structuralist research programs, pragmatists doing normal science, and lumpers developing a monopolistic center.

1.3. Foils in the Academy

While competition, pragmatism, and synthesis can offer three valuable perspectives on the multiple research communities in the social sciences, each can degenerate into intellectual folly.

Those who adopt a competitive perspective can reify the debate and hence contribute to irreconcilable confrontations. Such skirmishes, moreover, can degenerate into intolerance and ultimately war—a battle of the paradigms. Those who adopt the pragmatic perspective can ignore paradigmatic debates and create an isolated and insular cult seeking to become a hegemonic center. Searching for a very deep story within one's research tradition can lead scholars to the monotheistic conclusion that there is only one story to be told and hence only one intellectual path to be taken. Finally, those who adopt the synthetic perspective can transcend the debate and contribute to a messy center. Combinations of the three approaches can be ad hoc. Syntheses can ignore fundamental differences in ontology, methodology, and research strategy, resulting in theories that may be congruent with the real world but only because they are as messy and incoherent as that world.

Competitors, pragmatists, and lumpers nevertheless have valid places in the academy, despite the threat of degeneration. Consider MacIntyre's view of the university

> as a place of constrained disagreement, of imposed participation in conflict, in which a central responsibility of higher education would be to initiate students into conflict. In such a university those engaged in teaching and enquiry would each have to play a double role. For, on the one hand, each of us would be partici- pating in conflict as the protagonist of a particular point of view, engaged thereby in two distinct but related tasks. The first of these would be to advance enquiry from within that particular point of view. . . . The second task would be to enter into contro- versy with other rival standpoints, doing so *both* in order to exhibit what is mistaken in that rival standpoint in the light of the understanding afforded by one's own point of view *and* in order to test and retest the central theses advanced from one's own point of view against the strongest possible objections to them to be derived from one's opponents. . . . On the other hand, each of us would also have to play a second role, that not of a partisan, but of someone concerned to uphold and to order the ongoing conflicts, to provide and sustain institutionalized means for their expression, to negotiate the modes of encounter between oppo- nents, to ensure that rival voices were not illegitimately sup- pressed, to sustain the university . . . as an arena of conflict in which the most fundamental type of moral and theological dis- agreement was accorded recognition. (1990, 330)

Self-interest and the public good, in this account, dictate that some social scientists be pragmatists who advance claims from within their own tradition; that others be competitors who dispute claims from competing traditions, maintaining sufficient "ethical neutrality" and distance from any tradition so as to be able to listen to and react against alternative traditions; and that still others be lumpers who monitor the discourse among traditions and communities so as to assure an open and honest dialogue that identifies points of conver- gence.

A sophisticated understanding of political science, social science, and the academy thus leads to a healthy disputationalist position. Each perspective on foils, that is, has its scholarly value. Rational choice the- orists, the current contenders for hegemony, would do well to make more effective use of competing research frameworks: by ignoring their opponents and developing their approach as a *baseline model with boundaries;* by viewing their opponents' arguments as *worthy foils;* and by offering a *candidate synthesis* to resolve the tension between model and foil. The results are nested models to be evaluated against the evidence. Thus, as I will argue in the concluding chapter, rational choice theory needs a philosophy of science oriented toward competitive theory evaluation to complement a philosophy of social science oriented toward alternative rationalist, culturalist, and structuralist theories.

1.4. My Hope for This Book

My assumption throughout this book is that all research is conducted within a framework of theories, concepts, and methods and hence that theoretical criticism assists concrete empirical work. A more critical understanding of these frameworks—referred to as social theory—is therefore an important way to elaborate, reformulate, and extend substantive insights.[3] Indeed, the only way to overcome the trained incapacities produced by outdated philosophies of science and social science that twist us into knots (e.g., the microfoundation trap discussed in sect. 4.1.2) is to strive for a more secure philosophical foundation for what we do. Rationalists in particular need to reflect on their underlying presuppositions, to be reflexive and self-critical, and to be willing to publicly explicate and defend their commitments.

This book thus argues the disputationalist position that using competing frameworks can make better rational choice theories. Rational choice theorists have thrown down the gauntlet, so let them take the lead in stimulating a dialogue among the various research communities that produces creative engagements. Let them explore the different structure-action combinations of interests, identities, and institutions that guide inquiry. Let them operate as believers who raise questions and nonbelievers who wrestle with the answers.[4] The alternative is to be a community of theoretical philistines, in which case rational choice theorists will not be able to solve actual substantive problems.

There is a joke about a king who stages an opera contest—after hearing the first singer, he gives the prize to the second. Rationalists have acted as if they were similarly fatigued by the inadequacies of existing structural and cultural theories and hence wanted to move on to something else. The controversies that swirl around rational choice theory, however, cannot be addressed by ignoring other theoretical traditions and exploring only rational choice theory. Moreover, the best way to understand rational choice theory is to understand how it approaches other research communities. In the long run, only rationalists open to the similarities and differences among the various research traditions and communities can build better rational choice theories. And rationalists should be intellectually broad enough to admire—and study—the "other." In sum, a hegemonic rationalist social science does not serve the interests of rational choice theorists. As Heschel warned, "All power corrupts, including the power of reason" (1995, 196).

By exploring its foils—work not done in the rational choice tradition—this book therefore offers a unique and valuable perspective on rational choice theory.

Chapter 2

Three Types of Stories

I begin by discussing deep stories (sect. 2.1), exemplar theorists (sect. 2.2), ideal types (sect. 2.3), and the rational reconstruction of our protagonist research traditions of rationality, culture, and structure (sect. 2.4). I then turn to the trouble with ideal-type stories: since research communities are heterogeneous, they come in thin and thick versions (sect. 2.5). Finally, I discuss competing typologies of competing theories and explain why a genealogy of the competing typologies is valuable (sect. 2.6).

2.1. Deep Stories

How do social scientists understand and explain situations, events, and outcomes? Tilly refers to "standard stories."

> To construct a standard story, start with a limited number of interacting characters, individual or collective. Your characters may be persons, but they may also be organizations such as churches and states or even abstract categories such as social classes and regions. Treat your characters as independent, conscious, and self-motivated. Make all their significant actions occur as a consequence of their own deliberations or impulses. Limit the time and space within which your characters interact. With the possible exception of externally generated accidents— you can call them "chance" or "acts of God"—make sure everything that happens results directly from your characters' actions.
>
> Now supply your characters with specific motives, capacities, and resources. Furnish the time and place within which they're interacting with objects you and they can construe as barriers, openings, threats, opportunities, and tools—as facilities and constraints bearing on their action. Set the characters in motion. From their starting point, make sure all their actions follow your rules of plausibility, and produce effects on others that likewise follow your rules of plausibility. Trace the accumulated effects of their actions to some interacting outcome. Better yet, work your

way backward from some interesting outcome, following all the
same rules. Congratulations: you've just constructed a standard
story! (1999, 257)

A *standard story* is therefore a tale or fable about a small cast of self-
propelled characters who interact with one another over time in a
delimited spatial domain. The sequential narrative thus always has a
situational context—"once upon a time in a place long, long ago"[1]—
with facilities and constraints that help us to interpret the motivations
of the characters and thereby explain them. Children's encyclopedias
often construct a standard story of concrete historical events and outcomes, such as the French Revolution, World War II, or the New
Deal.[2]

Social scientists often mistake such accounts for abstract theories of
social revolutions, international wars, and policy regimes. However, a
standard story offers only commonsensical understandings of the
superficialities of social life and thus quickly becomes boring. A deep
story, by contrast, penetrates the surface to uncover the hidden secrets
and enigmatic truths of the human condition.[3] Such deep stories capture our attention and hold it as we continue to reflect on them and
probe their mysteries. Three types of social scientists go beneath the
ordinary to tell extraordinary stories.

First, rationalists engage in what Schelling (1978) refers to as "vicarious problem solving" and what Popper (1965) calls "situational rationality." While rationalist studies start with the individual and employ
assumptions about actors trying to maximize their advantage, they cul-
minate in questions about collective actions, choices, and institutions.
Looking beyond the standard story of directly willed consequences of
individual actions, they recognize that social outcomes do not mechanically follow from individual actions and interactions, and so they
focus on the complex emergent or downstream consequences of self-
motivated individual action. In other words, rationalists explore the
unintended, unwanted, unexpected, and also incoherent, chaotic, and
paradoxical aggregate consequences of intentional human actions.
Since their results show how rules, structures, and institutions aggregate individual choices in counterintuitive ways, we come to appreciate
the ironies and pathos of the workers, peasants, bureaucrats, and
politicians who make seemingly plausible decisions. Voting rules (e.g.,
two-party competition) and collective-action mechanisms (e.g., tit-for-
tat) are two prominent research foci. Following the path first charted
by Downs (1957) and Olson (1971), rational choice theorists address a

diverse set of problems: from electoral choice to revolutionary movements, from coalitions to political economy, and from institution formation to state building.

A second type of social scientist who seeks to deepen the standard
story includes social and cultural anthropologists such as Geertz
(1973). These culturalists maintain that there are no private languages,
preferences, and cognitions and hence that socially meaningful actions,
values, and beliefs are always oriented toward others. An individual's
subjective motivations to action are consequently only the surface
manifestations of deeper things. Culturalists thus move beyond the
standard story by providing thick descriptions of the intersubjective
webs of interpretation, meaning, and significance within which people
act. In this way Geertz and others come to understand varied ways of
life and systems of meaning in particular villages, workplaces, political
parties, and bureaucracies.

Structuralists, finally, have their own way of enriching the standard
story. Appearances can be deceiving, but by looking carefully one can
discover how actors are embedded in relationships that drive observable outcomes. These associations and connections are deep forces of
political power, called institutions, and hidden causal mechanisms,
called social order. Many structuralists emphasize the formal bureaucratic organizations of governments; some study state-society linkages
(political parties, interest groups, and social movements); some retain
Marx's concern with informal class relations; and others study civil
society (churches, gender roles, ethnic and communal stratification,
voluntary organizations, and age cohorts).

In sum, three ideal-type research traditions are active in contemporary comparative politics and historical sociology, just as they are astir
throughout political science and sociology and the social sciences more
generally. Each community of scholars deepens Tilly's standard story in
a particular way: rationalists focus on the complex consequences of individual action; culturalists study the meaning and significance of intersubjective values and beliefs; and structuralists seek the deep structures
of power and causation that drive superficial appearances and observable outcomes. Deep stories continue to hold our attention because they
penetrate into ultimate realities—hidden hands and microfoundations,
individual selves and collective consciences, and structural etiologies
and institutional forces. A compelling social science indeed must be a
"science of the invisible" (Schecter, cited in Sholem 1995, 252), albeit one
that can be narrated as a story with sequences of "observable implications" (King, Keohane, and Verba 1994).[4]

2.2. Exemplar Theorists

This book elaborates these three research communities abstractly, looking at *the* rationalist, *the* culturalist, and *the* structuralist, in an attempt
to rationally reconstruct (Lakatos 1970) internally coherent models and
foils that appear in social thought. A brief initial look at some concrete
texts that are paradigmatic or classic cases of the approaches will help
situate the discussion.[5] We find that each theorist thinks of himself or
herself as a member of a strong research community: Bates (1989)
argues that he is a rationalist, Scott (1985) identifies with the culturalists,
and Skocpol's (1979) work is determined by structuralist principles.
While each recognizes the value of synthesis and the cross-fertilization
of ideas, each is principally concerned with advancing a particular intellectual tradition and theoretical agenda that transcends his or her substantive inquiry. They have produced three of the most widely cited and
deeply respected works in contemporary social science: Bates's (1989)
Beyond the Miracle of the Market, Scott's (1985) *Weapons of the Weak,*
and Skocpol's (1979) *States and Social Revolutions.*

Bates's (1989) *Beyond the Miracle of the Market* explains how reason
shapes the political economy of agrarian development in Kenya. The
work offers a materialistic theory of political preferences: an actor's
location in Kenya's agrarian economy shapes his or her preferences
about economic and political institutions. Bates also argues that institutions shape the calculations of political entrepreneurs and hence
affect how material interests are defined, organized, and aggregated by
vote-maximizing politicians. Interests, in other words, are both materially and politically determined. The tragedy is that these reasoning voters and politicians, consumers and producers, create the drought,
famine, and subsistence crises that plague the people of Kenya. Rationalist solutions—democracy and capitalism—tend to stress that more
rationality, in terms of economic markets, social contracts, and political institutions, is needed to fortify reason and thereby overcome the
many pathologies of modernity. Bates therefore offers a seminal study
of "the impact of economic interests upon politics and the impact of
institutions upon economic interests" (46), one that explores both the
intended (and wanted) and unintended (and unwanted) consequences
of reason.

Scott's (1985) *Weapons of the Weak,* a study of a peasant village of
Sedaka in Malaysia, takes a very different perspective: "The peasants
of Sedaka do not simply react to objective conditions per se but rather
to the interpretation they place on those conditions as mediated by val-

ues embedded in concrete practices" (305). He argues that the discourses and practices of class conflict in Sedaka take the form of "everyday forms of peasant resistance" in which the poor and the well-to-do adhere to different norms and rules. Culturalist solutions to the problems of social diversity and political conflict tend to stress the nonrational, that the homogeneity of values and beliefs found in true communities facilitates the construction of more fully human identities that avoid many of the pathologies of modernity. In short, Scott offers a masterful analysis of the fragile ideological hegemony of the landed elite over the peasantry, one that traces the basis of a reasoning and yet irrational class order to the creation of identities and communities.

Skocpol (1979), in *States and Social Revolutions,* could have been addressing Bates or Scott when she rejects a "purposive image" of social causation that "suggests that revolutionary processes and outcomes can be understood in terms of the activity and initiation or interests of the key group(s) who launched the revolution in the first place" (17). Skocpol explains revolution by "rising above" the subjective viewpoints—the interests and identities—of the participants. She thus takes a structural perspective, or "an impersonal and nonsubjective viewpoint—one that emphasizes patterns of relationships among groups and societies" (18), in particular, "the institutionally determined situations and relations of groups within society and upon the interrelations of societies within world-historically developing international structures" (18). In considering France, Russia, and China, Skocpol argues that revolution occurred because the state was enmeshed in two sets of constraining structures: international relations, which consist of political and economic conflict among states, and domestic relations, which consist of conflict between dominant and subordinate classes. In probing issues of the inequality and inefficiency of the modern world, structuralists stress institutions and organizations. Skocpol thus argues that reformers need strong and rationalized state bureaucracies to cope with the economic and political competition that arises from the system of states and from the internal disorder that arises from conflicting social forces; radicals, on the other hand, need an organized group of like-thinking individuals to destroy and eventually remake the state. Skocpol's book is a classic comparative historical analysis that traces the reason (e.g., the development of democracy, markets, and state bureaucracies) and irrationality (e.g., the blind violence and human costs) of revolution to an "iron cage" of structural forces and relationships that operates behind the backs of individuals.[6]

In sum, Bates offers a rational/social choice study of how interests produced the dialectic of reason and irrationality in Kenya's political economy, Scott, a culturalist/interpretivist account of how communities and identities constituted Malaysia's class relations, and Skocpol, a structuralist/institutionalist analysis of how social forces caused the French, Russian, and Chinese Revolutions. Ultimately their stories are about the invisible: Bates tries to discover invisible human hands, Scott invisible cultural meanings, and Skocpol invisible social relations. Social scientists today have coalesced around these three competing research schools, as interests, identities, and institutions contend for theoretical primacy (Selznick 1992, 78; Garrett and Weingast 1993; Heclo 1994).[7]

2.3. Ideal Types

Weber's "ideal types" address general methodological problems throughout the social sciences ([1903–17] 1949). In this book we seek to understand the underlying issues that separate Bates, Scott, and Skocpol by exploring ideal-type rationalists, culturalists, and structuralists. Why use ideal types?

Since the chaos of our theoretical world is as pervasive as the chaos of our empirical world, it is impossible to study all the theories and approaches in contemporary social science in all of their complexity and flux. My typology permits a discussion of the nature of our overarching paradigms and their underlying assumptions in an orderly and purposeful manner that helps overcome the chaos (sect. 8.2.1).

An ideal-type taxonomy contains differentiations that facilitate comparisons. Indeed, because a thing is best understood via contrasts with the available alternatives, rationalists should explore the ideas of their culturalist and structuralist opponents. More concretely, an ideal-type classification can be used to generate four fruitful kinds of comparison among types (i.e., general theoretical traditions) and cases (i.e., particular theories).

First, one can compare and contrast among the types themselves. Weber, for one, frequently explores types and subtypes, sets and subsets, of cases. Moore (1966) contrasts bourgeois, fascist, and communist paths of development. I draw comparisons among rationalist, culturalist, and structuralist approaches. Second, one can compare cases. Weber argues that one needs clear concepts, typologies, and models before one can discern the similarities and differences between historical developments. His comparative analyses sought to discover how different people in different societies dealt with the same issue. Similarly, Moore (1966) contrasts democracy in England with fascism in Japan and communism in China. I draw comparisons among the theories developed by three exemplary theorists, Bates, Scott, and Skocpol.

Third, one can compare a type with a case within its range to show its applicability. Weber thus uses an ideal type as a yardstick for assessing historically concrete cases. By comparing the real with the ideal, Weber throws a case into relief, highlighting errors and assessing deviations, thereby showing how the ideal type works in practice. Moore (1966), for example, contrasts British, French, and American variants of bourgeois democracy. I draw comparisons between rationalism and Bates, culturalism and Scott, and structuralism and Skocpol. Finally, one can examine a single case from the point of view of several ideal types. Weber tries to explain the stream of historical events in particular cases by applying a battery of ideal types and theories. Actual cases, in other words, are distinctive and unique combinations of ideal types. Moore's (1966) three models of development appear in each of his cases; his analysis establishes why the bourgeois and fascist coalitions failed in China and hence why the communist coalition emerged. I dissect and extend a metaframework, Parsons's unit act, from rationalist, culturalist, and structuralist perspectives.

Weber uses these four sets of contrasts, analogies, and juxtapositions to produce a fascinating mix of the general and the specific, engaging theories and cases.

> The world itself is a mixture of many kinds of things; hence ideal types have to be shaped so that they can be used in combinations. They are something like tweezers, to grasp historical reality somewhere between different tendencies. Thus "bureaucracy" is an ideal type, a form of organization in which everything is done according to the rules, everyone has a strict position, there is a clear chain of command, and so forth. Of course most organizations never really fit this model, and Weber is quite aware of it. Hence, he pairs bureaucracy with another ideal type, "patrimonialism," which is a form of organization that is distinctly unbureaucratic, centered around personal networks and cliques. He can then characterize the history of various states as fluctuating somewhere between patrimonialism and bureaucracy (and of course various subtypes of these), and show the conditions that put it toward one end of the continuum or the other. History, in short, is an endless flux of particulars that we can never grasp in

their entirety. But by using the device of ideal types, we can pin down certain fixed reference points, and actually propose a definite theory about how it operated. (Collins 1986, 34)

The ideal-type approach thus facilitates general comparative and typological explication of particular events, situations, and outcomes and encourages a focus on cases of great substantive and theoretical significance. Ideal-type analysis, moreover, alerts social scientists to the pitfalls of moving from theory to case. Indeed, Weber warns that ideal types are only useful fictions that neither exhaust reality nor exactly depict it. Since they must not be reified into something "real" and should remain what they are—"nominal"—ideal types cannot be used to deduce cases, and they are not falsified by locating deviations from actual cases. I thus use the rationalist-culturalist-structuralist scheme to evaluate specific arguments advanced by each approach.

The set of ideal types also allows social scientists to suggest specific theories and address particular problems. Weber thus develops several classificatory schemes (e.g., class, status, and power; material and ideal interests; and traditionalist, rationalist, and charismatic bases of legitimacy) to support his own arguments and criticize those of others. I use the rationalist-culturalist-structuralist scheme to address problems that are significant for contemporary social theory: testing and evaluation, comparison and generalization, and structure and action problems.

Empirically oriented political scientists need ideal-type classifications of social theories, finally, because they typically do not devote entire articles or books to a single theorist. Since sociologists often write on Giddens but political scientists do not frequently write on Bates, political science needs typologies of its theories even more than sociology needs such typologies.

2.4. The Rational Reconstruction of Research Programs

The elaboration of ideal-type social theories in Parts II and III involves a rational reconstruction[8] of each research program (Lakatos 1970)—rationalist in chapters 3 and 4, culturalist in chapter 5, and structuralist in chapter 6. The core of a research program consists of a negative heuristic—a fundamental and unchallenged picture of reality that helps us understand how the world is constituted—and a positive heuristic—a methodology or explanatory strategy that indicates how the program is "articulated" (Kuhn 1970). Both heuristics tell us what counts as a "good" explanation and therefore tell us how the world should be investigated.

More specifically, I show how the traditions differ along four dimensions. The first is ontology: reasons, rules, and relations are the various starting points of inquiry. Rationalists study how actors employ reason to satisfy their interests, culturalists study rules that constitute individual and group identities, and structuralists explore relations among actors in an institutional context. Second, the traditions differ with respect to explanatory strategy: positivism, interpretivism, and realism are the possible philosophies of social science, as rationalists perform comparative static experiments, culturalists produce interpretive understandings, and structuralists study the historical dynamics of real social types.

Third, the research traditions differ on the issue of general laws. Rational choice theorists seek universal explanatory laws and use the power of mathematics to elaborate explanations with impressive scope. Culturalists, by contrast, offer nuanced, detailed readings of particular cases, frequently drawn from fieldwork, to understand the phenomena being studied; they eschew any need to tie explanations to general principles and abstract categories and discount the value of more "scientific" research. Although structuralists employ diverse patterns of reasoning, from mathematical models to verbal arguments, and use many modes of organizing empirical evidence, ultimately they are concerned with causal accounts of particular social types and hence seek to tie reliable descriptions to powerful generalizations about these types. And fourth, each research tradition faces its own set of internally generated problems. Core assumptions and explanatory frameworks produce characteristic aporia and lacunae. Rationalist thinking culminates in materialism, culturalist thought in idealism, and structural tenets in determinism. Each sacrifices something: hard-core rationalists lose values and contexts; true-believer culturalists, choice and constraint; and die-hard structuralists, action and orientation.

In sum, my rational reconstruction of ideal-type social theories establishes the value of an integral conception of the research traditions. Each ideal-type theory is logically coherent within its own internal structure of ontology, methodology, comparative strategy, and lacunae. The assumptions of each approach, that is, have an elective affinity for one another.

2.5. The Trouble with Stories: Thin and Thick Research Traditions

While the purpose of ideal types is of course to reduce the complexity of the real world, such efforts can be falsely interpreted as reifications of reality. In practice, rationalist, culturalist, and structuralist thought is heterogeneous. Each ideal-type research community does specialize—rationalists concentrate on action, culturalists, on norms, and structuralists, on conditions—but there can never be a pure rationalist, culturalist, and structuralist explanation, although some theorists— Bates, Scott, and Skocpol, for example—sometimes come close. Hence there is a danger when we apply ideal types to social theories and discover different deep stories: the ideal-type social theories become counterproductive as they become reified as narrow specialties.

Synthesizers argue that all research programs are synthetic anyway. A research community does not form a monolithic bloc but rather, in Wittgenstein's terms, shares a family resemblance: "Just as one can have a single cohesive rope with no single thread running its entire length, so one can have a unified research community without a significant hard core" (Hausman 1994, 205). Strict definitional exercises do not work because a program's scope and boundaries are not defined by necessary and sufficient conditions for its existence. Since paradigms contain a diverse set of claims, methods, goals, practices, and assumptions, an exploration of the variance of disciplinary matrices within and between research groups does not yield a definitive statement of what is in the core and what is beyond the periphery. Research schools overlap, even as they conflict. Much of the really useful scholarship is intertraditional and occurs at the perimeters.

Research programs, moreover, are not static; they develop over time through ongoing within-community conflict and debate. Similarly, scientists struggle with their tradition, challenging it from the inside in ways that members of the community understand.[9]

A research tradition's most important internal struggle is between those competitors or pragmatists who try to develop a thin version of their program and those synthesizers who wish to develop a thick one. Since purists believe that it is necessary to build a fence around a research tradition so as to allow it to develop and establish its capabilities, thin versions of research programs stick closely to their traditional cores. As they are relatively parsimonious, one can test them in a fundamental way. The problem, however, is that a thin program— whether rationalist, culturalist, or structuralist—is easily falsified: in slighting a great deal, it is often unable to explain the richness of social life. The aporia and lacunae of narrowly defined research communities thus lead to thick versions: researchers add elements from other programs and extend the boundaries of their approach with changes that are detailed and contextual (i.e., "realistic"). The consequence of intellectual imperialism is that one can test the program, though not in any basic way, as it is hard to know whether it is the core that is producing the really useful insights. There is also a tendency toward tautology as everything comes to be redescribed in the program's terms.

For example, rationalists study collective action and social choice. Thin rationalists are pure intentionalists who see reasons as causes. Their view of culture and conditions reduces them to individual desires and beliefs. They also typically take a materialist view of preferences and analyze beliefs from the viewpoint of perfect information. Thick rationalists extend their approach by deepening the micro and studying culture (preferences and beliefs) and by exploring the macro and examining institutions (conditions and constraints). Thick rationalists also explore different types of decision rules (Lichbach 1995, chap. 10).

Culturalists study values and beliefs. Thin culturalists analyze how an intersubjective culture defines choices and creates structures, or they explore how decision rules become part of choice and how actors are constituted by culture. Thick culturalists move toward the subjectivism of the rationalists by maintaining that actors make culturally informed choices, with material structures filtered through the individual's subjective ideas—values and beliefs.

Structuralists study relationships among actors. Thin structuralists study configurations of power—civil society, the state, and the international system of states—to understand large patterns of historical development. Because they minimize the significance of actors and their freedom to choose, they often ignore choice and culture. Thick structuralists expand the approach by studying how the reason and irrationality contained in structures is manifested in actions and orientations. In their exploration of the materially driven dynamics of the institutions behind collective action and social norms, they are concerned with contextualizing individuals and their relationships.

In sum: purists attempt to maximize between-tradition variance and minimize within-tradition variance, until the overlap between research communities is so small that there are no transparadigmatic issues to talk about, whereas monopolists minimize between-tradition variance and maximize within-tradition variance, until all research communities are the same.

Research programs in the social sciences probably thicken over time, and no research school remains rigidly orthodox. As each begins to incorporate a complex and many-sided internal dialogue about how to understand and explain the world, different types of rationalist (e.g., fig. 3.1 on human-nature and social-situation rationality), culturalist (sect. 5.1), and structuralist (sect. 6.1) theories emerge.

Rationalists, for example, debate the utility of relaxing the core assumption of individuals as maximizers of their self-interest. They also debate how to transform formal models into quantitative and qualitative accounts of events: some seek covering-law explanations, and others propose causal accounts. Rationalists thus come not only as thin and thick rationalists, or as human nature and social situation rationalists, but also as revealed-preference and institutional rationalists, universal and domain-restriction rationalists, deductivists and hypothesis testers.

Culturalists disagree about the theoretical importance of generalizations drawn from their fieldwork. May one derive or test general propositions from the analysis of a particular village? Do public opinion surveys provide a helpful picture of society's values and cognitions? They differ as well about the nature of explanation. Some culturalists reject any form of covering law or causal account, offering only interpretations of political life in particular places; others move toward social "science," incorporating values and systems of meaning into theories that adhere to standard positivistic forms of explanation. Section 5.1 notes that culturalism broadly construed encompasses survey research, interpretivism, constructivism, and postmodernism. While these approaches differ from rational choice in their emphasis on values and meaning, culturalists engage in bitter family quarrels over positivism.

Continuing the debate initiated by Marx and Weber, structuralists differ over the ontological status of their concepts. Are social class, the state, and ethnicity natural types? Are political processes best seen as determined and closed, or probabilistic and open-ended? Structuralists differ as well over the utility of nomothetic and causal explanations. Section 6.1 notes that structuralism encompasses Parsonian structural-functionalism, neo-Marxism, and state-centered historical institutionalism. While these approaches differ from rational choice in their holistic ontology, they position themselves differently on the nomothetic/idiographic divide. And structuralists, too, have fought bitter family battles over the level of conflict or consensus in society.

In addition to the diversity within each school, cross-fertilization occurs from one to the other. Scott influences Skocpol who influences Bates who influences Scott, and so on. Practicing social scientists thus employ a battery of ideal-type strategies in their concrete empirical work. As section 7.2 indicates, a great deal of work reflects combinations of the competing research programs:

- ◆ Inglehart's survey research = choice + culture;
- ◆ Almond and Powell's structural-functionalism = culture + structure;
- ◆ Przeworski's and Elster's analytical Marxism = structure + choice.

Theorists who blend ideal-type approaches wrestle with the resulting tensions. For example, survey research, which probes social norms by focusing on "public opinion," has been criticized on the grounds that individuals have opinions but that people collectively make judgments. This, in turn, raises questions about the nature of individualism in rational choice theory and collectivism in cultural theories.

In sum, ideal-type reconstructions of social theories can lead to the reification of deep stories. In practice, research communities are heterogeneous and thick; most practicing social scientists synthesize and combine ideas.

2.6. Typologies and Genealogies

In any particular research domain, one can therefore always make a case for other approaches to classifying theories. Domains are often divided into two rather than three basic theory choices: in studies of political violence, for example, Eckstein (1980) compares rational choice theory with cultural theory, and in the field of comparative politics, Steinmo, Thelen, and Longstreth (1992) compare rational choice institutionalism with historical institutionalism. Domains are also often divided into four rather than three basic theory choices: Hollis (1994, 19), for example, develops a 2 × 2 matrix of theories by distinguishing holism from individualism and explanation from understanding. In short, while rationality, culture, and structure are three approaches for building deep theories, other categorizations are possible, and social scientists indeed have developed many different typologies of many different sets of theories.[10]

Competing typologies of competing theories exist not only because of the heterogeneity of the theories themselves, but also because of the heterogeneity of the typologists. While my rationalist-culturalist-structuralist classification scheme juxtaposes the three most prominent research communities active today and takes account of the goals, perspectives, and ideas of the theorists themselves, typologists inevitably have interests and values, and typologies have what Weber calls "value relevance." In other words, typologies always define and frame questions and problems in particular ways, as typologists always design ideal types to address some problems and neglect others. Rather than providing exhaustive depictions of reality, they offer purposively selective, one-sided nominalist pictures that aim to highlight certain features and underplay others.

By dividing theories into three conflicting and all-encompassing intellectual traditions, I am not thereby claiming that rationality, culture, and structure are autonomous, natural, or given. The triad is not a timeless triangle of language and concepts with which to hold an ahistorical or transhistorical dialogue among every possible social theory in every possible empirical domain. The history of social theory is of course a history of changing intellectual contexts and problem domains.

If we project the debate among ideal-type social theories backward and forward, we uncover the value relevance and contextual significance of our competing typologies. Most important, we discover the struggles between the typologies. Which categorization of social thought became dominant, primary, and privileged at a particular time? How were these typologies maintained and reproduced? Why were certain distinctions established, and why did they remain powerful? Which voices were silenced, marginalized, or submerged? How did the choice of a typology ossify a particular agenda and prevent radical change? How were the dominant typologies eventually challenged and transformed? And does the history or genealogy of these typologies show gaps and discontinuities as manifested in major and abrupt changes?

In sum: while typologies are products of the way we think about the world, typologies come to fashion our understandings of the world; by categorizing our ideas they regulate our discourse. Since the self-image of a discipline is told through typologies of its theories, they are always contested. In fact, disciplines often emerge in battles over typologies. Consider international relations. Realism/idealism debates turned into neoliberalism/neorealism debates, and these are currently being challenged by a new "great debate" about constructivism. Hence, the development of typologies of theories in international relations was "not a pluralism without purpose, but a critical pluralism, designed to reveal embedded power and authority structures, provoke critical scrutiny of dominant discourses, empower marginalized populations and perspectives, and provide a basis for alternative conceptualizations" (Biersteker, quoted in Woever 1996, 157). New typologies allowed weaker perspectives to thrive and not be bulldozed by dominant paradigms. International relations theory therefore shows that debates over typologies of theories can structure and ultimately reconfigure a field. Woever even claims that "the discipline *was* the debate" (1996, 155).

Part of the political agenda behind my typology of social theories is to instigate such a struggle among typologies of theories, especially in comparative politics and historical sociology. My trinity is also designed as a set of ideal types that probe how currently popular rival paradigms struggle for hegemony throughout the social sciences, especially political science. My goal, in short, is to challenge the complacency of the discipline, as demonstrated in the *World Politics* symposium cited earlier, and show that there is a contentious struggle among theories, and even typologies of theories, rather than a messy center. I have therefore tried to recover the tradition in comparative politics, similar to the revival of political theory in international relations, that assesses metatheoretical controversies. My other political motive for developing a typology of social theories is to demonstrate that some theoretical arguments cannot be subsumed by rational choice theories; rational choice theorists, that is, cannot lay claim to having the single universal theory of social science. In fact, the only way that we can discover how rational choice analyses differ from culturalist and structuralist ones is to develop and criticize alternative typologies. I thus also hope to recover the idea of competing traditions as a defense against rationalist hegemony. In sum, I distinguish between types of social theorists with the goal of refocusing the current theoretical debate and providing alternatives to contemporary rational choice theory; the purpose is not to hold a timeless dialogue among randomly chosen rationalist, culturalist, and structuralist texts.

If I accomplish these goals, my typology will have demonstrated its value for dissecting a significant part of the social scientific world. I would also argue, of course, that my typology is the most well-elaborated taxonomy of general approaches to theory-building in contemporary social science, and especially in political science and comparative politics. Nevertheless, someone who does not like my typology or has another purpose in mind may critique it by adopting an existing classification scheme or proposing a new one. As has often been said in the philosophy of science, a null hypothesis cannot defeat a research hypothesis: one needs an alternative argument before one drops an existing one.

In conclusion: I combine various properties of social theories (e.g., ontology, methodology, comparative strategy, and lacunae) to rationally reconstruct three ideal-type research communities who tell deep stories about the invisible. I also distinguish pure and impure versions of each tradition: thin and thick rationalists (sect. 3.1), culturalists (sect. 5.1), and structuralists (sect. 6.1). I challenge the rationalist bid for hegemony by demonstrating incompatible invisibilities: the culturalist search for significant meanings and the structuralist search for power relationships cannot be subsumed under the rationalist search for microfoundational hands. The ideal types and the related range of cases developed here should be judged on pragmatic grounds: are they useful for elucidating this or that problem from this or that point of view? And if another set of ideal types successfully highlights different and (from another perspective) more significant aspects of the reality under investigation, it too should be pursued.

We turn next to part II, to the rationalist challenge to social theory, and then to part III, to the culturalist and structuralist alternatives.

Part II

The Rationalist Challenge

Chapter 3

Rational/Social Choice Theory

This chapter tries to "rationally reconstruct" (Lakatos 1970) a coherent set of themes that underlie the rational/social choice school.[1] The rationalist research program in comparative politics and historical sociology has developed from a thin one centered on human nature to a thick one focused on social situations (sect. 3.1). Rationalist ontology (sect. 3.2) depicts a world populated by rational individuals and operating in often irrational collectivities. Rationalist methodology (sect. 3.3) involves positivist comparative-static experiments that link structure to action.

3.1. Thin and Thick Rationalists

While rationalists share a common ontology and methodology, thin or human-nature rationalists and thick or social-situation rationalists incorporate different auxiliary assumptions.

Some rationalists begin with humankind and postulate an inborn and necessary human nature that structures experience. A transcendental ego or an absolute self, in other words, is defining or constitutive of all human beings. Such rationalists adopt a naturalist, rather than an empiricist, methodology. Reason, accordingly, is immanent in every human being: if A is a valid act for someone, it must be valid for everyone under similar conditions. The rational justification of an argument is thus public in that it is open to criticism by one and all. These rationalists therefore suggest that they can intuit a priori, purely by rational understanding and the exercise of reason, empirical truths about the nature of the person—truths that are independent of the senses and of experience, or that they have access to a world of ultimate reality that lies beyond the appearances of contingent and transient particulars. Since human-nature rationalists employ truths that are not demonstrated a posteriori by observation and evidence, no counterfactuals are involved: the truths are timeless and placeless, true in all possible or conceivable worlds. Self-verifying positive laws and global, universal moral rules are thus consistent from person to person, situation to situation, and society to society. Everyone everywhere everytime should believe in the same scientific laws, follow the same moral rules, and endorse the same political arrangements.

Human-nature rationalists consequently stress that there is only one rationality. An agent's decision rules are not "pursue the private interest in markets" and "pursue the collective interest in politics." While economics might involve a theory of markets, and politics a theory of government, the consumer-producer and the voter-taxpayer are nevertheless one and the same person. Much like Weber, who argued that the same people operate in the religious and the economic worlds, such rationalists explain the behavior of people in both spheres.

Many of the "universal laws" of economics favored by economists who do public choice (e.g., Becker 1976; Becker and Stigler 1977) are thus based on such simple assumptions as diminishing marginal utility, diminishing marginal rates of substitution, diminishing returns to scale, diminishing marginal productivity, irrelevance of fixed costs, substitutes and complements in choice, and the connectedness (transitivity) of choice. Political scientists see no problem in applying such laws to politics and imposing, for example, an assumption about marginal costs on a repression-dissent curve.

Those who challenge the human-nature rationality approach contend that there is no hardwired and universal rationality, and that instead human nature, the product of social context, is malleable and incomplete rather than unchangeable and final. As Kincaid puts it: "No fixed, universal nature of individuals will suffice to explain all social facts, because individual behavior itself depends on social context. . . . [S]ocial facts apparently are always involved in explaining individual behavior; the bare traits of human nature do not suffice" (1996, 150). Different human beings in different times and places therefore have different types of selves or egos. Structuralists and culturalists strongly oppose the idea of a universal human nature because it reduces the social (what they specialize in) to the status of a mere epiphenomenon.[2]

If the rationality postulate by itself yields few deductions (i.e., a simple biologically determined rationality is almost operationally meaningless), rationalists need to specify the situation in which a rational actor is found by coupling rationality with other assumptions about the constraints that rational actors face, especially the institutional facts they confront (Blaug 1992, 232). One can extend the boundaries of the rationalist approach by deepening the micro (studying culture, norms, and preferences) and exploring the macro (examining institutions, structures, and constraints) (Lichbach 1995, chap. 10). Rational-ists who subscribe to this social-situation rationality begin with a his-torically specific opportunity structure (e.g., time, resources) that defines desires, beliefs, and choices. The concrete situation, in other words, either constrains or enables action. Social-situation rationality thus produces conditional laws because human beings are defined by particular contexts.

Bates (1989), for example, begins with the historically specific opportunity structure that defines the desires, beliefs, and choices of Kenyans and then examines how Kenyans determine their historically concrete situation. Once he takes the economic, social, and political institutions of Kenya as endogenously determined by Kenyans, he then explores the behavioral and institutional outcomes of its political economy. Bates thus moves toward structure, by looking at conditions as both causes and effects, and toward culture, by also looking at pref-erences and beliefs as both causes and effects.

This move from biological human nature to worldly social condi-tions is then a move from rationalism (universalism) to empiricism (contextualism): from establishing truths by introspection and deduc-tion to establishing them by observation and experimentation (see table 3.1). Rational choice theory has oscillated between these two approaches.

Many early rationalists focused on a universal human nature. Social contract theorists such as Hobbes and Locke did not attempt to build their complex macrotheories of society from detailed comparative and historical sources. A reaction occurred, and in the eighteenth-century Scottish Enlightenment such social-situation rationalists as Smith, Ferguson, Millar, and Hume attempted to build complex macrocom-parative and historical theories of society (Seidman 1983, 40). Adam Smith, for example, was concerned with the broad comparative and historical development of capitalist industrial society. He viewed social

TABLE 3.1.   Two Types of Rationalist Argument

Human-Nature (Thin) Rationality	Social-Situation (Thick) Rationality
presocial or asocial	social
ahistorical and transhistorical	historical and comparative
universal	contextual
a priori	a posteriori
deduced from first principles	empirical
fixed	contingent

classes as agents of historical change and recognized that the social situation provides their motivations. His conclusion: the unintended outcomes of the materialist struggle among social classes shaped society, often in irrational ways. While there is a logic to history, it is one that often escapes its agents. Smith thus synthesized empiricism and rationalism, historiography and contract theory.[3]

The two competing schools of nineteenth-century economics contended over these approaches. The utilitarians, who argued that humans are outside of history and thereby interpreted social action in terms of the egoistic concepts of utility and self-interest, produced a universal social theory. The historical political economists, who stressed the social construction of human natures, were holists who saw specific societies as unique entities that could not be reduced to universal components. The discipline of sociology grew up in reaction to the utilitarians: nineteenth-century attempts to build complex macrotheories of society—Marx, Tocqueville, Weber, and Durkheim—were not based on rational choice.

The debate continues today: hard rational choicers are modelers who tend toward human-nature rationality, and soft rational choicers are comparativists who tend toward social-situation rationality.

3.2. Rationalist Ontology

All rationalists, however, are methodological individualists. They make six assumptions about individuals and collectivities.

First, the rationalist's key explananda lie at the macrolevel. Coleman argues that social scientists should explain aggregate rather than individual-level properties—"social phenomena, not the behavior of single individuals" (1990, 2). Since the goal is to account for social action, rationalists refer to their approach as social choice theory. Consider how Bates opens his book: "This book is about the political economy of development. It is about the politics and economics of agriculture. And it is about Kenya" (1989, 1). More generally, rational choice theorists study macroproblems: social movements, conflict, and revolutions;[4] political and economic development;[5] the emergence of democracy;[6] the operation of democratic institutions;[7] and macroeconomic policy.[8] Rationalist thinkers bring their core ideas to these issues and seek to explain the origins, operations, and outcomes of liberalism, markets, civil society, democracy, and the state.

Second, rationalists claim that macroscopic entities have no independent status apart from the individuals who constitute them. Only actors choose, prefer, believe, learn, and so on: society does not act independently of them. Consequently, the welfare of society depends solely on the welfare of its individual members. With rare exceptions, moreover, analysts must accept an individual's own judgments about his or her own well-being.

Third, rational choice theorists do not develop macrotheories of polities, societies, and economies based on macrounderstandings of these structures. Since the causal power of structures is derivative of individuals, "at best, the analysis of group interests leaves us one stage removed from the ultimate choice process which can only take place in individual minds" (Buchanan and Tullock 1965, 9).

Fourth, rationalists deduce consequences for the collectivity or system of individuals from their assumptions about individuals' desires, beliefs, and choices. They use microdata to reach meso- and macro-conclusions about how the individual actions of self-interested actors combine into collective actions, how individual preferences aggregate into common values, and how individuals' interactions join into social institutions. For rationalists, then, individual-level and not aggregate-level theories are the only valid explanations of macroexplananda.[9] Stinchcombe thus looks for the "mechanisms at the individual level or the situational level that make theories at the social structural level and at the level of longer time spans more supple, precise, complex, elegant, or believable" (1991, 367–68). Taylor writes:

> I take it that good explanation should be, amongst other things, as *fine-grained* as possible; causal links connecting events distant in space-time should be replaced wherever possible by chains of "shorter" causal links. This is an important reason for supplying explanations with causal links beginning and terminating at individuals. Structuralist and other holistic theories, where they take a causal form, are typically coarse-grained in this sense: they relate macrostates directly to macrostates without supplying a "mechanism" to show how the one brings about the other. (1988, 95, emphasis in original)

This search for the microfoundations of macrorelationships is illustrated by the Coleman-Boudon diagram shown in figure 3.1. The diagram shows that while collective causes are the origins of individual preferences and beliefs, individual actions explain collective consequences.[10]

Hobbes ([1651] 1988), Smith ([1776] 1976), Rawls (1971), and Nozick (1974) used this approach to explain the origin of the state, social order,

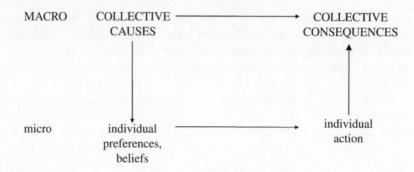

Fig. 3.1.   Coleman-Boudon diagram

social contract, group solidarity, and collective action. Contemporary comparativists are concerned, for example, with how personal dissatisfaction aggregates into a social movement, how fear aggregates into a mass panic, how private goods and endowments aggregate into market prices and quantities, and how personal transformation aggregates into social change. Bates (1989) thus uses the Coase theorem, a microeconomic idea that focuses on the transaction costs of individual exchange, to explore the efficiency of institutions, governments, and politics.

Fifth, rationalists argue that the aggregation of individuals into collectivities is not straightforward: one cannot simply sum individual preferences into collective preferences or add individual actions into collective actions. Since composition rules are complex and the whole is greater than the simple sum of its parts, it is a psychologistic fallacy to argue that complex human enterprises, like social revolution and regime reconstruction, are human nature writ large. For one thing, a rational actor's choices are a function of others' choices—action is always social action. Rationalist theories thus involve strategically interdependent decision making: one's actions depend on what one thinks others will do, and the preferences people reveal depend on the preferences they think others will reveal.

Social outcomes are therefore often the unintended consequences of intentional human action.[11] Schotter speaks of the centrality of these spontaneous invisible-hand outcomes for the social sciences: "If social phenomena showed no order except insofar as they were consciously designed, there would be, as is often argued, only problems of psychology. It is only insofar as some sort of order arises as a result of individual action but without being designed by any individual that a problem is raised that demands theoretical explanation" (1981, 20). The point is underlined as well by Hayek, who argues that the "aim [of the social sciences] is to explain the unintended or undesigned results of the actions of many men" (1979, 146–47). Popper (1965, 342) makes a similar point.[12]

A social choice explanation thus seeks to explain the irrational social consequences of action that is individually rational.[13] The invisible hand of rationality (Langlois 1986, 241) often leads to outcomes that are unintended, undesigned, and unplanned: the by-products, side effects, and secondary consequences of individual decisions. Sadly, these consequences are also often unwanted or Pareto-suboptimal results of independent decisions: given the difficulties of combining individually rational choices, better or best outcomes are unachievable or impossible. Tragically, these consequences are often the unavoidable and inevitable results of individually rational actions: The situation is opaque to the participants because these consequences are hidden, diffuse, distant, and invisible. And amusingly, the situation is often chaotic because these consequences are unexpected, unpredictable, and surprising. The only redeeming feature of the rationalist ontology is that these results are often short term because they are frequently in disequilibrium and hence unstable. As Goethe puts it, "There is nothing more illogical than absolute logic: it gives rise to unnatural phenomena, which finally collapse" (cited in Löwith 1991, 65). Social choice explanations thus focus on the emergent contradictions and paradoxes, comedies and tragedies, ironies and antinomies, and openness and contingency of individual reason. They explore the aggregation, transformation, coordination, and micro-to-macro aspects of interdependent decision making.

Rationalists thus eschew the belief that individually rational actors produce collectively rational action in a simple intentionalist manner. Rather, they argue that rational people inhabit an irrational society (Barry and Hardin 1982). And social choice theories assume rationality and then study irrationality. In explaining presumably irrational social outcomes by showing that they can be deduced from a model of individual rationality,[14] rationalists rescue the maintained hypothesis (rational action) from the anomalous finding (irrational outcomes), reconciling theory with observation and solving the substantive puzzle or riddle.

Finally, rationalists attempt to give these ontological assumptions bite by carefully choosing their research domain. Their approach will not work, as Riker (1990) recognizes, in an indefinite or ambiguous situation lacking precisely delimited temporal and spatial boundaries. If it is not clear what is included and what is excluded from an event, its emergent properties cannot command our attention. Riker thus argues that "you cannot specify the cause of a huge event like a war. A cause is a necessary and sufficient condition, and for a temporal event, a unique and necessary condition is the just-preceding event with the same spatial boundaries and the same movers as actors. The cause of a war is thus the entire state of the warring parties just before the war. Such states cannot, of course, be fully or even roughly specified" (1982a, 289). Rationalists must therefore carefully parse explananda. While they do try to explain macrophenomena, they do not try to explain such phenomena in their configurational entirety, for example the Russian Revolution or Iraq's decision to invade Kuwait, because such rare, large-scale, and complex events are the result of independent sequences of idiosyncratic events that converge and interact at a particular time and place. This conjunctural view implies that revolutions and wars are the result of many separate processes—not the inevitable product of large-scale historical forces but a result of idiosyncrasies of people, movements, institutions, and ideas.[15] For example, revolutions are the unintended consequences of complex strategizing and preference falsification under unforeseen contingencies. Revolution itself, moreover, is a process that unleashes many unintended consequences and by-products. Whereas individual properties and spheres of revolutions may be explained by general theories of collective action, the totality of a revolution's historical development and outcome cannot be so explained.[16]

Rationalists also parse structures. They do not try to develop laws that explain either particular large-scale and highly complex structural forms (e.g., France, India) or the general development of structural types (e.g., feudalism, capitalism, democracy, communism). As Riker argued previously, one cannot develop parsimonious but comprehensive explanations (a short list of causes) of very dense and complex social phenomena because the aim is too ambitious. Insofar as causal processes exist, they are limited in scope to the micro- or middle range. They concern well-defined institutions (e.g., federalism) and patterns of individual behavior (e.g., protest) that occur within grand historical structures, not the overall dynamics of the structures themselves.

In sum, rationalists disaggregate the historically concrete problem that interests them and focus on explanatory parts and not wholes.[17]

   1. Rationalists avoid hyperaggregation, overgeneralization, and

highly nominalist concepts that cover everything—that is, broad terms like *rationality, modernity,* and *elite.* In taking account of real historical variation, specific comparisons, and institutional particularity, they tend to use plural words rather than singular concepts (e.g., *states, policies, institutions, coalitions*).

2. Riker directs rationalists to focus on events and not structures. The most successful social scientists, he contends, concentrate on small events (e.g., strikes, crises, choices) rather than macrostructures (e.g., capitalism, social democracy, civilization). Indeed, "the primary advantage of the rational choice model is that it permits scientists to generalize about events (choices, actually) that are as small and precise as the events of price taking" (1990, 174).

3. Rather than trying to explain large-scale and complex historical outcomes and developments in their entirety, rationalists focus on individuals making decisions at key points. For example, they isolate the decision-making situation (institution) behind the choice of federal constitutional structures.

4. Rationalists study within-case relationships. They break down a big historical event into many observations, locate the internal causal processes, and make multiple predictions. King, Keohane, and Verba thus suggest that "the occurrence of a predicted revolution . . . is merely one observed implication of a theory, and because of the small amount of information in it, should not be privileged over other observable implications" (1994, 31). Rationalist claims are thus about specific, historically concrete variation within revolutions: they look for empirical consequences and observable implications that probe the theory within the case. Since rationalists examine within-case relationships, they offer the causal mechanisms and processes that can be used to deconstruct grand structuralist narratives.

5. Rationalists avoid between-case relationships; they test predictions of their theory *in* a case and not *for* a case. In other words, they make predictions about *aspects* of a case, not predictions that use superficial analogies and metaphors between theory and a case as a whole that ultimately redescribe the case in terms of the theory.[18]

Rationalists thus avoid large-scale aggregative predictions that derive from grand theoretical frameworks and stick to middle-range, but yet nomothetic, generalizations.[19] They avoid quick-and-dirty macrostudies of whole events or outcomes and are interested in careful local studies of global phenomena that show how structural factors drive local processes or how local processes interact to produce structures.[20]

3.3. Rationalist Methodology

Rationalists employ a distinctive explanatory strategy. They begin with *vicarious problem solving*—placing a set of people in some decision context and then trying to determine how rational actors would act in such a situation (Popper 1965). As Schelling puts it: "If we know what problem a person is trying to solve, and if we think he can actually solve it, and if we can solve it too, we can anticipate what our subject will do by putting ourselves in his place and solving his problem as we think he sees it" (1978, 18).

Rationalists thus assume that "rationality" is constitutive of the individual, that agents act in light of beliefs and desires that they are prepared to modify in the light of empirical experience. Rationalists make three more specific assumptions about rationality. First, actions are *purposeful* behavior directed toward attainment of a goal. Second, there is *choice,* so rational actors choose their strategies and tactics from among a repertoire of available alternatives. Third, given their situation, agents "quest for the best," their optimization or *maximization* problem being to choose the most desirable alternative available.

Rational choice explanations thus combine interpretive and causal understandings of action into an intentional explanation of human action (Davidson 1980). In other words, desires and beliefs are the reasons for action and in this sense the "causes" of action. Ideas play this "causal" role in the genesis of actions and at the same time rationalize action or make it intelligible. Ferejohn explains:

> We want social science theories to provide causal explanations of events in the same sense that scientific explanations of physical or biological phenomena seem to do. At the same time, we want social science theories to take account of the reasons for or meanings of social action. We want to know not only what caused the agent to perform some act but also the agent's reasons for taking the action. Good reason-giving explanations are supposed to show how it is that the action "makes sense" or is intelligible; such accounts may be thought of as rationalizations for or interpretations of action. (1993, 228)

The concept of interest follows from the idea that actions are done for certain reasons and those reasons motivate the action: "To say that doing x is in A's interest is to give A a reason for doing x" (Callinicos 1988, 123). Understanding this rational pursuit of individual interests is important, as indicated earlier, for understanding the all-too-common occurrence of irrational social outcomes.

Once theorists understand how rational actors would act in the decision situation, they perform a *gedanken,* or thought experiment (Bates 1989, 9–10). At first, the model is in a strategic or game-theoretic *equilibrium* in which actions depend upon the actions of others. More precisely, a Nash equilibrium of strategies is a self-enforcing institution (i.e., agreement) that is compatible with everyone's self-interest. Rationalists thus think in terms of a balance of forces, as in Newton's nature, rather than in terms of a normative or structural social order: society is an equilibrium outcome of natural forces, a compact geared to reaching social equilibrium through the reciprocal adjustment of interests. The equilibrium model is then subjected to comparative static exercises, a series of exogenous shocks.[21] Rationalists next observe the impact of these exogenous changes on the endogenous variables of concern.[22]

What sorts of exogenous shocks are possible? Rationalists refer to their intentionalist framework: given that beliefs and cognitions direct action, or that cultural ideas and material conditions drive social outcomes, desires and beliefs are the possible exogenous variables in social choice models. Hence, the constraints of the "objective external world" affect action because they influence the desires and beliefs of the "subjective internal world" of the actor. Rationalists offer, in short, materialist theories of preferences and beliefs and explore the conditions of choice: the shadow, relative, or opportunity costs (in terms of forgone material opportunities) of action. They tend to believe that they can conduct their comparative static exercises using only these "objective" shocks and avoiding "subjective" ones.

This is the approach applied by Bates: "In the early portions of this work, the shock is the colonial incursion. In the later portions, it is a failure of the rains. In the intermediate periods, the shocks include variations in access to land, cash crops, or productive ecological zones" (1989, 10). While Bates understands the culture of Kenya and factors it into his equilibrium model, his analysis is driven ultimately by independent and exogenous material shocks and forces, in other words by "a materialist conception of politics" (153). Empirically oriented rationalists like Bates are thus materialists in the end because material conditions are held to drive subjective consciousness—preferences and beliefs—and ultimately rational choice. Rational actor theories consequently have a parasitic relationship with material structuralist ones.[23]

This comparative static methodology that links structure to action is the ideal PGM—proposition-generating machine. Rationalists see individuals as hardheaded scientists who ground their preferences and beliefs in the material world. Similarly, rationalists see themselves as hardheaded scientists who conduct *gedankenexperimente* and then attempt to evaluate the success of the exercises. Because of their scientific approach, rationalists believe that they can specify what would constitute decisive evidence against their hypotheses: they think in terms of the observable implications of their experiments that are falsifiable (i.e., rationalists suggest null hypotheses and counterfactuals).

Bates (1989, chap. 4), for example, offers a series of regression equations that demonstrates that political institutions and public policies, by affecting Kenya's food stocks, stand between drought and famine. Refuting theories of unregulated markets offered by neoconservative development economists and of benevolently regulated markets offered by neoliberal development economists, he presents statistical evidence of a "policy-induced food cycle" (111). Institutions, that is, "may generate pressures that convert abundance into dearth and therefore translate droughts into food crises." Bates considers these lessons generalizable to agrarian politics in other third world countries. As he puts it, "This chapter has taught us about subsistence crises" (115).

The substantive results of social choice theorizing are among the most important and widely discussed hypotheses in political science. For example, Duverger's law (Riker 1982b) states that plurality electoral systems create two-party systems and that proportional representation systems create multiparty systems; Downs (1957) shows the conditions under which parties converge to the median voter; and Olson (1971) demonstrates the conditions under which public goods are underprovided.

In sum, rationalists are led, as if by an invisible hand, to quantitative methodologies and a positivist philosophy of science. They attempt to account for an explanandum (irrational social action) by fitting it into a structure of knowledge: initial conditions (about rational desires and beliefs) and general hypotheses (about their operation) allow them to deduce the anomalous (irrational) phenomenon in question. And while it is indeed true that every action or outcome is in some sense "rational," because there is always some intention, reason, or motivation behind it, rationalists avoid tautology by associating conditions with actions and thereby generating falsifiable predictions.[24]

Chapter 4

Rationalism and Hegemony

Section 4.1 discusses the micro- and macrodeficiencies of the rationalist research program, and section 4.2 shows how these lacunae generate hegemonic tendencies to take over all of social inquiry. Section 4.3 locates pluralistic countertendencies—rationalists who seek to define the baselines and boundaries of their approach explore culturalist and structuralist alternatives—and section 4.4 explains why rational choice theory lowers its positivistic pretensions. I conclude in section 4.5 that rational choice theory should be modest.

4.1. Why Rationalist Social Science Tends toward Hegemony

Nietzsche once wrote that "a state that cannot attain its ultimate goal usually swells to an unnaturally large size. The world-wide empire of the Romans is nothing sublime compared to Athens" (1982, 32). Rational choice theory suffers from micro- and macrodeficiencies that lead it to imperialism. At the microlevel, the insufficiency of reason leads rationalists to extend rationality and thereby take account of identity; and at the macrolevel, the inadequacy of microfoundations leads rationalists to explore institutions and thereby overcome disequilibrium. By engaging in these defensive maneuvers, rationalists subsume rather than engage their opponents, which leads them to claim that rational choice theory is the totality of social science.

4.1.1. The Micro: The Insufficiency of Reason

Many charge that people are not rational but are rather something else—arational, nonrational, irrational, extrarational, antirational, pararational, or boundedly rational. Since I have discussed the nature and limits of rationality elsewhere (Lichbach 1996, 227–34), including the important cognitive-psychological challenge to conventional rationality postulates, I will focus here on a more basic issue: the impoverished view of the self offered by rationalist social science, a problem that arises because of the way rationalists seek falsifiable hypotheses.

41

Recall how their positivistic comparative-static methodology leads to an "observable implications" perspective on hypothesis testing. Since every hypothesis must be evaluated by possible sense experience, the only comparative-static hypotheses that are relevant are ones produced by changes in the observable material constraints that supposedly affect unobservable preferences and beliefs.[1]

Rationalists thus wind up assuming that actors are machines that robotically calculate how external changes affect their fixed values and cognitions. This mechanical-behavioral view of subjectivity is a particularly anemic or thin version of intentionality and rationality. Rationalists who explain action in terms of exogenously changing prices thus inevitably slight questions of identity construction and of interest formation, both of which are treated as external to stable and orderly social relationships and interactions, rather than constitutive of them. In other words, exogenous structures influence the price of behavior but do not constitute or construct actors, that is, their interests and identities. As one critic puts it:

> Collective structures are portrayed as if they were external to individuals in a physical sense. These seemingly extra-material structures, political or economic systems, are said to control actors from without, whether they like it or not. They do so by arranging punitive sanctions and positive rewards for an actor who is assumed to be a calculator of pleasure and pain. Because this actor is assumed to respond objectively to outside influences, "motives" are eliminated as a theoretical concern. Subjectivity drops out of collectivist analysis when it takes a rationalist form, for it is then assumed that the actor's response can be predicted from the analysis of his external environment. This environment, not the nature or extent of the actor's personal involvement with it, is considered determinate. (Alexander 1987, 13–14)

By dichotomizing the objective and subjective parts of the choice problem, rationalist methodology produces a binary view of social life and a schizophrenic understanding of scientific inquiry.

The rationalist perspective is therefore "externalist" and "behaviorist": given that rational actors attempt to adapt efficiently to their material environment, the heart of the theory holds that external conditions and not human consciousness are central (Wendt 1999, 120–21).[2] Parsons thus maintained that rationalists, caught on the materialist end of the "utilitarian dilemma," thereby eliminate subjectivity: "Insofar as the conditions of the environment are decisive it does not matter what ends men may think they pursue; in fact, the course of history is determined by an impersonal process over which they have no control" (1937, 113).[3] This determinism is of course paradoxical: rationalists begin with an internalist explanation (i.e., intentions as causes)[4] but wind up with an externalist one: "It is not the agents' psychologies which primarily explain their behavior, but the environmental constraints they face" (Satz and Ferejohn, cited in Green and Shapiro 1994, 21). The rationalist theory of choice thus implies that actors have no choice but to follow the dictates of their material environment. Latsis refers to the rationalists' no-choice situation as situational determinism: "I shall call situations where the obvious course of action (for a wide range of conceptions of rational behavior) is determined uniquely by objective conditions (cost, demand, technology, numbers, etc.) 'single exit' or 'strait jacket' situations" (cited in Blaug 1992, 154).[5]

The materialistic determination of self-interest also leads to special puzzles. Bates suggests, on the one hand, that people are concerned with efficiency and Pareto optimality because mutual cooperation and social order can help everyone, including themselves: "In an almost Marxian manner, the theory contends that people devise institutions so as to unleash the full productive potential of their economies" (1989, 150). On the other hand, he recognizes that this focus might be taken to imply that actors are even more concerned about equity than about efficiency, about distribution than about production, and about individual property rights than collective outcomes. He thus asserts: "People see clearly where their interests lie. They invest in the creation of institutions in order to structure economic and political life so as better to defend their position within them. They invest in institutions so as to vest their interests" (151).[6] Ultimately, then, rationalists like Bates offer a materialist theory of preferences[7] according to which interests are an obstacle to social order rather than the basis for it.[8] And values (i.e., individualism) divide people rather than unite them. When rationalists sacrifice the subject and surrender the self, they undo the community and unmake the collectivity[9]—hence their felt need to synthesize more collectivist approaches like culture and structure.[10]

How do rationalists answer the charge that theirs is a particularly anemic version of subjectivity—that they lack a theory of preferences[11] or of cognition and that they view ends in a positive sense as random and in a normative sense as equal?[12] They argue that they focus on the important question of how reasonable people are constrained and empowered by their environment. Moreover, social-situation rationalists, who assume that institutions create and influence preferences and beliefs, are able to preserve both determinism and free will, objective reality and subjective perception (Crespi 1989, 15).[13] By equating individuality with rationality, they attribute to people subjectivity and agency, desires and the freedom to choose. The social-situation approach also acknowledges an objective reality: rational people form beliefs that reflect the material conditions they confront. The notion of objective constraints thus allows rationalists to avoid extreme subjectivism, and their notion of the freedom to choose allows them to avoid extreme determinism. Rationalists therefore believe that their interpretivist and structuralist critics have an oddly extremist view of subjectivity, a perspective, of course, that itself is not objectively universal but rather is socially and politically constructed. Finally, while rationalists are willing to work with a division of labor—they supply the laws of interaction, others supply the setting—the culturalists and the structuralists have not fulfilled their part of the bargain. Where is the empirically verified theory of preferences that they complain the rationalists lack?

Many rationalists recognize, however, that the materialism and determinism critiques of rational choice theory do hold for the thin versions of rationality and interests adopted by the neoclassical economists who tell us that there is no disputing taste (Becker and Stigler 1977). Marxists, for example, problematize the translation of objective into subjective interests. They adopt a thick or objective version of interest and thereby dispute the tastes of subordinate members of society. They remind rationalists that wants are different from interests: interests are "real" and hence agents may be unaware of, or mistaken about, their "true" interests (e.g., the debate on power in Lukes 1974). The Marxist message is hence that rationalists should thicken their conception of rationality to take account of the possibility of false consciousness: interests are more than revealed preferences and thus may ultimately be corrected and improved.

More generally, rationalists recognize that people can choose badly. Satisfaction and disappointment are the difference between desire and fulfillment. As the saying goes, the only thing worse than not getting what you want is getting what you want. Gaining an understanding of one's true interests involves careful reflection and the use of reason to guide action. Hirschman thus refers to the "disciplined understanding of what it takes to advance one's power, influence, and wealth" (1977, 38). Truly rational people pursue aspirations, appetites, and passions worth pursuing. Their prudence controls their greed and avarice.

Rationalists also acknowledge that a thicker conception of knowledge is another key to a thicker conception of rationality. Curiosity means that people seek out new information. Reflection means that people assess their own assessments (i.e., form second-order desires and beliefs) and employ external evidence, internal consistency, and ideal standards of satisfaction. And intelligence means that people alter their preferences and beliefs and then act on the basis of new information.[14]

Many rationalists thus concede that psychologists are right to challenge an exclusively materialistic and deterministic rationality, and hence they try to deepen the microfoundations of their models. However, in importing ideas about preferences and beliefs, rationalists appear to claim that they have appropriated whatever of value is to be found in culturalist approaches. Having exhausted cultural theory, this appropriately enhanced rational choice theory becomes all of social science, and its hegemony over the culturalist alternative is thereby established.

4.1.2. The Macro: The Inadequacy of Microfoundations

Rational choice theory has imperialist tendencies as well, because its methodological individualism seeks the intertheoretic reduction of holistic theories, that is, the microfoundations of macropropositions. The underlying claim is that only individual-level mechanisms can offer full explanations, so those are the mechanisms that social scientists should supply. The goal, for example, is to translate Marxism into individual-level terms and game-theoretic propositions. Is methodological individualism a valid approach to the study of large-scale social structures and long-term historical dynamics?

Holistic concepts and theories in fact bear a messy relationship to underlying microconcepts and theories. The intertheoretic reduction of macrooutcomes to microactions and interactions, which thereby eliminates social entities and social predicates in theories, is an impossible research program for numerous reasons.[15]

1. Macrooutcomes, having more than one microfoundation, are characterized by multiple realizability. As Wendt puts it:

Whether it is the relationship of particles to atoms, atoms to molecules, brain states to mental states, speech to language, or individual to social facts, there are often many combinations of lower-level properties or interactions that will realize the same macro-state. No particular state's actions create the tendency

toward balancing and institutional isomorphism. No particular, unchanging distribution of territory or citizens "is" the United States. No particular words are essential to English. World War II would still have been that if Germany had not attacked Greece. And so on. In each case certain unit- or interaction-level states of affairs are *sufficient* for the existence of a macro-state, but not *necessary*. Macro-states are "overdetermined."
. . . [M]acro-level facts often display "compositional and configurational plasticity" in which case macro-level regularities will be discontinuous with micro-level ones. (1999, 152, emphasis in original)

Since multiple possible causal mechanisms may bring about a single macrostructure, microfoundations are not unique, and multiple ones can exist.[16] With a little imagination, moreover, each macrostructure can be related to each micro- and mesofoundation, and vice versa. Any particular lower-level process may therefore be sufficient but not necessary for a macroregularity. Complicated biconditional bridge principles imply that complex systems can coexist at different levels of analysis and consequently that many different microprocesses can drive a big structural proposition.

Hence, a fundamental tension is involved in the rationalists' attempt to overcome the structure-action problem via a search for microfoundations: structuralist and rationalist metanarratives need not coincide because a one-to-one relation between structure and action (i.e., one macrostructure of society is associated with one microfoundation of action) need not exist. The structure-action relationship is many-to-many (i.e., one macrostructure may be associated with many microfoundations; one microfoundation may be associated with many macrostructures).

2. A macroregularity or outcome may not have significant microfoundations. Natural selection, for example, involves an important causal mechanism that does not operate at the microlevel.

3. The movement from structure to action is also indeterminate because microprocesses produce unintended macroconsequences.

4. The microfoundations of macropropositions may be context sensitive due to the way actors interpret their situation. For example, while a collective-action mechanism might underlie a repression-dissent proposition, political repression might beget violent protest under certain regimes and nonviolence under others.

5. By focusing exclusively on microfacts, rationalists may end up providing disparate explanations for events that in fact have a common macrocause (Kincaid 1988, 265).

6. Microfoundations might supply irrelevant detail and leave out the best explanation. The best explanation for a recession, for example, might be a decline in consumer spending that could result from a variety of microlevel forces.

7. Microfoundations are not needed for prediction. Macrofactors may permit better prediction because a theory based on microfactors may be incomplete, whereas the macrofactors may be proximate to the phenomena.[17]

8. Finally, intertheoretical reduction is an underspecified goal because the nature of mechanisms is poorly identified. As Kincaid puts it:

A first problem is that "the mechanism" has no definite sense. For any causal claim about aggregate variables, there are indefinitely many mechanisms. For any mechanism, M, that we cite between social variable A and B we can go on to ask again how M makes the connection between A and B possible. We can postulate both "horizontal" mechanisms—those between M and A or B—and "vertical" mechanisms, that is, the lower-level processes or structures realizing A and determining its causal capacities. In either case, we can go on asking about "the" mechanism as long as we have not reached the fundamental level of nature.

Thus demanding that we cite the mechanisms for macrosociological causation is inherently ambiguous. Do we need it at the small-group level or the individual level? If the latter, why stop there? We can, for example, always ask what mechanism brings about individual behavior. So we are off to find neurological mechanisms, then biochemical and so on. Unspecified "the mechanism" is of dubious sense. (1996, 179)

The search for microfoundations is thus ill defined.

In sum, intertheoretical reduction is an impossible research program, and the search for microfoundations, a chimera. Coleman's project of seeking the microfoundations of macrostructures, an important justification of rational choice theory, is therefore unachievable. Since structure and action are partially autonomous and partially interactive, exclusively microtheories are always incomplete. A social scientific explanation must contain more than individual-level elements. Social science needs both micro- and macrotheorizing, or a multilevel explanatory strategy that recognizes that causality operates at multiple levels of reality.[18]

Since many rationalists concede that the sociologists are right about the inadequacy of microfoundations,[19] they explore the macrostructures—social institutions and large-scale social processes—within which their models operate. For example, in Becker's human capital model, "the exogenous facts all seem to be social. Rational choice theory seems to presuppose rather than eliminate social theory" (Kincaid 1996, 158). Rational choice theories, in other words, inevitably let supraindividual collectivities into the analysis. Individual choice presupposes, after all, the existence of a structure of constraints within which individuals choose. This macrostructure of course provides the preferences and beliefs that help determine equilibrium.[20]

However, in incorporating macroarguments into their fundamental model of individual purpose, choice, and maximization, rationalists appear to claim that they have appropriated whatever of value is to be found in structuralist approaches. Thus enhanced, rational choice theory becomes the totality of social science, and its hegemony over the structuralist alternative is thereby established.

4.2. The Result: Theoretical Synthesis and Empirical Conciliation

Since many rationalists conceded that the culturalists are right about reason and the structuralists are right about microfoundations, they have attempted to subsume structure and culture—in other words, everything—into their approach. Rationalists who extend their paradigm by "exploring the macro" and examine structure, and rationalists who "deepen the micro" and examine culture (Lichbach 1995, chap. 10) accept Levi, Ostrom, and Alt's vision cited earlier: "We expect the next century to witness a major flowering of scientific achievement across the social sciences similar to the neo-Darwinian synthesis of this past century in biology" (1999, 337). Such rational choicers thus seek "the one great scientific system, a system of a small set of well co-ordinated first principles, admitting a simple and elegant formulation, from which everything that occurs, or everything of a certain type or in a certain category that occurs, can be derived" (Cartwright 1999a, 9). Their goal, in other words, is a complete theory of the whole: a few axioms that can deduce laws of unlimited or universal scope, laws that are unconditional and unrestricted, and laws that hold everywhere at all times in all domains. More specifically, rationalist hegemons seek theoretical synthesis by employing the socially embedded unit act and seek empirical conciliation by explaining stylized facts.

4.2.1. Theoretical Synthesis: The Socially Embedded Unit Act

What would a hegemonic rationalist synthesis—one that takes account of the aforementioned cultural and structural critiques—look like?[21] Rationalists make two basic arguments at two different levels of analysis:

> Collective Argument: preferences + institutions → outcomes
> Individual Argument: desires + beliefs → actions

Rationalists argue, in other words, that for individuals, actions result from the combination of desires and beliefs, and for collectivities, outcomes result from preferences filtered through institutions. If rationalist hegemons could reduce culture to individual desires and social preferences, and structure to individual beliefs and social institutions, both arguments would be connected and the goal of one social science achieved (i.e., the Coleman-Boudon diagram in fig. 4.1).

Whether rationalists recognize it or not, Parsons (1937) provided the tools, using the conceptual device of the intentional unit act to synthesize the ideas of several of the founders of social thought.[22] The "action frame of reference," part of his voluntaristic theory of action, was the first great effort to end the war of the rationalist, culturalist, and structuralist schools and integrate the conflicting paradigms. Synthesizers in the rationalist camp implicitly follow Parsons's approach when they recognize that both acts and contexts matter and hence that all acts are socially embedded. Rationalist hegemons thus extend the intentional unit act to take account of the structure-action problem of reconciling individuals and collectivities.[23] Figure 4.1 (Lichbach 1997a; Lichbach and Seligman 2000) has three layers: inner (the individual argument), middle (the collective argument), and outer (the rationalist, culturalist, and structuralist approaches).[24]

The inner or individual layer.   The socially embedded unit act involves a hypothetical person in a situation that is at least partially under his or her control. This actor has some agency—manifesting subjectivity, having purpose, possessing free will, and using reason to act. Agents thus have desires (goals, purposes, and ends) and beliefs (information and knowledge), and they make choices based on them. At this individual level—the individual argument—desires and beliefs direct action (Elster 1989c).

The middle or collective layer.   The socially embedded unit act also

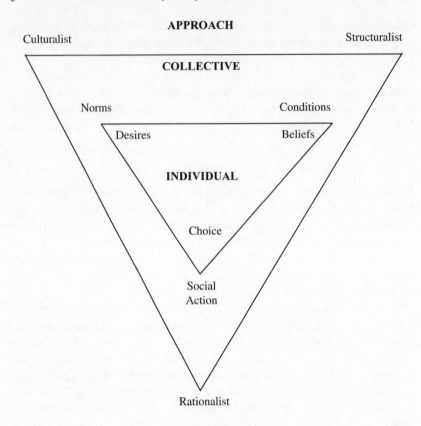

Fig. 4.1.   The socially embedded unit act

involves sets of individuals who constitute some collectivity. People, in other words, are part of some social order. The structure-action or individual-collective problem involves linkages between the three properties of agency and three corresponding properties of society. Individual desires reflect and produce social norms. Individual beliefs correspond to and ultimately influence material conditions. Finally, individual action aggregates into and also responds to collective action. At this collective level—the collective argument—cultural norms (the set of preferences) and environmental conditions (institutions) produce social action (outcomes).

   The outside or research-approach layer.   All grand syntheses, such as Parsons's (1937) voluntaristic theory of action, are subjected to close scrutiny and eventually yield to an intellectual division of labor. Specialists have therefore appropriated each of the components of the socially embedded unit act and spawned their own research communities.[25] Rationalists specialize in individual choice and social action, culturalists in individual desires and cultural norms, and structuralists in individual beliefs and environmental conditions.[26] As indicated by the outer layer of the diagram, each of the schools concentrates on one vertex of the triangle.

In sum, rationalist hegemons act "as if" they believed that the socially embedded unit act partnered with the Coleman-Boudon diagram offers a comprehensive synthesis of research schools. They achieve this synthesis by moving from the corners of the triangle in figure 4.1 to the sides and, finally, to the inside.

While the socially embedded unit act clarifies why rationalists believe that the three research communities complement one another, this multidimensional framework also reveals the tensions among the approaches. (Table 4.1 summarizes the key differences among the research communities discussed in Parts II and III.) While the ratio-

TABLE 4.1. Research Communities and Their Properties

Properties	Community		
	Rationalist	Culturalist	Structuralist
Ontology	rational actors intentional explanations actions, beliefs, desires methodological individualism	rules among actors intersubjective or common knowledge and values	relation among actors holism
Methodology	comparative statics irrational social consequences of individually rational action unintended, unwanted unavoidable, unexpected	interpretation meaning significance; culture constitutes interests, identities, institutions	social types with causal powers; structures with laws of dynamics
Comparison	positivism generalization explanation	interpretivism case study understanding	realism comparative history causality
Lacunae	instrumental rationality mechanical-behavioral view of subjectivity	tautology, teleology in existence and causal impact on outcomes	iron cage determinism voluntarism absent
Subtraditions	human nature rationalists social situation rationalists	subjectivists intersubjectivists	state/society pluralism-Marxism-statism
Exemplars	Bates	Scott	Skocpol

nalists' attempt to subsume their opponents is based on an individualistic understanding of culture and structure, the culturalist tradition cannot be reduced to the individual desires that drive choice, and the structuralist tradition cannot be reduced to the individual beliefs that direct choice. In short, there is more to culturalist and structuralist thought than personal preferences and individual understandings.

I will shortly show that the rationalist bid for hegemony bears some interesting parallels with culturalist and structuralist imperialism. Hegemonic rationalists incorporate culture by developing thick versions of rational choice theory that are compatible with thick culturalists who seek to incorporate agency. Section 5.1 shows that thin culturalists argue that thick culturalism comes too close to rational choice theory's atomistic reductionism. Since ideal-type culturalists eschew even thick culturalism, they will surely reject its cousin—thick rationalism—as an imperialistic pretender to culturalism. Section 6.1 argues similarly. Hegemonic rationalists incorporate structure by developing thick versions of rational choice theory that are also compatible with thick structuralists who seek to incorporate agency. As thin structuralists charge that thick structuralism comes too close to rational choice theory's atomistic reductionism, they will certainly reject its cousin—thick rationalism—as an imperialistic pretender to structuralism. In sum, while some culturalists and structuralists solve their structure-action problem by adding action (i.e., moving toward individualism), more paradigmatic culturalists and structuralists will forever reject the rationalists' bid for hegemony. And, of course, since culturalists conceive of culture as collective and structuralists conceive of structure as configurational, rationalists cannot go all the way to either the culturalist position or the structuralist position—study how actors are themselves constituted by values and cognitions or explore structural dynamics—and remain rationalists (see table 7.1).

Such schemes as the socially embedded unit act are therefore too clever for their own good. As Neurath puts it: " 'The' system is a great scientific lie" (cited in Cartwright 1999a, 6). Cartwright rails against "fundamentalism" or foundationalism and points to "the pernicious effects of the belief in the single universal rule of law and the single scientific system" (16). She argues that the unification of science under a single paradigm is impossible even in the natural sciences.

The laws that describe this world are a patchwork, not a pyramid. They do not take after the simple, elegant and abstract structure of a system of axioms and theorems. Rather they look like—and steadfastly stick to looking like—science as we know it: apportioned into disciplines, apparently arbitrarily growing up; governing different sets of properties at different levels of abstraction; pockets of great precision; large parcels of qualitative maxims resisting precise formulation; erratic overlaps; here and there, once in a while, corners that line up, but mostly ragged edges; and always the cover of law just loosely attached to the jumbled world of material things. For all we know, most of what occurs in nature occurs by hap, subject to no law at all. What happens is more like an outcome of negotiation between domains than theological consequence of a system of order. The dappled world is what, for the most part, comes naturally: regimented behavior results from good engineering. (1)

In natural science's "patchwork of laws" (Cartwright 1983), as discussed more fully in chapter 10, laws are "numerous and diverse, complicated and limited in scope" (Cartwright 1999a, 10). Understanding comes from a variety of competing and overlapping paradigms that cannot all fit together into one system whose parts stand in a fixed relation to one another. Rational choice theory will therefore fail "to take over the entire study of social and economic life" and become a "theory of everything" (3, 2n. 2).

4.2.2. Empirical Conciliation: Stylized Facts

Rational choicers also seek empirical conciliation with the middle-range theories, low-level hypotheses, and stylized facts of existing literatures. They try to subsume and thereby explain old ideas and old evidence. Green and Shapiro thus contend that "rational choice theory is nothing but an ever-expanding tent in which to house every plausible proposition advanced by anthropology, sociology, or social psychology" (1996, 254). They see rational choice theorists as advocating "a style of theorizing that places great emphasis on the development of post hoc accounts of known facts" (1994, 34). Seeking to explain already observed empirical regularities, rational choicers look for confirming examples, fit their theories to the data, and use case studies to illustrate their points.

Since many post hoc accounts are possible, this is not a good research design. In seeking to subsume existing propositions and observations on their own terms, rational choicers have a "tendency to ignore, absorb, or discredit competing theoretical accounts" (Green and Shapiro 1994, 203) rather than to test competing causal explanations or to evaluate alternative (i.e., cultural and structural) theoretical accounts. For example, many recent solutions to the collective-action problem extend the borders of rational choice explanations to explain or endogenize norms, trust, ideology, reputation, institutions, and leadership rather than take them as given (Axelrod 1984; Coleman 1990). Bates and Bianco thus observe the recent trend toward "the synthesis and reinterpretation of noneconomic variables that have traditionally been studied by the behavioral sciences" (1990, 351). Does pushing the rational actor paradigm to these new frontiers, as collated by Lichbach (1995, chap 4) as community solutions, represent "progress"? Miller argues that given the way many have tried to solve repeated Prisoner's Dilemma games, "the choices of 'homo economicus' in repeated, personal, norm-constrained, social interaction become virtually indistinguishable from the behavior attributed to 'homo sociologicus.' This leads us to ask if there is anything left in the classic distinction between economics and sociology" (1990, 343).

Rational choicers need out-of-sample predictions so that they explain more than the styled facts they began with. As Green and Shapiro put it: "Data that inspire a theory cannot, however, properly be used to test it, particularly when many post hoc accounts furnish the same prediction. Unless a given retroductive account is used to generate hypotheses that survive when tested against other phenomena, little of empirical significance has been established" (1994, 35). Even more important, rationalists need more credible alternatives than an ad hoc proposition or a null hypothesis of randomness. Green and Shapiro thus argue that "we should accord explanatory power to rational choice theories in priority to the credibility of the null hypotheses over which they triumph" (1994, 37). More "credible null hypotheses" means hypotheses that represent important and powerful alternative theories that emerge from well-articulated theoretical paradigms, like culture and structure, with which rationalists compete. Rational choicers thus need to confront powerful alternatives and plausible rival hypotheses more explicitly, and they need to make more effective use of counterexamples that can serve as benchmarks.[27]

Lacking out-of-sample predictions and confrontations with important foes, rational choice theory is only weakly supported—untestable and untested—with many complaining that it has failed to produce nonobvious and nontrivial empirical findings. Johnson thus writes: "I have tried to think of one book in which rational choice theory has been applied to a non–English-speaking country with results even approximately close to the claims made for the method. I cannot"

(1997, 173). Green and Shapiro (1994)[28] make several charges about the absence of an evidentiary base behind the rationalist paradigm:

- Successful empirical applications of rational choice models have been few and far between. (ix)

- Rational choice scholarship has yet to get off the ground as a rigorous empirical enterprise. (7)

- The case has yet to be made that these models have advanced our understanding of how politics works in the real world. (6)

- To date few theoretical insights derived from rational choice theory have been subjected to serious empirical scrutiny and survived. (9)

- Contrary to the assertions of Riker and others that rational choice theory fares well in political science because the field is theory poor, in fact rational choice theory fares best in environments that are evidence poor. (195)

- Rational choice theorists often seem to want to leave what they see as the mundane work of application and testing to unspecified others—who seldom materialize—and concentrate on the intellectual challenges of high theory elaboration. But no viable army can consist solely of generals, and even if theorists could really expect to delegate empirical work to others, the question remains whether such a division of labor is desirable. Arguably, mastery of the subject matter under empirical observation is required to guide and inspire innovative theorizing. (196–97)

Given the professed positivism of rational choice theorists, this is a severe indictment.

Rationalist attempts at theoretical synthesis and empirical conciliation therefore cannot succeed (also see sect. 10.4.1). Some rationalists, however, recognize that there exist powerful alternatives to rational choice theory and that not all empirical findings can be reconciled with a single theoretical synthesis.

4.3. Countertendencies: How Rationalist Social Science Defines Its Baselines and Boundaries

Not all rationalists are imperialists. Splitters rather than lumpers take rational choice theory as a baseline (sect. 4.3.1) from which to explore both the school's strengths and its weaknesses. They are therefore open to establishing boundaries to their approach (sect. 4.3.2).

4.3.1. Baseline Rationality

Davidson offers the key justification for the rationality assumption: "Irrational behavior only makes sense against a background of rationality" (cited in Callinicos 1988, 119). The social scientist therefore begins inquiry by assuming a "Principle of Humanity": actors are behaviorally and attitudinally rational (Callinicos 1988, 109, 119). Only after repeated failures or only after rationality is so "thickened" that it no longer makes sense should one abandon the baseline model and assume that actors are not rational.

Consider the scope or boundaries of rationality more closely. The debate over what is *really* a rational choice theory comes down to specifying core assumptions of what constitutes "rationality" and what "interests."[29] To this end, one may build upon Elster and distinguish five levels: intentionality, thin rationality, thick rationality, selfish and outcome-oriented rationality, and pecuniary rationality (1983a, 2–26; 1983b, 69–88; 1989a, 34–49).

Deeds may be intentional or nonintentional. Falling outside of the purview of rational actor theories is nonintentional and hence nonconsequentialist behavior—an unthinking action-reaction response to material conditions or a similarly unthinking affectual, traditional, or habitual reflection of social norms. Intentional action, by contrast, means that actors assess their situation in terms of their own desires and beliefs and act accordingly. These reasons explain or cause action. Intentional behavior itself may be rational or nonrational. Rational action at this level thus means simply consistency. Nonrational action—desires, beliefs, or a combination of desires and beliefs that are inconsistent—falls outside of the purview of rational actor theories.

Rational action in turn may be either thin or thick. Thin rationality meets the demands of a minimalist definition of rationality, that desires and beliefs are internally consistent and consistent with one another. This thin version of rationality has been termed *instrumental rationality* (Heap et al. 1992, 4). Others call it a *present-aim theory* because it implies the efficient pursuit of whatever aims one has at the moment (Parfit 1984, 117). Weber uses the term *zweckrational,* or ends-rational, to refer to the "rational consideration of alternative means to the end, of the relations of the end to the secondary consequences" ([1924] 1968, 24–26).

Because thin rationality can result in unintended and undesirable

consequences, actors may supplement thin rationality with thick rationality, or reason. People can do more than passively respond to choices
in a consistent way; they are free to choose and adjust goals and also
may be able to change the situation or constraints in which they find
themselves. This version of rationality that takes intentionality and
agency further has been termed *expressive rationality* (Heap et al. 1992,
21). It has also been called a *self-interest theory* of rationality because it
implies that a person's goals and beliefs efficiently promote the person's interests (Parfit 1984, 3). It is the basis of Parsons's (1937) "voluntaristic" theory of action. Weber uses the term *wertrational,* or value-
rational, to refer to the "self-conscious formulation of the ultimate
values governing" action that builds an individual's autonomy ([1924]
1968, 24–26).

In short, thin versions of rationality do not predict their content,
whereas thick versions give them some content because they inquire into
the rationality of desires and beliefs. Several considerations affect rational desires. There is one dichotomy between self-interest and self-transcendence and another between a process orientation concerned with
means and an outcome orientation concerned with ends. Finally, mater-
ial- or outcome-oriented action can focus on pecuniary (monetary) payoffs or nonpecuniary (general political, policy, or moral) payoffs.

Modifying Elster (1983a, 10), one can move from the core to the
periphery of the rationalist research program as follows. To explain a
given action, assume that it is economic (pecuniary). If not, assume
that it is at least selfish and outcome oriented. If not, assume that it is
at least thickly rational—expressive (of autonomous goal setting). If
not, assume that it is at least thinly rational (consistent). If not, assume
that it is at least intentional (reasoned). In short, the core of the theory
assumes an economic actor motivated by pecuniary self-interest, but
rationalists can legitimately move as far as the rational and even intentional actor. These five levels are displayed in figure 4.2.

The question of interests raises similar boundary concerns.
Hirschman indicates that interests can be "understood in the wider or
in the narrower sense" (1977, 40). He writes that historically

"interests" of persons and groups eventually came to be centered
on economic advantage as its core meaning, not only in ordinary
language but also in such social-science terms as "class interests"
and "interest groups." But the economic meaning became dominant rather late in the history of the term. When the term "interest" in the sense of concerns, aspirations, and advantage gained

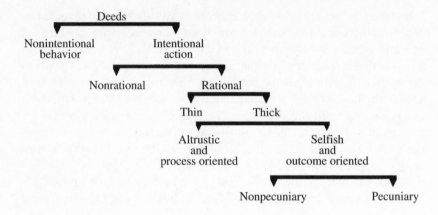

Fig. 4.2.   The core of the rationalist research program

currency in Western Europe during the late sixteenth century its meaning was by no means limited to the material aspects of a person's welfare; rather, it comprised the totality of human aspirations, and denoted an element of reflection and calculation with respect to the manner in which these aspirations were to be pursued. (32–33)

A thin sense of interest thus corresponds to the thin rationality described previously; a thick sense of interest corresponds to a thick version of rationality.

A related distinction is between subjective and objective versions of interest (Balbus 1971). Subjective or thin versions indicate that the actor finds something interesting or that he or she finds something pleasurable, because it satisfies his or her preferences or wants. This version of interest represents a "shallow" calculation of gain. Objective, or thick, versions of interest indicate "an interest in." That is, the person is affected by a "true" need rather than merely a "false" want for something: interests are thus really to his or her advantage or good. This version represents a "deep" calculation of gain.

All rational choice theories make one of the aforementioned assumptions with respect to rationality and interest. Why not move, in Hardin's (1982, 10) terms, from a narrow to a wide notion of rationality? Why not adopt, in Elster's (1983a, 1) terms, a thick rather than a thin notion of rationality? Why not propose, in Freud's terms, a synthetic theory that assumes that behavior is a function of id (impulse), superego (conscience), and ego (reason)? Collective action theories, for example, often expand the notion of rationality to include nonrational motivations designed to overcome pecuniary self-interest (Lichbach 1995, sect. 4.2). These theories combine various approaches to social order: political economy with political sociology, law and society with law and economics, resource mobilization with relative deprivation, or contingency with inherency (Lichbach and Seligman 2000). Synthesis appears to be the obvious solution to the controversy among research programs with alternative views of human nature.

While the expansion of rational choice theories to encompass nonrational motivations probably dominates applications, such expansion is usually not helpful. All social scientific theories must be based on some more or less explicit motivational assumptions about human nature. But if we permit too many motives, our assumptions become eclectic and thus inconsistent, and our theories become true only because they are tautological. As Jasay maintains: "We do not usually know for sure what is in people's heads. However, this is no license for ascribing to them unexplained dispositions, propensities, and aversions which can be turned to support almost any claim concerning behavior" (1989, 165). Considerations of parsimony thus dictate that we avoid indiscriminately "widening" and "thickening" rationality. The marginal benefits of additional bits of understanding do not approach the marginal costs of complicating the theory in an effort to redescribe reality.

This is also Harsanyi's reasoning: "If we make our motivational assumptions complicated enough, we can 'explain' any kind of behavior—which of course means that we are explaining absolutely nothing. To take an extreme example, we could 'explain' any conceivable action of a given individual simply in terms of some desire (or preference) on his part to act in this particular way. Obviously this would be a completely useless tautological explanation" (1969, 518). For example, it is not helpful to hypothesize that people commit suicide because they prefer death over life or that people help others because they prefer to do good rather than to do evil. Harsanyi thus cautions:

> We must definitely resist the temptation of postulating more than
> a very few basic motives in our theory, whether for the sake of
> "greater realism" or for any other reason. This is so because a
> theory which involves a *large* number of distinct motives, and
> therefore involving a *large* number of parameters to be estimated

from the empirical facts, cannot be used to explain these empirical facts without inadmissible circularity. This is of course just
another way of saying that if our theory is to have any real
explanatory power then our motivational assumptions must be
kept at a very low level of complexity—even if they do not have
to be made quite as simple as to postulate economic self-interest
as the *only* important motive of human behavior. (521, emphasis
in original)

It is all too easy and none too illuminating to argue, for another example, that what motivates dissidents against a regime, on the one hand, is
anger, frustration, despair, rage, hostility, resentment, vengefulness, and
hate; and that what motivates dissidents toward one another, on the
other hand, is love, a sense of belonging, and mutual interdependence.

Hardin, too, sees problems with thick notions of rationality. First,
he writes: "The results are too flimsy to be worth the effort, since most
of the relevant behavior may be explained already by the narrowest
assessment of costs and benefits, and the host of motivations underlying the additional elements of behavior to be explained is sure to be far
more crudely measured than the narrowest cost-benefit motivation."
Second: "The focus of the theory usually is shifted from explaining the
behavior of a particular group to explaining the behavior of those in
the group who *do* join in cooperative enterprise, especially in an interest group organization, so that it is not the logic, but the problem, of
collective action that has been modified." Third: "Only in an assumed
context can one sensibly be asked whether one's action was rational.
To make a more complete assessment would require packing the context and much of the social history that has brought that context about
into one's decision calculus. No decision theorist in his right mind
would attempt to do so." Finally: "In the modified logic of collective
action, the additional bits are minuscule, extremely costly, and of
painfully inferior quality. Qualitative accounts carry us farther than
such trivializing quantification" (1982, 14).

Rational action theorists therefore should not begin by attempting to
develop synthetic theories that expand rationality to cover all conceivable motivations. They do better first to adopt thin rationality as a baseline model in which self-interest is taken to be materialist and pecuniary
and then to assess errors. If necessary, they can try to explain systematic
deviations with microtheories drawn from psychology.

Elster articulates this baseline approach well: "When trying to
explain individual participation in collective action, one should begin

with the logically most simple type of motivation: rational, selfish, out-come-oriented behavior. If this proves insufficient to explain the phe-nomena we observe, we must introduce more complex types, singly or in combination" (1989a, 37). He proposes the following: "When setting out to explain a given piece of behavior, assume first that it is selfish; if not, then at least rational; if not, then at least intentional" (1983a, 10). Further:

> This [rational actor] model is logically prior to the alternatives, in the sense that the social scientist should always be guided by a postulate of rationality, even if he may end up by finding it vio-lated in many particular cases. This presumption is a "principle of charity". . . one should look very closely at apparently irra-tional behavior to see whether there could not be some pattern there after all. Needless to say, charity should not be stretched too far, and there may come a point where the observer simply has to state that to the best of his understanding the behavior has no rational motive. (1984, 116–17)

Weber is perhaps the earliest advocate of this approach: "In order to penetrate real causal interrelations, *we construct unreal ones*" ([1903–17] 1949, 166, 185–86, emphasis in original). One of these "unreal" causal relationships—Weber's "ideal types"—is *zweckrational,* a useful base-line from which to evaluate empirical cases. Olson (1971, 160–63) too recognizes that a thick notion of rationality makes a theory tautologi-cal while a thin notion offers a good starting point for inquiry.

Critics of rational actor theories are, however, skeptical that highly restrictive assumptions about rationality will carry the theories very far. In conflict studies (Lichbach 1995), however, there is evidence that collective action theories based on thin notions of rationality can explain a great deal, even if not everything, about collective protest. The accomplishments of the rational actor approach, as Harsanyi points out, are quite amazing.

> Of course, nobody denies that this one-motive theory of human motivation, which makes economic self-interest the only impor-tant objective of human behavior, represents a very drastic and unrealistic oversimplification of human motivation as we know it. It is really quite surprising—yet it is a clearly established and very important empirical fact—that a major segment of real-life economic and political behavior *can* actually be reasonably well explained in terms of this simplistic motivational assumption.

Nevertheless, in my opinion it is an equally clearly established empirical fact that many important aspects of everyday economic and political behavior *cannot* be explained in terms of this over-simple theory of human motivation. (1969, 519)

I therefore endorse the three-step research agenda outlined by the philosophers Elster and Hardin, endorsed by the game theorists Harsanyi and Rapoport, and applied by Weber and Olsen to their substantive work. Rational choice theorists should begin with thin theories (that assume pecuniary self-interest) as their baseline model, determine how much of the phenomena under question can be explained by such theories, and only then adopt thicker theories to account for phenomena that remain inexplicable. If the third step proves to be the most valuable—if additional microassumptions about motivation prove essential—so be it. But before they attempt to synthesize their major competitors, rational choice theorists should initially remain consistent with the core of rational actor theorizing.

Of course, other baseline models of human motivation besides rationality have figured prominently in the social sciences. For example, models of randomness, reproduction, and action-reaction exist in studies of domestic political conflict (Lichbach 1992). Economists sometimes advance a variant of the baseline strategy in the form of alternative baseline models (chap. 8).[30] But rational actor models of motivation, as generally the most productive in the social sciences, have earned a privileged position, and therefore the preceding three-step research agenda should be given priority.

4.3.2. The Boundaries

Given that pecuniary self-interest often proves to be an inadequate motivation, rational choice theories frequently take account of values and norms, bounded rationality and asymmetric information, nonpecuniary motives and other-regardingness. Given that the lack of structure often proves to be an inadequate starting point for comparative and historical analyses, rational choice theories often take account of political, social, and economic institutions. These limitations of rational actor theories have thus led the research program into territory beyond its economic base. But how far can rational action theories be pushed? What are the limits of rationality? What is the scope of rational actor models? The answer lies in exploring what the approach explains well and what it explains poorly.

Collective action theories, for example, offer better explanations of some aspects of collective action than others (Lichbach 1996, 242–44). They can better account for nonparticipation than for participation in collective action. And they work best

- ♦ in concrete situations (those with readily identifiable actors, actions, and outcomes)
- ♦ with actors who are unitary rather than collective
- ♦ if the coalitions and alignments among groups are not important
- ♦ with actors who possess fixed goals and who make stable evaluations of outcomes
- ♦ with a large number of actors or a small number rather than with an intermediate number
- ♦ when actions produce outcomes without a large element of chance
- ♦ when there are large differences in choice or when rational action matters much
- ♦ and with elites, leaders, and entrepreneurs (a theory of the supply of collective action) rather than with masses, followers, and foot soldiers (a theory of the demand for collective action).

But there is a great irony in all this: collective action theories work best when least needed and tend to work poorly in the most interesting situations. But then again, is any theory likely to explain the nonparticipation of complexly defined and highly interrelated followers in low-benefit, low-cost, chancy, and changing situations that occur in an ill-defined noninstitutional setting?

Indeed, one of the purposes of developing a research program is to discover its limitations, to establish what it does not know and what it cannot know. There is no shame in acknowledging trade-offs and delimiting boundaries. The first task of rationality, moreover, is to circumscribe its scope (Barry 1965; Hardin 1982; Elster 1989a; Mansbridge 1990). Elster is eloquent on this point when he writes that "as in Kant's critique, the first task of reason is to recognize its own limitations and draw the boundaries within which it can operate," for, he warns, "rationality itself requires us to recognize this limitation of our rational powers, and the belief in the omnipotence of reason is just another form of irrationality"(1989c, 17, vii). To quote him yet again: "It is only by the close consideration of reasons for failure that it will be possible to construct a more general account of human behavior in which the concept of rationality will have a privileged but not exclusive role" (cited in Levi et al. 1990, 1).

While establishing rational actor theory's trade-offs and boundaries is no great shame, it is no great honor either. Rationalists, as I will show in section 10.2.4, invest heavily in new applications that potentially transcend the following limitations of their theories: (1) they do not explain many things; (2) they explain some things less well than do other types of theories; (3) they can explain these things only if supplemented by additional microassumptions about culture and macroassumptions about structure; (4) they require auxiliary assumptions that do not fit well with the program and do most of the explanatory work. The beauty of an appropriately bounded rational choice explanation, however, is that it is useful even when wrong. If it can explain the outcome in question parsimoniously, we need do no more. If it fails to illuminate key aspects of reality, then that very failure may point the way to determining where its assumptions must be supplemented or its approach transcended, and hence how to construct a more complex and useful explanation.

4.4. Countertendencies: Why Rationalist Social Science Lowers Its Positivistic Pretensions

Methodological difficulties also push some rationalists in the direction of a more modest rational choice theory.[31] Rationalist social science has in fact developed an entire vocabulary to describe the insufficiency of reason. There are fundamental problems with equilibrium and disequilibrium; with initial and scope conditions; with dynamics (i.e., path dependency, punctuated equilibria, and learning); and with models based on comparative statics and nuts and bolts.

First, the notions of equilibrium and disequilibrium have some fundamental difficulties that must be addressed.

The equilibrium analysis of games has numerous technical difficulties. Rationalists specialize in action. While game theory is the science of how the action of one person depends on the actions of others, in all but the simplest of circumstances rationalists encounter the indeterminacies and disequilibria of choice. The welter of solutions in cooperative game theory has produced confusion, leading rationalists to turn to noncooperative game theory. But this branch of game theory has its own problems. If there is only one equilibrium point, rational choice theorists investigate factuals (why individuals took prescribed equilibrium paths) and counterfactuals (why individuals did not take nonequilibrium path actions). However, some noncooperative game theoretical models have no equilibria. The solution—mixed strategy equilibria—also has its problems (Ordeshook 1986, 136–37). Other noncooperative game-theoretic models, those having multiple equilibrium points, raise the problem of coordinating on the different outcomes of the game. New developments in extensive-form games—subgame-perfect equilibria—handle the multiple equilibria problem but raise thorny issues about the perceptions and expectations of actors that complicate the problem of falsifying and hence rejecting the models. Such models, for example, require one to conjecture about what would occur off the equilibrium path; it is a fascinating counterfactual but one that is difficult to investigate empirically. In short, knowledge of beliefs and their revision is too primitive to assure us that extensive-form modeling is correctly specified.

Disequilibria lead to strategizing and the dismal science. Given that games are often characterized by no equilibria or multiple equilibria rather than a unique, Pareto-optimal equilibrium, Riker argues that political science is "*the* dismal science" (1980, 443, emphasis in original). Since no determinate predictions of equilibria are possible, game-theoretic models are compatible with many outcomes. A political struggle to create an equilibrium is therefore likely, and hence "politics" is the practical implication of disequilibria. Strategic actors will attempt to manipulate the structural features of institutions to produce their favored outcome. Pivots, gatekeeping authority, and multiple veto points allow actors to employ threats, tit-for-tat, bluffs, first-mover advantage, bargaining, precommitment, promises, and signaling. Riker (1982a), for example, studies the politics surrounding particular historical events such as the Civil War by exploring preference falsification, agenda control, the change of institutions, the introduction of new voters, and the generation of new issues.

The fragility of equilibria thus leads to a strategic struggle over equilibrium institutions. The endogeneity of institutions, in turn, further increases disequilibria, creating outcomes that are doubly unstable and hence unpredictable. In sum, the forces that produce any one outcome are finally balanced and persist only in the short run.[32]

Second, the initial conditions and scope conditions affect equilibria in fundamental ways.

Initial conditions affect strategizing. Game-theoretic models rely on initial assumptions about preferences, beliefs, and endowments that partially determine the outcome. Change the initial structures and conditions, and you change the outcome. Models of chaos and complexity lead one to speculate that such models may be hypersensitive to initial conditions.

Scope conditions affect strategizing. Structure also matters in another way. Comparative statics does not produce universal propositions. As shown in section 10.2.1, no science has pure "if x then y" hypotheses. Since all propositions are derived from more general theories or sets of assumptions, hypotheses take the form "Given a, b, and c, if x then y." In other words, "In case i, which has characteristics a_i, b_i, c_i, and x_i, characteristic y_i follows." All seemingly general propositions are therefore actually context specific. Instead of studying how x influences y, social scientists study the variations (which involve context) in how x influences y. The scope, variance, and regularity of laws hence must be investigated rather than assumed. Given that conditionality, contingency, and context are always relevant, rationalist generalizations are limited.

Third, various types of dynamics—path dependency, punctuated equilibria, and learning—also affect equilibria in fundamental ways.

Path dependency occurs.   Equilibrium outcomes are path dependent. Once a strategic action is taken, it affects subsequent actions. Sets of actions become equilibria. An equilibrium institution, once arrived at, has lock-in effects: it influences subsequent activities by changing the context within which these activities occur.[33] Strategic situations are therefore turning points, branching spots, and critical junctures—decisive moments in social life—that shape subsequent developments by limiting counterfactuals (roads not taken, unactualized possibilities) and hence orienting future actions. They also create temporally ordered sequences of events.[34]

Punctuated equilibria exist.   Sequences of strategic equilibria—called punctuated equilibria—are moved along by the crises produced by external shocks.[35]

Learning happens.   Information is critical to rational choice models. Learning occurs as beliefs and expectations are updated.

Finally, the two major approaches to falsifiability—Samuelson's comparative statics and Elster's nuts and bolts—have fundamental problems.

Samuelson's comparative static approach rarely generates falsifiable propositions.   Rational choice theorists investigate exogenous shocks to an equilibrium system (e.g., the end of the cold war; unbalanced North-South economic growth in the pre–Civil War period) that alter equilibrium choices. Unambiguous comparative static predictions are rare because they require auxiliary assumptions about cross-partial derivatives that are much more interesting and important than the deductions themselves (Silberberg 1978, 164–67, 289–93). As Archibald argues, "It seems unfortunately to be the case that the general qualitative content of maximizing models is small, if not trivial. . . . [The] 'general' allowance of qualitative information is not sufficient for an unambiguously single prediction to be obtained" unless highly restrictive auxiliary assumptions are made (1965, 27). Becker's work, especially on crime, has been criticized along these lines (Blaug 1992, 222–28; Heineke 1978, 18–19; Simon 1987, 28–31). Moreover, the relationship between (typically) deterministic game-theoretic equilibrium predictions and stochastic empirical analysis is usually unspecified.

Elster's nuts-and-bolts alternative produces uniqueness and not generality.   If one looks at rational choice ideas as a toolbox or a set of "nuts and bolts" to explain outcomes (sect. 10.2), predictions of macrodevelopments and macrooutcomes by comparatively and historically inclined rational choice theorists must take account of four factors. First, static *combinations* or interactions can occur among general micromechanisms (e.g., the Tit-for-Tat, bandwagon, entrepreneurial, and patron solutions to the collective action problem; Lichbach 1995). Second, dynamic *sequences* can also occur among microrationalist processes. Third, static structural *circumstances* can interact with microfoundational building blocks in historically specific ways. Finally, dynamic *changes* in structural conditions, which include trends, cycles, and shocks, can surround a social outcome and thus also interact with general microfoundational building blocks in historically specific ways. In sum, static combinations and dynamic sequences of general microprocessual building blocks interact under static and dynamic environments to affect macrodevelopments and macrooutcomes in historically unique ways.

The vicissitudes of macrodevelopments and outcomes therefore result from the interplay of multiple general tendencies and the intrusion of specific internal and external forces. The causation of large-scale events linked through time, in other words, is a conjunctural unfolding of simultaneous and dynamic general process and specific contexts. Large-scale events are thus the result of independent sequences of small-scale events that converge at a particular time and place. A large event is a function of complex interactions of many factors whose conjuncture is crucial to the event's occurrence. Multiple streams of inputs and complex feedback channels influence a single output.[36] And such combinations within and across structure and action produce historical specificity.

Microprocesses are thus robust, repeatable, and recurrent building blocks that interact with one another such that outcomes unfold in particular ways. They are like Weber's ideal types: a battery of them may be applied to a single case, and one can study how their interactions and their combinations with environments produce historically unique results. Given that each microprocess has a somewhat autonomous internal logic and exerts a somewhat independent causal force, large-scale developments and outcomes are characterized by radical historical contingency.

Looking at rational choice theory as Elster's (1989b) toolbox rather than as Samuelson's (1947) comparative static proposition-generating machine, we therefore discover that reality is causally heterogeneous—there are many different overlapping and nonoverlapping causes. And since complex conjunctural and interactive conditions are at work, we also discover that these multiple causes have dense structuring conditions.

The implications are profound: there is no one comprehensive explanation of a social phenomenon, social scientific theories are never complete, and any one theory is inherently partial. As Little puts it, "There is no reason to expect that any single theoretical framework can explain a complex social or historical process" (1989, 27). Most important, there are always competing explanations, and neither deductive nor inductive logic can conclusively reduce them to a single one. Since conceptual and theoretical pluralism is inevitable, inquiry must be open-ended and conducted from a variety of perspectives. Weber ([1903–17] 1949, 72–81) holds that there are many different kinds of explanation, and each offers a different kind of understanding. Elster's toolbox methodology thus opens the door to the alternatives to rationalism—culturalism and structuralism.

In sum: rational choice methodology itself has shown the limits of reason in human affairs. Since the technical problems of game-theoretic solutions and the disequilibrium that ensues lead to endless political struggles, rational choice is the dismal science. Since strategies are greatly influenced by initial conditions, scope conditions, and past equilibria, reality appears to be an open-ended historical accident. Since path dependence, punctuated equilibria, and learning result in contingency, history is one damn thing after another. And since Samuelson's (1947) comparative statics does not generate simple generalizations subject to clear-cut falsifications, we are left with Elster's (1989b) nuts-and-bolts alternative, which reveals the complexity of social causation and the necessity of alternative perspectives. Every methodological innovation in rational choice theory has therefore opened new doors but also generated new problems.

All of this is fitting. Rationalist theory, designed to break down cul-turalist and structuralist metanarratives that are overly coherent, inte-grative, and totalist, does such a good job of showing that things are unintended, unwanted, unpredictable, and unstable that its own pre-tensions break down as well.

4.5. Modest Rational Choice Theory

It would then be foolish to pretend that rationalist theories offer the master key—a philosopher's stone or a Rosetta stone—that can unlock every problem in the social sciences. The theories neither resolve all fundamental problems, nor clarify all obscure puzzles, nor settle all outstanding controversies. Science (but not pseudoscience) seeks establish its perimeters. Only when we can "limit, specify, focus and contain" (Geertz 1973, 4) rational choice theories can we begin to appreciate their true value. They can explain a great deal, though clearly not all, about human behavior and social outcomes.

Modest rational choice theory thus abandons its positivistic preten-sions and tries to establish its limits by moving from thin to thick ratio-nality. Such a modest rational choice theory then concerns itself with important foils: plausible rival hypotheses against which to compare its baseline predictions and further establish its boundaries. The search for a modest rational choice theory therefore immediately raises the question: what are the alternatives? I now turn to culturalism and structuralism.

Part III

The Alternatives to Rationalist Hegemony

Chapter 5

Cultural/Interpretive Theory

Culturalists tackle social theory differently than rationalists do.[1] The alternative to assuming rationality is not to assume irrationality but rather to assume that rules and norms guide actions. Section 5.1 shows that culturalist thought comes in two versions. The subjectivist approach (e.g., Almond and Verba 1963, 1980 on civic culture; Inglehart 1977, 1990 on postmaterialism) is closer to rational choice theory than to structural theory in that it employs survey research on individual preferences, beliefs, and actions. Since my goal is to show that rational choice theory is not all of social science, I develop the intersubjectivist approach (e.g., Scott 1985)—which is closer to structural theory in that it employs fieldwork in a culturally holistic manner—as the ideal-type culturalist thought. *Culturalist* in this chapter and in this book therefore means *intersubjective culturalist*. Hence, culturalist ontology depicts a world dominated by intersubjective meaning (sect. 5.2); culturalist methodology consists principally of interpretive studies of meaning in which analysts try to discover the rules of social order (sect. 5.3); and the corresponding culturalist lacunae include what Parsons (1937, 732) calls "idealistic emanationism" (sect. 5.4).

5.1. Thin and Thick Culturalists

Culture is *both* inside *and* outside the individual. While it is interior in that individuals are socialized into it, culture is also exterior in that it is materially real and transmitted from the past. There are therefore two approaches to culture: subjectivists concentrate on the internal side and intersubjectivists on the external. I will consider each perspective in turn.

Subjectivists maintain that knowledge does not derive directly from the sensate, noncultural experience of the material world. There might be real world structures "out there," but knowledge does not directly reflect them because the mind is not a passive receptor. Our nervous system automatically leaves out characteristics of the events before us.[2] Moreover, the individual mind does not perceive things randomly and gather information haphazardly, but rather employs its structure-producing capabilities. A perceiving mind, that is, actively organizes the material world of space, time, and causality to allow the acquisition of knowledge. Subjectivists thus study how an intersubjective culture is internalized as a set of individual mental processes, including consciousness, intuition, understanding, reason, perception, cognition, feeling, and judgment, that structure experience. By investigating human consciousness, especially the facilities of the human mind that employ concepts and language, subjective culturalists offer a thick theory of the mind (self) that explains how we construct meaning out of the stream of our experiences.

Subjective culturalists thus hold that the outside world acquires meaning only through our interpretation of it. There are no simple facts independent of our perception, and the world is partly a personal invention.[3] Following Kant ([1781] 1964), they stress the importance of both subjective mental processes (phenomena) and objective reality (noumenon), as our experience involves elements constituted by us and the world. Though related, being and seeing are different.

And herein also lies the difference between behavior and action. Given that people must make sense of the external world, everyone finds himself or herself amid material objects that call for interpretation. Crespi's definition of behaviorism in stimulus-response terms should be read as a culturalist critique of rationalism.

> In order to analyze and interpret behavior it is sufficient to establish the connections between a given structure of the individual organism and the environment's structure, between the stimulus and the reaction to it: survival instincts, the fulfillment of biological needs, the orientation towards reproduction and the survival of the species can represent in this case forms of adequate interpretation. According to this perspective we can apply the content of behavior to a molecule, to a plant, to an animal, and even to man when we can leave out of consideration his more specific qualities. Economics and statistics can well analyze the *average* behavior of social actors in a particular environment. (1989, 5–6)

Subjective culturalists thus borrow from Weber ([1924] 1968), who distinguishes action from behavior in terms of subjectivity: internal orientation as intentionality. Animals *behave;* only humans *act.* Animals respond to internal and external stimuli; people attach subjective meaning to their actions. Because the same behavior lies behind an involuntary twitch of the eye, a wink of the eye, and a parody of the wink of the eye (Geertz 1973), subjective meaning must be understood in order to fathom action. Weber uses the analogy of the two bicyclists: "A mere collision of two cyclists may be compared to a natural event [in my terms, behavior]. On the other hand, their attempt to avoid hitting each other, or whatever insults, blows, or friendly discussion might follow the collision, would constitute 'social action' " (see Eisenstadt 1968, 5). Hence, action is not a direct response to facts but a response to meaningful and significant social facts. Since culture constitutes action, action may be distinguished from behavior by virtue of intention and goals or by virtue of social consciousness and other-regardingness.

Subjective culturalists, in sum, study culture primarily as the cognitions and motivations that produce actions (Almond and Verba 1963, 1980; Inglehart 1977, 1990; Barnes et al. 1979). Survey researchers, for example, argue that people undertake activities on the basis of complex psychological mechanisms that are often simplified into ideologies and belief systems. Liberalism, socialism, individualism, and Republican and Democratic party identifications affect all aspects of politics and society (e.g., individuals, groups, parties, policies, regimes, and nations) and govern all aspects of political and social action (e.g., trust, conflict, cooperation, voting, and participation).

While subjective culturalists argue that their view of culture is an advance over the rationalists' behavioralism, intersubjective culturalists believe that it suffers from a level-of-analysis, or micro-macro, problem. Consider an old joke: Two robbers stop someone in a dark alley and attempt to relieve her of her money and jewelry; a survey researcher comes along, hands out questionnaires, and subsequently discovers that public opinion favors redistribution of property. What makes this joke amusing? Since individuals are interdependent and not independent, and since culture is intersubjective and not subjective, the aggregation is inappropriate. The intersubjective approach to culture explicitly recognizes culture's transindividual and transsituational character. Culture is an intersubjective set of ideas, a common set of beliefs and values.

To understand this alternative approach, which is adopted by Scott (1985), one must further understand the problems with the subjectivist approach to culture. Critics charge that the subjectivist view of culture is reductionist because it adopts an atomistic focus on individual consciousness. The critics charge that subjectivists study attitudes and not culture, psychology and not sociology, the private and not the public world. Culture, by contrast, is socially established through signs, symbols, and structures of meaning. As Bakhtin maintains, "Ideology is not within us, but between us" (cited in Wuthnow 1992, 159). Values, by definition, must be held in common. Alexander argues similarly: "There is subjective order rather than merely subjective action because subjectivity is here conceived as framework rather than intention, an idea held in common rather than an individual wish, a framework that can be seen as both the cause and the result of a plurality of interpretive interactions rather than a single interpretive act per se" (1990, 1). Wittgenstein makes a parallel argument: language is communal; there are no private languages.

The consequence is that subjective culturalists of a Kantian sort take either a universalistic or a psychological approach to culture that assumes that only one set of a priori principles/structures are imposed by the mind. The idea of one conceptual framework—fixed, immutable, and constant across people—implies that culture is a general attribute of human nature and that there is only one possible set of these structuring categories. Subjective culturalists of the Nietzschean sort, by contrast, imply that there are as many conceptual frameworks as there are people. Culture is thus idiosyncratic or peculiar to an individual.

There is of course a third Weberian possibility: alternative conceptual frameworks or different forms of consciousness, each particular to a particular cultural group and historical period. As MacIntyre puts it:

> The role and function of desires in the self-understanding of human beings vary from culture to culture with the way in which their projects and aspirations, expression of needs and claims upon others, are organized and articulated in the social world. Where someone moves toward a goal deliberately and intentionally, it is not necessarily or always the case that this is destined to be because that person is moved by a desire or even, in some wider sense, by a passion. Whether it is so or not will depend in important part on the way in which in the relevant culture the relationship between the inner world of purposes, felt needs, pains, pleasures, emotions, desires, and the public world of actions, claims, excuses, pleas, duties, and obligations are organized. The inner world may mirror, be responsive to, be compensating for, or be reacting against the constitutive elements of the public social world. Even the possession of some conception of a universal inner self is not culturally necessary and one culture that functioned very well without it was that portrayed in the Homeric poems. (1988, 21)

If culture is communal rather than individual or universal, then the terms of that culture must be investigated. Intersubjective culturalists do so holistically rather than in the reductionist manner of the subjectivists. Wuthnow points out that an intersubjective (or more structural) view of culture

> pays relatively little attention to the individual. . . . Its emphasis is on the objectified social presence of cultural forms. Symbols— utterances, acts, objects, and events—are assumed to exist in some ways independent of their creators and to take forms not entirely determined by the needs of individuals. . . . Rather, the elements of culture are arranged in relation to each other, forming identifiable patterns. Understanding the structure of culture, therefore, requires paying attention to the configurations, categories, boundaries, and connections among cultural elements themselves. (1987, 332)

At a deeper (dramaturgic) level, the intersubjectivists are concerned with moral order.

> Although it remains important at this level to examine the patterns among symbols that give them coherence, these patterns are assumed to play an expressive role in dramatizing and affirming the moral obligations on which social interaction depends—the moral order. It is again assumed at this level of analysis that cultural elements are not exclusively (and perhaps not even primarily) shaped by individual motives and meanings. Rather, the *sociological* importance of cultural elements arises decisively from the fact that they take place within a matrix of moral obligations and are, in turn, shaped by the structure of social relations. (332, emphasis in original)

Hence meaning—the symbolic and expressive aspects of social life— is just like interpretation in that it must be understood in communal terms.

In sum: intersubjective (thin) culturalists argue that subjective (thick) culturalism comes too close to the atomistic reductionism of rational choice theory. Hegemonic rationalists incorporate culture by developing thick versions of rational choice theory that are at best compatible with thick culturalism. Since ideal-type culturalists do not even like thick or subjective culturalism, they will forever reject its cousin—thick rationalism—as an imperialistic pretender to culturalism.

Two approaches to culture—subjective and intersubjective—thus mediate between rationality and structure. The rationalists' "desires + beliefs = choice" framework maps beautifully onto survey research, and hence subjective culturalists are closer to the rationalists than to the structuralists. Common ideas are another type of relation among people, and hence the intersubjective culturalists are closer to the structuralists. Since this book attempts to demonstrate that rational choice theory can never become all of social science, I need to draw sharp contrasts with rationalist thinking. My ideal-type culturalist is therefore Scott, rather than Inglehart. Thin culturalists—those who stick close to the core of their research program—are therefore intersubjective culturalists. To make the text flow more smoothly, the term *culturalist* henceforth refers to *intersubjective culturalist.*

5.2. Culturalist Ontology

Culturalists argue that reason is conditional and contingent, not necessary and universal, and that it varies by culture, which means that the individuals in a group or community have common orientations, or ways of looking at the world. Cultural norms are to be found in all of society's institutions—political, religious, economic, and social—and in society as a whole. More specifically, a collectivity's intersubjective consciousness is composed of two elements: cognitions and conscience.

First, culture involves common knowledge about the past, present, and future construction of reality, or about the way the world operates, thereby providing individual agents with the shared cognitions (information, understandings, and beliefs) needed to make sense of their environment. Absent these things there is uncertainty, insecurity, and chaos—an inefficient social order. Durkheim thus refers to "collective representations," or to the ways society thinks, conceives, and perceives things and itself ([1893] 1933), and Searle refers to "collective intentionality," or to shared beliefs directed at something (1995, 23). Common beliefs can be about anything: values, ideas, resources, constraints, facts, arguments, causality, the self, or God. From these beliefs, members of a collectivity develop mutual expectations that take account of others' actions and hence enable them to coordinate their interactions. People sense that they are part of a larger project: what I do is part of what we do. For example, in football a lineman moves as part of a play, and in a concert a violinist performs as part of a symphony.

Second, society structures preferences so that they are not merely given, random, and idiosyncratic. With its common norms, values, and rules about the way the world should be, culture prescribes and proscribes behavior. Durkheim[4] thus argues that society becomes synonymous with morality, and Bacon refers to the natural prejudices to which people are liable, or the "idols" of the tribe (Hamlyn 1987, 126). More generally, norms are regulative and imply external control. Searle indicates that "some rules regulate antecedent existing activities. For example, the rule 'drive on the right-hand side of the road' regulates driving; but driving can exist prior to the existence of that rule" (1995, 27). Norms are also, more interestingly, constitutive: they are so accepted and internalized by the individual and the collectivity that they constitute the self and the group and thereby come to define the game of social life. In Hollis's words: "People could have gone fishing before there were rules to regulate this activity; but they could not have played chess without rules. Moves in a game have meaning only within the rules, as, for instance, words have meaning only within a language and within practices of communication" (1994, 18).[5] Change the rules and you change the game.[6]

In sum, culture involves both common knowledge (cognitions) and common norms (conscience) that allow people to manage the practicalities of daily life via the mutualities of collective action and social coordination. Powerful, organized, and systematic normative systems combine both common knowledge and common norms (Lukes 1985, 241). Scott thus refers to "the moral logic of tradition" in which custom and ritual define a community's meaningful roles or expectations (1985, 234). Religion, for example, unites norms and understandings, and political ideologies such as communism or liberalism define values and beliefs.[7]

Culture, more specifically, has five sets of properties that constitute social order and allow people to manage daily life.

1. Culture is structured, enduring, and hence autonomous.
2. Culture is an intersubjective language that enables communication.
3. While culture causes collective outcomes, it more importantly constitutes reality. All of the social world is thus socially constructed: individual and group identities, interests, actions, and ideas.
4. Culture legitimates social order. Conversely, it defines what is worth fighting over and hence characterizes the rules by which conflict takes place.
5. Culture provides a set of symbols that constitute shared signification and personal meaning.

I will now investigate these properties.

First, culture is structured, enduring, and hence autonomous.

Culture is structured.   It has an internal unity, logic, and order. Culturalists view culture as an integrated system in the same sense that material structuralists view structure as a system. Religion is an example: "In the early formative period of a religion's development, diverse interests and historical accidents affect the religion's conception of the divine and its promise of salvation. But, Weber argues, once a religion is sufficiently 'rationalized'—that is systematized and unified—its core religious ideas come to have a logic of their own" (Swidler in Weber [1922] 1991, xiii).

Culture is enduring.   It is transmitted from generation to generation via learning. Change is thus gradual. Inglehart, a survey researcher, recognizes this aspect of culture: "Cultural theory implies that a culture *cannot* be changed overnight. One may change the rulers and the laws, but to change basic aspects of the underlying culture generally takes many years" (1997, 19, emphasis in the original). The change that occurs, moreover, is principally generational: younger age cohorts (with a particular formative experience) replace older ones (with a different formative experience).

Culture is autonomous.   It is not just a dependent variable. Culture cannot be reduced to some other level but is independent of these other phenomena. Material structuralists are thus wrong in that culture is not an epiphenomenon of the material world. Culture is also autonomous of individuals and hence must be studied as a social fact governed by its own laws. Durkheim argues this point about the *conscience collective,* maintaining that it "has its own life," is "a distinct reality," possesses "its own distinctive properties," and has a characteristic "mode of development" (cited in Lukes 1985).

Second, culture is an intersubjective language that enables communication.

Culture is intersubjective.   There are intersubjective aspects and not only subjective components to culture. Searle (1995, 3) refers to institutional facts that are dependent on human agreement and hence are a human creation. Much of "objective" reality exists because of such human agreements; for example, something is money because we agree it is money. These institutional facts are to be distinguished from brute facts that exist independently of us.

Culture is a language.   The intersubjectivity of culture is best revealed by its linguistic aspects. In order for the single intentional act to have "meaning," actions must be materially and externally signed. Such communication of meaning to others can occur through verbal utterances, written statements, physical gestures, dramatizations, material artifacts, art, and music. Culture is a form of discourse that consists of all these signs, symbols, and codes. Culture also allows the communication of information that can reduce the uncertainties and risks of collective action. Since communication is based on shared symbols or rules, both enemies and friends understand what is meant by *reds, bleeding-heart liberals, the pigs, the establishment, fat cats,* and *the power elite.* In short, culture as a language has rules that people use and hence that scholars can study.

Third, while culture causes collective outcomes, it more importantly constitutes reality. All of the social world is thus socially constructed: individual and group identities, interests, actions, and ideas.

Culture causes collective outcomes.   Social action is not simply a function of external circumstances. Culture is an independent variable that can have major consequences for the state, the economy, and society. Ideas, under various sorts of conditions, have been hypothesized to influence forms of government policy, party systems, democratic stability, protest and rebellion, class conflict, and gender relations.

Norms and beliefs are not only causal. Culture also constitutes reality in that it is embedded in concrete processes, practices, and products—art, scientific works, religious symbols, clothing, and manners—that are part of the lives of the ordinary members of a culture. Since culture has symbolic meaning and yet operates within the material world, it is "observable" in several spheres.

Culture constitutes individual identity.   Contra Western thought and psychology, there is no inherent conflict between individual and group; rather, such conflict is socially constructed. Individualism is "a sociological account of individuals as a set of operative ideals, moral beliefs, and practices, indeed as a religion in which the human person becomes a sacred object" (Lukes 1985, 339, on Durkheim). Weber ([1904–5] 1985) thus studies how Western individualism was socially constructed. And Durkheim ([1893] 1933) argues more generally that individual identities are constructed by representations (conscience, cognitions) of society that allow one to differentiate one's self from others. As he puts it, "The individual is dependent on society" (cited in Lukes 1985, 286).[8]

Even the most individualistic idea is culturally constructed. Individual rights are defined by the collectivity. Durkheim thus criticizes natural rights theories that maintain that "the right of an individual depended on the notion of the individual as such [instead of] on 'the way in which society puts [the right] into practice, conceives it, and appraises it' " (cited in Lukes 1985, 271). Suicide is also a function of the collectivity, as Durkheim ([1897] 1951) argues, and anarchic suicide is related to social order. Anomie, moreover, is a function of societal development and hence is also culturally constructed. Finally, liberty is socially constructed because private contracts and public constitutions depend on society to define the conditions of their operation and the scope of their binding power.[9]

Some culturalists argue that the level of individualism is a function of the level of societal development. Durkheim suggests that as society becomes more complex "the conscience collective increasingly reduces itself to the cult of the individual" (Lukes 1985, 157, on Durkheim). The public sphere shrinks, becoming abstract and universal, rather than specific and concrete. While individualism is necessary for the advancement of society, it also prevents its further advancement, as Comte suggests: "The same principle that alone has enabled society in general to advance and grow threatens, from another point of view, to decompose it into a multitude of unconnected corporations which scarcely seem to belong to the same species" (cited in Lukes 1985, 141). As Durkheim (and Tocqueville before him) recognize, individualism and its associated autonomy and isolation challenge social order and social control because they deemphasize obedience and duty. Hence, individualism promotes social disorder, disintegration, and anarchy. Yet paradoxically, as individuals become increasingly autonomous (because of the division of labor), they become more dependent on society. Hence, individualism becomes the basis, indeed the only moral basis, of social solidarity (i.e., the division of labor produces organic solidarity).

Culture constitutes groups.   The self is really a "communal self" developed in interactions with others. Culture defines kinship, age, gender, ethnicity, and class, linking individual and collective identities as the basis of group life. It provides a group's shared understandings, common identity, and political community. It defines membership criteria, by distinguishing between insiders and outsiders and marking group boundaries (in-group/out-group distinctions), thereby managing intergroup relations and defining the permeability of groups. Culture provides we-feelings, distinctiveness of life-style, group identification, common fate, and social attachments. It defines "who lives with whom, who spends time together, to whom one is most attached emotionally, who controls scarce resources, how property is transferred between generations, and how work is organized" (Ross 1997, 48). Culture provides political resources for group entrepreneurs interested in organization and mobilization. It provides authority for implementing decisions and permits groups to discipline their members. It facilitates internal communications. It provides mechanisms for decision making. Finally, culture offers a political ideology for group action.[10]

Culture constitutes interests. Culturalists argue that interests are not given but rather must be interpreted. Hall indicates that "most people have multiple interests, often associated with the multiple roles they play in the world, some of which conflict with each other, and many of which are subject to multiple interpretations." The dynamic element of politics is persuasion: "Politics is fundamental to this process of interpretation. Much of what goes on in the political arena is, in fact, a struggle among political entrepreneurs to define the way in which the electorate or potential followers within it interpret their interests. . . . In short, politics is not only a contest for power. It is also a struggle for the interpretation of interests. . . . [I]nterests must be seen not as givens, but as objects of contestations" (1997, 197).

People thus have ideas about what is and what is not in their interest. These ideas also suggest causal patterns that indicate which policies will work toward their benefit. Ideas about Keynesian economics involve how the Keynesian policy system operates. Such ideas have implications about the policy's desirability and hence might fuel political action (Hall 1989). Does free trade, for another example, help or hurt the middle class?

Culture constitutes action. All three elements of the intentional act—desires and beliefs driving actions—are culturally constituted. Scott thus highlights the difference between mechanical behavior and meaningful action that I alluded to earlier:

> To confine the analysis to behavior alone, however, is to miss much of the point. It reduces the explanation of human action to the level one might use to explain how the water buffalo resists its drive to establish a tolerable piece of work or why the dog steals scraps from the table. But inasmuch as I seek to understand the resistance of thinking, social beings, I can hardly fail to ignore their consciousness—the meaning they give to their acts. The symbols, the norms, the ideological forms they create constitute the indispensable background to their behavior. However partial or imperfect their understanding of their situation, they are

driven with intentions and value and purposefulness that condition their acts. . . . How, finally, can we understand everyday forms of resistance without reference to the intentions, ideas, and language of those human beings who practice it? (1985, 37–38)

In other words, culture is a framework for interpreting the actions of others. After all, "few behaviors are so universal that they require little or no interpretation" (Ross 1997, 49).

Culture constitutes ideas.   Commonsense thought and scientific theories are socially determined. Culturalists would argue, for example, that there are no nonrelative, non–context- dependent criteria by which to evaluate truth, beauty, and justice.

Fourth, culture legitimates social order. Conversely, it defines what is worth fighting over and hence characterizes the rules by which conflict takes place.

Culture legitimates social order.   I have already discussed the consensual view of social order—community—that focuses on common knowledge and common values. Now consider the conflictual view of social order—hierarchy—that focuses on legitimacy. Since uncertainty and incomplete information characterize social life, the organizational or structural dimension of social life has the potential of being misperceived. Even more important, it can be seen as unfair and illegitimate. By framing alternatives and constraining opportunities, social order advantages some and disadvantages others. Values instill trust in hierarchies, regulate arbitrary power, construct meaning in authority systems, constitute common identity in stratified systems, foster solidarity among unequals, legitimate the social division of labor, establish justice for distribution systems, and validate superordination. Culture, in short, legitimates privilege and prevents the mobilization and countermobilization of resources in a free-for-all struggle for control and domination. Given that people cannot continually fight over who gets what, when, and where, culture offers the basic premises—the norms, rules, or laws—that make social interaction and hence social order repeatable and regular.

Culture and its concomitant community are thus the bases of social control. Viewed from one perspective, they provide standards of individual and collective obligation "that lie beyond immediate relations of production and serve both to create and to signify the existence of community—one that is more than just an aggregation of producers" (Scott 1985, 169). Roles dictate standards of social respect and mutual recognition, or "reputation, status, and prestige."

These, in turn, provide social sanctions that restrain self-seeking individualism, dog-eat-dog competition, and beggar-thy-neighbor strategies of survival.[11] As Scott puts it: "It is shame, the concern for the good opinion of one's neighbors and friends, which circumscribes behavior within the normal boundaries created by shared values." Hence, there is a "*collective* and *public* recognition that the village has an obligation to protect the livelihood of its members." Mutual expectations and preferences make the village, in effect, "one family" (234, 17, 212, 196, emphasis in original).

From another point of view, however, culture is a tool of domination used by superordinate groups. Lamont and Wuthnow are concerned with "how representations of social relationships, the state, religion, and capitalism contribute to the reproduction of colonial, gender, or class domination" (1990, 295). And Alexander makes the following Gramscian point about hegemony: "Although society is utterly hierarchical, the ruling class does not sustain itself mainly by force. Society is not primarily an economic or potential order but a 'moral-political bloc.' It is held together by what appears to be the voluntary adherence to dominant ideas" (7).[12]

Culture constitutes conflict.   While culture constitutes social order, Scott also argues that social order is contested. In contradistinction to the Parsonians, he offers a " 'meaning-centered' account of class relations" in the village of Sedaka (1985, xviii). Since class consciousness is constitutive of class relations and class conflict, the "public symbolic order" is based on a "symbolic balance of power" derived from class. Class conflict is therefore "a struggle over the appropriation of symbols, a struggle over how the past and present shall be understood and labeled, a struggle to identify causes and assess blame, a contentious effort to give partisan meaning to local history." For example, the breaking of accepted social conventions and behavioral norms leads to such symbols and exemplars as "the greedy rich" and "the grasping poor" (25, 22, xvii, 18).

The state of nature is therefore as much a competition over values as a contest over interests (Huntington 1996). Bloom writes that "cultures fight wars with one another. They must do so because values can only be asserted or posited by overcoming others, not by reasoning with them. Cultures have different *perceptions,* which determine what the world is. They cannot come to terms. There is no communication about the highest things. . . . Culture means a war against change *and* a war against other cultures" (1987, 202, emphasis in original).

In sum, culture is constitutive of *both* consensus *and* conflict. On the one hand, class struggle "requires a shared worldview. . . . [It cannot make sense] unless there are shared standards of what is deviant, unworthy, impolite" (Scott 1985, xvii). On the other hand, class struggle is contingent on the betrayal of shared worldviews: "What is in dispute is not values but the facts to which those values might apply: who is rich, who is poor, how rich, how poor, is so-and-so stingy, does so-and-so shirk work?" (xvii). Some conflicts thus occur within preexisting and accepted rules and reinforce culture; other conflicts occur about the rules and challenge culture. Some norms are designed to facilitate cooperation among friends; others, among strangers and even enemies.

The best way to demonstrate that culture constitutes a social order is, in fact, to show how it constitutes conflict within that social order. Searle writes:

> Even most forms of human conflict require collective intentionality. In order that two men should engage in a prizefight, for example, there has to be collective intentionality at a higher level. They have to be cooperating in having a fight in order for each of them to try to beat the other up. In this respect, prizefighting differs from simply beating up someone in an alley. The man who creeps up behind another man in an alley and assaults him is not engaging in collective behavior. But two prizefighters, as well as opposing litigants in a court case, and even two faculty members trading insults at a cocktail party, are all engaged in cooperative collective behavior at a higher level, within which the antagonistic hostile behavior can take place. (1995, 23)

Hacking argues that "whenever we find two philosophers who line up exactly opposite on a series of half a dozen points, we know that in fact they agree about almost everything. . . . If two people genuinely disagreed about great issues, they would not find enough common ground to dispute specifics one by one" (1983, 5). And Strauss writes that "every disagreement, we may say, presupposes some agreement, because people must disagree about something and must agree as to the importance of that something" (1989, 246).

Culture, moreover, is a tool of protest used by subordinate groups (Scott 1985). A revolutionary cadre of intellectuals can lead subordinate groups to reject dominant values and raise the level of their consciousness by reaffirming their group's perspectives and ideologies. Conflict thus involves cultural orientations derived from the mainstream and yet opposed to the dominant discourse (Ross 1993, 21–23).

Finally, culture provides a set of symbols that constitutes shared signification and personal meaning.

Culture is symbolic.   Human orientations are shared and mediated through symbols that are emotional and expressive (Habermas 1984), normative and value oriented (Parsons 1937), and ideological and political (Mann 1993). Culture and community underlie the symbolism of daily life and the world is thus constituted by social interactions and communicative acts endowed with deep and hidden significance. Kincaid indicates that "symbolic meaning refers, for example, to the meaning anthropologists sometimes attribute to rituals—as when Turner claims that the Ndembu milk tree stands for matriarchy or Geertz claims that the Balinese cockfight is a comment on Balinese class relations" (1996, 193). Geertz (1973, 89) defines culture as "an historically transmitted pattern of meaning embodied in symbols, a system of inherited conceptions expressed in symbolic forms by means of which men communicate, perpetuate, and develop their knowledge about and attitudes toward life."

Culture constitutes personal meaning.   Culture goes beyond shared symbolisms and provides interpretively felt and expressed meaning. Social order (hierarchy, inequality, power) is open and arbitrary, complex and incoherent, and ultimately incomplete. People thus need a feeling of mission and purpose, accomplishment and fulfillment—their own inner sense of worth and meaning—in their lives. A Weberian "calling" (Weber [1904–5] 1985) allows people to experience personal unity, integration, and identity. Without a calling, Durkheim ([1897] 1951) argued, life is empty and unfulfilled; individuals experience the loneliness, anomie, amorality, hopelessness, cynicism, frustration, anxiety, and depression of an externally directed life; and this state of moral emptiness can ultimately lead to suicide.

Selfish ends, in particular, are an insufficient motivation for action. People need to project meaning onto the world, to express their commitment to truth, beauty, and justice. The underlying significance and rationality of one's actions are thus derived from prevailing norms and beliefs. Humans need these moral commitments, ideals by which to live and die, and hence seek this ethical guidance. It is only through such self-transcendence that one can serve the self. In sum, people seek meaningfulness in their daily lives, and their work has meaning only if it serves some larger purpose, some intersubjectively binding moral structures, beyond themselves. Human beings therefore create and support institutions and traditions that express a conception of both the good life and the just society.

5.3. Culturalist Methodology

The upshot of these five sets of properties is that culturalists try to understand the common rules and expectations that give subjective and intersubjective meaning to life. As argued earlier, subjective culturalists, like their rationalist colleagues, adopt an intentionalist frame of reference, that desires and beliefs direct action. However, they take one step back from the rationalists and examine how the material conditions of existence (e.g., race, gender, class) drive the values and cognitions (e.g., liberalism, party identification) that guide action (e.g., voting, campaigning, protesting). As Antonio puts it: "Because humans are value-implementing beings, causal relations in the cultural sciences must be 'understandable' in terms of configurations of meaning that express typical motives of 'ideal type' actors in culturally defined situations" (1985, 21). This perspective thus leads to a survey research methodology and a positivist philosophy of science.

Other culturalists argue otherwise, that comprehending the material world is not the same as comprehending the social world and that the social world must be understood from within rather than explained from without. Analysts must go beyond establishing the external, materialistic causal connections sought by rationalist *gedanken* and instead should comprehend the self-understanding of human beings. These culturalists, in short, discard positivism and adopt an interpretive philosophy of science.[13] They ask of the person they observe, What is he doing? Gardening, taking exercise, preparing for winter, or pleasing his wife? The methodology of interpretation—hermeneutics or *verstehen*—differentiates itself from positivism by privileging the following.

Interpretation over motives.   Geertz rejects a focus on the subjective motives that cause action. Much more important than examining an actor's mental structures is making sense of his or her socially constructed interpretations of events. Anthropologists and ethnographers thus "read" discourses, interactions, events, and material artifacts to discover what they can tell us about intersubjective culture.

The concrete over the general.   Interpretivists seek to understand the significance, importance, and meaning of particular actions and events rather than to explain universal cause-and-effect relationships. They focus on "the temporal and spatial relatedness of historical particulars" (Griffin 1992, 417).

The collective over the individual.   Given that human actions are intentional, the human sciences should study emotions, purposes, attitudes, and other subjective dispositions (Scott 1985, 45) for the sole purpose of illuminating how an intersubjective culture constitutes reason, identity, action, and social order. Since the meaning of an action is a function of the agent's particular situation, the norms, forms, and practices of his or her society are relevant. Interpretation thus involves what Weber called value relevance: meaning relative to culture. MacIntyre consequently argues that intentional action needs a normative context or tradition to be understood: "We cannot, that is to say, characterize behavior independently of intentions, and we cannot characterize intentions independently of the settings which make those intentions intelligible both to agents themselves and to others" (1984, 206).

The subject over the observer.   Interpretations are infused with the analyst's purposes. Griffin writes that events consist of the "raw material of social action but are defined and constructed, from beginning to end, by the analyst. What is included as description of an event, then, is a problem of sociological historical purpose, and that is a property of the analyst rather than of history 'objectively given'" (1992, 417). Hence "theory infuses colligations, permeates events, and structures narratives" and "an event cannot be defined, much less explained, without recourse to historical concepts and categories" (420, 421). Culturalists thus suggest that there is no neat separation of sociology and history. Observation is infused with theory and, inversely, theory is infused with observation. Nevertheless, interpretive approaches are premised on the idea that participants' understandings might not be the same as scientists' understandings, making it essential to try to see things from the actor's point of view.[14] The goal is to arrive at an empathetic understanding of others—their consciousness and existence as meaningful experience.

The whole over the parts.   Interpretation involves a hermeneutic circle: the parts must be understood in terms of the whole and vice versa. Meaning thus must be established holistically: interpretivists begin with a set of prior meanings and use them to determine the meaning of particular actions.[15] Griffin (1992) calls these *colligations:* one interprets an entire system and not its parts.[16] Culturalists thus interpret the meaning of any concept in terms of its oppositional relationship to other concepts in the system (e.g., master and slave).

The constitutive over the causal.   Wendt writes that

ideas or structures have constitutive effects when they create phenomena—properties, powers, dispositions, meanings, etc.—that are conceptually or logically dependent on those ideas or structures, that exist only "in virtue of" them. The causal powers of the master do not exist apart from his relation to the slave; terrorism does not exist apart from a national security discourse that defines "terrorism." These effects satisfy the counterfactual requirement for causal explanations, but they are not causal because they violate the requirements of independent existence and temporal asymmetry. Ordinary language bears this out: we do not say that slaves "cause" masters, or that a security discourse "causes" terrorism. On the other hand, it is clear that the master-slave relation and security discourse are relevant to the reproduction of masters or terrorism, since without them there would not *be* masters or terrorism. Constitutive theories seek to "account for" these effects, even if not to "explain" them. (1999, 88, emphasis in original)

As Wendt's examples make clear, interpretation involves constitutive rather than causal thinking.

The unobservable and deep over the visible and superficial.   Finally, Gellner indicates that interpretation requires deep analysis: "It is *not* true that to understand the concepts of a society (in the way its members do) is to understand the society. Concepts are as liable to mask reality as to reveal it, and masking some of it may be part of their function" ([1962] 1970, 148, emphasis in original). Often interests are not given and transparent, and often motives need to be ferreted out of particular cultural contexts. Interpretivists thus investigate the multiplicity of human expressive forms—texts, text analogues, artifacts—because any single form may be puzzling, anomalous, incomplete, and contradictory. Taken together these forms may make the surface meaning of any single text clear (Huff 1984, 11).

5.4. Culturalist Lacunae

The empirical difficulties in ascertaining that a norm exists seem formidable. I will discuss the problems of evaluating arguments about the existence of norms and then the problems of assessing their causal significance.

Norms are bounded.   Norms occur within a culture or a community, but the latter is not a domain with readily recognizable boundaries. Core and periphery are poorly defined. Where, Ross asks, "does one culture stop and another begin?" (1997, 61). For example, what are the boundaries of Western culture? American culture? New England culture? Boston culture? Upper-class Boston culture? Moreover, cultures suffer from Galton's problem: the interaction of cultures affects each culture.

Norms are contested. Within-culture variation can be considerable. Conflict over norms occurs at multiple levels. First, within individuals: people hold multiple loyalties because they belong to more than one community. Second, among individuals: people disagree about norms, and individuals have different values. Third, among groups: sets of individuals might have homogenous values, but the groups in a single society might hold conflicting values. Fourth, between an individual and the society: an individual's values might be at variance with prevailing norms. Nonconformity to norms or deviance can occur, making individual violation of norms, or "contranormative" behavior, another possibility (Blake and Davis 1964, 466).[17] Finally, between a group and the society: subcultures might represent heresies and heterodoxies that involve the violation of norms.

Since culture is contested at every level, how can we establish that a norm exists? Cultures are always a mix of contradictory and competing, dominant and subordinate, norms. There are moralities, not morality: the meaning of truth, beauty, and justice is often disputed. While a holistic conception of culture leads to organicism and the anthropomorphizing of a "people," the questions "which values?" and "whose values?" must be asked. The operational issue is how wide a variance in the kinds and levels of norms a culture can incorporate. When is a value or belief no longer part of the culture?

Norms are multileveled. One must distinguish between norms and goals.

> The traditional [Parsonian] concept of the "ends" of action can be viewed as actually including two different levels of the internal, subjective reference of action, the levels of "goals" and "norms." This division is produced by the inherent tension between action's internal reference and its constraining objective conditions. Norms are the general conception of future expectations towards which action is directed. It is the opposition between normative ideals and conditions that generates goals. Goals are the specific ends pursued in any given act, those ideal states which are pursued with reference to particular conditions. (Alexander 1982, 66)

One must also distinguish between norms about proper rules and norms about proper acts, since act utilitarianism is different from rule utilitarianism. Finally, one must distinguish between actual rules (you should) and norms about rules (you should listen to shoulds)—second-order norms or metanorms.[18]

Norms are incomplete.   Rules are never exhaustive but must be operationalized and applied. Moreover, they are always subject to different interpretations: with some clever manipulating, almost anything can be made to conform to a rule, and almost anything can be made to conflict with the rule. As President Clinton once said, "It depends on what 'is' is." There are also variations in incompleteness. Rules are different from conventions in that the former are definite, codified, official, and formal, while the later are more ill defined.

Norms change over time.   A culture is a worldview that provides meaning to its history and pattern to its development. The moral themes of history are thus wrapped up with the ethos or spirit of a historical people. Jews are defined by Passover and Americans by the Fourth of July. However, this perspective can lead to a teleological conception of history: there is purpose and movement in history; the past and the future are wrapped in one evolutionary/cyclic view. Yet rules, values, conceptual schemes, and ideas can change abruptly, and new ideas are often adopted. More generally, there is the question of the historical development of norms. Nietzsche's (1989) genealogy of morals thus examines their development over time.

Part of this change is that norms are renegotiated and redefined, as Blake and Davis observe: "There are some people who regard certain rules as 'outdated' and 'unjust' and make efforts to change the rules; and there are other people who, feeling that the rules are adequate and legitimate, resist change. Because of this criss-crossing, many societies can undergo remarkable social transformation, all the while retaining an adequate degree of social control" (1964, 466).

Moreover, some norms prescribe change, for example, the American embrace of innovation and newness. When the norm is change rather than stability, one must locate a set of constantly changing norms—a daunting task. And if norms can be simultaneously the basis of cohesion and conflict and the source of stability and change, they are doubly hard to locate.

Norms are learned.   As indicated previously, some rationalists argue that norms are rooted in human nature and are thus natural, inevitable, and necessary. But culturalists tend to focus on learning: norms are held and instilled. Acceptance of norms may be rapid or slow. Moreover, what can be learned may be unlearned: rejection of norms can involve either sudden disabuse or gradual decay.

Norms are sometimes inconsistent.   Norms may not be homogeneous and coherent; the parts may even be incongruent and contradictory. Principles and duties can conflict. All normative systems, for example, must deal with the conflict between efficiency and equity.

Norms are sometimes weakly held.   The degree to which norms are internalized and systematized varies among individuals and groups. While some hold stable and consistent norms, others hold a hodgepodge of unstable and conflicting values.

Norms sometimes depend on context.   While some norms are unconditional (e.g., always turn the other cheek), others are contingent upon conditions (e.g., one's willingness to cooperate is a function of others' cooperation). Hence, there are both categorical and hypothetical imperatives: some moral judgments are fixed and unyielding, while others depend upon particular circumstances. Norms thus may be more binding or less so.

In addition to these formidable empirical challenges, there are three analytical difficulties in determining the existence of norms.

Norms are not directly observable.   If norms are thought of as private, they can be observed only through survey research (verbal reports) and subsequent written accounts. If norms are thought of as public, they are equally hard to assess. They produce artifacts from which one must infer transindividual desires and beliefs.

Insiders may see norms differently than outsiders see them.   Assessing whether one is following a rule can be done either by an outside observer or by the consensus of the community. Individuals make sense of their social world, and observers provide coherent accounts of the worlds of others whom they study. But the two may differ. Kincaid writes that "Geertz sees the Balinese cockfight as a 'sustained symbolic structure' or 'an ensemble of texts' that 'says something of something.' . . . [I]t is a 'metasocial commentary' upon the whole matter of sorting human beings into fixed hierarchical ranks. . . . Again his reading goes beyond anything the Balinese explicitly affirm." Kincaid thus concludes that "symbolists are committed to meanings that are meanings for no one" (1996, 215).

The owl of Minerva problem.   Norms are self-fulfilling prophecies that create reality, so following norms reinforces both the norm and the behavior. Searle thus writes that "institutions are not worn out by continued use, but each use of the institution is in a sense a renewal of that institution" (1995, 57). One might therefore conclude that disregarding norms weakens both the norms and the behavior. However, the nonuse of norms can be a self-denying prophecy as their violation can lead to their strengthening: as values come under attack, people proclaim moral outrage; they suddenly reflect on and understand their values; and hence norms are paradoxically reinforced. One must therefore conclude that norms are not dependent on practice, and, more important, widely accepted values are invisible while crumbling value are brought to the surface.

These empirical and analytic difficulties produce the besetting sins of culturalism—that arguments about the existence of norms are tautological and teleological.

Tautology.   Since norms can be a source of conflict and cooperation, stability and change, collectivity identity and individualism, indeed norms and normlessness,[19] the potential problem with normative explanations is apparent: tautology. Thus, the culture might promote conflict, and the norm might be struggle; the culture might produce change, and the norm might be innovation; and the culture might promote individuality, and the norm might be deviance.

Tautology is an ever-present danger because norms are tied to action, and one can always "explain" an action with reference to an "orientation" to that action. For example, citizens vote because of citizen duty, and people act altruistically because of altruism. Following or fulfilling a norm cannot be taken as evidence that a norm exists. To explain an action in terms of the norm that compels the action is redundant, as Blake and Davis argue: "If norms are taken to be regularities of behavior, they have no analytical significance at all; they are then merely another name for behavior itself, and cannot contribute to an understanding of behavior" (1964, 464).[20]

Moreover, norms may not even be related to action. Rules can permit a certain variation in their performance. Indeed, no norm is exceptionless. Since all rules are occasionally broken, and none applies or works in every case,[21] irregularity of behavior or the violation of a norm cannot be taken as evidence that a norm does not exist. Thus, a norm need not be followed to be a norm; it holds no matter how widespread and enduring the violation. In sum, the outcome of norms cannot be used to falsify or disconfirm arguments about the existence of norms. The presence of a norm cannot be deduced from conformity with it.

But the problem of equating norms and actions is only a part of the culturalists' propensity for tautology. Some culturalists, rejecting the idea of material structure, embrace a totalizing perspective and suggest that "everything is interpretation" or that "it is ideas all the way down" (Wendt 1999, chap. 3). Or in another version, they claim that everything is culture. Blake and Davis charge that "the term culture . . . is [sometimes] used so broadly as to cover all material products of man, all social behavior, all ideas and goals. Used in this way, it includes society itself, and therefore the cultural determinism of social phenomena becomes a tautology" (1964, 462). For some culturalists, that is, everything *is* ideas, norms, or culture. Culturalists thereby holistically absorb, define, or constitute two parts of the intentional act—choice and constraints—by reducing them to the third part—culture.

For this reason, cultural arguments have been called "the catch-all to end all catch-alls."[22] Mann criticizes them for a "totalizing idealism, eschewing causal analysis and, instead, redescribing entire social processes in cultural terms. This is the legacy of Hegel and of German idealism, carried into contemporary social science by discourse analysis and by writers like Foucault and Geertz" (1993, 168–69). Since individual and collectivity, cause and effect, and text and context are conflated, social constructivism does not generate falsifiable propositions. Idealists tend instead toward holism, either studying detailed concrete history or offering a philosophy of history (Parsons 1937, 475). Gellner parodies the idea that "everything is meaning, and meaning is everything, and hermeneutics is its prophet." He writes that "hermeneuticists tend to slide over quietly from the perfectly valid perception that concepts do constrain, to the totally indefensible idealist doctrine, or rather operational assumption, that *only* concepts constrain. Why? Could it be the intellectual's conceit and the pleasure at the thought that his own tools, i.e., ideas, are really that which controls the social order, and guides the pattern of history?" (1992, 24, 64, emphasis in original).

Teleology. How do learning, socialization, and reinforcement occur? How do norms become internalized in individuals? How do they become shared among people? Unless these mechanisms can be isolated, arguments about norms tend toward teleology—fulfilling the purposes of the culture or community. Thus, a culture or community must be held together by common norms, but in order for it to be held together, norms gradually develop for the very purpose of holding it together. Functionalist teleology thus substitutes for positivist etiology and becomes the dynamic counterpart of a static tautology.

In sum: the statement that a norm exists or that a person is following a rule can be true or false. The consequence of the aforementioned empirical and analytic complexities[23] is that testing arguments about the existence of norms is rendered impossible by culturalists who tend toward tautology and teleology.

This leads to the second major problem faced by the culturalists: testing arguments about the consequences of norms. Do norms produce action and outcomes? Murphey indicates that "within a given society there exists a structure of rules and systems of beliefs and desires which, where members of the society are committed to this cultural system, can be used to explain the actions of those members, and to explain why actions of members of one culture differ from those of another" (1994, 324). Norms are particularly attractive explanations of behavior because rules can explain repeated actions and sequences of actions.

While norms are action oriented and potentially explanatory and predictive, a rule by itself cannot explain action: motivation is also needed. To explain a behavior with a norm is therefore to give only half the story. As Münch argues, "Every explanation of 'the existence of norms' must simultaneously be an explanation of the source of the obligatory force of those norms" (1987, 20). Subjective culturalists, in fact, identify many motivations or plausible rival hypotheses about the causal mechanisms linking norms and actions.

One motivation fits the culturalist perspective best: oughts imply duty and not self-interest. Norms produce actions done out of obligation and a calling: one obeys norms for their own sake, not because they make someone a better person, fulfill one's sense as a human being, or build the self. But where does this ought come from?

One possibility is a social contract among rational individuals that provides a philosophical justification of their autonomously arrived at, yet obligatory nature (Kant). Morals thus involve reason, and oughts imply free will and moral agency. Existentialists tell us that making choices leads to building values: some norms respect autonomy in that people accept the obligation to obey. As Selznick puts it, morality is made for humans and not humans for morality (1992, 32).[24]

A second possibility is a heteronomously imposed desire that derives from and is ultimately imposed by a historically situated community.[25] Such a top-down perspective leads to determinism: the loss of free will or human volition. Individuals become mere carriers of value orientations and bearers of social roles; identity and self are totally penetrated by community; and people are oversocialized cultural dopes. As Giddens puts it: "*There is no action in Parsons' 'action frame of reference,'* only behavior which is propelled by need-dispositions or role expectations. The stage is set, but the actors only perform according to scripts which have already been written out for them" (1976, 16, emphasis in original). This is all quite ironic: culturalist arguments that start out subjectivist end up with as impoverished a view of subjectivity as that of rationalist opponents.

Selective material incentives and disincentives—rewards and sanctions—are also relevant motivations. Self-interest is thus a plausible rival explanation of behavior because norms are always backed by sanctions, and these, say the rationalists, are what really matter (Lukes 1985, 218).[26] Hence, an action (criminality) that breaches a norm (legal codes) is a function of the structure of rewards and sanctions (prisons). Hierarchy monitors and enforces norms, and people act out of self-interest, narrowly defined. In the end, the only effective norms are those that are utilitarian and self-centered.[27]

In fact, one can always probe the deeper question of what particular interests norms serve. Since we are driven by guilt (Freud), material interests (Marx), and survival instincts (Hobbes), norms are less ex ante sources of action than ex post sources of rationalization of self-interest. The result is that norms are subject to hypocrisy. Hayakawa indicates that "in all societies, the symbols of piety, civic virtue or patriotism are often prized above actual piety, civic virtue or patriotism" (1990, 24). Rational choice theorists would say they are subject to preference falsification.

A final motivation is habit. There is a difference between the commonplace (a statistical norm) and the internalized (a value norm). Unconscious rule-following includes automatic, habitual behavior like driving. To satisfy a rule, behavior must satisfy its prescriptions; but to follow a rule, one need not know the rule. If norms are no more than habits, they do not provide meaning to individuals or collectivities. Without free choice or a bit of rationalism, one has an amoral theory of morals: people never exercise their capacities for moral conscience and never show moral understanding of their situations.

One concludes, then, that the mechanisms that link culture to action are as complex as culture itself. Norms are neither necessary nor sufficient for action. They are not necessary: actions can be taken out of self-interest, strategizing, or habit. They are not sufficient: norms must be backed by self-interest, strategizing, or habit. Compliance with norms is thus overdetermined. There are many competing reasons for following a rule—reasoned choice, cultural training, or external constraints. But if self-imposed compliance, materially induced compliance, false consciousness, and semiconsciousness can all enter the picture, then of what value is the linkage between norms and actions?[28]

Since culturalist arguments that assert the unique power of norms face major problems, critics charge that rules neither explain nor predict action. And while supporters retort that rules help us understand action, the critics' rejoinder is that rules merely redescribe the facts that they seek to fathom. Geertz reflects upon the problem.

> The besetting sin of interpretive approaches to anything—literature, dreams, symptoms, culture—is that they tend to resist, or to be permitted to resist, conceptual articulation and thus to escape systematic modes of assessment. You either grasp an interpretation or you do not, see the point of it or you do not, accept it or you do not. Imposed in the immediacy of its own detail, it is presented as self-validating, or, worse, as validated by these supposedly developed sensitivities of the person who presents it. (1973, 24)

Culturalist methodology thus has its advantages and its disadvantages. On the positive side is something worth applauding: culturalists offer an understanding of meaning, and some culturalists produce useful arguments that link meaning to action. On the negative side is something to be deplored: action and the material world are swept up into the all-embracing Hegelian idealism, leading to teleology, tautology, and nonfalsifiability.

Chapter 6

Structural/Institutional Theory

Structuralists, who also come in thin and thick varieties (sect. 6.1), offer a second alternative to rational choice theory.[1] Structuralist ontology (sect. 6.2) depicts a world dominated by relationships; structuralist methodology (sect. 6.3) consists of positivist studies of how conditions produce action and realist studies of structural dynamics; and the corresponding structuralist lacunae (sect. 6.4) consist of nonvoluntarist and deterministic explanations.

6.1. Thin and Thick Structuralists

Structuralist thinking is widespread in the social sciences, as today's structuralists give theoretical primacy to many different kinds of relationships among actors. Thin and thick versions of structural theorizing again offer a useful distinction.[2]

Thin structuralists like Skocpol, looking to understand very large patterns of historical development, study broad configurations of power—states, social classes, national patterns of policy-making, regime structures, institutions of class compromise, and the international economy. They are concerned with historically specific issues such as modernity, globalization, and imperialism.

Some thin structuralists are concerned with formal and informal linkages between the state and civil society, or the "interorganizational networks of interest intermediation" that bind polity and society (Kitschelt 1989, viii). Interinstitutional connections and internetwork communications between political parties, interest groups, and state agencies influence the organization and strategies of each actor while also affecting policy outputs. In particular policy areas these linkages have been referred to as subgovernments, policy networks, and iron triangles; at the more general regime level they have been referred to as governing social coalitions, corporatism, pluralism, and consociationalism. Structuralists are interested in public policy, political economy, and interest representation because they involve transactions across supposedly bounded entities; they want to show how polity and society are related to one another. Since economic markets are a key component of society, thin structuralists are very concerned about how linkages among labor, capital, and government influence the strategies and organizations of these three groups. Domestic institutions that link capital-labor, capital-government, and labor-government include state networks (e.g., central banks) and social pacts (e.g., corporate interest-group arrangements). Since the state is embedded in a mesh of global relationships, global-state-society connections are also important to structuralists. International institutions that establish connections to the state and sometimes to civil society include multinational corporations, the IMF, WTO, and the World Bank.[3] Finally, since all of these relationships are most visible during times of crisis, upheaval, and change, structuralists study periods of reform and revolution.

The seminal structuralist in contemporary social science is Moore. Katznelson's account of Moore the structuralist is very illuminating.

> [Moore] did not slice and dice his cases into variables which themselves would be compared as if they were not enclosed and entwined inside cases of dense and distinctive complexity. He considered each with sufficient detail to stand alone as an analytically constructed, historically recognizable case study. Though deployed to a comparative purpose, each also was written as a coherent (and deliberately provocative) single-country investigation. (1997, 89)

Moore, in short, thought relationally and holistically.

Skocpol is Moore's most distinctively structuralist student.[4] Her classic work argues that state breakdown, peasant revolutions, and state reconstruction have structural causes. She offers a structure-conflict-change approach to state and revolution that emphasizes five structures. First, the international context: Skocpol studies international structures and relations—war and trade—and the world-historical circumstances in which states find themselves. Second, the nature of states: Skocpol explores states as "administrative and coercive organizations" (1979, 14) penetrating society and controlling people and territory. Third, intraclass[5] and interclass[6] conflicts: Skocpol is concerned with "*historically specific institutional arrangements*" (1979, 116, emphasis in original), such as "agrarian class and local political structures" (1979, 117). Fourth, the relations of states and classes: Skocpol is particularly interested in "the potential autonomy of the state" from dominant[7] and dominated[8] classes in society (1979, 24). Finally, the nature of the revolutionary crisis: the processes of state breakdown and of peasant revolts become legacies of the old regime that affect state reconstruction.

Structuralists like Skocpol reject rational choice's focus on the actors themselves as agential, voluntaristic, and reductionist. Skocpol thus criticizes an approach to revolution based on mobilizable groups and "the emergence of a deliberate effort" (1979, 15).[9] She argues that analysts should not assume self-conscious and purposive revolutionary vanguards or movements whose members share grievances and goals. Since revolutionaries do things they never intended, preferences, goals, and ideologies are not valid guides to outcomes.[10] Skocpol is very forceful on this point, arguing that "an adequate understanding of social revolutions requires that the analyst take a nonvoluntarist, structural perspective on their causes and processes." Hence, "any valid explanation of revolution depends upon the analyst's 'rising above' the viewpoints of participants" and taking "an impersonal and nonsubjective viewpoint." Skocpol prefers to instead "emphasize objective relationships and conflicts among variously situated groups and nations, rather than the interests, outlooks or ideologies of particular actors in revolutions." She focuses on the "structural contradictions and conjunctural occurrences beyond the deliberate control of avowed revolutionaries." Minimizing the ability of the ideologies of revolutionary leaderships (e.g., Jacobinism, Marxism-Leninism) to transform the state, she looks instead to the structural conditions under which elites struggle to consolidate and use state power, or the "specific possibilities and impossibilities within which revolutionaries must operate as they try to consolidate the new regime" (14, 18, 29, 291, 171).

Thick structuralists, as opposed to thin structuralists like Skocpol, care about highly general relationships that apply transhistorically. Examples include theories of contextual relationships (Huckfeldt and Sprague 1993), social interaction (Turner 1988), networks (Knoke 1990), actor-centered institutionalism (Scharpf 1997), social structure (Kontopoulos 1993), organizational ecology (Hannan and Freeman 1989), chaos, catastrophe, and complexity (Brown 1995; Holland 1995; Jervis 1997), systems (Easton 1965), cybernetics (Deutsch 1963), and authority patterns (Eckstein and Gurr 1975). Thick structuralists also study the operation of particular institutions—parties, interest groups, executive-legislative relations, electoral laws, courts, and firms—and their internal processes.

Thin structuralists like Katznelson (1997) argue that thick structuralism comes too close to rational choice theory's atomistic reductionism. Katznelson believes, in effect, that the structuralist research program has thickened over time and that structuralists should return to their original—Marxist and Weberian—core. Hegemonic rationalists incorporate structure by developing thick versions of rational choice theory that are compatible with thick structuralism. Since ideal-type structuralists do not even like thick structuralism, they will forever reject its cousin—thick rationalism—as an imperialistic pretender to structuralism.

6.2. Structuralist Ontology

Since structures constrain and empower individuals, structuralists maintain that analysts should study the cage rather than the prisoner. Structures have several features that make them arranged, configured, and patterned rather than disorderly, chaotic, and in disarray.

Structures are relational. Rationalists think of actors as situated within a multitude of isolatable variables that feed into a person's decision calculus. Human beings, however, do not think of themselves as facing a heap of disconnected variables; rather, they are aware of the rules and relationships within which they make choices. Structuralists, too, realize that analysts cannot study one time-space situation after another but rather must study the structures into which decision milieus are organized. Structuralists thus believe that actors are situated within historically concrete institutions and configurations of power. Structures are these patterned objects, and structuralists locate different configurations of bounded and patterned interactions. Rather than parsing entities into separable factors, disaggregating clusters of forces into isolatable parts, or "slicing and dicing" cases into distinct variables, structuralists search for "configurational complexity." To a structuralist the issue is not whether variable x matters more than variable y—as a causal hierarchy—but rather the issue is the relationships, connections, and transactions among the variables in the cases studied.

Since structuralists believe that there are interdependencies—networks and linkages—among the parts of some whole, their arguments are always concerned with relationships: individuals, collectivities, institutions, and organizations must be understood as standing in relation to one another.[11] As Grossmann indicates, "Structures are things in relations. Without relations, there are no structures" (1992, 51). Waltz argues that "in defining structures the first question to answer is this: What is the principle by which the parts are arranged?" (1979, 81). To show that a part is meaningful and intelligible only in relation to other parts, he offers the example of George and Martha in Albee's

Who's Afraid of Virginia Woolf? Their fate cannot be separated into individual-level components with independent existence but is rooted in their interpersonal (marital) relationship that produces mutual constitution and codetermination (74). Lawson points out that this example falls into one of two categories of relations.

> Two objects or aspects, etc. are said to be *externally* related if neither is constituted by the relationship in which it stands to the other. A barking dog and postman, or two passing strangers, provide examples. In contrast, two objects are said to be *internally* related if they are what they are by virtue of their relationship to the other. Thus, husband and wife, landlord and tenant, employer and employee, magnet and its field, are examples that come to mind. In each case, you cannot have one without the other; each, in part, is what it is and what it does by virtue of the relation to the other in which it stands. (1994, 275)

Structuralists are thus concerned with how things that seem to be externally related are, under close inspection, internally related.

Structures are positional.   Lawson points out that structural relations often involve social positions.

> If it is the case that prime ministers or presidents, say, exercise different rights, tasks, obligations, practices, duties and powers from the rest of us, or that, say, teachers exercise different practices and tasks, etc., from students, it is equally the case that the relevant rights, tasks and obligations, etc., exist independently of the particular individuals taking these roles. At issue then is a system of relationally defined positions-practices, i.e., a system of positions, with associated practices, obligations and power, etc., defined in relation to other such positions, and into which agents essentially slot. (1994, 275)

Structuralists thus describe individuals in terms of their social roles, as members of a class or group.

Structures are multilayered.   Social life is complex because it involves organizations of organizations, networks of networks, structures of structures, and frameworks of frameworks. Since institutions are often embedded in one another, social order has overlapping and relatively autonomous levels, layers, and strata. Higher-level organizations are composed of lower-level ones: substructures, subsystems, and suborders. Reality is stratified into many levels, from subatomic particles to the universe, and each level is structured in great relational complexity. Structuralists therefore focus on the larger institutional frame-work within which groups contend—the global order, the state, and civil society. They also show how the global structure of capitalism contains national markets, which, in turn, contain local firms.

Structures are wholes that are more than the sum of their parts. Fol-lowing from the fundamental principles that structures are relational, positional, and multilayered is the idea that we cannot understand a part in isolation, but must consider the whole, which is more funda-mental than its elements and is more than the sum of its parts. Indeed, the whole determines what counts as an element: there are no parts except those that the whole identifies and individuates. The ontology is methodological collectivism: individuals exist by virtue of structures that transcend those who momentarily inhabit them. Hence, the hermeneutic circle: to understand the parts one must understand the whole, and to understand the whole, one must understand the parts. As Hegel puts it, "The truth is the whole" (cited in Shand 1994, 181). Durkheim ([1893] 1933) thus argues that society is a structure, a reality sui generis, a whole object that is distinct from and greater than the sum of its parts.

Skocpol consequently opposes "strategies of analytic simplifica-tion" (1979, 294) as reductionist. Seeking to avoid approaches that focus on clusters of variables rather than on transactions among enti-ties, she argues that analysts should not concentrate "only upon one analytic feature (such as violence or political conflict)" that character-izes major social revolutions but rather should "look at the revolutions as wholes, in much of their complexity" (1979, 5). Instead of separating economic from political variables or state from society, a structural account thus shows how states rely on classes and how classes use states.

Structuralists also oppose individualistic and reductionist approaches that focus on self, subject, and agent. Skocpol therefore explores "objective structural conditions" rather than "politically manipulable subjective conditions" (1979, 16). As Ball puts it:

> It is simplistic at best and false at worst to conceptualize political relations in terms of observable relations between individuals. It is misleading, for example, to view power as a relation between individual agents (or, as Hobbes would have it, between an active "agent" and a passive "patient"). They do not meet as individuals but as actors located within a web of larger, relatively stable and enduring social structures which they did not create and over

which they have little, if any, control. It is by virtue of their location within larger structures of relations that political agents have and exercise power. (1987, 8)

The existence of a structure, that is, does not depend on the identity of the particular agents involved. Structures are not epiphenomena of microfoundations, and social life cannot be reduced to particles of matter that have laws of motion.

In sum: structures are fields of relations that embed agents at the supranational (e.g., war, trade), national (e.g., executive, legislature), subnational (e.g., city, region), and community (e.g., religious, ethnic) levels. Analysts must therefore look for deep structures—not the hidden hand of the market, nor cultural meanings.

6.3. Structuralist Methodology

Science can provide deep understanding of the world in two ways. First is the unification tradition common among positivists, who want to systematize knowledge by fitting diverse phenomena in some problem domain into comprehensive (global and universal) theories. Positivists contend that comprehension grows as the number of independently acceptable assumptions is reduced and as the number of independently verifiable conclusions is increased. The operational goal is to find lots of correlations that can be deduced, by ever-expanding chains of reasoning, from a small number of assumptions, or to locate the stylized facts that can be comprehended with a common core. Positivists therefore equate the correlation of event regularities—event x is regularly associated with event y—with causal necessity. To explain an event, one identifies its cause by placing it in a sequence where each event regularly gives rise to subsequent events in accordance with the laws of nature.

The second tradition in science, the causal-mechanical tradition, is commonly found—albeit often unrecognized—among structuralists who are best described as causal realists. In contrast to positivists who see cause as logical necessity, causal realists argue that causality involves natural necessity and hence logical relations are not explanations. Causal realists also argue that the constant conjunction of events—the statistical correlations touted by positivists—do not get at the causal mechanisms, relations, or processes that underlie phenomena. Realists maintain that science wants real causes and not just logical relations (Hempel's deductive-nomological laws) and empirical relations (Hume's constant conjuncture—correlations). Bombs explode because of physical forces governed by the laws of physics, and prices rise because of market forces governed by the laws of supply and demand. Wendt offers other examples of causal understanding in the social sciences: "Social interaction is in part a causal process of mutual adjustment that often has unintended consequences. Socialization is a causal process of learning identities. Norms are causal insofar as they regulate behavior. Reasons are causes to the extent that they provide motivation and energy for action" (1999, 82). Realists thus search for the causes that drive the world rather than for the theoretical unification of some problem domain.[12] Their realist philosophy of science is characterized by two basic principles.[13]

1. While the building blocks of science consist of real objects that are embedded in space and time, these structures are perhaps unobservable.
2. The form of a natural kind is a structure that produces recurrent causal processes and creates self-organizing types of entities.

Consider the first principle.

Theories are about the basic building blocks of the world, including their properties and interactions.   Realists thus adopt an ontology that is entity centered and not event centered: "Reality (ontology) conditions theory (epistemology)" (Wendt 1999, 60). Rather than discovering empirical regularities of the form "if event *x* occurs event *y* occurs," realists look for the underlying structures or fundamental entities in a domain of inquiry. Mature scientific theories typically refer directly to this world of objects and hence provide knowledge of reality "out there."

Real objects and entities exist in the world.[14]   Structures objectively exist in the external world apart from our perceptions of them. These objects are natural phenomena, units with matter, form, and properties that are "coherent, durable, self-propelling" (Hechter 1995, 1524; Tilly 1995, 1595). Labor organizations, bureaucracies, political parties, and corporations are real phenomena. Protest cycles, social movements, and revolutions are real things with internal structures. A police car is real, and so is the state; similarly, the UN charter is real, and so is the international state system.

These structures exist in time and space.   Realists try to understand events in a historically specific space-time region. Structuralists thus focus on historically rooted political, social, and economic connections among people and long-term and large-scale historical developments.[15]

While real objects and entities exist in the world, they may not be observable and hence may be known only by their effects.[16]   However real and important, structures are not easy to find. Because they have emergent properties, the whole may be greater than the sum of the parts. Another difficulty is that structures are often collective rather than common or shared; they are more than simply aggregates of actually existing individuals and interactions, yet they are often opaque or hidden from the individuals who inhabit them. In studying these unobservables, realists are detectives who emphasize the difference between outward appearance and deeper reality, between facade and essence, as they seek out the hidden but deep structures that operate behind the scenes independently of people's wills. Realists thus think of themselves as going beyond face value, penetrating surface illusion, and discovering the fundamental core of reality.

Realists thus assume that unobservable objects and hidden entities—known only by their effects—exist in the world. These unobservable structures are what produce the events, states of affairs, actions, and interactions that we observe. The term *gravity,* for example, refers to real, but unobservable, causes of observable motion. Boylan and O'Gorman offer the example of economics: "In this realist picture the observable economic world is like the face of a clock which has hidden mechanisms generating or causing the observable events on its face. Thus behind the observable economic work there are real but unobservable mechanisms which generatively cause the observable economic events. The aim of economics is to discover these generative unobservable causes" (1995, 2–3).[17]

Now consider the second principle: The form of a natural kind is a structure that produces recurrent causal processes and creates self-organizing types of entities.

Form is what makes a structure a certain kind of thing.   The form of a thing is structural and material and is what gives matter its determinate character. Structuralists are morphologists looking to get at the nature of a thing. They ask "what" questions—"what is this thing called?"—that aim to get at "how" questions—"how is this thing put together?" Piaget maintains that *"there is no structure apart from construction"* (cited in Lloyd 1986, 257). Scientists search for these real forms of entities—called *natural kinds*—in particular domains of inquiry. A natural kind is a differentiated structure or system with coherence and unity; it is more than an ad hoc collection of qualities. A dog, for example, is a natural kind, whereas a pile of sand or five randomly chosen objects on my desk are not. Little thus points out that "'water' refers to a natural kind, whereas 'air' does not; for (as we know) 'water' refers to the molecule H_2O, whereas 'air' refers to a mixture of oxygen, nitrogen, and trace gases. Pure air does not exist, but pure water does" (1989, 196–97). Natural kinds, therefore, are bounded; there are limits on how much they can vary without becoming another kind of structure.

Kinds of structures are defined by their causal processes.   Basic causal processes, real causal powers, and inherent causal mechanisms are associated with natural kinds. For example, chemistry looks for chemical elements (the periodic table) and the laws of chemistry; physics looks for elementary particles and their laws. Hence, structure, process, and outcome are linked: natural bodies or kinds have natural proclivities or powers that produce natural laws about observable regularities that operate in a variety of environments.

These causal processes recur in nature.   After each natural kind is examined, one develops generalizations—theories—about its essential features (its form and functioning). Since structures share causal features and can be found in many different contexts, they are general types and not particulars.[18]

Structures are then self-organizing kinds of entities.   Natural kinds follow natural laws of development. Since form determines the possibilities for change and development, scientists must discover the form of matter to understand how it will actualize its potential. This involves a focus on origins, or how a structure comes into being; on maintenance, or how a structure comes to be institutionalized; and on transformation, or how a structure changes. These lawlike processes thus involve production and reproduction, stability and change, and growth and development.

Since structuralists see reality in Aristotelian[19] terms as an ordered whole, each part of a structure is not homogeneous and interchangeable but rather has its own specific role in the functioning of the whole. One must therefore study the principles behind the differentiation and integration of the parts. In a system of differences—master-slave, husband-wife—each type of classified pattern has a theme or logic. It is the analyst's task to discover the rules of the configuration, the morphology of the pattern, and the principles that structure the relationships among the parts. This can lead to functionalism, the idea that structures survive because of implicit or hidden positive consequences. In other words, the purposes they serve—their effect on other institutions and the social whole—have feedback effects that contribute to their maintenance. But it can also lead to recognizing that structures contain potential conflicts and contradictions that are sources of movement and change and hence provide the dynamic mechanisms of becoming.

Little asks the key question for social science: "What, then is a *social kind*? . . . [W]e can provide a strictly parallel account to that of a natural kind. A social kind is a class of social phenomena, entities, or processes that possess similar internal structures and that consequently possess similar causal properties and are subject to the same causal laws. The entities that fall under a social kind, then, are similar in their causal or dynamic properties" (1989, 196–97, emphasis added). A social kind therefore shares a hidden structure; it is a homogeneous class of things with a set of similar causal properties that cohere and produce recurring dynamic patterns. According to Little, "Candidates for social kinds include 'riot,' 'revolution,' 'class,' 'religion,' 'share cropping land-tenure system,' 'constitutional monarchy,' 'market economy,' 'nationalist political movement,' 'international trading regime,' and 'labor union' as well as 'millenarian rebellion,' 'class system,' and 'commodity market' " (1993, 190).

Social kinds are studied through typologies.   Structuralists thus analyze social kinds with causal powers and hence study the historical dynamics of real structures. They discover social kinds by classifying types of political systems and exploring state building, war, capitalism, industrialization, and urbanization. The structural mechanisms that produce the historical dynamics of real social types include competition, conflict, consensus, division of labor, differentiation, diversity, distribution, inequality, stratification, polarity, size, density, and hierarchy.[20]

Aristotle was the first to propose classification of political systems, which tell us about the connections between the governors and the governed, the logic of how political processes operate, and their patterns of historical development. Others have followed his example. Weber, for example, explores the institutionalization of three types of systems of domination or authority—rational, traditional, and charismatic legitimacy ([1924] 1968)—and the logics of three types of systems of stratification—class, status, and party (1946). He also examines the development of the legal system ([1924] 1968), the dynamics of premodern and modern capitalisms ([1923] 1961; [1896] 1988), and the rationalization of religious belief systems (1951; 1952; [1904–5] 1985; [1958] 1992). He also argues that patriarchalism, domination by notables, political patrimonialism, feudalism, hierarchy, Caesaropapism, bureaucracy, charismatic community, church, sect, household, neighborhood, kin group, ethnic group, oikos, and enterprise have characteristic logics that produce characteristic developments ([1924] 1968).[21] Marx (1906) argues that capitalist-type societies have characteristic laws of development. And Durkheim ([1893] 1933) argues that modern-type societies are characterized by specialization and the division of labor.

Katznelson shows how the seminal contemporary structuralist, Moore, thought in terms of typologies.

> Nor did Moore treat "revolution" and "class struggle" as processes independent of time and place. Rather, he constructed and deployed a limited repertoire of developmental configurations . . . as a means to avoid becoming hostage either to historical detail or to rather too simple stories about historical trajectories even with respect to complex questions of historical change on a very large scale. He achieved this goal by constructing his cases to show how each was dominated by a particular configuration of class, revolution, and political regime, yet how each also contained subordinate combinations and arrangements which became primary elsewhere. (1997, 89)

Skocpol is also concerned with the concrete historical dynamics of types of states (1979, 304 n. 1). Which types of old-regime states were susceptible to social revolution? "Autocratic," "protobureaucratic," "imperial," "monarchies" that were "well-established," "wealthy," "politically ambitious," "historically autonomous," and in "noncolonial" states with "statist societies" and "agrarian" economies that faced "intense international military competition" from "economically developed military competitors" underwent social revolution (1979, 41, 161, 167, 285, 287–88, 304n. 4). What types of state were the outcomes of the social revolutions she studied? These were bureaucratic and mass-incorporating—autonomous and powerful.

Skocpol thus focuses on historically concrete types of cases: "This book does not, of course, analyze in depth all available historical cases of social revolution. Nor does it analyze a 'random' sample from the entire universe of possible cases. In fact, comparative historical analysis works best when applied to a set of a few cases that share certain basic features. Cases need to be carefully selected and the criteria of grouping them together made explicit" (1979, 40). She thus explains her case selection as follows: "It is the premise of this work that France, Russia, and China exhibited important similarities in their Old Regimes and revolutionary processes and outcomes—similarities more than sufficient to warrant their treatment together as one pattern calling for a coherent causal explanation" (1979, 41).

In sum, structuralists are not like positivists, concerned with logical necessity and constant conjunction, the basic components of the unification tradition in science. Rather they view structures as self-organizing entities and try to understand how types of structures cause and construct social life.[22]

Structures cause.   Structures are causally efficacious or creative.[23] Structural conditions are enabling and disabling because they have causal effects on agents. Constraints, circumstances, and contexts influence individual desires, beliefs, and actions. Structures therefore cause because they endow agents with powers. As Ball puts it: "Meta-scientific realists resolve the agency/structure problem by maintaining that agents and agencies, natural and social alike, have certain inherent causal capacities or 'powers' operating through structurally embedded 'mechanisms' that the social sciences must discover and describe" (1987, 8). Structural conditions also have causal effects on collective outcomes. A common and invariant set of essential properties of a unit (e.g., state institutions) produces common and invariant outcomes (e.g., revolution, social welfare policy). To apply this perspective, one looks for similar units with similar outcomes and structures. For example, federalism might influence how, what, where, and when political parties, interest groups, and social movements press government for policy change.

Structures construct.   We return to our original point about structuralist ontology: Unlike the rationalists, who believed that individuals, knowledge, and the self exist in the state of nature, structuralists maintain that the important truths are not to be found within ourselves but in the world of relations. Structures, more specifically, are constitutive of agents, defining individuals (identities, selves) and hence providing the grammar that makes agents and their interactions possible. Each actor is a "communal self," a social creature who exists only by virtue of relationships—parent-child, master-slave, worker-capitalist—and not by virtue of individual characteristics. More generally, the constituent units presuppose a social structure that enables choices but also constrains it by defining rules, roles, and relations.

6.4. Structuralist Lacunae

By emphasizing structure to the exclusion of choice and orientation, structuralists confront a characteristic set of difficulties. Since structural lacunae have clearer origins and consequences than culturalist lacunae, I will be briefer.

Structural theories emphasize that structures, not actions, produce outcomes. Extremists here argue a rigid methodological holist position: structure is significant, and individual actions, desires, and beliefs are not. Since structures determine individual preferences, beliefs, or actions, individuals have no choices and people are irrelevant; they are merely "bearers," "carriers," or "supporters" of functions determined by objective structures.[24] Culturalists thus charge that structuralists study history without a subject, turning human beings into mechanical robots forced to comply with the dictates of "the system." Structural theories, lacking people with agency, therefore produce a bloodless social science in which people are silent witnesses to history. Missing is human activity, creativity, and ingenuity.[25] In slighting people, structuralists also miss politics, the strategic interaction among goal-seeking individuals. Rationalists thus charge that structuralists ignore collective action and coalitional processes. And even when structuralists do consider individuals, they tend to homogenize them into Everyman, a characteristic individual who represents a collectivity, a role player lacking uniqueness. People, they hold, vary little over time or in a cross-section.

This depersonalized social science also means that structural theories are deterministic: given structure, outcomes follow. There are no surprises. Structural causes are so powerful that everything is predictable: there are imperatives and not possibilities, dictates and not contingencies. Structure is fate. This perspective leads to historical fatalism and an iron-cage defeatism. While action-based arguments tend toward contingency, structural arguments thus tend toward inevitability.[26] Finally, reification is a problem, with structures a reality sui generis, endowed with supraindividual, holistic, and macroscopic properties. Yet these features are often hard to demonstrate. A crude functionalism follows: a structure is treated as huge static entity that has conflicts but yet always manages to reproduce itself.

In sum, structuralist methodology has its advantages and disadvantages. On the positive side, structuralists understand structural dynamics in historical and comparative perspective and produce a variety of arguments linking structures to outcomes. On the negative side, action and the cultural world are slighted in the search for an all-encompassing and all-powerful set of morphological processes.

Part IV

The Debate about the Debate

Chapter 7

The Need for Synthesis: Structure and Action

As indicated in section 1.2, there are three approaches in the social sciences to one's intellectual opponents: competitors (splitters or relativists) explore competing research programs, pragmatists do normal science, and synthesizers develop a monopolistic center. The belief that rational choice theory can become all of social science is of course a belief in synthesis. This chapter deepens the debate by exploring the problem of structure and action and showing that rationalists are not the only imperialists in social science. The next chapter explores the opposite need for analysis. It shows why the pragmatists are right and that rationalists should use models, and why the competitors are right and that rationalists should use foils.

After developing the general argument for synthesis (sect. 7.1), this chapter explores the possible combinations of rationalist, culturalist, and structuralist subject matters—institutions and identities (sect. 7.2.1), identities and interests (sect. 7.2.2), interests and institutions (sect. 7.2.3), and interests, identities, and institutions (sect. 7.2.4). This chapter also discusses a related argument for synthesizing the traditions' subject matters—a structure/institution and action/process combination (sect. 7.3); explores one possible methodological synthesis of the traditions—positivism and interpretivism (sect. 7.4); and concludes by stressing the importance of synthesis to all three research schools (sect. 7.5).

7.1. For Synthesis

Many social scientists believe that a battle of the paradigms pushes advocates toward "abstract negation," attempts to supersede their opponents in a purely negative way (Hegel, cited in Alexander 1987, 121). True believers, they contend, caricature their opponents by stressing one-sided opposition, suppressing commonalities, and exaggerating differences. Their Manichaean worldviews ultimately degenerate into morality plays and intellectual holy wars. Paradigms become romantic allegiances based on aesthetics or ideology that discourage middle-range problem solving. Paradigms are thus responsible for generalizations that are so abstract and universal, and so impractically removed from the real world, that they are inevitably unfounded and unprovable. In exasperation, lumpers ask, Are not the approaches reconcilable and all research programs synthetic anyway (sect. 2.5)?

Syntheses are particularly attractive to practical social scientists seeking the common ground of a "messy center." These researchers, looking for the best explanation, attempt to evaluate how well a school comprehends a particular problem and accounts for some piece of reality. Creative synergisms—finding the combination of perspectives that works—are at the heart of this problem-centered approach. Hence, quantitatively inclined social scientists seek to explain 100 percent of the variance of some dependent variable, and qualitatively inclined social scientists seek to produce an airtight metanarrative of events.[1]

Certain philosophers of science endorse this search for intellectual harmony. Laudan, for example, argues that "a scientist can often be working alternatively in two different, and even mutually inconsistent, research traditions" (1977, 110). He observes that progressive synthesis is the "way that most so-called scientific revolutions take place . . . by the development of a research tradition whose novelty consists in the way in which old ingredients are combined" (1977, 104). Scientific progress does often arise from new ways of conceptualizing old phenomena (Toulmin 1967). Freud began with old data on myths, symbols, dreams, jokes, and slips of the pen or tongue. Darwin began similarly, applying his new ideas and interpretations to known empirical and theoretical material. Eckstein (1966) hopes for the same in social science, stressing that one test of new theories of conflict is what Kuran (1995) refers to as conciliation: can the new theory subsume many disparate old facts and thus produce cumulation?

Many social scientists therefore view research programs as complements rather than substitutes and look for integration, interdependence, and cross-fertilization. They borrow ideas and search for synergisms and convergences, with the goal of building bridges and fashioning a universal coalition, a hegemonic paradigm that will become the "common sense" of a field. With respect to social science in general, synthesizers seek one consolidated paradigm of social life; with respect to a particular research domain, they seek one unified theory of the phenomena in question; and with respect to a single case, they seek one complete explanation or understanding.

7.2. Types of Syntheses

Rationalists are not the only synthesizers. Each tradition fights a two-front war against the other two; each dyad can form a coalition to overcome the third; and the triad has wide appeal. I will therefore explore the possible syntheses of the subject matters of each pair of approaches—institutions and identities, identities and interests, and interests and institutions—and then of the grand interests-identities-institution coalition. Three connections among the approaches are possible. First, traditions may be autonomous. Some rationalists, culturalists, and structuralists consider interests, identities, and institutions to be sovereign entities that require independent investigation. Second, one tradition may be reducible to another. Materialists, for example, claim that social structure is regulative with respect to rational choice. Third, the traditions might be so interrelated as to be mutually constitutive. Identities, for example, might be inseparable from interests. To adopt the language of the positivists, traditions might be independent variables, one might be an independent variable and another a dependent variable, or traditions might be interacting variables.

7.2.1. Institutions and Identities

The debate between culturalists and structuralists is the age-old battle over the relative power and hidden unity of the mind and the body, the ideal and the material worlds, and the spiritual and the biological realms. Do ideas cause social change, or are material forces determinative?

Some analysts see the two spheres as autonomous. Culturalists who study only culture disregard institutions, and structuralists who study only structures ignore meanings. By specializing, each fails to attach significance to the other's core concern. Others privilege one sphere over the other. Some materialists claim that institutions determine ideas. A crude version of Marxism, for example, holds that the economic substructure of society generates a superstructure of values and beliefs. And some idealists claim that ideas determine institutions. A similarly crude version of Hegelianism, for example, holds that culture controls the evolution of the state.

Still other social theorists—the synthesizers—attempt a more equitable reconciliation. They argue that to separate the material world from meaning is to make it meaningless and unintelligible. Since structures are not material "things"—reified, static, and lifeless—Wuthnow et al. criticize "theories of culture which dichotomize human behavior into two realms, one characterized as concrete observable behavior or social structure, the other as thoughts, beliefs, and ideas which could be understood by attributing them to aspects of the former. [This is] reductionistic, based on a false bifurcation of the human condition, and counterproductive as far as understanding culture itself is concerned" (1984, 19). Sophisticated versions of both Marx and Hegel are dialectical in proposing that the material world be interpreted in terms of values and spirit, which, in turn, become "actualized" or "objectified" as the material artifacts of culture (e.g., texts, pottery). The later Parsons, for another example, contends that structure and culture are interdependent: the ideal and the material world are not distinct ontological processes but rather the constituent components of institutions. The structures that attach to norms and beliefs are said to be institutionalized.[2] Institutions, something more than mere forms or practices, embody two parts of the socially embedded unit act and, by shaping action, provide the context for the third. As cultural themes are interwoven and incorporated into structures, the material world becomes meaningful and intelligible.[3] As values and beliefs are embedded in practical material arrangements, social life becomes predictable and orderly.

This focus on the institutionalization of structures and symbols thus has major implications for social order, an issue that originally concerned Marx (class conflict and false consciousness), Weber (bureaucracy and legitimation), and Durkheim (the division of labor and conscience collective). How culture and structure combine to produce social order continues to concern many sociologists today, for example, Habermas (1984), Berger and Luckman (1966), and Giddens (1984).[4] Much of sociology continues to study the social mechanisms by which the carriers of culture shape institutional arrangements and hence by which culture becomes institutionalized as social order.

The combination of structure and culture is the true cage of reason, however. When identities and institutions combine, little scope is left for interests to define the rational choices for action. We therefore need to explore those other combinations of our trinity that involve the rationalists.

7.2.2. Identities and Interests

Individuals, groups, and whole societies may be controlled by ideologies, ideas, and identities rather than by incentives, incomes, and interests. This debate between culturalists and rationalists is partially the debate over nurture versus nature. Analysts who think of identities and interests as autonomous usually argue that interests and reason are defined by innate biology or human nature. Since rationality is universal and abstract, acontextual and ahistorical, one need not investigate its cultural roots. This is how human-nature rationalists (sect. 3.1) argue.

Others try to reduce identities to interests, or vice versa. Those "strong on identities and weak on interests" typically study interests in historical and comparative perspective, exploring how reason develops alongside large-scale social processes of identity formation. Ideas come to constitute individuals and therefore, as Wendt puts it, "ideas constitute interests." He thus maintains that "interests in power or wealth are themselves a function of beliefs about how to meet these needs, and as such are contingent on (largely) intersubjective contexts" (1999, 114). Hall argues similarly: "The social construction of identities . . . is necessarily prior to more obvious conceptions of interest: a 'we' needs to be established before its interests can be articulated" (1993, 51). Even some rationalists maintain that ideas about identities shape interests: "Credibility, moral codes and visions of the future, then, all affect a peasant's estimates that his investment will either contribute directly to collective goals or will bring an acceptable return of individual benefits" (Popkin 1979, 262). In this view, interests are socially and politically constructed and thus require interpretation.

Others who are strong on interests and weak on identities maintain that it is the other way around: interests shape ideals. Axelrod (1986), for example, demonstrates how norms rest upon rational choice. Rawls (1971), too, follows the Kantian tradition of finding an innate rationality that can serve as the universal basis for law and morality: morality is always subject to reason, and rational people are everywhere and every time the same moral beings. Scott (1985) offers a different perspective that could be interpreted as strong on interests and weak on identities: since norms are contested and become subject to strategic manipulation, rhetorical strategies disguise the private interest as the public good. Ideals are superficial, in short, because they are derivative of more fundamental interests.

Still others—the synthesizers—attempt to reconcile meaning and action by suggesting that identities and interests work together.[5] Thus, social action, says Weber, is a result of both orientation to meaning and motivation by interests. On one hand, he held that "the drive for power or material success was always the starting point for an analysis of ideas" (Bendix 1962, 481). On the other, he maintained that humans search for meaning. His comparative analyses of world religions—Catholicism, Protestantism, Confucianism, Taoism, Hinduism, Bud-

dhism, ancient Judaism, and Islam—examine how variations in soteri-
ologies, or theories of salvation, affect an actor's definition of his or her
situation, interests, and actions.

It is the task of analysts, then, to discover how both ideas and interests become mutually constitutive. Weber makes these points in a
memorable metaphor: ideas or images, like "switchmen, determine the
tracks along which action has been pushed by the dynamics of interest." Ideas, in other words, are the "switchmen of history" in that they
mark out the possible paths of societal development. The interests of
groups, in turn, give action its dynamic motivation along these paths.
Since alternative courses of action are usually available, one must
always remember that individuals are choice makers moved to action
by rational calculations of their interests. Without interests, therefore,
ideas can lead nowhere.[6] Weber adds, however, that interests are material and ideal and that neither is reducible to the other. Material interests fuse with ideal interests because both are rooted in ideas. As Bendix sums it up: "In analogy to Kant's famous dictum concerning facts
and concepts one can say that, according to Weber, material without
ideal interests are empty, but ideal without material interests are impo-
tent" (1965, 177).[7]

Identities and interests thus work together at the individual and collective levels. The dualism or bifurcation of individual identity between
self-interest and other-regardingness, an important part of modern
social theory, can be traced to the writings of Shaftesbury and Ferguson (Seligman 1992, 119). At the collective level, both interests and
identities are needed for social order.

> Neither the one nor the other by itself yields a concrete social
> order. Where pure means-end rationality reigns, no social order
> is possible. But if there is nothing but the categorical obligation to
> obey norms, with no interpenetration with the various spheres of
> ordinary self-interested action, the result will be nothing but a
> "sacred" order which will remain so removed from everyday
> behavior that it will be incapable of imposing a concrete order.
> Any order permeating all traces of social life can be expected only
> when the spheres of self-interested action and categorical obliga-
> tion interpenetrate. (Münch 1987, 20)

Social order is therefore a result of the interpenetration of self-interest
and norms: norms are a categorical imperative that sets the subjectively acceptable moral limits on self-interest (Münch 1981, 726). Nei-

ther norms alone nor rationality alone is a sufficient basis for social order or for social theory.

7.2.3. Interests and Institutions

The final combination of parts of the socially embedded unit act or spheres of society is the fusion of interests and institutions. Some think of interests and institutions as independent realities. These are typically human-nature rationalists (sect. 3.1) who believe that interests and reason are determined by a universal biology rather than being socially and politically constructed by institutions.

Other social theorists consider either interests or institutions to be dependent spheres. Either reason is caged (i.e., dominated by institutions) or creative (i.e., determines institutions). Those who are strong on structure and weak on choice believe that institutions confer interests on people (Lichbach 1995, 336–37). Material interests are defined and people are constituted by their place in the social structure. Rational choice Marxists, for example, argue that the class structure of society confers interests and that those interests are pursued in a rational manner (Carver and Thomas 1995). Historical institutionalists, for another example, argue that structures create and mobilize interests (Steinmo, Thelen, and Longstreth 1992). These structures can be class, but they can also be political institutions such as federalism. For example, while the organization of the British working class through trade unions has resulted in working-class interests being pursued on an industry-by-industry basis, in Germany a different institutional structure of labor has led to a greater concern with overall working-class interests. By contrast, those who are strong on interests and weak on structures maintain that interests determine structure. New institutionalists, institutional economists, and contractarians, for example, argue that institutions are founded upon self-interested action, albeit action that can produce unintended consequences. This leads to the modified Popper-Hayek program of unplanned then planned order (Lichbach 1996, sect. 7.3).

Still others—the synthesizers—suggest that interests underlie institutions and vice versa. Interest-group approaches to politics, for example, blend into institutional approaches when they focus on governing coalitions. The cleavage and coalition approach, that is, becomes structural when it studies ruling, governing, policy, or regime coalitions, especially state-class alliances. Examples of studies of how coalitions of interest groups institutionalize as structures of power include

Luebbert's (1991) work on the prewar and interwar years, Maier's (1975) study of interwar Europe, and Abraham's (1986) analysis of the Weimar Republic. By focusing on governing arrangements, Przeworski's (1985a) models of class compromise also take a structural spin on an essentially interest-group argument.

Weber offers a more general idea of how structure and action are mutually constitutive. He sees society as consisting of institutions and groups. Each institution he deals with—church, state, class, and science—controls a dimension of stratification. And the groups he deals with—peasants, workers, artisans, the bourgeoisie, Calvinists, Junkers, priests, and prophets—carry a particular vision of society and act on the basis of material and ideal interests. Groups struggle for power within and over institutions. An institution-group matrix in society therefore contains a more or less legitimated political struggle. Structures of domination and authority develop and stabilize social hierarchies by holding ideal and material interests in check and thereby regulating group and institutional conflicts. In sum, Weber explores three types of relationships: associational relationships based on material interests, communal relationships based on ideal interests, and authority relationships based on legitimacy. Any actual group of people is connected by institutions representing all three types of relationships.

7.2.4. Interests, Identities, and Institutions

Having now examined each approach individually and explored every possible pair of approaches, one can understand why rationalist hegemons want to create one social science. Since rationality, culture, and structure have their characteristic lacunae, and each pair of approaches makes a noble effort to overcome the deficiencies, why not then adopt the entire socially embedded unit act framework (fig. 4.1)? Synthesis would seem to be an attractive solution to the struggle in social science over the importance of reasons, rules, and relations: our plausible rival hypotheses include strategic action, shared norms, and resource constraints; our dependent variables involve combinations of actions (policies and programs), norms (values and ideologies), and structure (power and institutions); and our arguments indicate how institutions and identities influence interests, how structures and symbols sway strategies, and how cultures and constraints condition choices. We study, in short, how norms become internalized as identities and institutionalized as institutions and thereby affect collective action and collective choice. Habermas, affirming Weber, puts it as follows: "Interests have to be tied to ideas if the institutions in which they are expressed are to be lasting" (1984, 189).[8] The grand structure-action synthesis of choice, culture, and condition indeed offers important insights into individual, collective, and societal phenomena.

Individual. The action-mind-body problem pits behaviorists against spiritualists against materialists. But actions, beliefs, and desires work together. Reason mediates between the physical world of cause and effect (structure) and the mental world of preferences and beliefs (ideas). Morality mediates between rationality and structure, or between self-interest and the causal structure of the world. Finally, structure mediates between rational self-interest and culturally driven morality. Weber (1946, 61–65) thus suggests that reason navigates between ideal and material interests, Freud (1938) that ego navigates between id and superego, and Parsons (1937) that the rational and the nonrational are not two different types of behaviors but rather analytic dimensions of every intentional act. The interests-identities-institutions combination, moreover, holds important implications for individual freedom. Taken to their extremes, all three approaches deny liberty by suggesting that human beings are pawns of fate. The rationalist challenge to freedom is behaviorism, a materialist theory that says that mental phenomena are really physical phenomena, epiphenomenal by-products of brain activity. Similarly, the culturalist challenge to freedom comes in the form of socialization, a norm-driven theory that claims that actions conform to social dictates. The structuralist challenge to freedom is structural determinism, which holds that individuals are caged by material constraints. Freedom, however, means making morally autonomous and rational choices in the face of constraints, including the constraints of one's passions (culture) and others' power (structure). Freedom involves recognizing that we are not pawns of biology, norms, or structures; that interests, identities, and institutions are not determining; and that general causal laws are not always and everywhere decisive. Freedom can be understood, in short, only as particular combinations of rationality, culture, and structure.

Collective. The structure-perception-behavior paradigm is advocated by some culturalists. Social scientific theories need both structural and perceptual variables to explain behavioral variables. Because perceptions matter, objective conditions are not deterministic.[9] Dahl (1966) extends the structure-perception-behavior paradigm, linking the objective conditions of a social group, to subjective identification with the group, to attitudes associated with the group, and finally to group behaviors such as collective dissent. Hence, group formation involves a particular sequence of structure, culture, and action:

Objective → Subjective → Attitudinal → Behavioral
Group   Group   Group   Group

Objective social groups involve divisions based on observable manifestations—vertical divisions (stratification) like class position, and horizontal divisions (differentiation) like ethnic affiliation. Subjective group affiliation—shared feelings of community based on the awareness of homogeneity among its members (e.g., class identity, black identity)—is different from objective group identification in that the analyst asks whether members of an objective group identify with it. An attitudinal social group, defined as people sharing values, beliefs, and normative preferences, is different still, involving a further empirical question of whether its members share common opinions (e.g., on social issues or foreign policy issues). Finally, a behavioral social group is also different: for any objective, subjective, or attitudinal group the analyst chooses, a further empirical question is whether its members act in concert (e.g., vote, protest).[10]

Societal.   The three problems that put society at risk are scarcity, values, and power. Conflict thus occurs over interests (who gets what, when, and where), norms (the authoritative allocation of values), and structures (patterns of authority). Social order is therefore at risk from the pursuit of self-interest under conditions of scarcity; from moral conflicts over values; and from the accumulation of structural power. And social order holds in a situation of equilibrium of action, functions, and power relations, or via the coordination of action (system integration), norms (social integration), and structures (institutional integration). It is based on various combinations of instrumental reason, common values, and a hierarchical structure's imposition of material rewards and punishments (Lichbach 1996).[11]

More specifically, rational action produces unintended, unwanted, unexpected, unstable, and unpredictable outcomes—the antithesis of social order since these outcomes have no meaning and no structure. No social order, however, can endure only the unintended consequences of its actors. Norms provide the meaning and structure that control action. Norms and institutions can thus be looked upon as solutions to the rationalist dilemma of social disorder. In other words, the institutionalization of the unintended consequences of action occurs via norms.

Consider in figure 7.1, for example, this scenario with respect to revolution (Lichbach and Seligman 2000). In the first loop we begin with social order and observe how it influences individual desires and beliefs. This produces individual action that is aggregated to the macrolevel unintended consequence of revolution. But this social disorder has feedback effects. In the second loop new desires and beliefs produce new actions aimed at institutionalizing a new social order (i.e., relegitimating social order).

Structuralists focus only on what can be observed at the macrolevel. In the first loop social order produces revolution, and in the second loop it relegitimates itself. Structuralists thus study, as section 6.3 indicates, the historical dynamics—the equilibration and reequilibration—of social kinds.

Rationalist and culturalist perspectives illuminate different parts of this macroreality. From figure 7.1 one may say that

collective norms → individual values → individual action → collective action
$$\qquad (1) \qquad\qquad\qquad (2) \qquad\qquad\qquad (3)$$

Culturalists concentrate on linkage 1 (the "socialization" argument) and linkage 2 (the "motivation" argument); they focus their efforts, in other words, *before* the act. While their perspective tends toward idealism, it is an important approach to social order because norms are at once individual motivations and collective phenomena. Rationalists, by contrast, concentrate on linkage 3, which, they argue, is interesting because of the unintended, unwanted, and unexpected consequences of individually rational action. Rationalists focus their efforts, in other words, *after* norms. While their perspective tends toward materialism, it is an important approach to social order because outcomes do not follow trivially from individual interests and identities.

7.3. Structure/Institution and Action/Process

Another way to parse the socially embedded unit act stresses the value of synthesis: structure and action or institutions and processes.[12] Giddens suggests that "two types of methodological bracketing are possible in social research. In institutional analysis structural properties are treated as chronically reproduced features of social systems. In the analysis of strategic conduct the focus is placed on modes in which actors draw upon structural properties in the constitution of social relations" (1984, 288).

Action- or process-oriented approaches, which include rationalist and psychological varieties, are also referred to as individualistic,

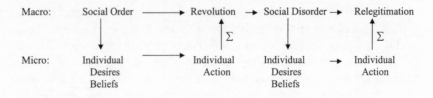

Fig. 7.1   Coleman-Boudon diagram of social order, revolution, and relegitimation

atomistic, or micro-oriented theories. The idea is that social systems are always dependent upon human action and that structure, system, or society is nothing more than a complex function of individual actions, interactions, and properties. People, moreover, can change the basis of social order as they reflexively monitor what they do. Agency theories of structural change thus emphasize humans as subjects who create and transform society by building institutions. In its most extreme version, this reduction of structures to action is methodological individualism—that social entities and processes can always be explained by the properties of people. This approach overemphasizes human autonomy, however. One cannot reduce structure to agency by referring only to actions and interactions. Since one cannot reason directly from individuals to collective outcomes like policy regimes and social revolutions, one needs a systematic starting point for individuals, a theory of structure. Therefore, all action theories either implicitly or explicitly add on structure and embed people in institutions (sect. 4.1.2).

Structure- or institution-oriented approaches emphasize that structures and not actions determine collective outcomes. Structure-oriented approaches, which include institutionalist and culturalist varieties, are also referred to as macro-oriented theories. The idea is that social systems cannot be reduced to their components and that structure, system, or society is more than a complex function of individual actions, interactions, and properties. In its most extreme version, this is methodological holism: structure is entirely deterministic of outcomes, and individuals have no choices. Since individual actions, beliefs, goals, and identities are determined by structure, people are merely "bearers" or "carriers" of functions determined by structures. As has often been said, this is history without a subject. Without agency, people are puppets. In fact, this approach reifies structure in the sense of attributing powers of agency to entities (sect. 6.4).

In sum, an action/process perspective focuses on the person as a transcendent and autonomous subject who gives meaning to objects. A structural/institution perspective, by contrast, dispenses with a subject and focuses on people as objects, or on the material and normative rules or laws of interaction. However, all extreme claims by action-oriented and structure-oriented theorists are implausible. One cannot ignore individuals any more than one can ignore structures. So synthesis is inevitable. Individualist and structuralist explanations are complementary. Process without structure has no cause; structure without process has no motivation. Social theories thus must take account of the conditioning powers of society and the agency powers of humans. Structures cause and constitute agency—actions and identity—and agents with identities, in turn, construct structures.

The central issue in social thought is thus the question of how to unite these two perspectives—the dialectic of subject and predicate, macrostructures and microfoundations, institutions and activities, structures and functions, contexts and actions, and processes and events. We willfully and purposefully attempt to make history, institutions, rules, and culture, yet these, in turn, continually make and remake us in the process. Individuals reproduce and transform structures, and yet structures constitute and change individuals. People use their ideas and experiences to influence society, and society constitutes individual desires, beliefs, and action. Structures do not act, yet people only act after they are structured. Human beings are the continually active subjects who make the eternally passive objects that limit their subjectivity. We are both autonomous creators and dependent creatures, innovators and prisoners. The world is both fact and counterfactual, constraint and construct.

Abrams's examples drive home the point.

Taking and selling prisoners becomes the institutions of slavery. Offering one's services to a soldier in return for his protection becomes feudalism. Organizing the control of an enlarged labour force on the basis of standardized rules becomes bureaucracy. And slavery, feudalism and bureaucracy become the fixed, eternal settings in which struggles for prosperity or survival or freedom are then pursued. By substituting cash payments for labour services the lord and peasant jointly embark on the dismantling of the feudal order their great grandparents had constructed. (1982, 2–3)

The structure-action problem is concerned, more specifically, with three issues.[13] There is first the aggregation problem: how unintended, unwanted, unexpected, unpredictable, and yet seemingly inevitable collective outcomes result from a set of more or less purposeful individual actions. Second, there is the institutionalization problem: how these emergent properties solidify over time into structures. Third is the contextual problem: how this solidified social order comes to constrain and enable individual consciousness and action. Hence, the structure-action problem has important normative[14] and positive[15] implications, especially about freedom and determinism or about the possibilities for rationality and nonrationality.[16]

Figure 4.1 (chap. 4) shows how the socially embedded unit act goes beyond the intentional unit act and clarifies these three issues. Looking vertically, one discovers that there are actually two structure-action problems: culture and rational action, and structure and rational action. Looking horizontally, there is one structure-structure problem: culture and structure. Legitimacy and social order, we find, rest on the harmonization of institutions and identities, identities and interests, and interests and institutions. In addition, the aggregation problem exists for all components of the socially embedded unit act—action (individual action and collective action), values (individual preferences and collective values), and beliefs (individual cognitions and institutional development). Further, rationalization occurs in the action sphere, where individual and collective action are reconciled through organization; in the ideal sphere, where the abstraction and systematization of values (substantive rationality) takes place; and in the material sphere, where bureaucratization (functional rationality) develops. The parts of the inner or individual layer of the socially embedded unit act (desires, beliefs, and action) are thus associated with the middle layer of spheres of society (ideal culture, material structure, and group action), something that was not clear in the intentional unit act. Hence, an individual's desires are a reflection of his or her ideal culture; an individual's beliefs are founded on the material structure in which he or she lives; and an individual's actions are a part of the activities of some collectivity. There are also individual-collective connections across the socially embedded unit act. One may investigate, for example, how individual actions reflect collective values. Hence, one may explore connections at the collective level, at the individual level, and across the individual-collective divide, both within and between parts of the socially embedded unit act.

Many social theorists, including Giddens,[17] Alexander,[18] Lloyd,[19] Turner,[20] Taylor,[21] and Wendt,[22] have argued that social science must combine structure/institution and action/process. Many different types of methodological positions, including models imbedded in a theory,[23] contextual analysis,[24] network theory,[25] and most different systems,[26] also recognize the importance of a combination. Rationalists have tried to combine structure and action by proposing situational analysis,[27] comparative statics,[28] partial equilibrium models,[29] game theory,[30] mechanisms and their environments,[31] processes within structures,[32] rational choice institutionalism,[33] transactions and institutions,[34] and microfoundations of macrostructures.[35] Culturalists, too, have tried to combine structure and action.[36] Finally, structuralists who have tried to combine structure and action include Skocpol,[37] Tilly,[38] Moore,[39] traditional Marxists,[40] rational choice Marxists,[41] historical institutionalists,[42] and causal realists.[43]

7.4. Methodological Synthesis: The Causal and the Interpretive

Interpretive/hermeneutic understanding is the search for meaning, and explanatory/causal understanding is the search for laws. Moon suggests that "the activities of explanation and interpretation presuppose and complement each other" (1975, 206). He explains that "for very good reasons analysts are seldom concerned with enunciating a general relationship between two variables, however impressive the observed correlation between them, without offering some 'theory' of why they should be related, a 'theory' couched in terms of the motivations and perceptions of the actors involved. These 'theories,' of course, are interpretive explanations, reconstructions of the practical inferences of the relevant individuals" (187). The link between explanation and understanding is therefore intentional explanation: "Fundamental concepts about human needs and purposes provide an essential element in the explanations of the theorizing provided that the presuppositions specify the decisional premises of the atoms which, together with description of their situations, provide the rationale for the actions which bring about the overall pattern of social behavior—conflict, violence, social change—that the theories desire to explain" (193–94).

Synthesizers argue that aggregate or structural propositions can be rooted in a microfoundation of rational choice that permits the interpretation of values and beliefs. Elster thus suggests that "the explanation of social events should take the form of 'mixed causal-intentional explanation'—*intentional understanding* of the individual *actions,* and causal explanations of their *interaction*" (cited in Callinicos 1988, 77).

General culturalist practice also conforms to this view:

A more satisfactory use of "values" in sociological analysis is to abandon them as causal agents and to recognize them frankly as sheer constructs by which we attempt to fill in the subjective linkages in the analysis of social causation. For example, the movement of peasants to cities during the process of industrialization is not "explained" by saying that they prefer the bright lights of the city to the drab monotony of the village. Only when the evolving economic and social situation in both village and the city are taken into account can we begin to explain this recurrent major social phenomenon. It helps us to understand the process, however, if we can get some inkling of how the peasant's feelings and thoughts take shape in view of these conditions; and so we try to put together a model of his mental reactions and test it out against various kinds of empirical evidence, including his verbal statements. (Blake and Davis 1964, 460)

Geertz is an example:

Geertz describes in detail how the Balinese see the world and what their institutions mean. To do so, however, he must likewise make standard naturalist judgments about the causal structure of Balinese society. For example, in arguing for his interpretation Geertz makes assumptions about Balinese political structure, about the social effects of wealth, about causal processes producing competitive struggles over access to social roles, about the social forces promoting cohesion, about the effects of kinship groups on politics, and so on. Understanding what people mean and understanding what forces shape their world go hand in hand. So "grasping the point" . . . may involve evidence based on insight, but Geertz tests that initial evidence by the usual methods of good science—and he of course involves standard natural causal explanations in the process. (Kincaid 1996, 208)

Scott (1976), too, offers a classic statement of how material conditions at the structural level drive culture and hence motivate individuals. He argues that subsistence conditions force peasants to be concerned with survival and not profits. Hence, peasants are not profit maximizers, and their decision rules are risk averse; they are reluctant to adopt new technologies that could increase crop yields but could also fail to produce any crops at all. Peasant conditions also work against individualism: since help from neighbors may be needed at any time, peasant decision rules also include reciprocity with the result that they share resources and come to their neighbor's assistance. Finally, because peasants are concerned about falling below minimum living standards, their decision rules include the right to subsistence with the behavioral consequence that they accept high taxes as long as they are structured to allow for survival in lean years.

Finally, structuralists also mix the causal and the interpretive. While Skocpol (1979) argues that postrevolutionary elites work within world-historical circumstances and are constrained by legacies of the old regime, she recognizes that their orientations toward state building—liberal, fascist, or Marxist—do matter.

It is Weber, however, who offers the most interesting syntheses of interpretive and scientific methodologies. He begins his lecture on "science as a vocation" with an examination of the external conditions of science: "We political economists have a pedantic custom, which I should like to follow, of always beginning with the external conditions . . . in the material sense of the term" (1946, 129, 134, emphasis in original). Conforming to this custom, he turns to his next task, an exploration of meaning: "I believe that actually you wish to hear of something else, namely, of the *inward* calling for science." Weber's ideal types, moreover, oscillate between institutions and their logic and individuals and their motives, combining rationalist, culturalist, and structuralist features. Ideal types thus consciously dramatize an agential actor's typical means and ends and the constraining and enabling situations within which actors calculate; they focus on the interpretation and cultural meanings actors attribute to their situations; and they account for the historical development of social formations. In sum, Weber remains sensitive to cultural meanings as he explores the causal role of the material forces that drive history.[44]

7.5. The Importance of Synthesis

The world is ordered, and hence a rational mind can explain it. The world is meaningful, and hence an interpretive mind can understand it. And the world has institutions, and hence an inquiring mind can discover power behind it. Synthesizers thus believe that the future of social science lies at the intersection of strategies, symbols, and structures; of interests, identities, and institutions; of reasons, rules, and relations; and of choice, culture, and conditions. The grand tripartite coalition is attractive for its ability to explain the richness of individual, collective, and societal phenomena: rationalist thought explores how self-interest overcomes scarcity, culturalist thought understands how norms define purpose, and structural thought comprehends how the freedom to choose is constrained by power.

But the elements of a Smith-Durkheim-Marx synthesis differ on how synthesis is to occur. To demonstrate the differences, we can work in table 7.1 with a 3 × 3 table whereby rationalists, culturalists, and structuralists define interests, identities, and institutions. Rational choice theorists define interests in terms of individual preferences and beliefs; culturalists define interests in terms of social identities; and structuralists define interests in terms of structural position. Rational choice theorists define identities in terms of autonomous preferences and beliefs; culturalists define identities as constitutive of individuals; and structuralists define identities as derivative of structural positions. Finally, rational choice theorists define institutions in terms of equilibria of strategic interactions; culturalists define institutions in terms of embedded norms; and structuralists define institutions in terms of deep power relations. Indeed, so intractable are the tensions, trade-offs, and contradictions among the approaches that consortium is rendered difficult or even impossible. Any hegemonic rationalist synthesis along the lines of the socially embedded unit act will therefore necessarily have its limitations.[45] Synthesis can, however, raise issues that analysts should be aware of, even if it does not settle them. It can locate research programs and theorists, even if it does not tell them which theories to develop. And it can clarify methodological difficulties, even if it does not solve them. Yet the limitations of synthesis mean that the door to analysis is open.

TABLE 7.1. How the Paradigms Differ

Dimensions	Paradigms		
	Rationalist	Culturalist	Structuralist
Interests	individual preferences and beliefs	social identities	structural position
Identities	autonomous preferences and beliefs	constitutive of individuals	derivative of structural position
Institutions	equilibria of strategic interactions	embedded norms	deep power relations

Chapter 8

The Need for Analysis: Models and Foils

The last chapter showed that rationalist hegemony is not the only imperialism in social science. Structure-action dialectics explain why synthesizers emerge in the rationalist, culturalist, and structuralist camps. Some, however, argue against synthesis and for analysis. After making the pragmatist's case for models and the competitor's case for foils (sect. 8.1), I state the case against the synthesizers (sect. 8.2). I conclude (sect. 8.3) by comparing the argument for analysis presented here with the argument for synthesis offered in chapter 7.

8.1. For Models and Foils

MacIntyre writes that "a tradition is an argument extended through time in which certain fundamental agreements are defined and redefined in terms of two kinds of conflict: those with critics and enemies external to the tradition who reject all or at least key parts of those fundamental agreements, and those internal, interpretive debates through which the meaning and rationale of the fundamental agreements come to be expressed and by whose progress a tradition is constituted" (1988, 12). He continues:

> Such internal debates may on occasion destroy what has been the basis of common fundamental agreement, so that either a tradition divides into two or more warring components, whose adherents are transformed into external critics of each other's positions, or else the tradition loses all coherence and fails to survive. It can also happen that two traditions, hitherto independent and even antagonistic, can come to recognize certain possibilities of fundamental agreement and reconstitute themselves as a single, more complex debate.

Theory evaluation thus sometimes focuses on predecessors or within-tradition variance. Some social scientists choose to work within an ongoing research tradition, elaborating its key insights and exploring its boundaries. In this vein Strauss writes that "within a living tradition, the new is not the opposite of the old but its deepening: one does not understand the old in its depth unless one understands it in the light of such deepening; the new does not emerge through the rejection or annihilation of the old but through its metamorphosis or reshaping" (1997, 24). Lakatos (1970) offers a philosophy-of-science version of Strauss's position. He suggests that scientists should work with models and evaluate their efforts in historical perspective using "additional and true" criteria: a new theory in an existing program is "progressive" (1) if it can account for previous findings in the field; (2) if it can predict "novel content," or some hitherto unexpected or counterintuitive observations in the field; and (3) if some of these excess predictions resist falsification. A new theory in an ongoing research tradition is "degenerative" if it is merely a patchwork to explain an internally generated anomaly of the program and hence offers no new substantive insights and accomplishments. Degenerative programs are, accordingly, autonomous and self-perpetuating, farther and farther removed from reality (see sect. 9.3.1).

Theory evaluation also focuses on rivals or between-tradition variance. In the philosophy-of-science literature, Popper (1968) advises scientists to work with foils and evaluate scientific efforts in comparative perspective. That is, one (1) studies a rival's position; (2) develops plausible rival hypotheses about a certain empirical domain; and (3) attempts to determine whether one's model is different from and better than the foil at explaining the relevant observations. A theory is successful only if it wins these competitive tests. Failed theories do not lose to the evidence so much as they lose to rivals (see sect. 9.3.2).

I first advance the argument for models and hence for historically oriented Lakatosian evaluation. I then advance the argument for foils and hence for comparatively oriented Popperian appraisal.

8.1.1. For Models

Rationalists, culturalists, and structuralists who employ ideal-type models draw on a Kantian-Weberian view of inquiry that stresses the necessity of perspective.

The "real" material world, they note, is complex, problematic, and ungraspable—in a word, irrational. Kant refers to it as the "thing-in-itself," and neo-Kantians argue that the phenomenal world appears as an infinite set of unordered, chaotic, and contradictory events, facts, and impressions. History is an immense flow of people, places, and periods—one damn thing after another across vast expanses of space and time—with the possible meanings of reality inexhaustible and in flux. Knowledge of the thing-in-itself is therefore impossible. Rikert writes:

> One need only make an attempt to "describe" reality *exactly* "as it is," i.e., to achieve a conceptual representation of it faithful in all its details, to realize very soon how futile such an undertaking is. Empirical reality [an immediate concrete situation] proves to be an immeasurable manifold which seems to become greater and greater the more deeply we delve into it and begin to analyze it . . . For even the "smallest" part contains more than any mortal man has the power to describe. Indeed the part of reality that man can include in his concepts, and thus in his knowledge, is almost infinitesimally small when compared to what he must disregard. (cited in Huff 1984, 8)

Weber agrees: "The absolute infinity of this multiplicity is seen to remain undiminished even when our attention is focused on a single 'object,' for instance a concrete act of exchange, as soon as we seriously attempt an exhaustive description of all the individual components of this 'individual phenomenon,' to say nothing of explaining it causally" ([1903–17] 1949, 72). Hence, one cannot reproduce concrete reality in a total and complete description of the whole of raw experience.

All knowledge then is partial. Of necessity, therefore, scientists always choose or sample a part of reality to serve as the object of scientific investigation. Laws of nature are thus not about total concrete reality but rather are about only carefully selected aspects of it: "What we formulate as scientific laws about 'nature' is not the total concrete reality even as humanly 'experienceable' but certain particular aspects, which can be expressed in abstract concepts" (Parsons 1937, 582). This being the case, the starting point of social analysis—the problem situation—is always how to comprise a domain of inquiry, that is, to identify the aspects of concrete reality in need of analysis. Moreover, these facts must be organized before they can constitute a subject matter. Just as evidence does not consist of facts standing alone but of patterns and connections among the facts, so, similarly, theoretical concepts do not consist of ideas standing alone but of patterns and connections among constructs. In Weber's classic line: "It is not the 'actual' interconnections of 'things' but the *conceptual* interconnections of *problems* which define the scope of the various sciences" ([1903–17] 1949, 68, emphasis in original). In scientific inquiry the problem is the problem, the question is the question, and the puzzle is the puzzle.

We therefore arrive at a key dilemma: "We cannot discover, however, what is meaningful to us by means of a 'presuppositionless' investigation of empirical data"; and

> trying to see how things look apart from the forms through which we perceive them is like trying to see what the world looks like when we are not looking at it. The attempt is self-contradictory. If we whirl around quickly to see how the "thing in itself" really looks behind our backs, our categories have come along with us. It is like trying to see the back of one's own head—not in a mirror, but as it really is. It just can't be done. (Weber [1903–17] 1949, 76)

A haphazard, passive, or purposeless sample of reality, in other words, is not significant to either the subject or the investigator. Concepts and frameworks are required to make data meaningful. By imposing order on the otherwise chaotic and unconnected impressions that constitute the phenomenal world, they allow us to grasp the infinite complexity and endless flux of that world. Scientists therefore need a viewpoint—presuppositions and a conceptual framework—about what is essential to observe. The point generalizes beyond scientists to all human beings: while biological processes provide sense experiences, understanding these experiences occurs only through a screen of subjective concepts and mental frameworks. In short, perception involves selection via conceptualization. This line of argument—evidence does not exist independently of the empirical world; sense data only become a reality with the application of a framework; whatever one knows of a thing is filtered through one's ideas; and one can never know a thing apart from the ideas one applies to it—was Kant's "Copernican Revolution" in epistemology.

A neo-Kantian view of inquiry, common among social scientists,[1] thus implies that science is built on concept formation, by which neo-Kantians mean the following:

♦ Facts are not intrinsic to the world, waiting to be discovered by rational inquiry. Rather than existing independently of the way scientists view the world, facts are always formulated within a conceptual schema and hence acquire significance only by virtue of the conceptual schemata used to understand them. Parsons makes the point succinctly: "The facts do not tell their own story; they need to be cross-examined" (1937, 698).

♦ Reality, in other words, is always mediated by frameworks and partially constructed by observers. Scientists thus produce a rational understanding of irrationality by means of selective sampling—the imposition of organizing principles called concepts.

♦ But these frameworks of concepts, presuppositions, and theories do not exhaust concrete reality or produce a mirror image of it: reality is too complex and diverse to be completely captured from the limits of one or even many conceptual schemes. Indeed, Weber prefers to focus on approximations of reality rather than on essences.

♦ There are consequently no such things as pure description and pure theory: both facts and concepts are constructions. Put otherwise: data do not emerge from the real world, nor concepts from theories, and hence the idea is not to bring data and theory in closer agreement so that reality is understood. Both facts and theory are equidistant from the real world. The objects and facts of a scientific discipline are constituted by the interpenetration of empirical observation and a conceptual frame of reference. As Kant would suggest, theory without evidence is empty; evidence without theory is blind.

♦ Moreover, concepts or ideal types—artificial constructions that do not capture, mirror, or represent the true, objective, or real world—at best refer to selected aspects of a concrete phenomenon but never to its totality.

♦ Nor are concepts concretely real or historically true, and reification, misplaced concreteness, or violent abstraction—the belief that *our* theory *is* reality—is the fallacy of treating abstract concepts as real entities. Weber himself warns against reifying his ideal types and treating them as "real" rather than "nominal": they cannot be used to "deduce" cases and are therefore not "falsified" by locating deviations from real cases.

♦ Finally, concepts are heuristic rather than descriptive, instruments for investigating entities and not stand-ins for the entities themselves. Since the concepts and theories of science are only useful fictions, the test of a concept is not its match to reality—its verification or falsification—but rather its utility in depicting what the scientist considers significant aspects of reality.

Science, according to this neo-Kantian view, is also built on problem formation, by which neo-Kantians mean the following.

♦ Scientists who lack principles of selectivity are overwhelmed by experience. Good scientists, never laborers and plodders,[2] therefore avoid the antlike drudgery of amassing facts. Levine thus writes that " 'the greatest enemy of any one of our truths,' William James once commented, 'may be the rest of our truths.' Truths crowd out truths; realities impinge on realities; facts clash with as well as complement each other" (1996, xvii).[3]

♦ So scientists must get their bearings in the vast ocean of facts by means of some perspective that allows them to know the important things. Hence, they select a theme about the phenomena that they study.[4] As Weber puts it: "Only a small portion of existing concrete reality is coloured by our value-conditioned interest and it alone is significant to us. It is significant because it reveals relationships which are important to us due to their connection with our values" ([1903–17] 1949, 76).

♦ Whereas reality is manifold, thought is selective: problems are always defined and developed from a particular point of view. Some parts of reality must be eliminated and others embellished according to the purposes and values of the investigator.[5]

♦ Because these different approaches vary, they will point to different problems and hence to different facts. For example, one approach might accept another approach's facts as true, but supporters of the first approach might well consider the second's facts to be irrelevant.

♦ The value of a plurality of theoretical systems is precisely that each theory explores a different aspect of concrete reality.

♦ Since there is no "objective" real world that can be understood scientifically apart from the scientist's "subjective" standpoint, there are no absolute and objective scientific laws, hypotheses that become secure, permanent, unchanging, unfailing, and final. And no *single* worldview or ideology can explain all of the world in a universal transhistorical and transcultural sense. The scientist is not a referee or umpire between warring paradigms—the Cartesian view from nowhere. And there is no synthesis that transcends thesis and antithesis.

In sum, concept formation and problem definition are the contexts of discovery. Models provide the starting points of these crucial aspects of scientific inquiry and thereby allow scientists to explore what they consider to be meaningful and significant.

8.1.2. For Foils

A research community almost never monopolizes a scientific field. The norm is dialogue and disagreement among competing research traditions or, as Laudan puts it, "permanent coexistence of rivals and the omnipresence of conceptual debate" (1996, 85). He documents "the rarity with which any one paradigm achieves that hegemony in the field which Kuhn requires for 'normal science.' . . . Indeed it is difficult to find any extended period of time (even on the order of a decade) when only one research tradition or paradigm stood alone in any branch of science" (1977, 134). A research tradition will always have its foil or nemesis.

This creative conflict is essential to science. Research programs tend toward medieval scholasticism, gathering true believers who choose faith over reason. Nonetheless, a tradition can also be self-reflective and open to scrutinizing its own assumptions. Reasoned inquiry in fact begins with skepticism, and progress occurs by resolving doubt. Good science is thereby characterized by conjecture and refutation, disputation and defense, question and answer, thesis and antithesis, point and counterpoint. And good scientists cross-examine what others think and how they argue. Since constructive engagement of alternatives is the best way to advance science, scientists need these dialectical confrontations, the mutual exchange of ideas that comes in open-ended discourse. Multiple perspectives produce doubt, and without skepticism important questions would never be asked and blind faith never be challenged.[6] Critical rationality (Popper 1965, 1968), in sum, becomes the main business of science, and scientists are comparativists who work with contending research programs.

Scientists also examine how competing principles work because such an examination often reveals how their own principles work. The process of testing their opponents, in other words, pushes scientists to test themselves. Newton-Smith observes that "we shall not fully appreciate the grounds in favour of our own theory unless we are forced to deal with objections to it" (1981, 132). Debate with one's rivals leads, for example, to the discovery of facts relevant to one's own theory, the understanding of one's own assumptions, and the delimitation of the scope of one's ideas. Scientists therefore use their strongest challengers to clarify, evaluate, and refine their own doctrines, with explicit theoretical critique serving to advance their own position as they define themselves partly in opposition to their foils.

The ancients recognized the value of intellectual conflict. The Socratic method of dialogue begins from generally held opinions, puts forward a hypothesis, and then tests it for coherence in conversation with others. Aristotle often began his inquiry with a critical survey of the relevant opinions held by others. Contemporary philosophers argue similarly. MacIntyre writes: "Knowing how to read antagonistically without defeating oneself as well as one's opponent by not learning from the encounter is a skill without which no tradition can flourish" (1990, 233). Hence, everyone must learn "how to test dialectically the theses proposed to him or her by each competing tradition, while also drawing upon these same theses in order to test dialectically those convictions and responses which he or she has brought to the encounter. Such a person has to become involved in the conversation between traditions, learning to use the idiom of each in order to describe and evaluate the other or others by means of it." Strauss puts it well: "No one can be both a philosopher and a theologian, nor, for that matter, some possibility which transcends the conflict between philosophy and theology, or pretends to be a synthesis of both. But every one of us can be and ought to be either one or the other, the philosopher open to the challenge of theology or the theologian open to the challenge of philosophy" (1989, 270). The same holds for rationalists, culturalists, and structuralists.

Elementary statistics and research design pick up on the philosophers and employ several simple rules of the scientific method to encourage dialogue among competing viewpoints (Hamilton 1996, chap. 8):

- ♦ replicate results with a wrinkle to establish their validity in a new domain
- ♦ think counterinductively (i.e., assume the opposite and defend, justify, and support that position) to challenge one's thinking
- ♦ employ null hypotheses to test one's research hypotheses
- ♦ entertain plausible rival hypotheses to eliminate the threats to one's pet hypotheses
- ♦ and conduct crucial tests to avoid building a single synthetic theory and fitting it to the currently available evidence.

The philosophy-of-science literature[7] suggests several parallel rules of thumb:

- ♦ employ foils to develop multiple working hypotheses

♦ adopt a rival theory to find refuting instances of one's pet theory
♦ use significant plausible rival hypotheses to advance a field
♦ manipulate data to distinguish between theories and their alternatives
♦ and do not give up something for nothing (i.e., if one's theory conflicts with the evidence, abandon the evidence until a better theory comes along).[8]

In sum: imperialism is the manifest destiny of research programs, and conflict among programs is inevitable, but the tensions between alternative paradigms are a source of great vitality and creativity. Laudan argues that "theoretical pluralism contributes to scientific progress" and that "dialectical confrontations are essential to the growth and improvement of scientific knowledge; like nature, science is red in tooth and claw" (1996, 87, 85). Competition against formidable alternatives brings out the best in one's own position, even if it ultimately does not survive intact.

The value of a creative confrontation of the approaches studied here may be appreciated by considering the culturalist perspective. Garrett and Weingast point out that "ideas are a dime a dozen. For every idea that appears to play a major role in politics, tens of thousands play no role at all. Rarely do scholars explain why the idea they study had an impact when so many others did not" (1993, 203). Berger poses the issue as follows: "Can culture be 'reduced' to social structure? Can it be adequately understood purely as a dependent variable even when the actions of persons that reveal and 'carry' culture are felt by them as willed and chosen from alternatives? Or is culture autonomous—or, like the state, 'relatively autonomous'? If so, relative to what and for how long?" (1995, 76). The key research question thus is, Given some situation, what aspect of rationality, culture, or structure is necessary or sufficient for what choice, consciousness, or condition?

8.2. Against Synthesis

If one combines the argument for models with the argument for foils, it becomes clear that reality is best understood from multiple points of view.[9] Since truth is partial, contingent, and contextual, social scientists need several perspectives in order to capture the complexity and variation of phenomena. Given that even multiple theories do not duplicate reality but rather look at the same phenomena differently, competing frameworks contribute to science by studying the different parts of the whole.[10] Hence scientists need to proliferate rival theories, engage foils, and differentiate ideas so that peripheral vision rather than tunnel vision wins the day. The case against the synthesis of different research programs is therefore strong, for many reasons: reality cannot be grasped all at once, paradigms conflict, especially in studying different subject matters, intellectual identities are forged in research communities, scholarly convictions lead to exploring important problems, syntheses are temporary solutions, and research design is neglected, as are questions of social theory.

The first reason draws on Kant and Weber: theories are only selective, partial probes of the world. No one theory can ever capture it all, and any one that tries will be nothing but a vague and unfalsifiable sponge—empirically descriptive, conceptually flabby, and theoretically incoherent.

Second, it is also the case that alternative paradigms may be in eternal conflict with one another because of fundamental or global incompatibilities in their values, assumptions, and standards. Transparadigmatic synthesis may be impossible; rival schools may be substitutes and not complements. Wendt suggests, for example, that

> some individualists are interested in identity and interest ("preference") formation, and some holists concede that agents have intrinsic attributes. Yet, even as they struggle to the center of the continuum, both sides cling to foundational claims that constrain their efforts. Individualist theories of preference formation typically focus on agents rather than structures, and holistic theories of intrinsic attributes typically minimize these as much as they can. (1999, 28–29)

Or to paraphrase Giddens: strong on interests, weak on identities and institutions; strong on identities, weak on interests and institutions; and strong on institutions, weak on interests and identities.

Consider the fundamental differences and trade-offs among the three approaches to social science. On the ontological level, there is the problem of reconciling individualism and holism. On the epistemological level, there is the problem of reconciling positivism and interpretivism. Perhaps most important, on the philosophy-of-science level, specialization leads to different methodologies justified by different philosophies of science. The choice of a research school determines the selection of an explanatory strategy.[11] Rationalists are positivists who suggest falsifiable propositions about how structure relates to action. Subjective culturalists (survey researchers) relate conditions to norms and then to action and hence also adopt a positivist methodology. Culturalists who stick to norms do not produce propositions and hence are not interested in their falsifiability. They advocate interpretive philosophies of science. Finally, structuralists focus on causal mechanisms, often relating these to outcomes, which leads them to adopt a realist focus on social kinds. While causal and interpretive arguments can reinforce one another (sect. 7.4), what metaphilosophy of science could possibly arbitrate among the full range of differences that characterize these fundamentally incompatible philosophies of science?[12]

Next in the case against synthesis, subject matter itself is constructed by approaches and often cannot be easily reconciled by a grand synthesis. Consider the field of contentious politics. Rationalists focus on well-defined groups acting in historically concrete situations. Culturalists broaden this explanandum quite considerably. Scott (1985), for example, studies "everyday forms of resistance" that include such symbolic forms of opposition as styles of speech and clothing. While culturalists, in other words, widen the study of conflict until, in Hegelian fashion, all history and action become inexorably embodied in meaning, rationalists narrow the study of conflict until the material conditions that drive interests become clear. The structuralists, as expected, position themselves in between the two. Thus Tarrow recognizes that "meanings are politically constructed" but notes that social movements are not merely symbolic crusades: "We must be wary of turning mass politics into no more than a form of political theatre" (1994, 119). He therefore broadens the explanandum beyond action to include such structures as social movements, protest cycles, and revolutions (1994, 4, 93, 101, 108, 181, 219–20 n. 5) but does not extend the subject matter as far as Scott does to "discursive communities" and "unobtrusive mobilization." Different approaches thus explore different domains within "contentious politics." Rationalists use the nuts and bolts of collective action theories—entrepreneurs, patrons, selective incentives, risk propensities, self-governing institutions, and so forth—to produce an approach focused on the action and organization of protest. Culturalists elaborate ideas about hegemony, frames, identity, legitimation, and domination into a broader focus on the normative underpinnings of conflict. Structuralists dispatch the alternative theories by locating the great material coalitions and power relationships that lay below surface changes and deterministically drive the structures of protest. Since each approach engages a different part of contentious politics, no single subject matter can ever serve as the basis of a synthetic theory.

Fourth, scientists need to engage in a dialogue with members of one particular scholarly community to build self-knowledge and make intellectual progress. MacIntyre argues that "one cannot think for oneself if one thinks entirely by oneself, that it is only by participation in a rational practice-based community that one becomes rational" (1988, 395). A scientist thus needs to be a part of some tradition and community. Attempts to remain unassociated with research communities, by adopting some suprastandard of rationality that is neutral, universal, and tradition-independent, in the hope of producing a synthesis lead to intellectual fragmentation and ultimately, as MacIntyre observes, alienation.

> Instead they tend to live betwixt and between, accepting usually unquestioningly the assumptions of the dominant liberal individualist forms of public life, but drawing in different areas of their lives upon a variety of tradition-generated resources of thought and action, transmitted from a variety of familial, religious, educational, and other social and cultural sources. This type of self which has too many half-convictions and too few settled coherent convictions, too many partly formulated alternatives and too few opportunities to evaluate them systematically, brings to its encounters with the claims of rival traditions a fundamental incoherence which is too disturbing to be admitted to self-conscious awareness except on the rarest of occasions.
>
> This fragmentation appears in divided moral attitudes expressed in inconsistent moral and political principles, in a tolerance of different rationalities in different milieus, in protective compartmentalization of the self, and in uses of language which move from fragments of one language-in-use through the idioms of internationalized modernity to fragments of another. (The simplest test of the truth of this is as follows: take almost any debatable principle which the majority of members of any given group profess to accept; then it will characteristically be the case that some incompatible principle, in some form of wording, often one employing an idiom very different from that used in formulating the first principle, will also receive the assent of a substantial fraction of that same group.) (1988, 395)

A focus on a manageable number of alternatives thus avoids the despair, cynicism, disconnectedness, and confusion that comes from the excessive fragmentation of the already chaotic, atomistic, and diverse theoretical world. Moreover, the liberal attempt to create all-inclusive knowledge paradoxically produces intolerance. "I have long

since become wary of impartiality, which is itself a way of being partial,"[13] says Heschel (cited in Kaufman 1992, 147). Syntheses thus
inevitably masquerade as singular objectivities. Structuralism in comparative politics, for example, is not the messy center portrayed by the
1995 *World Politics* symposium but is a particular research program.

Fifth, pragmatic synthesis leads to an indifferent neutrality—a
monotonous science without heroes or heroines. Some choices are
intractable, however, and harmony often impossible. Bloom thus
stresses the virtue of taking risks: "A difficult choice [means] to accept
difficult consequences in the form of suffering, disapproval of others,
ostracism, punishment and guilt. Without this, choice [lacks]
significance" (1987, 228). Great scientists make great choices that have
great consequences. Bloom continues that "in philosophy and morals
the hardest and most essential rule is 'You can't eat your cake and have
it too.' . . . Human nature must not be altered in order to have a prob-
lem-free world. Man is not just a problem-solving being, as behaviorists would wish us to believe, but a problem-recognizing and -accepting
being" (1987, 229).

Sixth, a grand synthesis is likely to generate questions about which
of its nested components are dominant and which secondary. As
Keech, Bates, and Lang indicate with respect to rational choice theory
and structural theory: "The 'value added' of adopting a choice-theo-
retic rather than a causal (or functional) perspective has seemed small
and the loss in richness of understanding potentially large" (1991, 233).
Skocpol's critique of Taylor's (1988a) effort to amend her structural
analysis with collective action theory is illustrative.

> Taylor is very careful to say that he is reconstructing the argu-
> ments in [*States and Social Revolutions*], and in no way contra-
> dicting them. And indeed he presumed the entire analysis in my
> book about the breakdown of state power that made the peasant
> community rebellions possible. In short, Taylor's analysis is
> partly a gloss on mine and partly a complement to it.
>
> There have been intelligent commentaries linking individual-
> level processes with macroscopic conflict and institutional
> processes. What rational choice theorists have not done, how-
> ever, is to create successful general theories of phenomena such as
> revolutions or democratization or the rise of authoritarian
> regimes. Hechter and others are all promise and no delivery on
> this score. And it seems unlikely that microlevel models will ever
> completely displace historical-institutional analysis of macro-
> scopic patterns of political conflict and change. (1995, 42)

Partisans of different approaches, in short, eventually tear apart any synthesis and propose competitive tests to establish theoretical primacy.

Synthesis, moreover, complicates Popperian-type competitive testing. For example, it is conceptually possible to construct such wide definitions of interests, identities, and institutions that they encompass everything. Monopolists thus claim that "everyone everywhere is always rational" or that it is "ideas all the way down" or that "in the end structure is determinate." Synthesizers who wish to expand their empire thus eventually become imperialists, with each approach claiming to mediate the others. Rationalists claim that norms and conditions motivate choice. Culturalists claim that individual actions and collective situations must be interpreted. Structuralists claim that structure controls choices and passions. The result is tautology: a norm that includes structures and practices is probably too thick; a rationality that includes nonpecuniary process benefits is also probably too thick; and a structure that includes collective actions, beliefs, and desires is probably too thick as well. If one thickens programs in these ways, one never competitively tests the programs in a fundamental way. The first job of rationality, culture, and structure is to circumscribe their own limits (sect. 4.3).

Finally, a single messy center of synthesis perpetuates a key problem of much of contemporary social science: we do not take our theories or our theorists seriously enough. Synthesis leads to fuzziness, splitting intellectual differences rather than analyzing their analytical consequences.

In sum: one size never fits all. There is no single approach to understanding the world, no all-encompassing social theory, no final solution that provides ultimate truth, no complete vantage point that neutrally incorporates all perspectives, no single way to explain 100 percent of the variance, and no single metanarrative that incorporates all events. If we can not have the unity of science, how can we have the unity of social science?[14] Social scientists have to recognize the possibility of either/or and not both/and. Like the theologians who distinguish between heaven/earth, light/day, and evil/good, scientists need sharp distinctions in their theories. I conclude this section with a nod to Nietzsche, who understood the significance of heroes and villains, friends and enemies.[15]

> You should have eyes that always seek an enemy—your enemy . . . you may have only enemies whom you hate, not enemies you despise. You must be proud of your enemy.

I only attack causes that are victorious; I may even wait until they become victorious.

If a temple is to be erected, a temple must first be destroyed.

The creation of a fashionable synthesis is less honorable than the judicious use of ideal-type models and foils.

8.3. Conclusion: Synthesis and Analysis

This chapter has demonstrated that all scientists work within a more or less well defined research tradition that holds important consequences for their research. Since family quarrels within a research community and antagonism between research communities are inevitable, social scientists also live with the tensions between protagonists and antagonists of particular viewpoints. If we embrace these creative confrontations among the strongly defined research traditions—rationalist, culturalist, and structuralist—that exist in social science, reflexive understandings by theorists of their theories will flourish and better explanations of the world will be developed. The starting point of inquiry in the social sciences should therefore always be a model and a foil. Accordingly, my foil in this chapter is the lumper who wants to overcome a dialogue between models and foils and create a hegemonic synthesis at the level of a research paradigm, social theory, or empirical explanation. And my model is the splitter who wants to use the dialogue, debate, and disagreement between models and foils to advance a field.

While there will never be a single research tradition accepted by an entire social scientific discipline, a single theory acclaimed by everyone who works in some empirical domain, nor a single explanation believed by all those interested in a particular case, synthesizers are happy to work toward a postparadigmatic world that is no longer disturbed by debates among Marxists, functionalists, pluralists, historical institutionalists, and so on. Part V thus continues to deepen our understanding of the rationalists' bid for hegemony. It studies contemporary philosophy of science to understand how the rationalist, culturalist, and structuralist traditions can peacefully and fruitfully coexist. Chapter 9 rejects all bids for intellectual hegemony and advocates multiple perspectives about generalizations in the social sciences. Chapter 10 rejects the traditional positivist philosophy of science and argues that the three traditions provide the models and foils needed by social science.

Part V

The Philosophy of Science

Chapter 9

The General and the Particular

Social scientists grapple with questions about the general and the particular concerning concept formation, theory building, and case selection.

♦ *Concept formation.* How do concepts carry across cases? Are properties abstract and universal or located in time and space? Is there something common to the many instances of the same property? Can one and the same property be a property of several things?

♦ *Theory building.* What is the scope of theories? Are there trans-historical and transcultural uniformities? Do law-governed causal social processes occur across countries? In other words, "Is it possible to construct a science of history (for example, as a sequence of modes of production) or a science of society in general (universal laws of social organization and change) or a science of a given society as a whole (such as British society in the nineteenth century)?" (Little 1989, 216).

♦ *Case selection.* What is the proper use of case-specific information for theories that cover many cases? How does the choice of cases affect general propositions? Are there requirements that define the number of cases that need to be included in an analysis? Is it possible or desirable to include all relevant instances in the analysis? Is it possible to devise an adequate methodology that permits powerful generalizations based on the observation of a small number of cases? Can a single-case study speak to general sets of phenomena? How, in short, does one establish external validity or justify generalizations beyond the case or cases being observed?

These questions point to long-standing battles between generalists and particularists, between a universalizing perspective and one that is bounded in time and space. Per Verba (1967, 117): "The dilemma of comparative analysis is clearly posed: reality seems to demand a configurative approach; generalizability seems to demand a more analytic approach."

The debate between nominalists/particularists and realists/universalists marks the divide. Nominalists argue that there are no abstract things: all things that exist are particular, universals are just names given to groups of individuals, and hence all classifications are arbitrary. Realists classify because they believe that properties are universal and that things do share a common property of "one over the many." In other words, while nominalists say that each human has its own essential property—human 1 and human 2—realists maintain that one can abstract from particulars to universals and that the universals exist—human 1 and human 2 may be distinguished from tiger 1 and tiger 2.

Where do our protagonist research traditions fall on this question of the general and the particular? Section 9.1 discusses the positions advocated by each research program. Section 9.2 discusses how Weber employed universalistic, classificatory, and particularizing methodologies. Section 9.3 expands on the value of joining generalist and particularist perspectives.

9.1. The Research Programs

Rationalists, structuralists, and culturalists diverge on the appropriate mix of the global and the local.[1] Rationalists are positivists who conduct comparative static exercises in which particular structural and cultural conditions drive general action processes. They employ a deductive-nomological or covering-law framework to demonstrate the universality of explanation: each case is understood as a particular manifestation of general laws. Structuralists are realists who study how real types of structures contain causal processes and dynamics. They employ a typological framework of explanation that classifies all cases into a set of mutually exclusive and exhaustive social kinds: each case is understood as part of a general classificatory scheme. Intersubjective culturalists are interpretivists who study idiosyncratic developments. They employ a highly path-dependent mode of understanding in which processes interact with one another and with particular structures, both statically and dynamically, in highly individualistic ways: each case is therefore different and unique. In sum, rationalists are drawn to generalist or universalist modes of theorizing; culturalists are attracted to particularist or historicist arguments; and structuralists split the difference (between all and each lies some) and think like typologists or

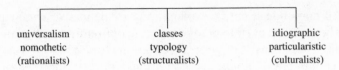

universalism	classes	idiographic
nomothetic	typology	particularistic
(rationalists)	(structuralists)	(culturalists)

Fig. 9.1.   Research programs and methodology

contextualists. In terms of a continuum, we have the connections shown in figure 9.1. We can thus say that some social scientists look for similarities in spite of differences, others for differences in spite of similarities, and still others for kinds of similarities and differences. We now explore these positions in greater detail.

9.1.1. Rationalists and Universality

Rationalists, and especially human nature rationalists, believe that a relatively homogeneous and undifferentiated human condition creates behavior that is regular and repeatable (i.e., normal and typical) and thus fashions the laws and generalizations that underlie the multiplicity of historical instances.[2] Rationalists therefore have nomothetic aims: they seek similarities in order to establish parallels among cases, abstract in order to get at universals, and search for cross-cultural regularities to reveal timeless and placeless truths.[3]

And they adopt Hempel's (1966) covering-law model of deductive-nomological explanation, the purpose of which is to show that an event or process that occurs at a particular time and place is, under the circumstances, necessary or predictable. As Hempel puts it, "The explanation fits the phenomenon to be explained into a pattern of uniformities and shows that its occurrence was to be expected, given the specified laws and the pertinent particular circumstances" (50).[4] Why, for example, did France have a revolution in 1789? A general statement of which the French Revolution is one instance must be true; the statement must support prediction ex ante and explanation ex post; and all countries placed in similar conditions must have revolutions. The covering-law model has been critically applied to all types of explanations (Suppe's 1977 critique of Hempel), including social scientific explanations (Hollis's 1994 critique of Przeworski and Teune 1970) and rational choice explanations (Bohman's 1993 critique of Hempel).

The Hempelian form of explanation combines universality, context, and particularity in subtle ways.

♦ All bona fide scientific explanations are deductive arguments. They are sets of statements consisting of premises or explanantia. These consist of general conditions (one or more testable general laws), boundary conditions (one or more testable statements of facts), and a conclusion or explanandum (a statement of the fact or regularity to be explained).

♦ In the covering-law model, a given event or regularity can be subsumed under one or more deeper and more general regularities. Just as one explains specific laws by grander theories, one explains specific observations by grander laws.

♦ The covering-law model employs a particular notion of cause and effect: whenever a particular event of a certain kind x occurs (the initial conditions and the explanans), another event of kind y occurs (the explanandum)—that is, same cause, same effect. Because of the general laws involved, the phenomenon to be explained was not accidental; given the circumstances, it was necessary. Historically specific cause-and-effect statements thus become general laws.

♦ Covering-law explanations are processes within structures: the constants drive the variables, the exogenous forces determine the endogenous forces, the boundary conditions affect the laws, the parameters set the context, and the environments control the mechanisms.

♦ Theory comes in two parts. Something descends from above: laws, hypotheses, and propositions. Something else is on the ground: institutions, situations, environments, Kant's middle term, boundary conditions, auxiliary assumptions, scope conditions, bridge principles, special theories, and auxiliary hypotheses. Rationalists thus parameterize universal laws, extend core hypotheses to fit particular topics and issues, and show how general propositions produce similar outcomes in different situations. Reality is therefore a combination of the general and the specific: uniqueness arises from initial conditions that are specific to each case; universality comes from general laws developed from the comparative study of many cases.

♦ Theory is always operationalized, as Hempelians ask how the process or theory works out in a real situation. For example, rationalists operationalize their theories in a structural context that specifies the actors and their preferences, beliefs, and actions.

♦ The theory is different from the reality. Since structures intervene, there is no one-to-one correspondence between a rationalist model and the truth. Rationalists thus try to keep their models *simple* and *different* from the real world: complexity is added when they apply the model, rather than when they build it initially.

♦ In dealing with specific cases, strict deductions from general theories can be made. Hence, rationalists interpret cases logically as being implied by theories: law + case = outcome. Valid theories therefore compel particular explanations of cases and rule out others. As the generalist Eckstein puts it: "The present task of study is, however, not merely to add up determinants to yield plausible accounts of specific cases—nothing is easier— but to discover the general circumstances under which each of the conditions discussed above may be of special significance" (1968, 451).

♦ Since "human behavior is contextual" (Kincaid 1996, 62), all "explanations come to an end" (Wittgenstein, in Shand 1994, 288). Ultimately, rational choice theorists have to be content with a description of conditions. As Keynes puts it: economics must "begin with observation and end with observation" (in Blaug 1992, 73).

♦ There is no contradiction between understanding historical context and developing general theories. Theorists and historians are part of the intellectual division of social scientific labor.[5] The reason for the complementarity is that there are no unambiguous comparative static hypotheses: all falsifiable predictions are tied to specific contexts, and contextual factors always limit the scope of general laws.[6] For example, repression does not decrease dissent everywhere, every time, and under all conditions. Rationalists thus test $x \rightarrow y$ statements by probing the ceteris paribus conditions for the scope of the law, hoping to find important qualifications and exceptions.

In sum, while rationalists are positivists, sophisticated rationalists recognize that no explanation is unlimited and invariant. And as all theories are subtly contingent, they seek to explain historical particularity. The Holy Trinity of rationalist methodology has therefore become models, statistics, and cases (Huber 1996). But even sophisticated rationalists are opposed by two sets of antipositivists: culturalists[7] who study meanings (the subjective critique) and structuralists[8] who study institutions (the objective critique).

9.1.2. Culturalists and Particularity

Consider the Hebrew Bible. The Bible is not like systematic Greek philosophy but rather is closer to historical narrative. It presents examples or situations under varying conditions and then works out the application of general (moral) principles—the lessons of history. The Bible thus finds the universal in the particular, the eternity in the moment. The whole truth, the Bible seems to be telling us, can be grasped only in particular truths.

Particularists, for example, Bloom,[9] think that this is the way to study social life.[10] The reason goes back to the nature of culturalism: since the meaning and significance of a person's actions are tied to his or her culture, social scientists must study particular cultures. As Weber writes:

> The type of social science in which we are interested is an *empirical science* of concrete *reality*. . . . Our aim is the understanding of the characteristic uniqueness of the reality in which we move. We wish to understand on the other hand the relationships and the cultural significance of individual events in their contemporary manifestation and on the other the causes of their being historically *so* and not *otherwise*. . . . It too concerns itself with the question of the *individual* consequence which the working of these "laws" in a unique *configuration* produces, since it is these individual configurations which are *significant* for us. Every individual constellation which it "explains" or predicts is causally explicable only as the consequence of another equally individual constellation which has preceded it. As far back as we may go into the grey mist of the far-off past, the reality to which the laws apply always remains equally *individual,* equally *undeducible* from laws. ([1903–17] 1949, 72; emphasis in original)

Since individual configurations of reality, in other words, are meaningful and significant for us, we need to understand the characteristic uniqueness of each reality. Simmel thus refers to "finding in each of life's details the totality of its meaning" (cited in Scaff 1989, 195).

Here then is the difference between rationalists and culturalists: while

rationalists are concerned with transhistorical, abstract truths, culturalists are concerned with individual historically specific realities—concrete things and events. Culturalists thus study the actual state of the
real world, not an idealized, equilibrium, or long-run version of it. And
they leave questions of external validity to the rationalists.

Little makes the culturalist argument against global and universalistic theories and for localist and contextually relativist ones.

> Consider one example—efforts by comparative sociologists to
> analyze collective violence in diverse societies. The concept of a
> "grain riot" may be useful to characterize bread riots in medieval
> England and rice riots in Qing China. Each is an instance of col-
> lective violence stimulated by an immediate food shortage and,
> perhaps, a popular sense of injustice. This concept enables the
> social scientist to analyze and discuss events from different cul-
> tures. But from beginning to end, the social scientist must bear in
> mind the facts of historical contingency and cultural diversity;
> thus it will be important not to force the English and Chinese
> events into an overly sparse conceptual space of food shortage
> and collective violence. The concept of a grain riot is a useful tool
> with which to probe the historical particular, but it does not pro-
> vide a basis for deciding the necessary course of development of
> the phenomena that fall under it. So social science knowledge
> does not typically take the form of unified deductive theories;
> instead it is a theoretically informed effort to analyze historical
> particulars. (1991, 226)

For the culturalist, the rationalist effort to locate parallels or analogies
that can be used to construct laws and regularities that hold for all
members of a class of phenomena is only the beginning of inquiry,
offering benchmarks or orienting devices to probe the particular and
hence culturally significant manifestations of general social processes.

Culturalists thus relish heterogeneity, diversity, and multiplicity—in
other words, the variance and not the mean. Nolte argues that "to
understand means to grasp the differentiated within its context" (1965,
x), and Bloch, that "comparative history has a duty to bring out the
'originality' of the different societies" (1967, 58). In stressing configurative paths, culturalists move beyond the point that all societies have a
division of labor to show how the division of labor differs from one
society to the next. They seek to establish sharp differences rather than
vague similarities,[11] not to "flatten" but to "illuminate" divergence.
The social sciences should therefore focus on origins and outcomes to

understand divergent histories and historical particularities, respecting the unique historical integrity of each case. This often comes down to studying one case. By contrast, those who study one hundred cases are likely to discover what the cases have in common.[12] Culturalists thus explore deviant or nonparadigmatic cases that challenge existing theoretical generalizations (Eckstein 1975 on most-likely and least-likely cases); historically seminal cases that, via path dependence (i.e., contingency and contextuality), affect all others (Weber [1904–5] 1985 on the unique origins and world-historical importance of the West); and paradigmatic cases (Marx [1895] 1964 on France).[13] MacIntyre,[14] Moore,[15] and Skocpol,[16] though not all culturalists, have offered classic criticisms of generalizing social science.

9.1.3. Structuralists and Classification

Whereas rationalists universalize and culturalists particularize, structuralists typologize, employing classification, history, comparative history, and world-historical context.

Classification.   Structures are patterned configurations. Structuralists thus divide the objects they study into species and genera, classifying their similarities and differences into "comparable situations" or "contrast sets" (Rule 1988, 231–32). Elements and classes thus take on identity and importance in relation to the rules of the typology—other classes or kinds in an entire classificatory scheme. Taxonomy, moreover, has explanatory aims: while structuralists cannot predict what will happen, they can classify the various possible outcomes on the basis of the dynamics of the class to which a case belongs.[17]

History.   Skocpol writes: "One cannot simply develop a general model and go out and apply it universally, in place after place" (1995, 39). Structuralists thus "share a suspicion of theories that generalize at too great a remove from specific cases (explicitly recognizing that relations among variables cannot be consistent from case to case)" (Katznelson 1997, 92). Similar to the culturalists, structuralists believe that one should study historically concrete relationships in particular social formations that produce unique outcomes. They prefer theorizing about federalism and Protestantism, for example, to theorizing about political opportunity structures and cultural frames (McAdam, Tarrow, and Tilly 1997) because the relations in the former are more real and concrete. Thompson, for another example, suggests that "class is a social and cultural formation (often finding institutional expression) which cannot be defined abstractly or in isolation, but only in terms of relationship with other classes; and ultimately the definition can only be made in the medium of time—that is, action and reaction, change and conflict" (cited in Kaye 1984, 232). Skocpol (1979), for a final example, focuses on the historically concrete forms of the state so as to assure a "tighter fit between concepts and situations" (Katznelson 1997, 90).

Unlike culturalists, however, structuralists focus not on a particular detail, event, or outcome, but rather on the relationships among the great many details of the historical record, especially if these facts have not been recognized as interconnected. Seeking to explain a concrete historical configuration of situations and events, they weave these many threads into a larger pattern and more coherent whole that respects the historical integrity of the case. Structuralists thus consider each case in detail, mining their sources to accumulate many specific points that joined together yield a historically recognizable case study.

Structuralists thus typically begin their work with a set of historically interrelated puzzles. They probe conventional historiography— historical debates, controversies, and problems—for the collection of observations to be explained, the set of challenges to theory, and the complex of issues or questions to be analyzed. Goldstone thus advises: "It is essential for comparative historians to engage fully the secondary literature of the cases they study in order to be aware of the historical arguments, uncertainties, and issues at stake. A comparative historian does not approach historical scholarship as a miner approaches a mine. Instead, he or she approaches the literature as a historian would, to engage in a conversation about what happened" (1991, 54).

For structuralists, the country-level context is essential. Katznelson recommends that "agents always be understood as embedded in institutional milieus; that causal relations of elements and variables always are patterned by context and circumstance; and that historical developments are contingently shaped by choices taken by actors about the content of the institutional links connecting state, economy, and society at key moments of historical indeterminacy" (1997, 104). Derry puts it bluntly: "To understand fascism in Norway, it is first necessary for us to try to understand Norway" (1981, 223).

Structuralists also study narrative sequences of historically interrelated events in which one tells what happened and why. Moore speaks of process tracing in this way: "Though I too would reject any thorough historical determinism, I do not believe that the significant facts of history are mere mechanical aggregates. Instead, they are connected with one another over time" (1958, 132). Since concrete outcomes have concrete causes, explanation is dependent on time and place. At each point in time structuralists consider the factual of what happened and the counterfactual of what did not happen but might have happened. They explore a case's causes (setting, origin, or how it came to be), its courses (operation, mechanism, or interactions with other variables), and its effects (dependent variables).

Comparative history. Putting the last two arguments together, structuralists approach their historical problems comparatively, by juxtaposing different histories. As Katznelson puts it, "The method deployed to grapple with the tensions inherent in the relationship between such [general] propositions and specific historical instances is that of a continuous oscillation 'between alternative explanatory hypotheses and comparisons of relevant aspects of the histories of two or more cases'" (1997, 92).

Structuralists thus classify cases into a number of categories, all fundamentally different from one another, and then investigate the historical dynamics associated with each class. Similar processes, sequences, and laws occur in similar structures or social kinds; different processes, sequences, and laws occur in different structures. The result is the identification of a small and hence manageable number of typical paths or historical trajectories of development and change.

Structuralists doing comparative history think causally. They examine counterfactuals, or why things were not so. The goal is not merely to identify analogy or generality—the search for parallel histories— but to account for difference. Structuralists thus typically study geographic neighbors and historical contemporaries, countries close to each other in space and time.

Comparative history can begin with some striking differences where one might have expected similarities. While there are global influences on local developments—common roots, origins, and causes—there are also variations in response to common external developments. If both society A and society B have similar causes, dissimilar effects intrigue us. Despite having a depression in common, fascism became dominant in Germany and Italy but not in England and the United States. Why?

Comparative history can also start with striking similarities where one might have expected differences. If both society A and society B have similar effects, dissimilar causes intrigue us. For example, the French, Russian, and Chinese Revolutions occurred in different historical periods. Skocpol (1979) argues that the similarity is that all these states failed to cope with external pressures either because of inadequate economic development (Russia) or because powerful elites blocked the changes necessary to improve state efficiency (China, France).

The exercises are often combined. Because of differences in initial conditions and contexts—institutions, structures, groups—similar causes or shocks (e.g., wars) can produce dissimilar effects in the different systems.[18] Yet different contexts within a similar overall type can produce similar outcomes.[19] According to Skocpol (1979), for example, state breakdown and peasant revolutions operate differently in agrarian bureaucracies than they do in postcolonial regimes. Comparative history involves being both a *why* political scientist and a *how* political scientist: explanation and narrative. Structuralists thus contextualize developments or root phenomena in space and in time, in a period and in a place, often long ago and far away.

World-historical context.   Since structuralists are concerned with multilayered relationships, every country for them is situated in a larger holistic pattern. Structuralists thus maintain that reality is understandable only in terms of its world-historical context: there is a time and a place for each real-world phenomenon. Consider, for example, fascism: it is not a fixed quality that occurs in a static and mechanical natural order but instead means different things in different contexts. An account of fascist movements should therefore not involve ahistorical and acontextual abstractions but dynamic developments rooted in particular histories. For example, it should try to explain the origin and nature of fascism in interwar Europe by the failure of concrete democratic institutions, the development of particular political crises, the evolution of certain social conflicts, and the mobilization of unique political groups.

An explanation or interpretation of a single country is therefore interesting and important only if it situates the particular case among others and shows how its individual history fits into a global pattern of development via intersections, linkages, and relationships. Moore[20] thus establishes the significance of a case by exploring how its external relations—for example, contagion, diffusion, imitation, and competition—affect its particular configuration of interests, identities, and institutions.[21]

9.2. Weber's Approach

Weber[22] is a generalist, a typologist, and a particularist. He demonstrates the value of employing multiple methodologies.

Generalist.   While Weber appears to be uninterested in transhistorical and transcultural generalizations, there is a sense in which he has nomothetic aims. He refers to the generalizing sciences as follows.

The logical ideal of these disciplines is to differentiate the *essential properties* of the concrete phenomenon subjected to analysis from its "accidental" or meaningless properties, and thereby to establish intuitive knowledge of these essential features. The attempt to order phenomena into a universal system of concrete "causes" and "effects" which are immediately and intuitively understandable commits these disciplines to an increasingly sophisticated explication of concepts. These concepts are meant to *approximate* a representation of the concrete actuality of reality by selecting and unifying those properties which we judge to be *"characteristic."* ([1903–6] 1975, 57, emphasis in original)

Weber's ideal types have such generalist ambitions and look remarkably like the rationalists' comparative statics (Burger 1987, 160–61). Since they are nominalist working tools rather than realist depictions of the world, ideal types serve as orienting models to define and frame general questions and problems with a one-sided emphasis that captures the typical or invariant characteristics of phenomena.

Weber abstracts, for example, historical particulars and focuses on the ideal-type characteristics of Calvinism, Catholicism, Lutheranism, Chinese literati, Brahmin intellectuals, the polis, the caste system, ancient capitalism, the medieval city, the clan, the neighborhood, the *oikos,* bureaucracy, patrimonialism, patriarchalism, Caesaropapism, feudalism, and charisma. He also uses ideal types as heuristic devices to generate nomological hypotheses and causal laws. *The Sociology of Religion,* for example, links social status to the religious orientations of peasants, warriors, intellectuals, bourgeoisie, and nobility, while his *Economy and Society* explores many general concepts such as the state.

Typologist. Weber, however, rejects the idea that there are universal truths about overall societal change. History, he believes, has no teleology but rather is full of contingencies. Since there are no grand theories of history, one should undertake historically grounded comparisons and establish similarities and differences in paths of change. Rather than proposing elaborate evolutionary, deterministic, or developmental theories, Weber thus examines the change and dynamics of particular types of cases. His ideal types contain the alternatives and contrasts inherent in concrete structural configurations.[23] Ideal types are consequently transformed through internal conflicts and thereby show typical patterns of historical development. For example, the ideal type of bureaucracy leads to a theory of bureaucratization, and the ideal type of charisma leads to a theory of the routinization of charisma.

Weber's ideal types, moreover, are tied to specific sociohistorical relations and not to whole societies. As he studied, for example, bureaucratic, patrimonial, feudal, and charismatic social relations, Weber developed such famous classifications as paths of salvation, solutions to the problems of evil and suffering, and the bases of legitimacy. As indicated in section 1.3, these ideal types permitted four types of comparisons: among ideal types, among cases, between a type and a case within its range, and between a case and several ideal types. These comparisons allow Weber to confine the scope of his theory to the type of case involved.

Particularist.   Weber believes that social scientists can study only selected parts of reality, not all of it. He thus refers to

> knowledge of *concrete reality,* knowledge of its invariably qualitative properties, those properties responsible for its peculiarities and its uniqueness. Because of the logical impossibility of an *exhaustive* reproduction of even a limited aspect of reality—due to the (at least intensively) infinite number of qualitative differentiations that can be made—this must mean the following: knowledge of those aspects of reality which we regard as *essential* because of their individual *peculiarities.* ([1903–06] 1975, 57, emphasis in original)

The parts of reality that social scientists find worth studying are thus those having meaning or significance for the actors involved. Weber's ideal types are therefore interpretive frameworks based on subjectively meaningful action. He believes, moreover, that the values that give meaning to action are a product of historically specific processes of development. A culture therefore is a worldview—an ethos, spirit, or *Geist*—that imparts meaning to its entire history and pattern to its whole development.

Weber often analyzes one case in depth, taking a general concept or idea and considering all of its ramifications for a particular society's economy, social structure, and government. Coming at his case with a definite point of view, Weber characterizes the essence of the societies he studies: "He defines a particular society and period in terms of its dominant classes, institutions, and values. The three are inextricably related for Weber and influence each other reciprocally. This give his approach and his work remarkable focus; Weber does not describe, he 'interprets.' When he deals with a society he imputes a definite direction and character to it, from which necessarily follow certain inherent strengths and weaknesses (*Agrarian Sociology*, p. 25)" (Bendix 1962, 276).

In analyzing a single case, Weber focuses on divergent paths of development and historical singularity, attempting to isolate and abstract individual elements of a case that distinguish it from all others and then comparing the case with the appropriate ideal type. Weber's ideal types thus establish the unique, specific, peculiar, distinctive, and original aspect of a case. They serve as yardsticks against which to measure empirical cases to discern how and why they differ from the ideal. Ideal types thus alert us to individuality and differences and not only to universalities, similarities, and averages.

Another way Weber establishes particularity is through broad historical comparisons of cases. He wants to know, for example, "what, after all, constitutes the indubitable peculiarity of Israelite religious development" ([1917–19] 1952, 428) and "how that peculiarity is historically conditioned" (Weber, cited in Fahey 1982, 63). Most famously, Weber examines the West: by comparison and confrontation with the major historical alternatives, he establishes the world-historical significance of a case.

Theory for Weber is thus not a goal of inquiry but rather a means for the analysis of concrete historical cases. He uses theories to explain the unique outcome of each case, to compare for the purpose of establishing important differences and not to discover superficial similarities. Using such an orientation, the individual case becomes important rather than crude, subtle, and dull.

> Let us assume that we have succeeded by means of psychology or otherwise in analyzing all the observed and imagined relationships of social phenomena into some ultimately elementary "factors," that we have made an exhaustive analysis and classification of them and then formulated rigorously exact laws covering their behavior. What would be the significance of these results for our knowledge of the *historically* given culture or any individual phase thereof, such as capitalism, in its development and cultural significance? As an analytical tool, it would be as useful as a textbook of organic chemical combinations would be for our knowledge of the biogenetic aspect of the animal and plant world. In each case, certainly an important and useful preliminary step would have been taken. In neither case can concrete reality be deduced from "laws" and "factors." . . . The real reason is that the analysis of reality is concerned with the *configuration* into which those (hypothetical!) "factors" are arranged to form cultural phenomenon which is historically significant to use. Fur-

thermore, if we wish to "explain" this individual configuration "causally" we must involve other equally individual configurations on the basis of which we will explain it with the aid of those (hypothetical!) "laws." ([1903–17] 1949, 75])

Weber thus argues that "if we strive for intellectual understanding of the reality about us, of the way in which it was by needs individually determined in a necessarily individual context, then the analyses of those *parallels* must be undertaken solely from the viewpoint of elucidating the specific meaning of concrete culture elements with regard to concrete, intelligible causes and consequences. In this case the parallels would merely be a means of comparing several historical phenomena in their full individuality for the sake of identifying their specific character" (cited in Roth 1971, 254). He concludes:

> A genuinely analytic study comparing the stages of development of the ancient *polis* with those of the mediaeval city would be welcome and productive. . . . Of course I say this on the assumption that such a comparative study would not aim at finding "analogies" and "parallels," as is done by those engrossed in the currently fashionable enterprise of constructing general schemes of development. The aim should, rather, be precisely the opposite: to identify and define the individuality of each development, the characteristics which made the one conclude in a manner so different from that of the other. This done, one can then determine the causes which led to these differences. It is also my assumption that an indispensable preliminary to such a comparative study would be the isolation and abstraction of the individual elements in each development, the study of these elements in the light of general rules drawn from experience, and finally, the formation of clear concepts. . . . Without these preliminary steps no causal relationship whatever can be established. ([1896] 1988, 385–86)

In this way, Weber links the analysis of the general with an analysis of the particular: "One can only define the specific characteristics of, for example, the mediaeval city . . . after one has established which of these characteristics were lacking in other cities (classical Chinese, Islamic). That is a general rule. The next task of historians is to give a causal explanation of those specific characteristics" ([1896] 1988, 21).[24]

In sum, Weber's ideal types combine the rationalist search for explanatory laws, the structuralist concern for classification, and the culturalist search for interpretive meaning. Recognizing the limitations of each approach, he teaches social scientists to take account of both the individual, historical, or concrete and the general, common, or average. His work is sensitive to broadly conceived lines of analysis and to complex detail and thus stands as a model of social science in the service of history, and history in the service of social science.

9.3. The General and the Particular in the Social Sciences

Hayakawa observes that literature is often stuck at a particular level of abstraction—overly detailed, insignificant, and disjointed at a low level and overly ambiguous, vague, and irrelevant at a high level. One needs instead an interplay of levels: "A 'significant' novelist or poet is one whose message has a high level of general usefulness in prodding insight into life, but he gives his generalization an impact and persuasiveness through his ability to observe and describe social situations and stages of mind" (1990, 165). For natural science, too, wisdom is in the particular and the universal.[25] As Alfred North Whitehead put it: "It is the large generalization, limited by a happy particularity which is the fruitful conception" (cited in Bell 1973, 13–14). The notion of an operational definition of course implies that the natural scientist needs to climb up and down the abstraction ladder, to develop generalizations *and* explain particular cases. This position is consistent with how mathematicians work.[26]

While some rationalists have followed Weber and tried to bridge the idiographic-nomothetic divide, it is the comparativist Eckstein who has been particularly outspoken: "The end of inquiry, as I see it, is a close joining of broad and deep studies, but doing so on the scale ideally required is beyond the scope of any single work or any single scholar. What is needed is a long, deliberate, mutually sympathetic dialogue by those whose tastes run to the general and those who prefer to deal with special cases" (1966, v–vi). Maintaining that general theories help inform the analysis of individual cases, and particular cases help the construction of general theories, he makes a plea for tolerance that bears repeating in full.

> Either mode of study entails shortcomings. The generalizer sacrifices sure mastery of detail, the narrower scholar relevance of theory and the excitement of imagination that comes from broad horizons. For that reason alone the work of using specific studies to inform general ones, and of the latter to inform the former, can never be fully and finally done. Especially in the early stages of

inquiry, the special studies available for pursuing any broad concern are likely to be very incomplete and to a large extent irrelevant. That problem can be progressively reduced only by a serious interest in general theory on the part of those preferring to work on special cases, but is unlikely ever to be removed completely. Then too, when special studies are used for general purposes, it is only too possible that the generalist (who, like any human being, is limited in time, energy, and background) will misunderstand or merely be superficial, or be misled by mistakes or biases of specialists that he cannot detect himself. Only constant criticism by specialists will help reduce this problem, provided that they understand the generalist's concerns and that the latter is willing to take well-informed criticisms into account. Hence, the interplay of general and special work in political study must be unrestrained, sympathetic, and above all continuous. But to continue, it must begin. And to begin one must be prepared to write on a level of great tentativity and very insufficient knowledge, hoping that others will not misunderstand one's intentions. (vi)

More than thirty years later, Eckstein's hopes—which could encourage dialogue among rationalists, culturalists, and structuralists—remain unfulfilled.

Chapter 10

Models and Foils: A Modest Philosophy of Science for Social Science

Is rational choice theory all of social science? No. To see why social science needs modest rational choice theory, I progressively deepened our understanding of the rationalist bid for hegemony. I began by studying the rationalists and showing how the rationalist synthesis is rooted in the weaknesses, not the strengths, of rationalist thought. Rationalist lacunae, in other words, lead rationalists to incorporate the competing paradigms of culture and structure in a subordinate fashion. From rational choice theory I moved to its intellectual opponents. By showing why multiple research communities exist in the social sciences, I demonstrated how the rationalist attempt to subsume its opponents is based on an individualistic reduction of culture and structure. Since culturalists conceive of culture as collective and structuralists conceive of structure as configurational, culturalists and structuralists will forever reject rationalist hegemony.

I then moved from competing social theories to the philosophy of social science. I explored the structure-action problem and explained what leads some rationalists, culturalists, and structuralists to synthesize the alternative research traditions into one meta-approach that aims to monopolize a discipline or field. I also explored debates about transparadigmatic testing and evaluation and explained what leads other rationalists, culturalists, and structuralists to analysis, or to analytically split research alternatives. I argued that social science needs multiple perspectives and that the three research traditions studied here provide the necessary models and foils.

If social science will forever be a multiple-paradigm science, how can the three traditions coexist peacefully and fruitfully? Part V explores how the contemporary philosophy of science can deal with the multiple-paradigm nature of social science. Chapter 9 showed how the multiple perspectives about generalizations in the social sciences constitute a useful intellectual division of labor. Social science needs rationalist generalizers, structuralist typologizers, and culturalist particularizers.

This final chapter deepens the debate about rationalist hegemony one last time by showing how rationalist aims are rooted in three principles of the traditional positivist philosophy of science.

◆ *Theory* is deductive-nomological: it begins as abstract, axiomatic, and foundational; it becomes subsuming, integrating, and unifying; and it ends as organized, comprehensive, and encyclopedic.

◆ *Evidence* is oriented toward falsification: scientists attempt to reject a hypothesis; after one possible explanans is discarded, they investigate another to see if it can account for the explanandum.

◆ *Evaluation* is therefore based on deductive and nomological laws that resist falsification: these laws establish the ever-expanding domain of a theory; science therefore succeeds when it discovers universal laws that are true.

This philosophy of science might suit rational choice theorists who operate as a hegemonic research community in search of a one-size-fits-all theory. If rationalists seek baselines and boundaries (sect. 3.3), it will not work. Modest rational choice theory requires a modest philosophy of science that instead consists of three different principles.

◆ *Theory* consists of research programs that contain nuts and bolts; these causal mechanisms are combined into models of a theory that suggest lawful regularities.

◆ *Evidence* establishes the applicability of these models of a theory for the models of data that exist in particular domains; the elaboration of a theory thus delimits the theory's scope.

◆ *Evaluation* grapples with the problem that the science that results from following the first two principles is prone to non-falsifiability and to self-serving confirmations. Confrontations between theory and evidence are thus evaluated in the context of larger structures of knowledge. For pragmatists who work with a thin version of one paradigm, Lakatos's (1970) "additional and true" standard, which lets them explore rationalist, culturalist, and structuralist approaches on their own terms, is applied. For competitors who employ alternative paradigms, Popper's (1968) "different and better" standard, which lets them conduct competitive evaluations among alternative rationalist, culturalist, and structuralist explanations, is employed. And for hegemons who synthesize the different paradigms into one thick paradigm, "nested models" that combine the two standards, and thus let them compare syntheses to their components (models and foils), are used.

Section 10.1 discusses theory; section 10.2, evidence, section 10.3, some mistaken ideas about theory and evidence, and section 10.4, evaluation. I conclude by showing how a modest rationalist evaluates theory and evidence.

10.1. Theory

Strauss writes that

method brings about the leveling of the natural differences of the mind, and methods can be learned in principle by everyone. Only discovery remains the preserve of the few. But the acquisition of the results of the discovery, and especially of the discovery of methods, is open to all. And there is a very simple proof: mathematical problems which formerly could not be solved by the greatest mathematical geniuses are now solved by high-school students. (1989, 236–37)

Social scientists, confirming Strauss, indeed seek heuristic devices to guide inquiry. Like the mathematician Polya's (1957) *How to Solve It,* they seek social scientific algorithms. Many social scientists thus view theory as a set of explanatory devices or model types (Lloyd, cited in Kitcher 1993, 18).[1] Members of all three research communities have advocated this view of theory.

Rationality. Robinson views economics as a "box of tools" (1933, 1). Schumpeter says that "it is the sum total of such gadgets . . . which constitutes economic theory" (1954, 15). This view is represented in mainstream economics by the supplementary books on problems in microeconomics (e.g., Miller, Benjamin, and North 1998) that usually accompany microeconomic textbooks. These texts address a set of historically concrete issues—taxi medallions in New York City, rent control during wartime, or the OPEC oil cartel. By putting the nuts and bolts, causal mechanisms, and ultimately the models of economics to work in different problem areas, these texts help students understand the relevance and scope of microeconomic theory. A related approach to economic theory is known as MIT-style theory, also called exemplary theory, exemplifying theory, modeling by example, applied modeling, or domain- or context-specific modeling (Akerlof 1984). The idea is to take a broad and important problem and reduce it to something narrow and tractable—a concrete institution, case, or data set. For instance, while one might really be interested in a general model of lemons, one captures the generalities with the specifics of the used-car market. One then generalizes back to the original and broader problem and thereby demonstrates how the specific substance illuminates the general principles. The model's basic stylized results are thus shown to conform to several empirical situations, to explain many events and institutions, and to yield many specific applications.

Culture. Swidler (1986) argues that a culture is a "tool kit" for its members. For students of the culture, its tool kit contains the nuts and bolts that can be used to create the subplots of larger narratives. Aminzade, moreover, indicates that "analytic narratives—theoretically structured stories about coherent sequences of motivated actions"— are basic to social science (1992, 458). And Weber's ideal types (sect. 9.2) are of course culturalist constructions.

Structure. Structuralists study how long-term processes and trajectories unfold and combine in different cases. For example, Moore (1966) works with a set of neo-Marxist nuts and bolts that produces causal propositions about development: specific modes of labor repression are behind the bourgeois, fascist, and communist coalitions that forge the historical paths of the commercialization of agriculture and the industrial development of a country. Structuralists often draw on his insight that each historical case can be examined as a potential combination of three modes, coalitions, or paths (e.g., the United States could have become authoritarian had its budding fascist coalition not been destroyed by the Civil War).

Many philosophers of science also advocate a nuts-and-bolts view of theory. While Kuhn (1970) sees paradigms as heuristic devices based on exemplars, Lakatos (1970) views research programs as cores that generate hypotheses in peripheries. Realist philosophy of science (Miller 1987) offers a problem-oriented approach to explaining phenomena that supplies a description of the relevant causal mechanisms. Realists thus maintain that

> when the search for hidden mechanisms is successful, the result is often to reveal a small number of basic mechanisms that underlie wide ranges [and diverse types] of phenomena. The explanation of diverse phenomena in terms of the same mechanism constitutes theoretical unification. For instance, the kinetic-molecular

> theory of gases unified thermodynamic phenomena with New-
> tonian particle mechanics. The discovery of the double-helical
> structure of DNA, for another example, produced a major
> unification of biology and chemistry. (Salmon et al. 1992, 34)

According to realists, science achieves theoretical leverage when it can
explain diverse outcomes as a function of the same basic causal
processes.

Just as the unity of physical science consists of discovering connections among the causal mechanisms that underlie electromagnetism,
gravity, and light, the unity of social science might consist of discovering the connections among the causal mechanisms that underlie voting, membership in political parties, contributions to interest groups,
and protest activities. The rationalist, culturalist, and structuralist
research programs offer the crucial causal components (the nuts and
bolts) that can be used to construct models with great explanatory
power. The rationalist collective action research program (Lichbach
1995), for example, offers a rich framework that has entered the general
social science lexicon: risk aversion, incomplete information, team
competition, bandwagons, Tit-for-Tat, entrepreneurs, patrons, federal
group structure, and selective incentives. Culturalists work with such
causal mechanisms as cognitive dissonance and social roles, and structuralists work with types of state autonomy, modes of production, and
systems of labor control. Social scientific research programs therefore
locate unobserved causal mechanisms that can explain observed correlations between events. Since they stand between an input/explanans
and an output/explanandum, these mechanisms tell a deep story that
unlocks black-box correlations between observables.

The world is more than a jumble of nuts and bolts and a grab bag of
causal mechanisms, however. Reality is patterned and ordered in many
overlapping ways; the parts stand in relation to one another in interrelated sets of systems. These patterns, moreover, have a historical
dimension in that they are often stable and fixed. Focusing only on the
bits and pieces produces disconnected snapshots of reality, with nothing belonging anywhere and with each part, in effect, in solitary
confinement. A science of *only* nuts and bolts and causal mechanisms
is therefore no science at all.[2] Scientists who work only with nuts and
bolts are therefore like my son playing with his clock: he is bright
enough to rip the clock apart and reveal all the cogs and wheels that
make it tick, but he cannot put it back together and make it work.[3]

It is therefore important to recognize that the structuring and order-
ing power of well-articulated scientific programs gives nuts and bolts

significance and coherence: programs show how causal mechanisms associate and combine with one another to form characteristic bridges and links that permit larger causal explanations and narrative understandings.[4] Thus, rationalist nuts and bolts in Bates 1989 are connected by hidden hands that produce unintended consequences; culturalist nuts and bolts in Scott 1985 hold together because of the meaning and significance of a society's collective values and beliefs; and structuralist causal mechanisms in Skocpol 1979 are tied together because of deep structures of political power and social causation.[5]

In sum, rationalist hegemons have been misled by a positivist philosophy of science that seeks theory that begins as abstract, axiomatic, and foundational; becomes subsuming, integrating, and unifying; and ends as organized, comprehensive, and encyclopedic. Modest rational choice theorists, as well as modest culturalists and structuralists, recognize that all scientific explanation involves research programs that contain sets of nuts and bolts or causal mechanisms that can be combined into models of a theory that help explain and understand phenomena.

10.2. Evidence

While rational choice theorists are committed to a general research paradigm, their commitments need not compel a search for universal theory. Paradigms can also yield middle-range theories: as a law is elaborated, its scope and boundaries are delimited. Rather than confirming or falsifying a general theory, evidence therefore establishes the theory's applicability to particular cases and domains of inquiry.

10.2.1. Traditional Philosophy of Science

This understanding of evidence is in some sense consistent with the traditional positivist philosophy of science that rationalist hegemons find so appealing. While laws in Hempel's deductive-nomological framework are general and universal, their operation is restricted to specific domains by initial assumptions, boundary conditions, and ceteris paribus contexts. Hempel elaborates the idea that auxiliary hypotheses link general hypotheses to particular situations by suggesting that theories contain two types of principles.[6]

> Internal principles characterize the basic entities and processes involved by the theory and the laws to which they are assumed to conform. Bridge principles indicate how the processes envisaged by the theory are related to empirical phenomena with which we are already acquainted, and which the theory may then explain,

predict, or retrodict. . . . Without bridge principles . . . a theory would have no explanatory power. Without bridge principles, we might add, it would also be incapable of test. For the internal principles of a theory are concerned with peculiar entities and processes assumed by the theory (such as the jumps of electrons from one atomic energy level to another in Bohr's theory), and they will therefore be expressed largely in terms of characteristic "theoretical concepts," which refer to these entities and processes. But the implications that permit a test of those theoretical principles will have to be expressed in terms of things and occurrences with which we are antecedently acquainted, which we already know how to observe, to measure, and to describe. In other words, while the internal principles of a theory are couched in its characteristic theoretical terms (nucleus, orbital electron, energy level, electron jump), the test implications must be formulated in terms (such as hydrogen vapor, emission spectrum, wavelength associated with a spectral line) which are antecedently understood, as we might say, terms that have been introduced prior to the theory and can be used independently of it. Let us refer to them as antecedently available or pretheoretical terms. The derivation of such test implications from the internal principles of the theory evidently requires further premises that establish connections between two sets of concepts; and this, as the preceding examples show, is accomplished by appropriate bridge principles (connecting, for example the energy released in an electron jump with the wavelength of the light that is emitted as a result). Without bridge principles, the internal principles of a theory would yield no test implications, and the requirement of testability would be violated. (1966, 72)

All theories, in other words, employ auxiliary assumptions to generate observable implications.

The consequence, Hempel writes, is that "a scientific hypothesis normally yields test implications only when combined with suitable auxiliary assumptions" (1966, 31). Using H (Hypothesis), A (Auxiliary Assumptions), and I (Implications), we may write:

If both H and A are true, then so is I.

But (as the evidence shows) I is not true.

H and A are not both true.

Falsification thus provides limited information: "If the test shows I to be false, we can infer only that either the hypothesis or one of the auxiliary assumptions included in A must be false; hence, the test provides no conclusive grounds for rejecting H."

10.2.2. Two Types of Science

The traditional positivist or received philosophy of science therefore yields a disturbing implication known as the Duhem-Quine thesis: "Hypotheses never confront experience singly but only as parts of larger packages, involving other hypotheses, initial and boundary conditions, and the like. . . . According to Quine, what gets refuted is the entire complex of assumptions used in generating a mistaken prediction. Quine and other relativists are adamant that we cannot draw any inference from the failure of the complex as a whole about the falsity of any one of its constituents" (Laudan 1990, 42).

Rational choice hegemons typically adopt an approach to the Duhem-Quine problem that holds that the assumptions behind a theory are universal and hence self-evident, a priori truths (sect. 3.1). If assumptions are unfalsifiable in principle, one cannot "test" their implications but only discover whether they are satisfied. Rational choice theorist Bueno de Mesquita thus comments on the role of empiricism in theory evaluation as follows.

Yet theories must be logically true or logically false. Theories are no more than a priori reasoning about the relations among variables. The truthfulness of such modeling depends on whether it shows logical flaws in arriving at its deductions. If a deduction follows logically from a set of assumptions, then that deduction is necessarily true for all circumstances that comply precisely with the assumptions of the theory. Hence the truthfulness of a deduced relationship among variables in a world that complies with the theory's assumptions is a logical, and not an empirical, question. Consequently, empirical relations have little relevance for the truthfulness or falseness of a theory per se.

To be sure, situations of an empirical case that are inconsistent with one's logically derived expectations are reason for reflection. Such a case may be inconsistent for one of two reasons. Either a logical flaw exists, or else the case does not conform precisely with the theory's assumptions. If the logic is flawed, the theory is false and can be rendered true only by eliminating the logical flaw. . . . If the cause of the inconsistency is an assumption that excludes the particular empirical case from the purview of a theory, then one must determine whether a theory that excludes such a case is useful. That is, are the assumptions so far-fetched that the events the theory addresses seldom occur in the real world? Evaluating a theory's usefulness is a difficult task. (1981, 9)

Musgrave concurs: "We do not falsify a theory containing a domain assumption by showing that this assumption is not true of some situations. . . . [W]e merely show that the assumption is not applicable to that situation in the first place" (cited in Cartwright 1994, 283). The existence of wind resistance thus does not falsify the theory of gravity but rather shows that the theory works only in a vacuum. If tests merely show that assumptions do not apply, failed attempts to fit theory to data are probably not worth reporting and published refutations will be few and far between.

An alternative approach to the Duhem-Quine problem is to hold that scientists investigate the empirical validity of a theory's assumptions, expressed in a particular model of the theory, in order to reduce the distance between universally applicable laws and thorny multiple realities. Diermeier thus argues that science tries to avoid precise laws and inaccurate predictions, or implausible theories with scant predictive power.

> The key idea is the distinction between fundamental and specific laws. Fundamental laws apply to all intended applications, specific laws only to subsets. . . . Newtonian mechanics perfectly exemplifies this distinction: its fundamental law is Newton's Second Law, linking force, mass, and acceleration. Special laws include the law of gravitation, whose intended application, or domain, is the set of large bodies, such as planets; and Hooke's Law, which applies to phenomena such as springs. Specific laws link the fundamental law to measurable phenomena. The fundamental law systematizes a variety of previously unrelated and more specific laws. (1996, 67)

By this account, the goal of social science is to use theory as a toolbox for probing evidence and to develop models of a theory that can engineer useful applications.

Others, such as Mill,[7] Hacking,[8] and Cartwright,[9] have recognized these two approaches to science. The first—adopted by rationalist hegemons—treats universal theory as primary and auxiliary assumptions as secondary. Auxiliary assumptions, that is, are merely nuisance factors that confound theory: laws apply only ceteris paribus, or in the absence of disturbances to the generating assumptions. The second—adopted by modest rationalists—treats auxiliary assumptions as primary and universal theory as secondary. Contextual factors, that is, are essential to modeling research domains: laws apply locally and not globally. As usual, priorities make all the difference. Since I want to turn rationalists away from their drive to hegemony and toward a search for more modest rational choice theory, I will now elaborate the virtues of the latter postpositivist position.

10.2.3. Structures, Mechanisms, and Events

I begin with a realist ontology (sect. 6.2). Bhaskar argues that "the world consists of things, not events. Most things are complex objects, in virtue of which they possess an ensemble of tendencies, liabilities and powers. It is by reference to the exercise of their tendencies, liabilities and powers that the phenomena of the world are explained" (1997, 51). Realists understand the structure of things by classifying them into characteristic "natural" types. Bhaskar writes that "the justification of our systems of taxonomy, of the ways we classify things, of the nominal essences of things in science thus lies in our belief in their fruitfulness in leading us to explanations in terms of the generative mechanisms contained in their real essences" (1997, 210). For example, democratic states contain voting systems and patrimonial states contain patron-client ties that constitute these states' structures.

The nuts and bolts of things, the "generative mechanisms of nature" (Bhaskar 1997, 14), combine to produce the actual flux of phenomena (outcomes or events) in the world. Hence, "this is the arduous task of science: the production of the knowledge of those enduring and continually active mechanisms of nature that produce the phenomena of our world." Bhaskar indicates that "there is a distinction between the *real* structures and mechanisms of the world and the *actual* patterns of events that they generate." Hence, "the world consists of mechanisms not events. Such mechanisms combine to generate the flux of phenomena that constitute the actual states and happenings of the world." Since outcomes are conjunctures of a multiplicity of radically different kinds of mechanisms, "science consists in a continuing dialectic between taxonomic and explanatory knowledge; between knowledge of what kinds of things there are and knowledge of how the things there are behave" (46, emphasis in original). While pure or abstract theory locates structures and mechanisms, empirical work studies the outcomes they generate.

The basic problem of empirical work, according to realists, is that events in the world are only weakly related to the nuts and bolts or causal mechanisms of generative structures.[10] Electoral rules only weakly structure electoral behavior in democracies, and patron-client ties only weakly structure clientelistic behavior in patrimonial states. Lots of factors confound the linkages between electoral rules and elections, and patron-client ties and clientelism. Lawson thus writes:

> Universal constant conjunctions of events are rare even in natural science and more so in the social realm. But if this is so how can economic mechanisms be identified? This is the question that is bound to be asked. The point that warrants emphasis is that just because universal constant conjunctions of the form "whenever event *x* then event *y*" are unlikely to be pervasive it does not follow that the only alternative is an inchoate random flux. These two possibilities—strict event regularities or a completely non-systematic flux exist—merely constitute the polar extremes of a potential continuum. Although the social world is open, certain mechanisms can come to dominate others over restricted regions of time-space, giving rise to rough-and-ready generalities or partial regularities, holding to such a degree that *prima facie* an explanation is called for. Thus, just as autumn leaves do still fall to the ground *much* of the time, so women are *concentrated* in secondary sectors of labor markets, and productive growth in the UK over the last century has *frequently* been slower than that of other comparable industrial countries. Such "stylized facts" can serve both to *initiate* investigation and also in the assessment of the relative *explanatory* powers—the relative abilities to illuminate a range of empirical findings—of competing hypotheses that may, in due course, be constructed. (1994, 276–77, emphasis in original)

Empirical work thus demonstrates how the universal causal mechanisms that inhere in structures come to dominate outcomes in specific space-time domains.[11]

Realists would add that that these applications must be to *natural kinds:* "What one finds . . . is the development of families of models together with exemplary applications to the behavior of particular kinds of systems" (Giere 1988, 105). And here is the key to physics: domains of application are to *natural kinds of systems*—the moon, the planets, artificial satellites.

Hacking believes that the results of social science are fragile compared with those in the physical sciences because the latter have not located stable structures, called *social kinds,* that can generate causal laws.

We can diagnose doubts some of us share about the social sciences. Those fields are still in a world of dogmatics and empirics. There is no end of "experimentation" but it as yet elicits almost no stable phenomena. There is plenty of speculation. There is even plenty of mathematical psychology or mathematical economics, pure sciences which have nothing much to do with either speculation or experimentation. Far be it from me to offer any evaluation of this state of affairs. Maybe all these people are creating a new kind of human activity. But many of us experience a sort of nostalgia, a feeling of sadness, when we survey social science. Perhaps this is because it lacks what is so great about fairly recent physical science. Social scientists don't lack experiment; they don't lack calculation; they don't lack speculation; they lack the collaboration of the three. *Nor, I suspect, will they collaborate until they have real theoretical entities about which to speculate— not just postulated "constructs" and "concepts," but entities we can use, entities which are part of the deliberate creation of stable new phenomena.* (1983, 248–49, emphasis added)

Cartwright agrees, arguing that a realist understanding of social kinds often escapes social science.

The results derived may be rendered as regularities claims, but the relationship between the structures described by the model and the regularities it gives rise to is not again itself one of regular association. So our whole package of sophisticated techniques— mostly statistical—for testing regularities claims are of no help in the decisions about choice among models. How do we decide? As far as I can see we have no articulated methodology, neither among philosophers nor among economists (though we may well have a variety of unarticulated methods). (1999a, 149)

Cartwright wonders further whether "free-standing probabilities," those calculated on an arbitrary sample of cases, can be the basis of robust causal laws (1989; 1999a, chap. 7). Since this sort of exercise constitutes a good deal of social science, the question is whether it has any value and whether social science has any alternatives, that is, whether social kinds, as structuralists believe, exist.

Empirical analysis could discover, for example, the types of democracies and the types of patrimonial states in which, respectively, certain electoral rules influence certain electoral outcomes and certain patron-client ties influence certain clientelistic outcomes. One could investigate, that is, laws of the following form: given democracies of type D, electoral rules R influence electoral results E; and given patrimonial states of type S, patron-client ties P influence clientelism C.

10.2.4. Theories, Models, and Problem Situations

Science therefore involves a three-step process. First, scientists speculate about a new application of a theory.[12] A key theme of this book is of course that the context of discovery is a more or less well defined research program or paradigm.[13] Since rationalists approach problem situations from a particular point of view, they should always have been wary of positivism.

Second, in order to assess how the initial conditions, boundary assumptions, and ceteris paribus understandings of the theory hold in the new case or domain, scientists investigate and calculate, matching theoretical speculations with experimental results. Since scientists typically need to do some empirical fudging to make the theory fit, they reach into their toolbox and pull out models of the theory—sets of nuts and bolts, cogs and wheels, and building blocks—that can deal with the new problem situation. *Scientific progress occurs when scientists can adjust off-the-shelf models of a theory to fit the new situation and social science is challenging because new situations arise all the time.* Since extraneous forces are usually involved (e.g., while the theories assume frictionless planes and perfectly elastic collisions, adjustments take account of the deviations), scientists employ a small number of well-known fudge factors in novel ways to engineer the application. Cartwright thus writes that "it is no theory which needs a new Hamiltonian for each new physical circumstance. The explanatory power of quantum theory comes from its ability to deploy a small number of well-understood Hamiltonians to cover a wide range of cases" (1983, 139). Hacking writes that "this is a standard move in physics. In order to make the equations fit the phenomena, you pull from the shelf some fairly standard extra terms for the equations, without knowing why one rather than another will do the trick" (1983, 211). Social scientists work similarly. As Morgan writes, econometricians "do not aim to refute, they aim to make the thing work. Thus the testing here is not really a notion of accept or reject; it is a testing of how good is the quality control of the model we've got" (cited in Simkin 1993, 171).

In short, scientists work within general frameworks called *research programs* and then interpret them with specific problem formulations called *models*. Research programs, in Cartwright's (1999a, 4) terms, are "nomological machines" that allow scientists to combine the nuts and bolts or models of a theory to investigate empirical regularities or laws in particular problem situations. As idealized and abstract theories are developed, they are thus elaborated and interpreted through practical models designed to engage local contingency. Models thus translate or bridge theory and data; theory is used to model a domain; and the models of a theory approximate particular local realities. Theories are indeed important only when scientists can construct models that connect them to families of situations in the real world. Otherwise they are merely abstractions bearing no relation to reality. A theory, to repeat, is a set of models (nuts and bolts that could be construed as causal mechanisms) plus the knowledge of how to apply the models to particular cases and domains.

A nuts-and-bolts view of science, in which "models occupy center stage" and theories are "a family of structures" (van Fraassen 1980, 64), is consistent with the textbooks of the various sciences in which scientists present themselves as modelers rather than as theorists or empiricists. To use Kuhnian language: normal science extends the exemplars of a paradigm to solve new problems and puzzles. Scientists are trained to use the paradigm's models to go out and solve problems. Giere (1988) suggests that they learn how to select from the causal repertoire of a theory to explain phenomena.[14]

We can now better understand the aforementioned distinction between two types of science: scientists do not deduce testable propositions about the world and see if they fit; since they approximate the real world with models, theory and observation mutually adapt. To use a formula: *Theories model problem situations.*

Third, after scientists study several problem situations to see if they work as the theory predicts, they end up with a list of various types of cases: in case x, the theory is true using one model; in case y, the theory is true using another model; and in case z, no model of the theory fits well. General speculations eventually emerge about the types of cases under which the theory holds. Scientists then make new experiments to evaluate novel applications of the theory, and we are back to step one.

As scientists engineer models of a theory to fit the world, they are establishing the domain or boundaries of the theory. Herein lies the justification for the search for the modest rational choice theory advocated earlier in section 4.5. Rational choice theories are toolboxes that allow theorists to standardize and generalize their local achievements in modeling a theory—say collective action theory—to different local contexts, especially new and important situations that have created interesting possibilities for investigation. Modest rational choice theorists thus move from local knowledge to local knowledge, transforming that knowledge in the application, with the goal of encompassing a variety of phenomena in different problem areas.

10.3. Theory and Evidence

The philosophy of science just articulated clarifies some mistaken ideas that rationalist hegemons have about theory. I first discuss their confusion about generalization and then elucidate the nature of laws and theories.

The general and the particular. Since mechanisms work in particular environments and come to dominate specific domains, a theory does not hold under all conditions, circumstances, or contexts. A theory holds only when a model of the theory applies to a particular case or to a class, set, or type of case. Showing, therefore, that the model is true in one domain does not mean that it is true in other domains, and it is the task of science to delineate the range of situations to which the model applies. Testing, appraisal, or evaluation thus involves domain clarification: where, when, how, and why a particular set of evidence fits the models of a theory. As empirical work establishes a theory's boundaries, the domain or applicability of the theory shrinks or expands. Moreover, the effectiveness and accuracy of a theory can even vary over its useful range—from classes of cases to classes of cases, from case to case within a class, and even within a case.

In sum, theories do not a priori determine their domain—the situations to which they apply; science does not search for general laws—universal (ahistorical and acontextual) generalizations—that inhere in a theory; scientists do not move deductively from one general thing to many particular things, nor inductively from local knowledge to universal statements. Science instead proliferates local models, working out what happens from situation to situation. Since there are only relative generalizations, partial universalism, structured variations of theories, characteristic logics of substantive situations, and middle-range theories, rational choice theory must be modest.

Laws. The movement from Hempel 1966 to Lakatos 1970 is a move away from theory as understood by rationalist hegemons—deductive-nomological laws—and toward theory as understood by modest rational choice theorists—a toolbox of nuts and bolts (causal mechanisms) that scientists combine into models that generate lawful regularities in particular domains. Rouse thus suggests that theories are research strategies for explaining phenomena: "The question is not how we infer one statement from others, but how we generate research opportunities and resolve them, drawing upon and reinterpreting prior concrete achievements" (1987, 22–23). This perspective places models and not laws at the center of inquiry.

Science in fact does not have laws in the form of the universal generalizations that characterize Hempel's deductive-nomological theory. As Giere writes: "An examination of even the simplest textbook example shows, however, that if considered as general empirical statements, the laws of motion must be judged either as false or at best irrelevant to the science of mechanics." He continues: "This is not to argue that generalizations play no role in mechanics. I claim only that *universal* generalizations play no role. What one does find is catalogues of cases in which various force functions yield models that fit tolerably well. Putting all these catalogues together yields a truly impressive range of cases. This finite, and not well defined, range of cases constitutes the empirical content of classical mechanics" (1988, 76, 103). If even the laws of motion of physics are best understood as families of models rather than as universal laws,[15] the search for universal generalizations in science is indeed fruitless. "Laws, where they do apply, hold only *ceteris paribus,*" and "even our best theories are severely limited in their scope. For, to all appearances, not many of the situations that occur naturally in our world fall under the concepts of these theories" (Cartwright 1999a, 4, 9).

Laws thus require "shielding" to be observed. As Cartwright indicates, it "is not enough to insist that the machine have the right parts in the right arrangement; in addition there had better be nothing else happening that inhibits the machine from operating as prescribed" (1999a, 57). In nonexperimental situations, scientists need to locate "cases where nature fortuitously resembles one of our special models without the enormous design and labour we must normally devote to making it do so" (3). Rationalist hegemons also need to understand that laws in economics, just as in physics, are exact in formulation but narrow in application: "The kind of precise conclusions that are so highly valued in contemporary economics can be rigorously derived only when very special assumptions are made [specific structure is added to general theory]. But the very special assumptions do not fit very much of the economy around us" (149).

In sum, there are no universal laws that are true and nonvacuous: if precise enough to be informative, they have significant qualifications that yield useful applications; if general enough to be true, they are vacuous. Laws, at best, are rough generalizations covering particular environments: holding in particular times and places, they are local and not global. And they are rooted in robust mechanisms that scientists try to fit to different bodies of evidence. Cartwright stresses the modesty of this approach: "Fundamentalists . . . want laws; they want true laws; but most of all, they want their favourite laws to be in force everywhere. I urge us to resist fundamentalism. Reality may well be just a patchwork of laws [holding in classes of circumstances]." She thus urges "local realism about a variety of different kinds of knowledge in a variety of different domains across a range of highly differentiated situations" (1999a, 34, 23).

Social science should be seen in this light. As scholars from the various research traditions use their nuts and bolts, they propose laws. There are many examples of such propositions in the social sciences,[16] some of which come from the rationalist paradigm.

1. Holding income constant, as the price of A increases relative to the price of B, less A and more B is consumed.
2. In a two-party system, party positions converge to the median voter, regardless of the electorate's preference distribution; in a multiparty system, party positions diverge as parties' products differentiate them from each other.
3. In democracies with winner-take-all electoral systems, two parties emerge; in proportional representation systems, more than two parties emerge.
4. If a social movement seeks a public good, less than 5 percent of the people who identify with the group make costly contributions to the group.

Other general propositions come from the culturalist tradition.

5. Anomie produces political protest and revolution.
6. A Protestant ethic accounts for the rise of capitalism in the West.
7. The growth of postmaterial value orientations disrupts traditional left-right party systems.

Still others come from the structural approach.

8. For OECD countries, corporatism, small size, and leftist party control are associated with lower unemployment.

9. After a state breaks down during a social revolution, peasants rebel on their own only if their communities display solidarity and are autonomous from landlord control.
10. No bourgeoisie, no democracy.

There are also many propositions that are widely thought to have been falsified by contemporary social science and hence are no longer in their toolboxes. Some are consistent with rationalist thinking.

1. The higher the level of political repression, the greater the number of people actively engaged in political dissent.
2. Democracies have less political dissent that do nondemocracies.

Some are consistent with culturalist thought.

3. Those who engage in protest feel relatively deprived.
4. Stable democracy requires cross-cutting cleavages.
5. Fascism flourishes only in mass society.

And some are consistent with structuralist ideas.

6. Economically advanced states in the core of the world economy are the strongest states.

While social science therefore has laws that are moribund, it also has laws that succeed in many ways: they are relatively simple (e.g., they avoid nonlinear relationships among variables, probabilistic outcomes, and nonparity in the size of cause and effect); they are theoretically and substantively important; they are of wide but not unbounded scope (i.e., they apply to a definite but large number of cases); they are supported by underlying causal mechanisms; and they can be evaluated empirically because they imply clear counterfactuals, relevant plausible rival hypotheses, and test implications that yield relatively clear and falsifiable predictions. But social science does not have universal laws any more than physics has such laws. The successful generalizations listed previously are best understood as lawful regularities that have emerged from applying models of theories to classes of situations. For example, supply-demand analysis does not provide abstract universal laws such as envisioned in deductive exercises (e.g., the comparative statics of demand curves), but rather offers various models of a particular economic theory (e.g., oligopoly) that can be applied more or less fruitfully to a variety of situations.[17]

Theories. The syntactic or received view of theories accepted by rationalist hegemons claims that the syntax of theory is pure and abstract: theory, in other words, is a body of theorems derived from a set of assumptions and stated in the formal language of logic. The semantics of theory (i.e., its meaning or interpretation) is given by an additional set of definitions called *correspondence rules* that make the theory's axioms true. As we have thus seen, Hempel (1966) argues that theory involves internal principles, bridge principles, and their deductive consequences. The bridge principles allow us to interpret the concepts of the theory, which, of course, are only partially defined by the internal axioms. Logical empiricism therefore encompassed the logical structure of theories and the empiricist idea of meaningful language. Following Hilbert's formalized geometry, Peano's axiomized arithmetic, and Russell and Whitehead's attempt to reduce mathematics to logic, some positivists hoped that all scientific theories could be reconstructed as axiomatic systems in which a syntactical structure was interpreted via a semantics. In short, the theory/model distinction in science was taken to be the syntax/semantics distinction in linguistics.

The problem with the syntactic view of theory is that there is no one-to-one relation between formal theory and its correspondence rules: meanings are not fully captured by a narrowly defined set of bridge principles. Many different procedures can attribute meaning to theory, and models of theories come in many different types. Kuhn 1970 and Lakatos 1970, for example, stress paradigms and research programs. A system based only on axioms is therefore too limited a basis to express theories. The search for the axiomatic foundations of theory is consequently not an important part of science. The reconstruction of Newton's laws of motion or Marshall's supply-and-demand curves on a Hempelian axiomatic basis is not central to science.

The syntactic view of theories was therefore replaced by the semantic view (Suppe 1977; van Fraassen 1980). Instead of seeing theory as composed of axioms and interpretations, theory was seen as the models that provide the interpretations of the formalisms. It is the models, in other words, that make the theory's axioms true and relevant. Since theory provides the fundamental building blocks from which to construct the acceptable models, the language in which the theory is expressed (i.e., formal and axiomatic) is not as relevant as the models that interpret the formalisms. As Suárez puts it, theory equals model: "Theories *are* models: they are really nothing but collections of models" (1999, 171). Each model in the set embodies an interpretation of the formal system that makes the assumptions true. In the semantic conception of theory, there are consequently many models of a theory that can be expressed in many different languages (van Fraassen 1980, 44).

The problem with the semantic view of theories, however, is that the set of models cannot be precisely delimited. Diermeier thus writes:

> Theories should be interpreted as ordered pairs consisting of a *core,* C, which expresses the mathematical content of a theory, and a set of *intended applications,* I. The empirical claim of a theory then consists in the statement that C can successfully be applied to I. Theories can be modified by changing either the mathematical core or the intended applications. Progress will consist in either strengthening C or extending I. Regress consists of relaxing C or restricting I. All these variants are common procedures in empirical sciences. (1996, 66)

Cartwright characterizes this semantic view of theories as follows: "To apply the theory to a given case we have to look through the models to find one where the initial conditions of the model match the initial conditions of the case" (1999b, 246). But as the models of a theory are never well defined, they have no necessary or sufficient conditions for their specification: one cannot specify a priori the intended domain as part of a formal theory. Since the models are at best held together by a family resemblance or elective affinities, Cartwright criticizes both the syntactic and the semantic view of theories.

> Both are cases of the "vending machine" view. The theory is the vending machine: you feed it input in certain prescribed forms for the desired output; it gurgitates for a while; then it drops out the sought-for representation, plonk, on the tray, fully formed, as Athena from the brain of Zeus. This image of the relation of theory to the models we used to represent the world is hard to fit with what we know of how science works. Producing a model of new phenomena such as superconductivity is an incredibly difficult and creative activity. It is how Nobel prizes are won. (247)

She argues further that the "vending machine" view of theories is excessively Platonic in that it displays

> fascination with theory *per se,* with the details of formulation and exact structure of a heavily reconstructed abstract, primarily mathematical, object: theory. . . . [T]hese philosophers are not interested in what the world is like. Rather they are interested in a world that is not our world, a world of appearances, but rather

a purer, more orderly world, a world which is thought to be represented "directly" by the theory's fundamental equations. (255)

Many philosophers of science (Hacking 1983; Cartwright 1983; Giere 1988) thus prefer the "models as mediators" view of theory articulated earlier. More humble than a syntactic or semantic view of theories, this view befits a modest rather than a hegemonic rational choice theory.

To futher appreciate this view, we must understand how the philosophy of science that I have articulated also clarifies some mistaken ideas that rationalist hegemons have about evidence. I first discuss the confusion about induction and deduction and then clarify the nature of testing and falsification.

Induction and deduction. Methodological disputes among scientists often revolve around whether one should model economic theories (i.e., deduction) or data-generating processes (i.e., induction) (*Economic Record* 1988, *Journal of Econometrics* 1988, *Econometric Theory* 1990, and *Scandinavian Journal of Economics* 1991). Comparativists are similarly divided (e.g., see the debate over analytical narratives between Elster 2000 and Bates et al. 2000). There are, broadly speaking, three approaches to this dispute.

First consider deduction, or models of theory. Hempel (1966) thought that once scientists supplied the initial conditions of a case, they could explain the case deductively. Samuelson's (1947) comparative statics, in the spirit of Walrus and Jevons, also assumed scientists could deduce cases from theories: one can specify the assumptions of a mathematical model, derive its equilibrium conditions, and perturb that equilibrium with some exogenous variable. The comparative statics of the equilibrium constitute a falsifiable deduction, specified in terms of an estimating equation, that explains a set of cases. In other words, after one establishes basic premises, uses rigorous proofs, produces a conclusive test, and summarizes the model as a fully specified whole, one tweaks assumptions and deductively interrogates the theory.

Now consider induction, or models of data. Hesse writes that "the subject matter of science is not raw observation but *models of data.* In the case of mathematical science, these come as sets of measurable quantities representing observable properties derived from idealizations of the real world, and not from raw experience" (2000, 302, emphasis in original). Hendry (1993) thus looks for the data-generating process that can be derived from a data set. Several theories of statistical inference are available (Barnett 1999), as is a plethora of stochastic models, for this type of exploratory data analysis. The idea is that the theory and the data-generating process are separate, with the former providing little information on the latter: one should therefore let the data "speak" in a relatively unconstrained way. Friedman and Schwartz characterize the approach as follows: "Start with a collection of numerical data bearing on the question under study, subject them to sophisticated econometric techniques, place great reliance on tests of significance, and end with a single hypothesis (equation), however complex, supposedly 'encompassing' . . . all subhypotheses" (1991, 39). In other words, one ends with a variable or set of variables to be explained in regression-like fashion in one final model.

Neither procedure captures scientific modeling. Deductivists argue:

theory → models of theory → models of data → data

However, the search for a seamless web from the logical assumptions of a formal model, to its equilibrium conditions, to its comparative statics, and finally to an estimating equation, is chimerical (Morton 1999). As Morrison and Morgan put it: "Theory does not provide us with an algorithm from which the model is constructed and by which all modeling decisions are determined" (1999b, 16–17). Models are not strictly deduced from theories, nor are empirical tests strictly deduced from models. The idealist search for a pure theory, a set of Platonic truths with which to explore the world, is too fanciful.

Inductivists argue:

data → models of data → models of theory → theory

The purely inductive search for data-generating processes or models of data is similarly flawed. The pragmatic attempt at curve fitting considers data everything. It assumes, in effect, that there is no "truth" in general and that every situation (i.e., data set) is sui generis.

A linear and closely knit theory-model-reality relationship therefore does not hold in either direction. Is there a middle way between deduction and induction? This third approach, used, for example, by Friedman and Schwartz (1991) and in the realist spirit of Marshall and Keynes, is eclectic: it recognizes that while theory without evidence is empty, evidence without theory is blind. Scientists are thus modelers who focus on an important nut and bolt, such as the quantity theory of money, and examine its robustness in a variety of contexts in a variety of different ways. Friedman and Schwartz summarize the procedure as follows: "Examine a wide variety of evidence, quantitative and non-quantitative, bearing on the question under study; test results from one body of evidence on other bodies, using econometric techniques as one tool in this process, and build up a collection of simple hypotheses that may or may not be readily viewed as components of a broader all-embracing hypothesis; and, finally, test hypotheses on bodies of data other than those from which they were derived" (1991, 39). The scientist as modeler thus bets on a limited number of simple yet robust models that derive from one or more central theoretical principles. He or she then speculates about applications to various domains, investigating the general mechanism in a plethora of special cases by trying to make the models fit. One is ultimately persuaded by the weight of many pieces of evidence. In contrast to deduction, which might be called idealist, and to induction, which might be called materialist, this approach might be called realist: it explores the interaction of theory and data in which revision and updating is an iterative procedure.

In this mixed inductive/deductive approach, models do not stand on their own. They require a complex interpretive calculus based on in-depth study of particular cases or domains, deep familiarity with data (the nature of sources and measurement), detailed testing, and the use of natural experiments thrown up by history. The result is an overall understanding of the problem, often in narrative form. Friedman and Schwartz thus produce an "analytical narrative" (a term used in Katznelson 1997, 99 to refer to Moore's work) of U.S. monetary developments from 1867 to 1960 (1963, xxi) and a comparison of Britain and the United States (1982).

So we end here where we began back in chapter 1: good models are good stories. Hartmann indeed writes that "there is no good model without a story that goes with it." He considers storytelling essential to physics.

> A story is a narrative told *around* the formalism of the model. It is neither a deductive consequence of the model nor of the underlying theory. It is, however, *inspired* by the underlying theory (if there is one). This is because the story takes advantage of the vocabulary of the theory . . . and refers to some of its features. . . . Using more general terms, the story fits the model in a larger framework (a "world picture") in a non-deductive way. A story is, therefore, an integral part of a model: it complements the formalisms. To put it in a slogan: *a model is an (interpreted) formalism + a story.* (1999, 344, emphasis in original)

Similarly, Cartwright suggests that "fables transform the abstract into the concrete, and in so doing, I claim, they function like models in physics. . . . [T]he relationship between the moral and the fable is like that between a scientific law and a model. . . . [This] picture of the relationship between the moral as a purely abstract claim and the fable as its more concrete manifestation . . . mirror[s] what I think is going on in physics" (1999a, 36–38). Joined to the use of a major foil, models/stories have an oppositional and critical style that is quite compelling.

Extending Boumans (1999, 92), we can therefore contrast three views of models (see fig. 10.1). These diagrams make it clear why we should consider "models as mediators" (Morrison and Morgan 1999a). Models do not constitute theories—they are not strictly models of theories. Models do not descend from theory and hence are not reducible to it: they are not a lesser version of theory (e.g., a tentative hypothesis). Nor do models constitute data—they are not strictly models of data either. Models do not ascend from data and hence are not reducible to it, so they are not a more abstract version of data (e.g., a data-generating process). Models instead mediate between theories and the empirical world. Morrison and Morgan thus write that "it is because they are neither one thing nor the other, neither just theory nor data, but typically involve some of both (and often additional 'outside' elements), that they can mediate between theory and the world" (1999b, 10–11). With respect to models, the theoretical/phenomenological or discovery/justification distinction is never clear. Since models are hybrid, mixed, and open-ended, they act as "autonomous agents" in inquiry and are used for trial-and-error discovery and investigation (Morrison 1999, 44). Suárez thus suggests that "a mediating model mediates between high level theory and the world by conveying some *particular* or *local* knowledge specific to the effect or phenomenon that is being modeled" (1999, 170, emphasis in original).

Lots of things besides strict deduction and induction thus go into the construction of models. As Hartmann writes, "There is, however, more to models than formalism" (1999, 328). Since models are intermediate levels of inquiry standing between abstract theory and raw data, they combine many elements. Morrison and Morgan maintain, moreover, that the combination is fairly ad hoc: "There are no rules for model building. . . . [P]erhaps this is why modeling is considered in many circles an art or craft" (1999b, 31). A model is thus a mixture and not a compound: in building a model, one integrates a list of ingredients deemed important. Boumans thus writes that "model building is like baking a cake without a recipe. The ingredients are theoretical ideas, policy views, mathematisations . . . , metaphors and empirical facts" (1999, 67).

One-dimensional (models are deduced from theory or induced from data):

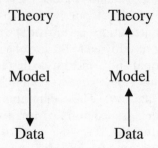

Two-dimensional (models capture theory-data interaction):

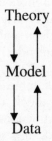

Multidimensional view (models are a recipe of many ingredients)

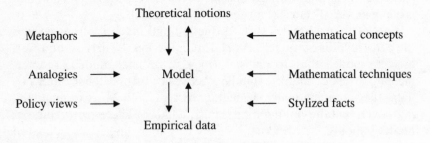

Fig. 10.1. Three views of models

The practical implication of the realist view of models is that scientists should not begin inquiry with a set of theoretically derived hypotheses that they plan to "test." One cannot deterministically and automatically deduce cases from theories. A priori hypothesis testing holds great dangers: a rigid preconceived model does not do justice to the nuances and complexities of cases and domains. Similarly, scientists should not proceed inductively, assuming that nothing, or almost nothing, is known in advance. Rather, they should take models of their theories from one concrete case to the next, or from one research domain to the next, engaging new empirical materials, extending and refining preconceived rules to cover new cases, and testing the new rules against new evidence, as each new case or domain challenges preconceived ideas. Modeling is thus open-ended and dialectical, redefining existing models and developing new ones through continuous concrete analyses. Goldstone thus claims that "it is an empirical inquiry to discover what happened and why" (1991, 52), and Hall indicates that "theories *can* only develop in the process of trying to explain reality" (1986, 1–2, emphasis in original).

Engineers thus stand between theorists and practitioners because they use the nuts and bolts from theories to construct workable characterizations of reality, and craftsmen stand between scientists and artists because they adjust preconceived plans as they work. Although they are not the strict deductivists or inductivists found in the austere formulations of positivism favored by rationalist hegemons, science loves engineers and craftsmen.

Testing. Suárez writes that "models provide theories with genuine empirical content, by 'filling in' the abstract descriptions afforded by theory, hence making it possible to apply theories to natural phenomena" (1999, 168). As Cartwright says with respect to physics, "Newton's principles for mechanics are to be thought of as rules for the construction of models to represent mechanical systems, from comets to pendulums" (1999b, 249). She notes, moreover, that scientists need to "*customize* the general model produced by the theory to the special needs of the case at hand" (248, emphasis in original). Hence, as Giere (1988) says, theories = models + hypotheses about the model's similarities to real systems. The problem, as Cartwright (1983) notes, is that there is more ad hocery in physics than nonphysicists think. The power of a model of a theory is usually not great: they do not stretch very far and must be adapted to fit a new domain.

So, contra Bueno de Mesquita's (1981) ideas cited previously (sect. 10.2.2), it is models of theories and not theories per se that are applicable or not: "You cannot show that the predictions of a theory for a given situation are false until you have managed to describe the situation in the language of the theory. When the models are too bad a fit, the theory is not disconfirmed; it is just inapplicable" (Cartwright 1999a, 26). The difference is subtle but crucial: whereas rationalist hegemons see testing as purely deductive exercises, Cartwright thinks that experimenters fudge models.

Falsification. Science does not reject theories as a whole; it falsifies the hypothesis that a particular model of a theory fits a particular set of data. Since another model of the theory can usually be constructed, theory development is open-ended. Representations of situations are thus typically modified: if a model of a theory does not fit the facts, it is revised. Falsification therefore means that a particular model of the theory is inapplicable rather than wrong, impractical rather than rejected, or useless rather than disconfirmed.

Since post hoc theoretical alteration is the basis of science, scientists are verificationists who search for confirming evidence: once basic principles are generally accepted, science consists of overcoming deviations and exceptions and thereby discovering applications to new situations. The corroboration of the models of a theory thus establishes the value of the theory.

10.4. Evaluation

Hirschman recounts the following: "In an old and well-known Jewish story, the rabbi of Krakow interrupted his prayers one day with a wail to announce that he had just seen the death of the rabbi of Warsaw two hundred miles away. The Krakow congregation, though saddened was of course much impressed with the visionary powers of their rabbi. A few days later some Jews from Krakow traveled to Warsaw and, to their surprise, saw the old rabbi there officiating in what seemed to be tolerable health. Upon their return they confided the news to the faithful and there was incipient snickering. Then a few undaunted disciples came to the defense of their rabbi; admitting that he may be been wrong on the specifics, they exclaimed 'Nevertheless, what vision!'" (1977, 117).

Are scientists different? Physical and biological scientists who cling to the heuristic power of their "vision" of the world often fit their theories to the world in order to "save" the phenomena in question. Curve-fitting—aligning theory and observation—is easy, and Davis and Hersh describe the classic scientific parallel to the disciples of the rabbi of Krakow:

In the Ptolemaic system, the earth is fixed in position while the sun moves, and all the planets revolve around it. Fixing our attention, say, on Mars one assumes that Mars circled about the earth in a certain eccentric circle and with a certain fixed period. Compare this theory now with the observations. It fits, but only partially. There are times when the orbit of Mars exhibits a retrograde movement which is unexplainable by a simple circular motion. To overcome this limitation, Ptolemy added to the basic motion a second eccentric circular motion with its own smaller radius and its own frequency. This science can now exhibit retrograde motion, and by careful adjustment of the radii and the eccentric and periods, he can fit the motion of Mars quite well. If we require more precision, then a third circle of smaller radii still and a yet different period may be added. (1981, 75)

The Duhem-Quine thesis explains why such things happen in science and hence why science can be no different than religion: when a theory is found wanting, it not clear what has gone wrong. Scientists thus use ad hoc explanations, post hoc adjustments, and tautologizing alterations to immunize their theory from falsification due to its inaccurate predictions. Analysts, eager to prove their pet theories correct, ignore the facts and instead turn to these fudge factors: arbitrary domain restrictions, empty prevarications, face-saving linguistic tricks, and exception barring. Scientists who claim to know the cases before they see them eventually interpret cases in terms of theory, conflate evidence and generalization, and equate the empirical and the analytical. Even when they consider plausible rival hypotheses, such scientists often engage those other theories on their own terms, carefully privileging their own theory by setting up their opponents as a straw figure.

Rapoport thus argues:

Mathematically, you can cook up anything. You can imagine any sort of situation and represent it by a mathematical model. The problem becomes that of finding something in the real world to fit the model . . .

There was a man who liked to fix things around the house, but the only tools he could use were a screwdriver and a file. When he saw a screw that wasn't tight, he tightened it with his screwdriver. Finally, there were no more screws to tighten. But he saw some protruding nails. So he took his file and made grooves in the caps of the nails. Then he took his screwdriver and screwed them in. To paraphrase Marshall McLuhan's famous remark, "the medium is the message," the mathematician could well say, "the tool is the theory." (In Weintraub 1985, 35)

Rule agrees: "For many thinkers, seeing one's theory 'fit' (any slice of reality that catches his/her fancy) is reason enough for acceptance of the theory, indeed for preferring it to others. But . . . we need a more rigorous standard. If one embraces a theory on the grounds that it 'fits' evidence that might as well support a version of other theories, the choice is more a statement of one's own inner world than about a shared exterior one" (1988, 86). By reinterpreting an appropriate set of stylized facts, a determined theorist can always locate supporting illustrations and rationalize belief in the face of contrary evidence. As Tolstoy caricatured the point: "He was one of those theoreticians who so love their theory that they lose sight of the theory's object—its practical application. His passion for theory made him despair all practical considerations and he would not hear of them. He positively rejoiced in failure, for failures resulting from the theory only proved to him the accuracy of his theory" (1968, 771).

If physical and biological scientists are eerily like the disciples of the rabbi of Krakow, social scientists may be worse. Consider rational choice theory. Some economic theories are comprehensive, unified, and elegant: Arrow-Debreu general equilibrium theory is the most prominent example. Other economic theories are frameworks or toolboxes that organize our thinking by housing many different models for analyzing various problems. Dixit offers oligopoly theory as an example.

> There are so many different issues that arise in the study of competition among a small number of firms that there is no hope of constructing a single analytical model of oligopoly on par with the standard elegant model of perfect competition. However, most people would agree that oligopoly remains a useful conceptual umbrella for sheltering the large variety of models that examine specific issues such as tacit collusion, strategic commitments, and preemption. (1996, 35)

Arrow—the general equilibrium theorist—identifies a problem with this perspective.

> I think there is a tendency in . . . this methodology to say, "here is a particular problem, I will make a set of assumptions, and here are the consequences; ah! yes in this case they worked out well." But I say, if these assumptions are true, they should be true for

the next problem. In other words, there is a tendency to look only at the consequences that one happens to be studying at that moment, and not asking whether these assumptions can imply something quite different, whether they can be used in another field. In other words, it is not enough to test the assumptions in one field, one has to test them in others as well—something that Popper, for instance, would insist on. (1987, 226)

A related foible in economic methodology is what Schumpeter (1954, 472) refers to as the Ricardian vice: strong exemplar cases and self-evident truths lead to a theory that assumes too much and produces tautologies, yet is applied to the world to make theoretical and policy inferences (Pheby 1988, 17). Green and Shapiro (1994, 1996) locate another similar problem: rational choicers use a style of theorizing that advocates arbitrary a priori and a posteriori domain restrictions, so when their theory does not fit a case, the case is not treated as a disconfirming instance. Rational choice theorists, in other words, treat ceteris paribus conditions as "open ended escape clauses" (Kincaid 1996, 63).

The twin dangers of self-serving confirmation and nonfalsifiability bedevil rational choice theorists for yet another reason: their models are often deliberately heuristic rather than realistic. They may have, that is, instrumental value in probing the world rather than intrinsic value in mirroring it. Suárez draws a valuable distinction between the two approaches to approximating the world.

There are, broadly speaking, two methods for approximating theory to the world. One is the approximation of the theory to the problem situation brought about by introducing corrections into the theoretical description—the theory is refined to bring it closer to the problem-situation. . . . [T]his is a form of approximation toward the real case: the corrections introduced into the theoretical descriptions are intended to account for the imperfections that occur in the problem situation.

The other is the approximation of the problem-situation to the theory by means of simplifications of the problem situation itself. . . . We idealize the description of the problem-situation, while leaving the theoretical construction unaffected. . . . [T]his process can come in either of two forms. It can come first in the form of conceptual redescriptions of the problem-situation, performed only in thought, and not in reality. In such "thought-experiments" complications are idealized away and the result is a simplified description of the problem-situation. Secondly, there is also the possibility of physical "shielding" of the experimental apparatus.

In the latter case the theory is left untouched, while the problem-situation is altered; in the former case the converse is true: the problem-situation is left untouched, while the theoretical description is corrected. (1999, 174)

Such approximations to a problem-situation may have great heuristic value but come at the cost of realism.

In other words, a rationalist model might not approximate the world at all. Indeed, it might be counterfactual to the average occurrence of reality (Reuten 1999, 198). Gibbard and Varian suggest that economic models often deliberately distort in order to emphasize some part of reality (1978, 667, 676). They thus speak of caricature models that present "even to the point of distorting—certain selected aspects of the economic situation. . . . Often the assumptions of a model are chosen not to approximate reality, but to exaggerate or isolate some feature of reality" (665, 673). Mayer comments that "the value of such a model is that it brings out an important feature of the economy that was previously not given enough attention, and that it is robust with respect to the exaggerated assumptions" (1993, 126). Modeling in economics is thus often heavily dependent on interpretive context, emphasizing significant features of the world and not describing it as a whole.

Other social scientific research communities also face the twin dangers of self-serving confirmation and nonfalsifiability. With respect to the culturalists, Durkheim often said "the facts are wrong" when confronted with evidence that contradicted his theories (Lukes 1985, 33, 52). With respect to the structuralists, the explanatory modesty of structuralists regarding the scope of their "historically concrete" arguments comes down to the assertion "that the theory should apply only where the evidence happens to fit, while instances of discordant evidence should simply be ignored" (Rule 1988, 71). While a theory with a limited domain is common in science, some maintain that one that "holds only for certain special cases is not very exciting *unless* we can specify in advance what those cases will be. Perhaps what Weber said of the materialist theory of history holds for theories in general: They are not conveyances to be taken and alighted from at will" (Rule 1988, 89, emphasis in original). Hence, the Marxist theory of revolution is often saved by lengthening the time span: the revolution is *always* coming.[18] Shades of Cartwright's fundamentalists!

Thus social science—whether practiced by rationalists, culturalists, or structuralists—often displays "built-in justification" (Boumans 1999) that produces the ex post validation of ad hoc modifications of failed theories. In other words, if a social scientist acts as if he or she can neither accept nor reject a theory, but rather acts as if the boundary, scope, or domain of the theory is defined in its application and elaboration, there is a danger of self-serving confirmations and non-falsifiability. Unless scientists have a way to evaluate the application and elaboration of a theory, a science consisting of models of a theory (nuts and bolts) that mesh with models of data to explain particular problem domains is no science at all.

To return to the metaphor with which we began this book: Why is one story preferable to another? How do we know when we have improved an existing story? What does a set of stories generated from one or more approaches tell us about the approaches?[19] Unless social scientists can separate real knowledge from mere opinion, every social scientist can claim that his or her story is guided by data and evidence and that his or her opponents' stories, too invested in misguided theories or ideas, are driven by dogmatic beliefs. Social science therefore needs criteria of theory appraisal that stand somewhere between positivism and relativism.

To clarify the problem of induction: empirical inquiry faces two fundamental and interrelated logical difficulties. First, facts, data, or observations are overdetermined by theories, hypotheses, or propositions, and the supply of plausible rival hypotheses that can fit the same body of evidence is in principle infinite—social scientists, after all, can readily invent different theories to explain the same piece of reality (e.g., lots of causes of capitalism in the West or of economic success—and now failure!—in Japan). Hence, there are always several alternative and incompatible ways to account for the facts: one can explain 100 percent of the variance in more than one way, divide the sample space with more than one approach, and locate multiple paths to the same outcome.

Second, theories are underdetermined by empirical evidence. On the one hand, we cannot conclusively verify theories or prove them true. The fallacy of affirming the consequence means that there will always be the possibility of committing a Type I error—rejecting a true null hypothesis. On the other hand, we cannot conclusively falsify theories either. The Duhem-Quine problem of auxiliary hypotheses means that we test theories as whole; if a test fails we do not know whether the test hypothesis or an auxiliary hypothesis is false. Hence, the probability of committing a Type II error—accepting a false null hypothesis—also cannot be reduced to zero. Any theory can thus be reconciled with some evidence.

The implications of these twin problems of induction run deep. Hume writes that *"we have no reason to draw any inference concerning any object beyond those of which we have had experience"* ([1739] 1984, 189, emphasis in original). King, Keohane, and Verba offer a modern restatement: "We can never hope to know a causal effect for certain" (1994, 79). In other words, extrapolation from experience, from the present case to another case, is never completely justified. Probabilistic and nonprobabilistic theories of confirmation and falsification (Howson 2000) and the very notion of verisimilitude (Brink 2000) have deep philosophical problems. There are even empirical grounds for this skepticism about empiricism. The pessimistic induction—"any theory will be discovered to be false within, say, 200 years of being propounded" (Newton-Smith 1981, 14)—or, alternatively, science is "one damn theory after another" (Rouse 1987, 4), seems to fit the history of science quite nicely.

We are left with Maher: "The history of science is a history of false theories, and yet we want to say that science is making progress" (1993, 218). Nagel, hoping to overcome Hume's problem, thus writes that the "basic trouble" with the philosophy of science is that "we do not possess at present a generally accepted, explicitly formulated, and fully comprehensive scheme for weighing the evidence for any arbitrarily given hypothesis so that the logical worth of alternative conclusions relative to the evidence available can be compared" (1953, 700). The twin problems of induction tell us that just as there can be no methodical routine for doing creative work (i.e., a master science of discovery), neither can there be an inductive science of justification. Nagel's (1953) hope for a unique scientific method for making the uniquely rational choice among the limitless number of contending theories, and hence a method that could explain and justify the change in scientific theories, is an impossible dream: the search for a computer program that can conclusively decide between competing theories is a chimera; the search for Algorithor, the philosopher of science who discovers the one true method, cannot succeed (Newton-Smith 2000, 4); and the search for "the methodologist's stone" (1981, 77) is fruitless. Scientists cannot quantify "degrees of confirmation," in effect "adding the weight" of many studies so that propositions are established "more or less." There is no algorithmic way to assess verisimilitude: how close (or closer) to the truth one hypothesis is, compared to another hypothesis.

This then is the fundamental indeterminacy of empirical work: important questions can not be entirely arbitrated by the sciences of deductive and inductive logic.[20] Logical empiricism, the positivist view favored by rationalist hegemons, overestimated the power of formal logic and measurement strategies to adjudicate competing theoretical claims.

So we must ask: How can observational data provide reasons for accepting or rejecting[21] a hypothesis that transcends the data? What principles can scientists use to weight evidence and make inferences that allow them to accept hypotheses that are true and to reject hypotheses that are false? If we cannot answer these questions, the disciples of Bates, Scott, and Skocpol are no better than the disciples of the rabbi of Krakow.

Following van Fraassen (1980), "constructive empiricism" does not aim at "true" theories but only aims at empirically adequate theories—everything it says about observables is "true." As best as they can, scientists rely on judgment to establish that a model of a theory is consistent with a model of the data. Newton-Smith thus writes that

> a practicing scientist is continually making judgments for which he can provide no justification beyond saying that is how things strike him. This should come as no surprise in a post-Wittgensteinian era. Wittgenstein repeatedly drew attention to the fact that we cannot specify usable, logically necessary and sufficient conditions for the application of many commonly employed predicates.
>
> The time has come to model at least some aspects of the scientific enterprise not on the multiplication tables but on the exercise of the skills of, say, the master chef who produces new dishes, or the wine blender who does deliver the goods but who is notoriously unable to give a usable description of how it is that he does selection [of] the particular portions of the wines that add up taste-wise to more than the sum of their parts. (1981, 232)

Since it is so difficult to assess the epistemic value of a theory, scientific judgment involves "beauty" and "justice" in addition to "truth" (Lave and March 1975). Pragmatic or aesthetic values—consistency, parsimony or simplicity, and fruitfulness, fertility, scope, or unifying power—thereby enter science.

Let us focus here, however, on empirical criteria of theory evaluation.[22] Since facts are overdetermined by theories and theories underdetermined by facts, something else must determine our choice of explanatory theories. Absolute standards of theory evaluation are not available, so relative ones must be found. I therefore offer an approach to evidence that focuses on larger structures of knowledge. For those pragmatists who work within one paradigm to fit its models of theory (nuts and bolts) to models of data in a new problem domain, Lakatos's (1970) additional and true standard should be used; for those competitors who use the nuts and bolts that come from alternative paradigms, Popper's (1968) different and better standard is appropriate; and for those who synthesize different paradigms into one favored paradigm, nested models that combine the two standards are relevant.

10.4.1. Lakatos

The philosopher of science Imre Lakatos (1970) proposes a standard for evaluating a single research program. He suggests that scientists characterize each modification of a research program (i.e., an attempt to apply a program's nuts and bolts to a new problem domain) as "progressive" if (1) it can account for previous findings; (2) it can predict "novel content" or some hitherto unexpected or counterintuitive observations; and (3) some of these excess predictions resist falsification. A modification of a research program is "degenerative" if it is merely patchwork to explain an internally generated anomaly of the program and offers no new substantive insights into the new problem domain. Degenerative programs are, accordingly, autonomous and self-perpetuating, farther and farther removed from reality.

Consider an example from the rationalist approach to collective action. Lakatos's additional and true criteria ask the following: What, besides that protest groups do form and that their participants are rational, does the collective action research program tell us about a new case of collective dissent? Each new application of an existing solution to the free-rider problem must tell us something additional and true about the protest. Solutions are potentially rich in their implications, focusing as they do on the group's actions (e.g., rhetoric, deeds), internal organization (e.g., membership characteristics, entrepreneurs), and external relations (e.g., competition with enemies such as the regime, cooperation with allies such as patrons). Showing that the collective action research program can tell us more about a new conflict than simply that rational people rebel demonstrates the heuristic value of the approach. It reveals the range of observations or the multiple outcroppings (Webb et al. 1981, 66–68) about conflict that the approach can explain. It also enables us to take a fresh look at existing theoretical arguments and empirical evidence.

Consider, for example, the selective incentives idea. The application of this solution to the Rebel's Dilemma could reveal many stylized facts about a new instance of protest or rebellion. (1) Rioters typically loot stores. (2) Voluntary members of a dissident group often attempt to become paid staff and make a career out of their participation (i.e., over time protest is professionalized). (3) Long-lived dissident organizations usually become oligarchical, with leaders receiving the majority of the benefits. (4) Government commonly co-opts leaders and buys off followers, and thus long-lived dissident organizations regularly become deradicalized. (5) Organizing manuals written by protest leaders frequently stress appeals to self-interest, and hence to immediate, specific, and concrete issues, rather than to altruism, and hence to ideology, programs, and self-sacrifice. (6) Organizational meetings and protest demonstrations routinely include food, drink, and entertainment.

These ideas tell us more than that participation in the new instance of collective dissent is rational. The existence of selective incentives determines what the various actors (e.g., participants, opposition leaders, government, patrons) do and how opposition groups become corrupt and change over time. While the selective incentives solution to the free-rider problem was initially designed to explain why rational people participate in rebellion, it explains much more—why protest and rebellion take particular courses and have particular consequences. The focus upon additional and true statements about protest is thus a particularly useful perspective for evaluating the new application of this old nut and bolt.

The Lakatosian approach is not without its critics, however. Many would argue that the deductive fertility of a research program—the variety of propositions that it can yield about a new problem domain—is a necessary but not sufficient condition for its value.[23] While valuable and important, there are four reasons why one should not overestimate the significance of any research program's ability to produce additional and true observations about a new domain of inquiry.[24]

First, a research program is only one of many research programs. Each has a more or less fertile agenda of topics for study. Some parts of the agendas of different research programs do not coincide. "Breakdown theories" of protest, for example, tell us that protest will occur during periods of personal pathology and antisocial behavior; the concomitants of protest will therefore be suicide, divorce, alcoholism, drug abuse, and vagrancy. Nothing in the collective action research program leads one to study these phenomena as covariates of protest. Other parts of the agendas of different research programs do coincide. Both collective action and grievance theories, for example, have been used to explain the same observations about the impact of economic inequality on collective dissent (Lichbach 1989, 1990).

Second, almost all the proponents of a given research program claim that the program can explain much of the empirical world by subsuming the important parts of competing research programs. Consider, once again, the case of collective dissent. Gurr is obviously correct, from a philosophy-of-science perspective, when he argues that "one determinant of the adequacy of theoretical generalization is the degree to which it integrates more specific explanations and observed regularities" (1970, 321). But claims about the deductive fertility and integrative capacity of the core ideas of research programs in conflict studies have been heard too many times. Gurr, for example, too easily integrates status discrepancy, cognitive dissonance, value disequilibrium, and relative deprivation ideas under the frustration-aggression rubric (1970). Tilly thus likens *Why Men Rebel* to a sponge and maintains that "the spongelike character of the work comes out in Gurr's enormous effort to subsume—to make every other argument, hypothesis, and finding support his scheme, and to contradict none of them" (1971, 416). Students of conflict are thus justifiably suspicious about claims by supporters of the latest research program that the program is the key that "unlocks all conceivable doors" (Hirschman 1970, 330). Exaggerated claims succeed "only in provoking the readers' resistance and incredulity" (331). The derivation of innumerable "true" propositions from a research program is thus seen as a breathless search for cognitive consistency between new information and old perspectives, with all the inevitable elements of gimmickry and gadgetry. Hirschman (1970) understandably counsels modesty in the difficult search for truth and understanding. In fact, only a simple-minded positivism would lead one to try to subsume all theories under a single favorite theory (Lloyd 1986, 216).

Third, it is always easy to make deductions that support theories. Hence, accounts of the beginning of protest always seem to confirm culturalist theories, and accounts of the end of protest always seem to confirm rationalist theories. If, for example, collective dissent occurs, culturalist theories conduct an ex post facto search for grievances while rationalist theories look for collective action solutions. If instead collective dissent does not occur, culturalist theories conduct an ex post facto search for the weakness of grievances, and rationalist theories look for the Rebel's Dilemma. An example from Thompson illustrates the point: "Yorkshire Luddism petered out amidst arrests, betrayals, threats, and disillusionment" (1966, 572). Collective action theorists are trained to read "selective disincentives" and the "improbability of making a difference" into Thompson's diagnosis of why Yorkshire Luddism failed. Runciman's warnings against "self-confirming illustrations pre-emptively immunized against awkward evidence" are quite relevant here (1989, 367).

Finally, it is easy to produce numerous deductions by adding numerous assumptions. Much "like a conjurer putting a rabbit in a hat, taking it out again and expecting a round of applause" (Barry, cited in Hechter 1990, 243), it is an approach that deserves no honors. Research programs in the social sciences often appear deductively fertile only because of an inelegant eclecticism: their assumptions are hedged so as to be able to account for much of the empirical world. But unless the assumptions behind a research program are parsimonious and precise, nothing of value has been accomplished, for anything can be derived from everything.

The consequence of eclectic theories is therefore that testing becomes impossible. Eckstein (1980) discovered this truth in conflict studies when he tried but failed (not *his* fault) to separate two important research programs, Gurr's (1970) version of culturalist theories and Tilly's (1978) version of rationalist theories, by determining which theory better explains the known facts about how social cleavages, the economy, repression, urbanization, and so on influence collective dissent. Eckstein points out that Gurr and Tilly surrounded their core assumptions with a "protective belt" by arguing that grievances and mobilizable resources are required for collective dissent. Both theories thus turned out to be eclectic.

10.4.2. Popper

Given these difficulties with the "additional and true" criterion, scientists often try to answer a second question about models of theories derived from their pet research program: Compared with other approaches, does my approach tell us things that are unique and more valid about the new problem domain under investigation? Scientists must show, in other words, that the implications of their pet theories are (1) original and pioneering and hence unexpected and counterintuitive, given other traditional wisdom in the field and (2) more valid than that traditional wisdom. The additional and true propositions about the new conflict derived from rational choice theories, for example, must also be different and better than those offered by alternative theories of conflict.

Truth, Popper (1968) tells us, comes out of the confrontation of ideas. A research program's models must therefore be tested against those of the competition. A scientist is consequently less interested in finding the best hypothesis from his or her pet program than in comparing the competing theories from different programs in a subject domain, a point well recognized by both philosophers of science[25] and practicing social scientists.[26]

The "different and better" criterion is particularly relevant because of the imperialistic tendencies of research programs. Many rational choice theorists, for example, have tried to push back the limits of their explanations (Bates and Bianco 1990, 351; Miller 1990, 343). Rapoport thus comments on Riker's minimum-winning coalition prediction of the election of 1824: "How seriously are we to take these calculations? Are not the conventional political interpretations of the Clay-Adams alliance more convincing? I do not know. If we could find situations where the predictions of 'conventional' political theory and the behavioral scientist's interpretation of n-person games seem incompatible, we could pit one against the other. In the above instance they are compatible and the question remains open" (1970, 300).

In attempting to be integrative and eclectic, scholars often miss the value of Popperian-type crucial tests among paradigms in advancing middle-range theories and concrete explanations (Lichbach 1995, sect. 9.3). In their widely cited studies, however, Eckstein (1980) and McAdam (1982, chap. 4) develop "explanation sketches" of two or three alternative models of contentious politics and then explore several substantive domains to discover competing test implications. How do the paradigms differ? Do they yield competing predictions? Can we develop and test the predictions in a new problem domain, whether a broad sample, a carefully chosen set of comparisons, or a crucial case study?

Nonetheless, there is a problem with the "different and better" criterion. Researchers who consider themselves "problem driven," "puzzle directed," or "question oriented" often argue that synergisms of research traditions are valuable. Since this type of social scientist is interested in developing middle-range theories in some substantive domain (e.g., protest cycles) or historically concrete explanations of empirical happenings (e.g., fascism in Germany and Italy), he or she wants to draw freely upon rationalist, culturalist, and structuralist approaches to develop a single comprehensive theory or explanation.

10.4.3. Nested Models

As such scientists mine different approaches to construct explanations that address concrete problems and puzzles, they create the possibility for substantive syntheses. Similarly to how Weber used ideal types, scientists can draw on the nuts and bolts available in different schools to explain a historical puzzle. The combination can, to use a chemical metaphor, be a compound, mixture, or something in between like a colloidal suspension; or the combination, to use a biological metaphor, can range from true symbiosis to mutual coexistence. However intellectually cohesive the result, creativity comes from the reconciliation of differences and the attempt at synthesis. Section 4.3.1 therefore argued that modest rational choice theory moves cautiously from thin to thick rationality—incorporating cultural and structural alternatives into an individualistic decision-calculus—in an attempt to establish baselines and boundaries.

There is a research methodology that allows scientists to evaluate the results: nested models. In this approach, splitters develop a set of competing predictions that complement the set of predictions produced by the synthesizers. For example: What do rationalist theories predict about regime transition? Or culturalist theories? Or a rationalist-culturalist consortium? Nested models enable scientists to evaluate the limitations of the pure theories and the value added of the combined one. This approach therefore allows creative competitions in new problem domains. Some combinations might work better in some of these domains than others (Lichbach and Seligman 2000, chap. 4).

At the level of paradigm, middle-range theory, or empirical explanation, such creative confrontations are to be preferred to flabby and facile syntheses. Rationalist and culturalist paradigms, for instance, can be used to generate ideal-type theories about regime transition that can serve as the models and foils that make theoretical and empirical work interesting and worthwhile. The dialogue between paradigms should therefore stress struggle over synthesis and competition over consortium; even syntheses and consortia, via the nested models, can enter the struggle and the competition. Contending theories should always guide our research.[27]

The critical assumption here is that metastandards of evaluation exist, and hence transparadigmatic connections can be fashioned. Popperians and those who use nested models thus search for this neutral language—an Archimedean point of the ideal observer, a transparadigmatic norm, and a theory-independent standard of comparison—that does not privilege one tradition over the other. Partisans counter, however, that there are often real differences among research schools, that competing theories do not share meanings, and that different theories cannot be translated into one another. The incommensurability or otherness of theories, that is, dooms interparadigmatic translations and transparadigmatic syntheses, and researchers are trapped in their particular self-contained discourses. Since there is no metaframework, higher-order language, first philosophy, foundation, or independent tribunal that can facilitate comparison of the separate local languages, the only standards are within-paradigm standards. Hence there can be no conversations among traditions, competitions among communities, and rational choice among paradigms.[28]

Davidson (1973–74) challenges this dogma of the separation of conceptual schemes and maintains that a conceptual scheme can be made intelligible to someone else. Wittgenstein adds that one can see the fly in the fly-bottle only if one's perspective is different from that of the fly (cited in Bhaskar 1997, 8). Following Weber's point that one does not have to be Caesar to understand Caesar, one does not need to speak with Caesar to understand Caesar. More generally, there are analytical and empirical arguments against relativism and for the kind of transparadigmatic comparisons advocated by the synthesizers.

The analytical argument is that conflict implies mutual understanding or a common language within which disagreement can occur—a metastandard of comparability and translatability. As MacIntyre puts it: "A precondition of the adherents of two different traditions understanding those traditions as rival and competing is of course that in some significant measure they understand each other" (1988, 370). MacIntyre continues: "To be able to recognize some alien system of belief and practice as in contention with one's own always requires a capacity to translate its terms and idioms into one's own. The adherents of every standpoint in recognizing the existence of rival standpoints recognize also, implicitly if not explicitly, that those standpoints are formulated within and in terms of common norms of intelligibility and evaluation" (1990, 5). Implied in incommensurability and incompatibility, or in disagreement and conflict, is therefore some mutual understanding.[29]

The empirical argument against relativism is also straightforward: where is the evidence that scientists on opposite sides of a theoretical fence fail to comprehend one another? Commonsense observation implies the exact opposite: scientists often understand their disagreements and conflicts quite well. To write a history of science, moreover, is to assume that conceptual frameworks different from one's own can be made understandable. Gellner thus maintains that traditions or "cultures are not terminal. The possibility of transcendence of cultural limits is a fact; it is the single most important fact about human life." He continues: "Organic, self-contained social and conceptual cocoons cannot cope with either their internal or external conflicts. The notion of a culture-transcending truth emerges partly to cope with the resulting problems, partly to help explain the culture-transcending achievements of science" (1998, 187, 191).[30]

10.4.4. Summary

A common complaint about theories is that what is new is wrong and what is right is old; we therefore want models of theories (nuts and bolts) that grow out of a single research program to be additional and true (i.e., new and right) explanations of a new problem domain. Another common complaint about theories is that what is different is wrong and what is right is the same; we therefore want our models of theories to confront alternatives and to be different and better (i.e., different and right) explanations of a new problem domain. A model of a theory thus must ideally satisfy two criteria: it must account for some additional and true observations about a subject matter, and it must explain these observations differently and better than competing models of theories. If the theory is synthetic, both criteria should be applied to its component parts and the resulting consortium.

Rational choice theorists therefore should elaborate their research program to discover its utility in explaining new problem domains; they should also compare its deductions to a stylized version of an alternative research program and to a synthesis of the two programs. We again arrive at the theme of this book: the success of rational choice theory depends on how it treats its foils. Weber's (1946) "pedantic political economist"—one who begins with external conditions and then considers material and normative orientations to those conditions—needs rationalist, culturalist, and structuralist ideas.

Foils matter. We social scientists can begin with our research interests and then turn to our colleagues who can further those interests: "When I start a new piece of research, the first thing I ask myself is, 'Who should I take to lunch?'" (Bates, cited in Shafer 1994, 4). We can also begin with our colleagues who can help us define our research identities: "He who walks with wise men becomes wise" (Proverbs 13:20). Whether our research interests/identities are the goals and our colleagues the means, or our colleagues are the goals and our research interests/identities the means, we need wise colleagues to serve as our models *and* foils. They are the foundation of a modest philosophy of social science that buttresses modest rational choice theory.

10.5. How a Modest Rationalist Evaluates Theory and Evidence

To sum up:

♦ *Theory.* Science employs research programs to develop models—combinations of nuts and bolts (in realist terms, causal mechanisms)—of a theory that yield lawful regularities in particular problem domains.

♦ *Evidence.* Science investigates how well models of a theory explain models of data in different domains.

♦ *Evaluation.* Science employs foils as well as models and hence asks not only whether existing models from a favored program offer additional and true insights into a new problem domain but also whether the models are different and better than the foils and combinations of the models and foils.

While several philosophers of science, including Bacon,[31] Kuhn,[32] Lakatos,[33] Hacking,[34] and Cartwright,[35] could accept this relatively modest view of science, some social scientists seem reluctant to do so. Luce and Raiffa thus indicate that a domain-specific model

seems to be regarded by many social scientists as a terrible inadequacy, and yet it is a common difficulty in all physical science. It is analogous to a physical prediction of gas using boundary conditions which may be subject to change during the process, either by external causes or through the very process itself. The prediction will only be valid to the extent that the conditions are not changed, yet such predictions are useful and are even used when it is uncertain whether the assumed invariance actually holds. In many ways social scientists seem to want for a mathematical model more comprehensive predictions of social phenomena than have ever been possible in applied physics and engineering. It is almost certain that their desires will never be fulfilled, and so either the aspirations will change or formal deductive systems will be discredited for them. (1957, 8)

Other social scientists, including Weber,[36] Stinchcombe,[37] Boudon,[38] Hechter,[39] Shubik,[40] George,[41] Burnham,[42] Verba,[43] Goldstone,[44] Tilly,[45] and King, Keohane, and Verba[46] recognize the limitations of scientific theory and evidence and offer more modest approaches to evaluating the two.

Earlier rationalist modeling, for example, reflected an ambitious positivism that failed to appreciate the limitations of generalization and falsification. Tullock (1971) and Bueno de Mesquita (1981) thus sought general theories, or the cross-domain generalizability of rationalist models. More recent reflections (Shepsle 1979) on modeling in the social sciences, similar to what was referred to earlier as MIT-style theorizing, stress contextualized, domain, or institution-specific models: one begins testing with a well-defined historical case and then very carefully moves to a second case and eventually to a well-defined set of cases.

Many rational choice theorists (Riker 1982a; Cox 1987; Bates 1989; Levi 1997; Rosenthal 1992; Greif 1998; North and Weingast 1989; Popkin 1979; Geddes 1994; Root 1987; Golden 1997; Ames 1987; Aldrich 1995) recognize some of the aforementioned difficulties of rational choice theorizing and adhere to this more modest modeling tradition. Their models (Bates et al. 1998) yield what might be called *rationalist narratives:* historical and comparative analysis of strategic decision-making situations. These efforts should have six components.

1. One begins with a single concrete case (e.g., nation, city, international organization). The motivation for selecting the new case is that, from a rationalist point of view, it is either paradigmatic or deviant in its problem domain.

2. Out of the narrative stream of happenings, events, and episodes in the case, rationalists locate separable interactions: collective action and collective choice situations (sect. 3.2). Each case thus consists of a set of chronologically linked strategic situations—episodic crises, recurring problems, periodic challenges, or key turning points in the case's history. Weingast (1998) shows how the pre–Civil War equilibrium was punctuated by a series of crises. Bates (1998) focuses on critical events in the formation, operation, transformation, and ultimate termination of the Colombian coffee cartel. Levi (1998) studies a series of legislative actions in France from 1793 through 1872, each of which altered conscription laws. Greif explains stylized factors about "the nature of Genoa's economy and its inter-clan relations before 1154" (1998, 22), the transition from pirates to traders from 1154 to 1164, the civil wars from 1164 to 1194, and the institutionalization of the *podesteria* organization after 1194.[47]

3. Each historical episode is probed with rationalist nuts and bolts. Analytically, one can do equilibrium analyses and comparative statics to explain why some interactions turn out one way instead of another.

4. More generally, one can derive many observable implications about the recurring pattern of politics (i.e., strategizing) manifested in the case's particular events, individuals, issues, groups, conflicts, regions, or time periods. Weingast (1998), for example, tells us about the political use of slavery (the Riker thesis), the political difficulties of pure majority rule, the implications of institutional compromises supporting the balance rule, and the North's tenuous commitment to property rights in slaves. Levi (1998) uses the comparative statics of her model to arbitrate among a set of exogenous forces thought to cause change in conscription policy: war-induced changes in government demand for troops, experience with past conscription policies, democratization of political institutions, nation building, and state building (especially of repressive capacity). Rosenthal (1998) matches his model against stylized facts about the goals and strategies of various actors and the resulting possible and actual institutional changes. He claims that "the model is therefore consistent with much of the public finance of Early Modern France" (9). While the overall historical narrative of sequential situations is interspersed with these sorts of models and data, an overall thesis, or metanarrative, illuminates the general pattern or overall stylized facts of the case. A protest cycle, the interrelationship of politics and institutions underlying democratic stability, the political foundations of economic development, or state (institution) building thus molds the strategic situations into an overarching narrative structure. And the short-run equilibria compound to produce a long-run equilibrium, and the series of within-case studies compounds to produce the overall case study.

5. Significant foils are investigated. What would historians of Italy make of Greif's explanation of Italian trade and development? Does Rosenthal engage the historiography of Old Regime France in a way that demonstrates the superiority of his model? How is Weingast's explanation of the U.S. Civil War different from and better than other accounts? Has Levi explained conscription in France differently and better than alternative explanations? Is there reason to think that Bates explains the Colombian coffee cartel differently than the culturalists and better than the structuralists?

6. One draws conclusions about the conditions under which thin and thick versions of the theory's assumptions apply, for example, about rationality. Lichbach (1995) thus argues that collective action

theory consists of theoretical possibilities or possibility claims: nothing in the theory says that people facing a collective action problem will always find it in their interest to use the collective action solution under investigation. The presence of solutions, that is, does not guarantee that they will be used. To find out whether they will be used and the consequences that will arise, one examines concrete strategic situations in specific historical contexts.

In sum, a modest rationalist narrative explains the historical sequence of major decision-making situations, as well as many general aspects of the historical record. There are variations of this strategy: Rosenthal (1998) structures his narratives of France and England with a single integrated model of the division of institutional control over taxation and policy control over war making between an elite and a crown. Greif (1998) develops a single model and one variation for one time period. Levi (1998) looks at a single model but in multiple cases (i.e., in this important variation, she produces a set of comparative case studies of the historical sequences of strategic situations in each nation case). Weingast (1998) proposes two integrated models—a spatial model and two interrelated sequential game models, but of one case. Bates (1998) uses a battery of different types of rationalist models in a single case. Hence, there is a range of ways in which a rationalist narrative "seeks to use history to construct the theory and to flesh out its implications" (Rosenthal 1998, 2). The important point, however, is that *the work of modest rationalists, especially those who engage major foils, is far from a deductive-nomological treatment of theory and evidence.*

This chapter has consequently suggested that we use ideas drawn from Lakatos and Popper to evaluate the rationalist's bid for hegemony. Lakatos asks whether sticking pragmatically to a thin version of rationality allows rationalists to develop a research program that is progressive: successful hegemons should develop models that yield additional and true hypotheses about new problem domains. Popper asks whether a baseline model of thin rationality allows the rationalist program to beat culturalists and structuralists in competitive empirical tests: successful hegemons should also develop models that are different and better than their foils. And it is possible to evaluate nested models according to Lakatosian and Popperian criteria: successful hegemons should synthesize rationalist, culturalist, and structural explanations—that is, develop thick versions of rationality that incorporate culture and structure into an individualistic decision calculus— and create rationalist models that yield additional and true hypotheses about new problem domains that are different from and better than their component parts. The different types of theorists and the different types of theories can thus compete in ways that benefit everyone.

As a proponent of rational choice theory, I am betting that modest rational choice theory will yield a progressive research program and a program whose nuts and bolts can often (but not always) prove better in explaining new problem domains than the nuts and bolts found in other programs. Hopefully, the rationalist bid for hegemony will not turn culturalists and structuralists away from disputing my claims and thus engaging in an exciting debate about the models and foils that characterize social science.

Notes

The authors of the epigraphs that appear at the beginning of the book are Roth (cited in Weber [1924] 1968, lxvii), Parsons (1937, 490), Rorty (1989, 9), Taylor (1991, 72), MacIntyre (1984, 164), Levinas 1982 (cited in Ouaknin 1995, 160), Feyerabend (cited in Redman 1993, 49), Arendt (cited in Bernstein 1996, 106), and Weber (1946, 155).

Preface

1. Most of the hegemons are in political science. Rational choice theory tried to make disciplinary inroads in sociology (e.g., Coleman, Hechter), but has not been nearly as successful. Since Parsons positioned sociology as the disciplinary answer to "economists" and "utilitarians," most sociologists have seen themselves as studying normatively guided action within institutional orders. In other words, sociologists think of themselves as studying the antidote to rational choice theory. My efforts to engage sociologists include a book, *Market and Community: The Bases of Social Order, Revolution and Relegitimation,* coauthored with a sociologist, Adam Seligman; a debate with a prominent sociologist—Chuck Tilly—about rationalist, culturalist, and structuralist approaches to the field of contentious politics (Lichbach 1997b; Tilly 1997); and a review essay that positioned rational choice theory among sociological approaches to social order (Lichbach 1998a).

2. I use the terms *research communities, traditions, languages, schools, approaches, paradigms, programs,* and *frameworks* interchangeably.

Chapter I

1. Success would also have meant, as I will show in section 4.2.1, that there was just one unit act rather than a Weberian typology of unit acts based on different norms or decision rules (e.g., one for actors concerned with pecuniary self-interest and another for actors concerned with group interest).

2. Tradition, encyclopedia, and genealogy partially correspond to premodern, modern, and postmodern forms of inquiry.

3. While philosophical reflection can eliminate some mistaken ideas and avoid some wasted time, it is necessary but not sufficient for good social science. Good social science—inventing new nuts and bolts or discovering new problem domains for old nuts and bolts—requires a creative spark.

4. Interest in the battle of the paradigms was once strong in comparative

politics (Holt and Turner 1970; Merritt 1971) but has weakened. In international relations the debate between neoliberals and neorealists helps structure inquiry and inform scholarly identities. A literature has evaluated the meaning and significance of this latter controversy (Keohane 1986; Baldwin 1993; Kegley 1995), and students of international relations are well aware of the value of social theory in sharpening theoretical lenses (Wendt 1999). Social theory also thrives in sociology (Alexander 1987), and the philosophy of economic theory now prospers in economics (Blaug 1992). While the underlying purpose of this book is to invigorate theoretical reflection throughout the social sciences and political science, I specifically hope to encourage a subfield in comparative politics called comparative theory that is as significant as economic theory, social theory, and international relations theory (Munck 2001; Lichbach 1997a).

Chapter 2

1. One need not search for the far-off and inaccessible. One can also question the surface of the simple things surrounding us: "To have a philosophical mind is to be able to be astonished by everyday events and objects. . . . [T]he more a man is intellectually inferior, the less existence is mysterious for him. Everything seems to him to contain the explanation of its how and why" (Schopenhauer, cited in Ouaknin 1995, 97 n. 35).

2. Scott also stresses the importance of stories: "A certain amount of storytelling seems absolutely essential to convey the texture and conduct of class relations" (1985, xviii). Larger theoretical "considerations require, I think, the flesh and blood of detailed instances to take on substance. An example is not only the most successful way of embodying a generalization, but also has the advantage of always being richer and more complex than the principles that are drawn from it" (xviii). Scott thus opens his book with two wonderful stories of social outcasts: Razak, the symbol of "the grasping poor," and Haji Broom, the symbol of "the greedy rich" (18).

3. Artists have a similar goal: "Art does not reproduce the visible, it renders visible" (Paul Klee, cited in Ouaknin 1995, 151). Foucault's genealogy seeks to recover hidden patterns of power beneath seemingly normal or ordinary daily actions. And of course science tries to ignore accidental and contingent surface phenomena and discover the hidden, innermost patterns in nature—the "real" essence of things. While nowadays many political scientists eschew "variable analysis" focused on correlations among variables and prefer to focus on the processes that generate outcomes, earlier giants—Smith and Marshall, Freud and Nietzsche, and Marx and Engels—also valued depth and hence wrote deep stories.

4. There is an oft-cited dictum: "Your true philosopher will not believe what he sees." Hegel says that social life involves processes that go on behind the backs of human agents. Marx's view is that "all science would be superfluous if the outward appearance and the essence of things directly coin-

cided" (cited in Parkin 1982, 28). Nietzsche writes that "it is by invisible hands that we are bent and tortured worst" (1954, 42).

5. There are, more specifically, three reasons for starting off with Bates, Scott, and Skocpol. First, while there is considerable between-tradition variance, there is also much within-tradition variance. Rather than focusing exclusively on a priori thought, it is thus valuable to have a concrete statement and clear domain to criticize. Second, since conceptual concerns are embodied in specific disputes about empirical problems, one can see how rationalists, culturalists, and structuralists practice what they preach. Finally, the mixture of the thick and the thin—concrete examples discussed in the context of a set of general ideas—will prevent the discussion in the bulk of the book from becoming too dense and integrative.

6. In Weber's use of the term, an *iron cage* consists of ideas that eventually come to be supported by material forces ([1904–5] 1985, 181).

7. For the significance of the rationalist-culturalist-structuralist dialogue in comparative politics, see the contributions to Lichbach and Zuckerman 1997 that examine substantive research areas. Hall (1997) shows that the field of comparative political economy involves a lively struggle among perspectives oriented to interests, ideas, and institutions. McAdam, Tarrow, and Tilly (1997) indicate that the three main concepts used to explain contentious politics—political opportunities, mobilizing structures, and cultural frames—embody rationalist, culturalist, and structuralist elements. Migdal (1997) maintains that rational choice and culturalist perspectives have been marginal to comparative studies of the state but are now challenging the hegemonic structuralist perspective. Finally, Barnes (1997) observes that the survey research tradition in the study of voter turnout and partisan choice has been affected by all the perspectives but has come to rely recently on the (declining) rationalist approach. If space permitted, the footprint of the three-way conversation could be traced in comparative studies of democratization, globalization, modernization, and many other substantive problem domains.

8. This is a bit more elaborate than an explanation sketch (Popper 1968) or a paradigm (Kuhn 1970) in that the core and the periphery of the program, and hence thin and thick versions, are given more careful consideration. The danger of producing a cartoon rather than an adequate characterization remains, however, whenever one generalizes over very many individual contributions to produce an ideal-type approach. I therefore cite, at appropriate points, relevant theorists and texts.

9. MacIntyre indicates that "when an institution—a university, say, or a firm, or a hospital—is the bearer of a tradition of practice or practices, its common life will be partly, but in a centrally important way, constituted by a continuous argument as to what a university is and ought to be or what good farming is or what good medicine is. Traditions, when vital, embody continuities of conflict. Indeed when a tradition becomes Burkean it is always dying or

dead" (1984, 222). MacIntyre suggests further that such conflict is inevitable and necessary:

> It is out of the debates, conflicts, and enquiry of socially embodied, historically contingent traditions that contentions regarding practical rationality and justice are advanced, modified, abandoned, or replaced, but that there is no other way to engage in the formation, elaboration, rational justification, and criticism of accounts of practical rationality and justice except from within some one particular tradition in conversation, cooperation, and conflict with those who inhabit the same tradition. There is no standing ground, no place for enquiry, no way to engage in the practices of advancing, evaluating, accepting, and rejecting reasoned argument except from that which is provided by some particular tradition or other. (1988, 350)

10. I have also made cases for two basic theory choices (Lichbach and Seligman 2000; also see sect. 7.3), when the distinction between structure and action seems important, and for four basic theory choices (Lichbach 1995), when important issues of social order and of collective action call for it. The connections between the different typologies run as follows.

Two Types	*Three Types*	*Four Types*
action	rationalist	market
	culturalist	
	subjective	contract
structure	intersubjective	community
	structuralist	hierarchy

As Weber suggests, different sets of ideal types have different purposes.

Chapter 3

1. There are many useful evaluations of the rationalist approach. On the microfoundations of macrooutcomes, see Nozick 1974, chap. 2, and Coleman 1987; on collective action, see Olson 1971 and Lichbach 1995, 1996; on collective choice, see Downs 1957, Riker 1982a, and Schwartz 1987; on public choice and public finance in democracies, see Mitchell 1983 and Aranson and Ordeshook 1985; and on institutional choice, see Bates 1989, North 1990, and Wittman 1995. For an overall evaluation of the rationalist approach, see Moe 1979, Little 1991, chap. 3, and Hollis 1994, chap. 6.

2. The nature-nurture debate—while there are enormous cultural differences among societies, there are startling similarities in human beings—is not confined to rational choice theorists. Durkheim ([1893] 1933) in effect argues that individuals are tabula rasa; the world is created de novo; and people are completely malleable by culture. Nurture thus matters more than nature; a priori theory is not helpful; and the similarities among people are superficial. Lévi-Strauss (1966), by contrast, stresses nature and natural man: differences

are overwhelmed by what human beings have in common; the universal features of humankind reflect the underlying properties of the mind; and important things are inborn and objective.

3. Swingewood summarizes an argument from Adam Smith that illustrates this line of reasoning:

> Thus discussing the development of commercial society, Smith described initially the structural forces which led to the decline of feudal society and property and the necessary evolution of trade and manufacture. The key to understanding this transition, Smith argued, was the actions of two contending social groups, the rich barons whose concern with social status and ornament led to their gradual impoverishment and the more secular, and efficient, merchant class whose manufactured goods brought the ruin of the great landowners. The rising merchant class replaced the landed groups, buying their agricultural holdings and making them efficient and profitable. Smith's assumption here was that wealth from agriculture was more durable than that derived from commerce, but his more significant point is that social change was unconsciously effected by social groups pursuing their own interests and without the slightest regard for the public good: "To gratify the most childish vanities was the sole motive of the great proprietors. The merchants and artisans, much less ridiculously, acted merely from a view to their own interests, and in pursuit of their own peculiar principle of turning a penny wherever a penny was to be got. Neither of them had knowledge or foresight of that great revolution which the folly of the one, and the industry of the other, was gradually bringing about." (1991, 26)

4. Lichbach (1995) explores rebellion and revolution; Opp, Voss, and Gern (1995), revolution in Eastern Europe; Tong (1991), rebellion in ancient China; Hardin (1995), group conflict; Rogowski (1974), rational legitimacy; Brustein (1996), how modes of production lead to class relations and conflict; Przeworski, class conflict in capitalist societies (1985a) and economic reforms in transitional societies (1991); Cohen (1994), regime change; Hunter (1997), military regimes; Root (1987; 1994), revolution in states and markets in France and England; Ramseyer (1996) and Ramseyer and Rosenbluth (1995), institutional choice and economic performance in Japanese history; and Popkin (1979), revolution in Vietnam.

5. Almond, Flanagan, and Mundt (1973) explore crises and political development; North (1981), the origins of the West; Olson (1982), the rise and decline of nations; Colburn (1986), postrevolutionary society; Gambetta (1993), mafias; Laitin, culture (1986) and language (1992); and Posner (1980), the origin of law in primitive societies.

6. Aldrich (1995) explores the origins and transformations of political parties in the United States; Cox (1987) and Kiser and Barzel (1991), democratic development in England; Riker, the origins of federalism (1987), the

U.S. Constitution (1996), and the U.S. Civil War (1982a); and Tsebelis (1990), the origins of party factions and consociational democracy.

7. Mueller (1996) studies constitutional democracy; Shugart and Carey (1992) and Taagepera and Shugart (1989), constitutions and elections; Laver and Schofield (1990), Laver and Shepsle (1994, 1996) and Strøm (1990), parliamentary coalitions; Tsebelis and Money (1997), bicameralism; Laver and Hunt (1992), spatial competition; Rae (1971) and Cox (1997), electoral laws; and Kitschelt, social democracy (1994) and the radical right (1995).

8. Rogowski (1989) studies free trade and protectionism; Frieden (1991), democracy and third world debt; Keohane and Milner (1996), globalization and domestic politics; Simmons (1994), the domestic sources of foreign economic policy during the interwar years; Levi (1988) and Kiser (1994), the relationship between rule and revenue in states; Geddes (1994), policy-making in Latin America; Ames (1987), leadership strategies in Latin America; Kuran (1995), social structure and the development of public policies; Bates (1981, 1983, 1988, 1989, 1997), Ensminger (1992), and Firmin-Sellers (1996), the political economy of development policies; Waterbury (1993), public enterprise; Wade (1994), village collective action; Golden (1997), union responses to job loss; Kato (1994), tax politics in Japan; Milner (1994), social democracy; Pierson (1994), neoconservatism; and Lewin (1988), Swedish politics.

9. For an example of how this might be done with Skocpolian comparative history, see Lichbach and Seligman's attempt to show how structural forces drive collective action processes (2000, chap. 3).

10. Evidential methodological individuals add that all valid confirmations/falsifications must refer to individuals.

11. Hirschman argues that analysts also need to study intended but unrealized effects.

> Curiously, the intended but unrealized effects of social decision stand in need of being discovered even more than those effects that were unintended but turned out to be all too real: the latter are at least here, whereas the intended but unrealized effects are only to be found in the expressed expectations of social actors at a certain, forgotten, fleeting moment of time. Moreover, once these desired effects fail to happen and refuse to come into the world, the fact that they were originally counted on is likely to be not only forgotten but actively repressed. This is not just a matter of the original actors keeping their self-respect, but is essential if the succeeding power holders are to be assured of the legitimacy of the new order: what social order could long survive the dual awareness that it was adopted with the firm expectation that it would solve certain problems and that it clearly and abysmally fails to do so? (1977, 131)

12. Historical sociologists are also aware of the paradoxes and ironies of social choice. Merton (1936) studies unintended consequences, Marx ([1895] 1964), contradictions, and Hegel (1975), the cunning of reason. Abrams argues

that "history is made by the action of individuals in pursuit of their intentions; but the variety and conflict of those intentions and the weight of the past in the form of ideas and institutions shaping and setting limits to the possibilities of action ensure that in practice history becomes a record of the *unintended* consequences of individual action" (1982, 34). Bendix indicates that "as Herbert Butterfield has observed, it is the *clash of wills* which is necessary for the emergence of the present, and the final result of that clash is unknown to the participants" (1984, 55). Elias asks: "How does it happen at all that formations arise in the human world that no single human being has intended and which yet are anything but cloud formations without stability of structure?" (1982, 230). Engels indicates that "men make their own history, whatever its outcome may be, in that each person follows his own consciously desired end, and it is precisely the resultant of these many wills operating in different directions and of their manifold effects upon the outer world that constitutes history" (1962, cited in Abrams 1982, 34). Skocpol understands revolution as "a complex unfolding of multiple conflicts that ultimately give rise to outcomes not originally foreseen or intended by any of the particular groups involved" (1976, 169). Mosse says students of fascism attempt "to analyze the irrational through rational study" (cited in Payne 1995, xiii). Finally, Weber shows how revolutionary charisma is routinized into bureaucratic organization; rule-oriented bureaucracy becomes captured by vested interests; political patrimonialism, an effort at centralization, produces decentralization; and the Protestant ethic becomes the spirit of capitalism ([1904–5] 1985; [1924] 1968).

13. Social choice has also shown that is possible for irrational individuals to inhabit a rational collectivity. Becker's (1976, chap. 8) study of randomness in choice demonstrated that one can start with random individual choice and end up with downward-sloping demand curves that help produce Pareto-optimal market equilibria. Aggregate supply-and-demand functions thus hold up under assumptions of nonrationality (Kincaid 1996, 240). In addition, biases pulling in different directions may produce a collectively unbiased outcome.

14. This goal of social choice theorists is widely misunderstood. Skocpol (1979), for example, takes voluntaristic theories of revolution to say that individuals possess knowledge about the consequences of their actions and that revolutions are the result of conscious planning. Social choice theorists need not make such an argument: revolution could be the unintended (irrational) consequence of interactions among intentional (rational) human beings and groups. Analysts therefore cannot assume that if revolutionary class action occurs, there must have been class-conscious workers, or if well-ordered institutions exist, there must have been socialized actors.

15. Fiorina offers other examples:

When NASA put astronauts on the moon (and brought them back), its scientists and engineers did not rely on a single overarching model. They relied on literally hundreds of models and theories to construct the equipment, train the personnel, design the organization, and make the round trip. No single model would have accounted for more than a few aspects of the total enterprise. Analogously, there will never be a single RC [rational choice] model of any real presidential campaign, of the U.S. Congress, or of the federal regulatory process. What we are engaged in is the construction of scores of models that focus on different aspects of political institutions and processes. One or two models might be able to explain a specific feature of an institution or process . . . but the explanation of broader institutional patterns normally will require several models used in combination. (1996, 289)

16. This approach coincides with several arguments about revolution. Some maintain that revolution and normal politics are not radically different (Tilly 1978; Gamson 1990; Tarrow 1994). Tilly thus suggests that "revolution turns out to be a coherent phenomenon, but coherent in its variation and in its continuity with nonrevolutionary politics, not in any repetitious uniformity" (1995, 1605). Others suggest that revolution is really the sum of many other forms of collective dissent (coups, riots, secession, state breakdown, civil war). Still others suggest that all forms of dissent are highly interrelated. Three empirical predictions follow. First, revolution is a large blip in a long time-series of protests and rebellions. Second, collective action processes should occur in all forms of dissent. Third, protest and rebellion take many different forms, even as all Skocpolian states face international pressures, recalcitrant elites, reforming leaderships, and social communities that are autonomous and cohesive.

17. Fiorina thus suggests that rationalists focus on "explanatory parts, not wholes":

When being trained in RC [rational choice], students are taught to focus—to restrict their attention to one or two aspects of a situation or process (a "stylized fact" or two), and to explain it on the basis of one or two considerations. That is simply the nature of the enterprise: tractability requires simplification. As a consequence of this tradeoff, a RC model, even in principle, is ordinarily only part of an explanation. RC scholars work out "logics," "principles," and problems and seek to apply them to situations. But that is not to assert that only one logic or principle is operative in a situation. Only an empirical test that gets 100 percent of the variance can show that. (1996, 89)

Salmon et al. suggest that the rationalist approach is simply good science.

By and large, the events that happen in our world are highly complex, and we hardly ever try to explain every aspect of such an occurrence. For example, in explaining the explosion of the Challenger vehicle, we are not concerned to explain the fact that a women was aboard, the fact that she was a teacher, or the fact that her life had been insured for a million dollars. When we speak of a particular fact, it is to be understood that this term refers to certain limited aspects of the event in question, not to the event in its full richness and complexity. (1992, 10)

18. Snidal critiques Snyder and Diesing for violating this principle in their modeling.

Snyder and Diesing use game models of 16 historical cases to investigate bargaining in international crises. Their technique is to reconstruct the game structure underlying each crisis from a historical analysis of events. . . . Such a challenge, however, is only a test of their skill in reconstructing a crisis in game terminology, and not a test of the theory itself. Indeed, because Snyder and Diesing use the totality of the crisis (including the outcome) to generate the descriptive game model, their use of game theory does not produce any predictions that could be empirically falsified. None of the deductive power of game theory is employed. Thus, their work is not an example of the empirical application of game theory even though it illustrates the purely descriptive use of game models. (1985, 27)

19. Little writes:

Consider the role of causal laws in classical Marxism. At one extreme, Marxism offers generalizations about the sequence of modes of production and the dynamics of development to be expected from each mode. These function as highly general assertions about the social processes within feudalism, capitalism, the peasant mode of production, and the like. At the other extreme, however, Marxism rests on a range of hypotheses about the causal processes at work within a class society—hypotheses about the circumstances that affect the organization of the firm, the political behavior of the proletariat, the economic choices of the peasant, and the like. These hypotheses are couched in the level not of the mode of production but of the local-level processes through which individual behavior and social institutions interact. My suggestion here is that the social scientist is on the surest ground when providing analysis of the latter process and is also in the best position to offer cross-cultural generalizations at this level. When the social scientist turns to higher-level claims about the social system as a whole—for example, the pattern of development to be expected of any capitalist economy—both the basis of the generalizations itself and its projectability to the social contexts is most shaky. (1989, 199–200)

20. Little endorses this focus on

local processes of change—local politics, features of organization, and the particulars of agent motivation. The best of the studies examined here—Scott, Popkin, and Perry—have argued for fairly generalized conclusions about certain processes of social change, but they have done so on the basis of detailed attention to data drawn from local studies and to local mechanisms of political and economic change. There is a conjunctural unfolding of specific historical processes: capitalism, state building, parliamentary conflicts, war making, tax collection, the rise of private associations. (1989, 25)

21. Since actors try to change the structure of games, rationalists also investigate alternative assumptions about the structures that produce different games or models. For example, the district attorney creates the Prisoner's Dilemma situation or fails to create it (e.g., he or she does not stop retaliation for finking). Since the Prisoner's Dilemma, like all games, is socially and politically constructed, it can be reconstructed. The quest for the best thus leads rationalists to question the optimality or efficiency of positive equilibria.

22. Guessing where the model's assumptions hold or do not hold also produces comparative statics. Diermeier offers an example.

Thus, in rational choice theories of candidate competition, some researchers assume policy-motivated candidates, while others follow Downs's suggestion and assume pure office-seeking motivation. . . . The former assumption may be more appropriate in cases where disciplined parties compete for office, the latter where the competition is among political entrepreneurs. Both assumptions are, of course, untestable, yet they allow us to link the rational actor assumption to empirical realities. In the particular case of candidate competition under uncertainty over voters' ideal points, these assumptions, in conjunction with the rational actor assumption, lead to different empirical implications: convergence in the Downs model, nonconvergence in the Calvert-Wittman model. So, in conjunction with a particular assumption concerning motivations, the rationality assumption generates precise and testable implications. (1996, 67)

Stinchcombe provides another example.

We may be able to establish that, for example, the conditions of perfect (or at least equal) information for the important actors, similar ranking of the utilities of outcomes, equilibrium prices, and the like *evidently* obtain in the larger stock markets, in certain futures exchanges, and so on but do *not* obtain in the market for takeovers (because of different knowledge of probabilities of getting control), in international currency markets (because of intervention of central banks), in the market for patents (because patents are worth much more to the company that did the R&D because they have a near monopoly over the technical competence to explore "nearby" technical options), in the market for sexual services (because of the widespread presence of pairwise sexual monopolies), and so on. That is, we may be able to provide a *list* of social structure phenomena where we know that the conditions necessary for the operation of rational mechanisms do (or do not) hold. (1991, 376, emphasis in original)

23. This methodology is made clear in Coleman 1987 and Boudon 1987. Nonrationalists also understand it. Wendt (1999, chap. 3) argues that rational choice theory studies how external constraints or material structures condition action. Smelser (1992, 23) suggests that rational choice theory is basically a heuristic intervening variable or mechanism used to explain how an agent's actions result from aspects of his or her objective environment.

24. Because rationalists see their experiments as questioning their assumptions, they argue that researchers should spend, say, 50 percent of their time debating assumptions and 50 percent examining the conclusions that follow from those assumptions. True believers, of course, spend 99 percent of the time on the deductions; militant nonbelievers spend 99 percent of the time on the assumptions.

Chapter 4

1. As C. Turner suggests: "It is to the mechanisms of that conditionality—and those mechanisms alone . . . [that] positivist science addresses itself. The facts of human action with which science is concerned contain no reference to the facts of what is valuable to human beings because there are no such facts. The only facts which 'exist' are facts about the conditionality of action" (1992, 22).

2. Abelson argues the contrary, or that rationality is socially constructed: "Instrumentality is a mindset that is learned (perhaps overlearned), and can be situationally manipulated; because it is valued in our society, it provides a privileged vocabulary for justifying behaviors that may have been performed for other reasons, and encourages the illusory belief in the universality of rational choice" (1996, 25). Green and Shapiro carry the social construction argument to its logical conclusion and suggest that rational choice theorists can create what they study.

> In some circumstances rational choice theories might actually produce the behavior in people that they believe they have discovered. Studies suggesting that the propensity for strategic behavior increases with the study of economics, or that the introduction of selective incentives into children's games can make continued play dependent on those incentives where previously it was not, raise potentially worrisome possibilities. It may be that agency problems can be created, where previously they did not exist, simply by drawing people's attention to their possibility. Likewise with agenda manipulation and free riding: research may help create the possibility they describe by pointing out and legitimating as "rational" certain forms of strategic behavior. (1994, 269)

3. The ultimate materialism of rationalists (especially human-nature rationalists, see sect. 3.1) is also revealed in their preoccupation with a universal human nature. Hume writes: "It is universally acknowledged there is a great

uniformity among the actions of men in all nations and ages, and that human nature remains still the same, in its principles and operations. The same motives always produce the same actions. . . . Mankind is so much the same, in all times and places, that history informs us of nothing new or strange in this particular. Its chief use is only to discover the constant and universal principles of human nature" (cited in Harris 1992, 4). Rationalists focus on the conditions of biological existence (i.e., an innate, hereditary nature) so that they can avoid the problems that a study of the social and political construction of desires and beliefs would raise for their theories. This materialism also explains the rationalist preoccupation with the market—another structure over which the individual presumably has no control. As Wendt perceptively comments, a Hobbesian struggle for survival thus characterizes two harsh material environments: human biology and economic markets: "At least five material factors recur in materialist discourse: (1) human nature; (2) natural resources; (3) geography; (4) forces of production; and (5) forces of destruction. These can matter in various ways: by permitting the manipulation of the world, by empowering some actors over others, by disposing people toward aggression, by creating threats, and so on" (1999, 23). The reductio ad absurdum of materialism is "you are what you eat," a line with philosophical implications (Solomon and Higgins 1996, 229).

4. There is a problem here too: explanations that take reasons to be causes face the problem of the causal indeterminacy of reasons. Because they leave the sources of preferences open, rational explanations of action are therefore not causally adequate.

5. In explaining preferences, some economists have therefore retreated to a purely behavioral position: nothing goes on in the mind of the agent. They have therefore moved from cardinality to ordinality, from interpersonal comparisons to noncomparability, from preferences to revealed preferences or behavior, and finally from behavior to production (i.e., Becker's household production functions; see Rosenberg 1992, 152).

6. The problem of social order thus arises. Given the subjectivism and ultimate materialism of intentional explanations of action, how is it possible for intersubjectivity and community to occur among actors? How can actors, in other words, avoid a Hobbesian struggle of subjective wills?

7. A related criticism is that they also have a materialist theory of beliefs.

8. Since subjective interests must be largely random and unstructured (Parsons 1937), rationalists typically argue that conflicts of interests can be resolved through some procedure rooted in liberal social choice (e.g., political democracy and economic markets).

9. Here is a Jewish story demonstrating that the material distribution of resources is irrelevant to cooperation and conflict and that the cultural orientation to the distribution is decisive.

There were two brothers. One was married and had eight children; the other was a bachelor and lived alone. They farmed adjacent fields. The married brother thought to himself: "My brother is all alone. His life is much harder than mine, so I will give him an extra bale of wheat." The bachelor thought to himself: "My brother has eight children. His life is much harder than mine, so I will give him an extra bale of wheat." So at midnight the married brother carried one bale of wheat to the unmarried brother's storage shed, and the unmarried brother carried one bale of wheat to the married brother's storage shed. Nothing had changed. The next night both brothers carried two bales of wheat to each other's storage shed. So again nothing had changed. On the third night, as they were carrying three bales of wheat to each other's storage shed, they bumped into each other. They immediately knew what had happened and embraced. On that site it is said the Bais Hamigdash (the first Jewish Temple) was built.

Thirty-five hundred years later there was another pair of brothers. One was married and had eight children; the other was a bachelor and lived alone. They farmed adjacent fields. The married brother thought to himself: "My brother has no children and I have eight. My life is much harder than his, so I will take one bale of his wheat." The bachelor thought to himself: "My brother has eight children to help him with his field and I have none. My life is much harder than his, so I will take one bale of his wheat." So at midnight the married brother took one bale of wheat from the unmarried brother, and the unmarried brother took one bale of wheat from the married brother. Nothing had changed. The next night both brothers took two bales of wheat from each other's storage shed. So again nothing had changed. On the third night, as they each were taking three bales of wheat from each other's storage shed, they bumped into each other. They immediately knew what had happened and fought. On that site it is said that the Knesset (Israel's parliament) was built.

10. Alexander summarizes the "utilitarian dilemma" as follows: "If Utilitarianism wishes to maintain subjectivity and freedom, it has to remain individualistic. If it wishes to explain order in a more positive way, it has to eliminate agency and fall back to an emphasis on the unalterable elements of human interaction, to either heredity (biological instincts) or environment (material conditions). The latter are conditions the actor cannot control, things which have nothing to do with his identity or will" (1987, 26). Alexander adds that what he calls the "individualist dilemma" pushes rationalists toward synthesizing collectivist thought.

To maintain an approach to order that is individualistic in a clear, consistent, and honest way, a theorist must introduce into his construction a level of openness to contingency that makes his explanation of order approximate randomness and unpredictability. But whatever the theorist's formal commitment, and whether or not this contingency is seen eventually to lead to collective order, few individualist theorists are, in the end, fully satisfied with such randomness. . . . [W]hatever its sources, this dissatisfaction pushes individualist theories toward more collective ideas, for despite their formal commitments they try, in one way or another, to embrace some aspect of supraindividual order. (179–80)

11. Hausman (1992) argues that the idea that preferences are exogenous follows from the idea that economics is a separate science. The justification for this latter assumption is *de gustibus non est disputandum* (Stigler and Becker 1977). As Hobbes puts it: there is no "common Rule of Good and Evill, to be taken from the nature of objects themselves" ([1651] 1988, 120). Since rationalist or utilitarian thought implies that "desires are random" (Parsons 1937, 89), rationalists must have an exogenously supplied theory of preferences. If rational choice theories are to be useful and not tautological, moreover, they must separate tastes and preferences from choices and actions.

12. As Parsons put it:

There is nothing in the theory dealing with the relations of the ends to each other, but only with the character of the means-end relationship. If the conceptual scheme is not consciously "abstract" but is held to be literally descriptive of concrete reality, at least so far as the latter is "important," this gap is of great significance. For the failure to state anything positive about the relations of ends to each other can then have only one meaning—that there are no significant relations, that is, that ends are random in the statistical sense. (1937, 59)

13. The common knowledge problem is how rational agents model—form, maintain, and alter—beliefs about other rational agents' beliefs. Rational expectations theory thus employs empirical models of the world to proxy expectation formation.

14. Wendt argues that "desires plus belief plus reason equals actions" (1999, 126).

15. Further problems of theoretical reduction are discussed in Weldes 1989, 360–66.

16. Kincaid offers another good example.

My belief that London is a wonderful city probably involves various neurological connections that do more than just process thoughts about London. If this many-many relation holds, then we have no way of equalizing kinds or descriptions one by one. That means we cannot reasonably substitute individualist descriptions for particular social ones. The explanation for a particular social process is always the same: the totality of individual processes. Reduction fails. (1996, 150)

17. Coleman offers two examples: "In meteorology, for example, predictions based on immediately prior weather conditions in the vicinity may be better than predictions based on interactions among many component parts

(various air masses and land and water surfaces). Similarly, macroeconomic predictions based on leading indicators that have known statistical association with subsequent system performance may give better predictions than will economic models based on interactions among parts of the system" (1990, 3).

18. Jackson and Pettit (1993) conclude that smaller and smaller mechanisms do not yield better and better explanations. The type of mechanism sought should correspond to the question asked.

19. Given these difficulties, some rational choice theorists reject extreme methodological individualism. For example, Taylor writes that "the proposition that explanatory changes 'behind' an explanandum must always terminate at individuals is implausible. [He rejects] views of institutions and social structure as formed by and explained *solely* in terms of individual action and takes little or no interest in the explanation of the actions or the desires and beliefs that inform them" (1989, 149). Stinchcombe adds that "where there is rich information on variations at the collective or structural level, while individual-level reasoning (a) has no substantial independent empirical support and (b) adds no new predictions at the structural level that can be independently verified, theorizing at the level of mechanisms is a waste of time" (1991, 380). I have advocated an alternative approach to collective action theorizing. Rather than seeking, say, the Coleman-Boudon microfoundations for Skocpol's theory of revolution, I suggest that rationalists are better off seeking the causes and consequences of collective action processes (Lichbach 1995). A collective action theory of revolution thus need not be parasitic on a structural theory, nor does it need to justify itself by intertheoretical reductionism. Lichbach and Seligman (2000, chap. 4) thus provide microfoundations and then seek their macrodeterminants.

20. But if individual preferences, resources, and actions are taken to be a function of macrostructures, contexts, and environments, where do the latter come from? Were they generated by individualism, in which case they are redundant, or did they come from outside individualism, in which case the individualistic approach is insufficient? Since a rationalist's theory is parasitic on truths about social entities and events, he or she must have a theory about the aspects of a social situation that are relevant.

21. Game-theoretic equilibria offer another attractive way to think about a rationalist synthesis. Equilibria are combinations of interests, identities, and institutions, or of choices, values, and facts. A set of actions are in equilibrium when they are based on a common set of beliefs and can function as a rule, institution, or agreement that constrains and channels individual actions. A Nash equilibrium is thus an agreement not to change strategies, or an institution that locks everyone in place and that is enforced by self-interest. Since there is often no unique path to cooperation, moreover, institutions generate expectations and hence serve as focal points for action. Interests thus set parameters, ideas pick out which parameter is relevant, and institutions coordinate equilibria by helping actors select among their interests.

22. For nearly two decades Parsons's (1937) unit act and related conceptual schemes dominated a great deal of social science. For example, many of the paradigms that became popular during the early flirtation of comparative politics with theory and generalization in the 1950s and 1960s were rooted in Parsons (e.g., structural functionalism). Parsons eventually moved from a general theory of action (a view of social order as resulting from the contingency of individualistic decision making and the voluntaristic interaction of isolated individuals in some larger framework of norms and values) to a structural-functional scheme (a systems theory of social order based on functional or systemic imperatives). My brief discussion of course does not encompass the entirety of Parsons's thought. For a review of his work, see Sculli and Gerstein 1985. An important recent contribution is Camic 1989.

23. Parsons (1937) in fact presents the unit act as mixing individual and collective levels. Actors have goals. The situation in which they find themselves is paired into two parts—conditions and means. Conditions are the material elements that cannot be molded to the actor's purposes; they are the obstacles that constrain agency about which actors develop beliefs. Means are the choices or actions undertaken by the actor that enable agency. Finally, actors approach the situation with certain norms. They use their own subjective judgments or standards to interpret or understand their situation. The pursuit of goals and the choice of means is therefore judged by normative considerations, ideal standards, or value expectations.

24. Parsons (1937) recognizes the value of his unit act framework as a synthesis. Hence, there are subjective and objective components of the socially embedded unit act: ends and norms can be described in a subjective way; conditions and means can be described in an objective manner. Parsons thus writes that

> action must always be thought of as involving a state of tension between two different orders of elements, the normative and the conditional. As process, action is, in fact, the process of alteration of the conditional elements in the direction of conformity with norms. Elimination of the normative aspect altogether eliminates the concept of action itself and leads to the radical positivistic position. Elimination of conditions, of the tension from that side, equally eliminates action and results in idealistic emanationism. Thus, conditions may be conceived at one pole, ends and normative rules at the other, means and effort as the connecting links between them. (732)

All (rational) action therefore emerges from the tension between subjective (cultural) and objective (structural), in other words, idealistic and realistic or normative and instrumental, considerations. Parsons thus tried to unite two basic streams of Western thought: positivism and idealism, normative and utilitarian approaches to social order. In the corpus of his work he explored the interdependence and interpenetration of values and conditions on individual and collective action.

25. This helps explain why today's battle of the paradigms is taking place among rationalists, culturalists, and structuralists and not among functionalists, systems theorists, and Marxists, as was the case in the 1960s. Theoretical thinking has sharpened, and the issues are now crisper. There is now a certain symmetry among the competing positions that was missing from the earlier "war of the schools."

26. There are of course several individualistic, micro-, or action approaches to inquiry besides rational choice. Subjectivist approaches (e.g., modern survey research), for example, offer a richer focus on the cognition, reasoning, motivation, and existential meaning that the individual actor attaches to his or her action. There are also richer intersubjective approaches to consciousness that emphasize praxis, or the enactment and performance of social acts.

27. Many rational choice theorists in comparative politics do recognize the need for plausible rival hypotheses and understand that the significant ones are structure (Geddes 1994, 6) and culture (Golden 1997, 77). For example, Laver and Shepsle indicate that "the ideal yardstick of course, would be to compare the performance of our theory against serious competitor theories" (1996, 159). Bates (1989, 10, 159) argues that some plausible rival hypotheses derive from simple game models and that others derive from dependency theory, neoclassical economics, international regimes, and systemic theories. Golden's (1997, 11) two foils are a median-voter model of union behavior (an existing rational choice theory) and a structural model of union behavior (a competing theory). Other rational choice comparativists recognize the alternatives posed by historical institutionalism (Ames 1987; Levi 1997).

28. Green and Shapiro (1994, x) also point out two related empirical problems with rational choice theory. First, rational choice theorists, in looking for a universal approach to politics, willingly "soak and poke" to fill in the big picture, i.e., the details of how rational choice theory applies. Second, excessive technical virtuosity produces ideas that are empirically intractable. As Golden indicates:

> The models of strikes that have been developed using the theory of incomplete information are often technically highly complex, while nonetheless based on radically simplified assumptions about the situation and the actors. This combination of mathematical complexity and conceptual simplicity tends to make these models difficult to use in empirical investigations. The assumptions bear only a vague approximation to real-world situations, the results are difficult to interpret, and critical variables almost impossible to operationalize. (1997, 6)

Green and Shapiro thus argue that there is a trade-off between rigorous formal modeling and insightful empirical work. Rationalists are driven first to impose drastic analytic simplifications—to reduce complexity, chaos, and disorder—in order to understand reality and then to change reality to fit the simplifications: "Empirical research becomes theory driven rather than problem driven, designed more to save or vindicate some variation of rational choice theory rather than to account for any specific set of phenomena" (1994, 6). Green and Shapiro thus charge that rationalists employ "a method-driven rather than problem-driven approach to research, in which practitioners are more eager to vindicate one or another universalist model than to understand and explain actual political outcomes" (33).

29. This section draws upon Lichbach 1996, sect. 1.4.2. See also Lichbach 1996, sect. 8.2.

30. Rapoport suggests that

> one of the useful results of game-theoretic analysis is that it provides specific contexts in which the different meanings of rationality can be defined. Those definitions, then, can serve as base lines. Situations having a reasonable resemblance to games can be studied with reference to these base lines of rationality. It is the departures from these base lines, especially systemic pattern-forming departures, which call for explanations in psychological, sociological, perhaps even pathological terms. (1970, 285)

From there, the issue, as Plott suggests, becomes one of relative accuracy: "Rather than inquire whether a theory is true or false, [economists] ask if the magnitude of error in the prediction of market phenomena is acceptable; or, if no concept of degree of acceptability is readily available, the question becomes which of several competing models is the most accurate, fully realizing that the best model might still be 'poor'" (1990, 147).

31. Nonrational choice analyses—chaos and complexity theory—have shown that causality is complicated. For example, although changes in initial conditions and scope conditions may be small, the effects may be large. The nonparity of cause and effect, perhaps due to nonlinearities, complicates equilibrium analysis. There is symmetric and asymmetric causality (King, Keohane, and Verba 1994, 89): causal effects differ when an explanatory variable increases as compared with when it decreases.

Other nonrational choice analyses—time-series models—have shown that social systems are open. Unexpected events, shocks, or triggers interact within a system and ultimately become incorporated into it. In addition to exogenous shocks, the equilibria of partially isolatable processes are upset by cycles and trends, and they become incorporated into them. Rather than structure, there is conjuncture. Hence, nothing social is absolutely exogenous, and it is difficult to isolate social phenomena experimentally.

32. The lack of explicit measurement, moreover, means that "it may be impossible to determine empirically whether a system is temporarily or permanently out of equilibrium" (Green and Shapiro 1994, 40).

33. Lipset and Rokkan (1967) offer the classic example of how the founding moments of institutions affect subsequent developments. They demonstrate that the initial alignments created by political parties outlast their origins and constrain subsequent electoral politics.

34. In sum, heritage is fate, and time matters. Weber uses the analogy of the loaded dice to understand the problem of historical legacies ([1903–17] 1949, 182–85).

35. Libecap offers an example.

For any given amount of mine output there appear to have been short-run equilibrium levels of legal support—levels at which there were no private net gains from further change. Additional ore strikes upset each equilibrium by raising both the benefits of exclusive control and owner-ship uncertainty. The latter was due to increased competition for the more valuable land. This led to lobby activity by owners who sought fur-ther legislative and judicial guarantees until a new short-run equilibrium was reached. This progression occurred until a stable long-run equilib-rium of support was obtained where uncertainty was minimal, regard-less of the amount of mine production. (1996, 57–58)

36. Ragin refers to "multiple conjunctural causation": several distinct combinations of causal forces can generate the same outcome in a set of cases (1987, 20). King, Keohane, and Verba (1994, 89) refer to multiple causality. There is also the issue of equifinality in general systems theory: the same out-come can be produced by different combinations of independent variables (e.g., for factory workers, high income can be earned by a college degree or four years of seniority).

Chapter 5

1. On culture, see Sahlins 1976; Wuthnow 1987; Wildavsky 1987; Laitin and Wildavsky 1988; Chilton 1988; Archer 1988; Alexander and Seidman 1990; Little 1991, chap. 4; Münch and Smelser 1992; Hollis 1994, chaps. 7–9; Calhoun 1994; and Berger 1995. On comparative political culture, see Kim 1964; Merkl 1970, chap. 3; Mayer 1972, chap. 9; Bill and Hardgrave 1973, chap. 3; Elkins and Simeon 1979; Inglehart 1988; Eckstein 1988; and Chilcote 1994, chap. 6. On interpretive approaches to the social sciences, see Geertz 1973; Berger and Luckman 1966; and Winch 1990.

2. The narrow span of human attention has cognitive roots:

The human eye and ear are highly parallel devices, capable of extracting many pieces of information simultaneously from the environment and decoding them in their significant features. Before this information can be used by the deliberative mind, however, it must proceed through the bottleneck of attention—a serial, not a parallel process whose informa-tion capacity is exceedingly small. Psychologists usually call this bottle-neck short-term memory, and measurements show reliably that it can hold only about six chunks (that is to say, six familiar items of informa-tion). (Simon 1985, 302)

3. An important corollary: since the human mind can operate independ-ently of experience, it can tie itself in knots. This produces the language

games of Wittgenstein—the talk of talk, the theory of theory, the methodology of methodology, and the philosophy of philosophy.

4. Lukes's excellent summary of Durkheim bears repeating.

> Durkheim saw society as the end and the source of morality. He thought of morality as "social" in a number of senses. Moral rules are social in origin ("the rules of morality are norms that have been elaborated by society"); they are general within a given society ("there is a general morality common to all individuals belonging to a collectivity"); they presuppose human association ("Let all social life disappear, and moral life will disappear with it"); they impose socially given obligations on the individual ("the obligatory character with which they are marked is nothing but the authority of society"); they provide an external framework for the individual ("like so many moulds with limiting boundaries into which we must pour our behavior"); they attach him to social goals ("Man . . . acts morally only when he takes a collectivity as the goal of his conduct"); and they necessarily involve altruism ("The basis of the moral life is the sentiment that man does not belong to himself alone"). (1985, 22)

5. Searle thus indicates that

> some rules do not merely regulate, they also create the very possibility of certain activities. Thus the rules of chess do not regulate any antecedently existing activity. It is not the case that there were a lot of people pushing bits of wood on board, and in order to prevent them from bumping into each other all the time and creating traffic jams, we had to regulate the activity. Rather, the rules of chess create the very possibility of playing chess. The results are constitutive of chess in the sense that playing chess is constituted in part by acting in accord with the rules. If you don't follow at least a large subset of the rules, you are not playing chess. (1995, 27)

Searle is making the point that "institutional facts exist only within systems of constitutive rules. The system of rules creates the possibility of facts of this type; and specific instances of institutional facts such as the fact that I won at chess or the fact that Clinton is president are created by the application of specific rules, for checkmate or for electing and swearing in presidents, for example" (1995, 28).

6. As Jackson notes, "If four strikes were permitted in baseball, we should expect not only different stratagems and plays on the part of coaches and players but also longer games and very likely more hits and runs. Even the skills and players would be affected by this rule change: the balance between pitching and hitting might be tilted in favor of the latter" (1993, 111–12).

7. Where there are obligatory beliefs and nonobligatory values, one finds lip service commitment, e.g., superficial democrats who go through the motions of voting. Where are nonobligatory beliefs and obligatory val-

ues, one finds unthinking cultural dopes, e.g., lower classes unaware of their false consciousness.

8. Löwith writes: "I therefore confess that the great duty 'know thyself,' which sounds so important, has always seemed to me to be suspect, like a trick of priests in a secret conspiracy who would like to confuse man through unfulfillable demands and lead him away from his proper activity in the external world to a false interior contemplation. A man knows himself insofar as he knows the world, which he perceives only within himself, and himself only within it. Every new object, properly examined, reveals a new organ within us" (1991, 10).

9. Lukes thus indicated that

> Rousseau's man was free through collective and impersonal forces liberating him from both personal dependence on others and from his own imperious desires: "the truly free man desires only what is possible and does as he pleases." For Rousseau and Durkheim, man "is free only when a superior force compels his recognition, provided, however, that he accepts this superiority and that his submission is not won by lies and artifice. He is free if he is held in check." As Durkheim frequently said, "liberty is the fruit of regulation." (1985, 284)

10. For example, Cohen argues that "religion provides an ideal 'blueprint' for the development of an informal political organization." He explains:

> [Religion] mobilizes many of the most powerful emotions which are associated with the basic problems of human existence and gives legitimacy and stability to political arrangements by representing these as part of the system of the universe. It makes it possible to mobilize the power of symbols and the power inherent in ritual relationship between various ritual positions within the organization of the culture. It makes it possible to use the arrangements for financing and administering policies of worship and associated places for welfare, education, and social activities of various sorts, to use these developing the organization and administration of political functions. Religion also provides frequent and regular meetings in congregations, where in the course of ritual activities, a great deal of informal interaction takes place, information is communicated, and general problems are formulated and discussed. The system of myths and symbols which religion provides is capable of being continuously interpreted and reinterpreted in order to accommodate it to changing economic, political and other social circumstances. (Cited in Ross 1997, 53)

11. By definition, not everyone can be an eccentric genius or a bohemian counterculturalist.

12. Searle offers an interesting story about how the rule or monopoly of force rests on consent.

The armed might of the state depends on the acceptance of a system of constitutive rules, much more than conversely. This was apparent at the time of the well-televised street riots in Los Angeles in 1992. Looters walked out of stores carrying valuable property while the police pointed their guns at them and ordered them to stop. The looters simply ignored the police, with no further consequences. The police power of the government is usable only against very small numbers, and even then only on the assumption that nearly everyone else accepts the system of status-functions. Once the number of lawbreakers is more than tiny, the police typically retreat to the station house or put on a ceremonial show of acting as if they were enforcing the law, as in Los Angeles, or quite often arrest the law-abiding citizenry . . . during the main period of rioting and looting, a store owner was arrested because he had armed himself with the intent of defending his store, and this arrest occurred while looters robbed nearby stores unhindered by the police. (1995, 90)

13. Durkheim, however, maintained that both objective external circumstances and subjective internal consciousness lend themselves to rigorous analysis. He writes that "the science of ethics" can supplement age-old moral and legal philosophies and holds out the possibility of developing descriptive and causal hypotheses about the origins, operation, and outcomes of rules in particular contexts ([1893] 1933, 35).

14. Weber offers a classic rejoinder to this perspectivism: "One does not need to be Caesar to understand Caesar" (cited in Calhoun 1995, 48).

15. This sort of holism is seen in some philosophies of science. It is present in the Duhem-Quine thesis and in Kuhn's (1970) background assumptions.

16. As Griffin writes: "Colligations are relational constructs that unify a number of past or contemporaneous actions and happenings that might otherwise have been viewed as discrete or disparate into a coherent, configured whole that gives *meaning to* and *explains* each of its elements and, simultaneously, is constituted by them." The New Deal, the Civil Rights movement, and an account of a particular space launching are all colligations. Such "colligations are analogous to systems: both are reconstituted by the relationships among their parts, and the parts of each are themselves parts per se rather than something else (or nothing) because only in their relationships do the parts form the whole" (1992, 417, emphasis in original).

17. A thick-headed version of norms ignores this problem and eliminates the tensions between individual and society. As Alexander puts it: "Moralistic and idealist theories often underestimate the ever present tension between individual volition and collective order. There is a strong tendency to assume an innate complementarity between the social self and that self's world—in religious terms, between the individual soul and the will of God, in political terms between individual will and collective will" (1987, 14–15).

18. The culturalists' efforts to locate a norm/rule for contravening norms/rules is similar to the rationalists' effort to locate a higher-order reason to deal with the problems of first-order reason.

19. Anomie, just like individualism, can be a social norm and hence norm-lessness the norm. This would be, as has been said, a society of Sartres.

20. This has important implications for normative approaches to social order. Widespread compliance does not prove that the system is legitimate: there can be an enforced armistice. Widespread rebellion does not prove the system is illegitimate: changing opportunities can be responsible for the dissidence. On the flaws of the common value solution, see Lichbach 1996, 211–13.

21. There are even rules about exceptions (Edgerton 1985).

22. Weber writes that "the appeal to national character is generally a mere confession of ignorance" ([1904–5] 1985, 88). Moore explicitly rejects culturalist arguments as follows: "To explain behavior in terms of cultural values is to engage in circular reasoning. . . . The problem is to determine out of what past and present experiences such an outlook arises and maintains itself. If culture has an empirical meaning, it is as a tendency implanted in the human mind to behave in certain specific ways 'acquired by man as a member of society' " (1966, 486).

23. Rationalists would add that observations about the existence of norms must confront the problems of preference falsification (what is said is not necessarily what is believed; Gibbard 1973; Satterthwaite 1975), revealed preference (what is done is not necessarily what is valued; Samuelson 1954), and preference aggregation (what is decided is not necessarily what is agreed; Arrow 1963).

24. While some norms are self-imposed by personal altruism (love, empathy, sympathy, and we-feeling), others are self-imposed by impersonal altruism (duty, commitment, principle, and conscience). Kant's idea of duty for duty's sake is a deontological (some actions are right or wrong, and hence the "right" is primary) rather than teleological (an action is right or wrong because it produces good or bad consequences, and hence the "good" is primary) view of morals.

25. A third possibility is a communicatively arrived-at rationality that bridges the two (Habermas).

26. If conditions matter to the exercise of norms, moreover, then perhaps the conditions are the real determinants of action.

27. Of course, the real test of a norm comes when there is a conflict between duty and inclination—habit and incentive. Norms are subject to convenience because of moral weakness, lack of self-discipline, and weakness of will.

28. A related problem: How does one separate the power of ideas from the power of the carriers of the ideas? Can ideas, for example, persuade independently of the power of their proponents? The ideas of key actors, moreover, often become relevant only after they become institutionalized in groups and organizations.

Chapter 6

1. On structural theories in the social sciences, see Skocpol 1979, chap. 1; Lloyd 1986, 1993; Alexander et al. 1987; Little 1991, chaps. 5, 6, 9; Hollis 1994, chap. 5; and Kontopoulos 1993.

2. Dreyfus and Rabinow suggest that "there are two kinds of structuralism: atomistic structuralism, in which the elements are completely specified apart from their role in some larger whole . . . and holistic or diachronic structuralism, in which what counts as a *possible* element is defined apart from the system of elements but what counts as an *actual* element is a function of the whole system of differences of which the given element is a part" (1983, xx, emphasis in original).

3. Other foci are possible. Mosca (1939), Pareto ([1920] 1980), and Michels ([1919] 1962) are concerned with the internal dynamics of elite coalitions and with the connections between elites and masses. While recognizing that the growing structural differentiation of society and the increasing division of labor affect political order, Huntington (1968) reversed the then dominant concern of modernization theorists and emphasized political institutionalization. Goldstone (1991), for a final example, explores how demographic patterns are behind revolution.

4. Two other thin structuralists deserve mention: Wallerstein (1974) studies world systems—large-scale structures of world capitalism set in world-historical perspective—and Braudel (1980) explores civilizations—societies of global significance.

5. Intraclass relations include what Skocpol calls "the degrees and kinds of solidarity of peasant communities" (1979, 115).

6. Interclass relations include what Skocpol calls "peasant autonomy from direct day-to-day supervision and control by landlords and their agents" (1979, 115). While rentier agrarian class relations—those with absentee nobles and a landed peasantry—beget numerous peasant conflicts, large estates managed by nobles and worked by serfs or landless labor resist peasant rebellions. Interclass relations also involve the political structures of local government and their relation to the peasantry and to the national government: "Those vulnerable agrarian orders also had sanctioning machineries that were centrally and bureaucratically controlled" (117).

7. In "statist societies" the state was autonomous from the nobility and hence better able to push through needed reforms (e.g., prerevolutionary Russia modernized more than prerevolutionary China).

8. Skocpol argues that peasant rebellions are a function, first, of whether the state penetrated the peasantry and consequently did not rely on local elites for social control and, second, of "the relaxation of state coercive sanctions against peasant revolts" (1979, 115).

9. Skocpol maintains, more specifically, that voluntaristic theories of revolution go wrong in four ways. First, they get the process wrong: revolutionary intentions develop in the course of revolution. Second, they get the coun-

terfactuals wrong: such theories imply a voluntaristic conception of political order and stability. Third, they get the causes wrong: revolutionary crises simply occur rather than being "made" by revolutionary movements. Finally, they get the outcomes wrong: states are not constructed by the revolutionary agency of vanguard parties.

10. Similar to the rationalists, however, Skocpol looks at revolution as the unintended consequence of the interaction of self-interested actors: "Revolutionary conflicts have invariably given rise to outcomes neither fully foreseen nor intended by—nor perfectly serving the interests of—any of the particular groups involved" (1979, 18). The term she uses is *conjuncture:* "the coming together of separately determined and not consciously coordinated (or deliberately revolutionary) processes and group efforts" (1979, 298 n. 44). Rather than focusing on explicitly formulated intergroup coalitions, she concentrates on "the conjunctural, unfolding interactions of originally separately determined processes" (320 n. 16).

11. Lloyd writes that "social history should be primarily concerned with the *causal explanation* of the history of recurrent *relational structures* of social life (i.e., the relatively enduring small- and large-scale structures of organized human relationships such as families, institutions, and economies)" (1986, 7, emphasis in original).

12. Whereas the logical necessity of thought, ideas, and language is not the same as the causal necessity of natural properties, powers, and processes, there is overlap between the deductive-nomological and causal-mechanism traditions. Salmon et al. thus write: "When we find that the same mechanism underlies diverse types of natural phenomena this ipso facto constitutes a theoretical unification" (1992, 39). Hence,

> when the search for hidden mechanisms is successful, the result is often to reveal a small number of basic mechanisms that underlie wide ranges of phenomena. The explanation of diverse phenomena in terms of the same mechanism constitutes theoretical unification. For instance, the kinetic-molecular theory of gases unified thermodynamic phenomena with Newtonian particle mechanics. The discovery of the double-helical structure of DNA, for another example, produced a major unification of biology and chemistry. (34).

13. Realism should be distinguished from positivism and idealism. As Bhaskar indicates, realism

> regards the objects of knowledge as the structures and mechanisms that generate phenomena; and the knowledge as produced in the social activity of science. These objects are neither phenomena (empiricism) nor human constructions imposed upon the phenomena (idealism), but real structures which endure and operate independently of our knowledge, our experience and the conditions which allow us to access them. Against empiricism, the objects of knowledge are structures, not events;

against idealism, they are intransitive (in the sense defined). On this conception, a constant conjunction of events is no more a necessary than it is a sufficient condition for the assumption of the operation of a causal law.

[Hence] there are three philosophies of science. Under classical empiricism, Hume sought knowledge of atomistic events and their relationships (constant conjunction). Theory is descriptive, instrumentalist, and fictionalist; the goal is to accumulate confirmed or not falsified facts. Under transcendental idealism, Kant saw ideas as artificial constructions; constructions of mind and community. The goal is to construct models of phenomena. Under transcendental realism, structure and understanding is of the different enduring general mechanisms that generate or produce specific phenomena. (1997, 25)

Hence realists claim that "the ultimate objects of scientific understanding are neither patterns of events nor models but the things that produce and the mechanisms that generate the flux of the phenomena of the world" (66).

14. Nominalists, for example those who employ ideal types, assert that universals are only names, mental concepts, and human-made conventions and not real entities. Universals are thus useful cubbyholes to classify and describe social phenomena. Description requires concepts, but there are many points of view. Which conceptual framework is employed is a pragmatic question rather than a question of truth.

Realists counter that one cannot eliminate the thing-in-itself. Structures are natural entities that have objective facticity. If our concepts are mental, subjective, and conventional, if our linguistic references have no real ontological counterparts, and if the natural order is not independent of our minds, alternative conceptual schemes proliferate and science becomes anarchical. The alternative concepts, moreover, will have no common ground in objective reality and hence will be incommensurable and irreconcilable. Realists thus reject the idea of nominalist classifications that are imposed by observers, created by the mind, and given by language. Divisions are discovered and not invented. Scientists must find the real and objective divisions in the world and divide nature at its joints.

15. Structures thus include *conjunctures:* the short-term confluence of various events, contingencies, and trends. Examples include "prices, taxes, rents, subsistence crises, trade cycles, contractions and expansions—in short, singular occurrences and short- and long-term movements and convergences chiefly of an economic character" (Zagorin 1982, 122–23).

16. Occam's razor expresses the opposing nominalist position: "Entities are not to be multiplied beyond necessity." A basic nominalist principle is thus simplicity: ceteris paribus, postulate the existence of observable rather than nonobservable entities. Realists oppose this view and suggest that there is something beyond the lawlike connections between observable appearances.

17. Inference to the best explanation is the foundation of realist argument

about unobservables: given that electron theory is the best explanation for a wide range of observable effects, it is reasonable to infer the existence of electrons as the cause.

18. As Lloyd writes:

Science is not on the whole concerned with the supposedly unique features of phenomena, whether they be particular particles, atoms, molecules, cells, organisms, animals, persons or social or natural systems. Science is primarily concerned, rather, with universals, i.e., with the general defining characteristics, modes of being and causes of types, classes, and patterns of phenomena. Without a notion of related types of entities, which have discoverable, relatively fixed dispositions, powers, and potentialities, there can be no scientific enquiry, since such enquiry consists fundamentally of uncovering such properties and in showing how actual phenomena relate to those properties. (1986, 34)

19. Many structuralists thus follow Aristotle's teleology: All objects have a natural tendency to fulfill their inner purposes or natures; nature, a kind of potential to be realized, is a collection of substances constituted by essential qualities and ends; the end state is rest and fulfillment; and equilibrium is the natural state of bodies.

20. Note that rationalists focus on a different set of structural logics: contradictions, paradoxes, and ironies involving unintended consequences. Smith thus argues that society organizes itself in the pursuit of private gain and thereby produces a market governed by the laws of supply and demand ([1776] 1976).

21. Common outcomes thus may be the result of common causal histories. Little indicates that one

characterizes a collection of events or occurrences in terms of a hypothesized common causal mechanism. The term *crater* illustrates this type of theoretical construct in natural science. A crater is not merely a circular formation on the surface of a planet; rather, it is a circular formation with a particular causal etiology (having resulted from the impact of a large object). Classifying a given formation as a crater, therefore, brings with it a hypothesis about the causal history of the formation; if that hypothesis is falsified, then the attribution of the concept to the formation must be withdrawn. (1989, 193)

Little further indicates that "examples of a causal etiology concept in the social sciences include Marx's conception of a crisis of underconsumption and Naquin's concept of a millenarian rebellion. Each involves a hypothesis about the causal antecedents of the crisis of rebellion to which the concept is applied" (193).

22. Wendt maintains that "structures can have two kinds of effects, causal and constitutive. A causal effect means that X causes Y or that X produces Y.

A constitutive effect means that X presupposes Y or that X is X because Y is Y. The latter describes how X's properties make a Y what it is. For example, the structure of the master-slave relationship causes slaves to rebel when the master becomes abusive. By defining them as the property of the master in the first place, the structure thus constitutes them as slaves and their protests as rebellion" (1999, 25, 27, 78, 372–73).

23. Some argue that the structures of the human-made world are derivative of material conditions in the natural environment. Moore (1966), for example, attributes the difference between English and French development to environmental facts that promoted the cultivation of wool rather than wine.

24. In practice, of course, the level of constraints varies from situation to situation and may produce choices that are more or less limited. Inglehart thus points out that

> on one hand, one can conceive of situations so totally rigidly structured that virtually nothing the individual can do affects his or her fate. The situation of a prisoner in a concentration camp may be very near this extreme. On the other hand, one can also conceive of situations in which what happens mainly reflects the individual's behavior; a libertarian society with lavish and well-distributed resources might approach this ideal. In the real world, one is almost never at either extreme; outcomes reflect both internal orientations and external constraints. (1990, 18)

Hence, action is both subjective and conditional. The levels of structure and action in any problem, moreover, vary over time: both are historical products and constructions. Luckmann thus writes that "perhaps the ratio of personal actions to institutional processes which determines the course of history is not unchangeable but varies historically itself. Perhaps at different times in history, under different forms of social life, the portion of human action (as against the portion of social institutions) which determines history grows or diminishes significantly" (1975, 6). Hence, in eras characterized by a high level of individualism, rational action perspectives may be more valuable.

25. Bendix retorts that anyone can "refuse simply to submit to both the conditions and their consequences, but rather to respond to them and hold oneself responsible" (1984, xvi).

26. On the efforts of contemporary structuralists to counter determinism, see Alexander 1988, 91–93.

Chapter 7

1. Is there is a cultural process at work here? Bloom notes the appeal of "an impossible synthesis of opposites" for a society "that wants to be told that it enjoys all good things." He suggests that "our desire for conflict reduction accounts for the great popularity of the word 'dialectic'—in our sense, the Marxist's sense—for, beginning in opposites it ends in synthesis, all charms and temptations united in harmony" (1987, 229). He continues:

Conflict is the evil we most want to avoid, among nations, among individuals and within ourselves. Nietzsche sought with his value philosophy to restore the harsh conflicts for which men were willing to die, to restore the tragic sense of life, at a moment when nature has been domestic and men become tame. That value philosophy was used in America for exactly the opposite purpose—to promote conflict-resolution, bargaining, harmony. If it is only a difference of values, then conciliation is possible. We must respect values, but they must not get in the way of peace. Thus Nietzsche contributed to what he was trying to cure. Conflict, the condition of creativity for Nietzsche, is for us a cry for therapy. (238)

2. The idea of function captures this mix of institutions and values. Structures always serve some purpose that involves normative judgments and a prior assignment of value. For example, there is value to human life, survival, reproduction, and health; hence the function of the heart is to pump blood, and a malfunctioning heart does not perform its valued function. There is value to private property in economic life; hence, the function of a court system is to protect valued property rights.

3. There may be unintended consequences at work here. Wuthnow, Hunter, Bergesen, and Kurzweil point out that "cultural products or artifacts are often objectivated in the social world in very different ways than their producers originally intended. Subjective or intended meanings, in different words, need not correspond with cultural products. Herein is strong justification to follow the cue offered by the structuralists, namely to view cultural artifacts as concrete observable objects not reducible to subjective meanings and to analyze them as such" (1984, 73).

4. The poststructuralism of Michel Foucault and Jacques Derrida is a combination of structure and culture that involves decentering the subject. Poststructuralism, that is, reacts against the primacy of the self or against a transcendental and existential ego that takes precedence over the relationships that condition the self and constitute its meaning, choices, and freedom.

5. Medieval scholasticism tried to join faith and reason by suggesting that religion can be rational or that there are rational grounds for faith.

6. Goldstein and Keohane argue that interests affect the institutionalization of ideas via the creation of further interests: "Once ideas have influenced organizational design, their influence will be reflected in the incentives of those in the organization and those whose interests are served by it. In general, when institutions intervene, the impact of ideas may be prolonged for decades or even generations. In this sense, ideas can have an impact even when no one genuinely believes in them as principles or causal statements." The origin of this process is power: "Although this institutionalization may reflect the power of some idea, its existence may also reflect the interests of the powerful." Hence, "politically relevant ideas are not formulated independently of interests and power," and "an idea that becomes institutionalized essentially for

reasons of power and interest ultimately has an independent impact" (1993, 20). Science, for example, is an institution that creates reward structures (norms and incentives) such that rational individuals attempt to promote the ends of science. It is therefore in the interests of scientists to be perceived as engaged in research programs that are fertile (Laudan 1990, 155); in turn, a "progressive" rather than "degenerative" research program is a widely accepted scientific norm (Lakatos 1970). Scientists who are served by this norm have a collective action problem in trying to protect their interests.

7. Weber's analysis of status groups demonstrates the sophisticated connections that can be drawn between interests and identities. For Weber, "The world view of a status group is never solely a response to material conditions or a product of economic interests. It is also the product of ideas that are the result of human inspiration in response to a spiritual challenge" (Bendix 1962, 260). Weber thus suggested that groups have an "elective affinity" for certain types of ideas. As Gerth and Mills put it:

> The decisive conception by which Weber relates ideas and interests is that of "elective affinity," rather than "correspondence," "reflection," or "expression." . . . For Weber, there is hardly ever a close connection between the interests or the social origin of the speaker or of his following with the concern of the idea during its inception. The ancient Hebrew prophets, the leaders of the Reformation, or the revolutionary vanguard of modern class movements were not necessarily recruited from the strata which in due course became the prime bearers of their respective ideas. Only during the process of routinization do the followers "elect" those features of the idea with which they have an "affinity," a "point" of "coincidence" or "convergence." (In Weber 1946, 62–63)

Groups are attracted to particular symbols, Weber argues, because of the material challenges they face. Different status groups are therefore attracted to different symbols on account of their occupational experiences: magic appeals to peasants, religions of the book to city dwellers, and fatalism to warriors. The Prussian Junkers, for another example, responded to the frontier society of Eastern Europe by idealizing a military way of life.

However, one cannot reduce the ideas of a status group to its material interests. So one must also study the group's ideal interests.

> Weber emphasized that the collective actions of *Junkers* as well as of farm workers could not be understood in economic terms alone. It also was necessary to analyze the ideas derived from the subculture of each group—in Weber's terms, its "style of life"—which entered into the evaluation of its economic interests. In this sense the farm workers were as much a *Stand* as the *Junkers,* for their resistance to personal subservience had become as ineradicable an element of their whole outlook as the patriarchal manner had become part and parcel of the *Junkers'* way of life. (Bendix 1962, 85)

8. Many others recognize that social science involves all three perspectives. Kant's triad is man (soul) or the rational individual, world or structure, and God or culture/meaning (Kaufman 1992, 38). Selznick indicates that Weber's main concern was with "ideas, interests, and institutions" (1992, 78). Parsons argues that there are "three great classes of theoretical systems . . . systems of nature, action and culture" (1937, 762). Hall indicates that "ideas have real power in the political world, however . . . they do not acquire political force independently of the constellation of institutions and interests already present there" (1989, 390). Heclo indicates that "whatever the preferred political science approach, the three common building blocks are ideas, interests, and institutions"; he thus refers to the "codependency among ideas, institutions, and interests" (1994, 375, 380). Padgett and Anseell suggest that "rules induce roles, which induce interests, which induce strategic exchanges, which lock in patterns of collective action that depend on the rules" (cited in Katznelson 1997, 107). Wendt argues that "the structure of any social system will contain three kinds of elements: material conditions, interests, and ideas. . . . [I]dealists and materialists disagree importantly about their relative weight, with interests being the central battleground. . . . Materialists privilege material conditions, and try to show that they largely determine interests. Idealists privilege ideas, and try to show that *they* largely determine interests" (1999, 139–40, emphasis in original). Interests, in other words, originate in ideas (culture) and/or material power (social and human structure). Finally, McAdam, Tarrow, and Tilly's (1997) theory of collective action weaves together action ("acting collectively"), culture ("framing collective action"), and structure ("political opportunities" and "mobilizing structures").

9. The case of protest is instructive. Kitschelt suggests that the cultural construction of meaning affects dissent.

> The central argument forwarded by cultural analysis of social movement mobilization is that there is no one-to-one relationship of social modes of production, concrete grievances, and opportunity structures to particular types of collective action. That is, the symbolic interpretation of social institutions may affect the relative strength of movement mobilization as well as the types and objectives of collective practices. Variations in the meanings manufactured by social movements are attributed to an ongoing, freewheeling cultural definition of claims by social actors. (1985, 301)

But also crucial to behavior is how the world is "really" constructed. Eckstein comments: "A structural hypothesis singles out, so to speak, 'objective' social conditions as crucial for the occurrence of internal war; aspects of a society's 'setting,' such as economic conditions, social stratification, and mobility, or geographic and demographic factors" (1965, 148).

10. Weber's critique of Marx is that these linkages are weak, or that class situation does not necessarily produce class action. As Weber puts it: "The rise

of societal or even of communal action from a common class situation is by no means a universal phenomenon" (1946, 183). Moreover:

> That men in the same class situation regularly react in mass actions to such tangible situations as economic ones in the direction of those interests that are most adequate to their average number is an important and after all simple fact for the understanding of historical events. Above all, this fact must not lead to that kind of pseudo-scientific operation with the concepts of "class" and "class interests" so frequently found these days, and which has found its most classic expression in the statement of a talented author, that the individual may be in error concerning his interests but that the "class" is "infallible" about its interests. (184–85)

11. Rationalists also recognize that social order occurs when norms or identities direct action or interests into paths that sustain structures or institutions. Garrett and Weingast thus suggest that

> in order to succeed, institutions must employ and perpetuate a *normative system* that translates the general idea for capturing the gains from cooperation into specific expectations and behavior that make it possible to capture them. It is a normative system because it requires the institution to define what constitutes cooperation and defection and hence good and bad behavior. . . . The necessity to create a successful normative system in turn places strong and direct bounds on the decisions and constructions issued by the institution. In the context of a set of actors voluntarily participating in an attempt to cooperate, the system must not only capture the potential gains from cooperation but distribute them in a manner that makes all better off. Otherwise, participation would fall off and the attempt would fail. (1993, 204–5)

Ferejohn offers an example.

> Parliamentary institutions, as collectivities, can become effective participants in governing only to the extent that they can create and sustain internal hierarchical or vertical relations of power among independently chosen members that permit them to react promptly and effectively to external events. Each such creation rests on a set of shared supporting beliefs and expectations that serves both to explain and to justify the inequality of powers to relatively equal members. This structure of beliefs and expectations must have the property that all the agents find it rational to act in such a way that the institutional structure is sustained. (1993, 208)

Ideas (values and beliefs) become embedded in institutions and therefore guide individual and collective action by defining interests and identities. The carriers of ideas are then groups who act in their collective interest in some institutional context.

12. This section draws upon Lichbach and Seligman 2000.

13. On the structure and agent problem in international relations, see Wendt 1987.

14. The individual-society issue is important normatively. All societies must deal with value conflicts among individuals and harmonize social norms. All societies must establish principles of the good life and reconcile them with the principles of the good society. And all societies must create an ethical totality in the face of fragmentation, polytheism, and a relativistic "everything goes" mentality. Societies must, in short, establish legitimacy. However, our Western values lead us to wish to preserve agency, as did Weber. One element of the structure-action problem thus revolves around individuals: free will versus fate. The question is how to mix voluntaristic action with structural determination. Action implies freedom but structure implies constraint. Duesenberry captured the difference: "Economics is all about why people make choices, and sociology is all about why people don't have choices to make" (quoted in Van Den Berg 1998, 230). Humans must deal with their fate (structure) and their freedom (action). People are morally free but social life is determined by laws. The individual-society issue therefore cuts to the core of the liberal agenda.

15. The individual-society or structure-action problematique is associated with several major issues in positive political theory: personality (being, autonomy, existence, alienation), culture (legitimacy, trust, morality, justice, ethics), economics (market, socialism, equity, efficiency, welfare), society (civil society, contract, corporatism, community), conflict and cooperation (peace, war), and politics (the state, democracy, liberalism).

16. The structure and action problem can be understood historically. Montesquieu's aphorism is that "it is men who first make institutions, thereafter institutions form men" (cited in Welch 1980, 200). Marx's aphorism (see note 40, this chapter) is "Men make their own history, but they do not make it just as they please." Moore argued that "there is no need to deny the historical significance of moderate and intelligent statesmen. But it is necessary to perceive the situation within which they worked" (1966, 39). In other words, social structures, the result of past human agency, preexist action, but persist and change because of current reproductive and transforming actions of human agents. To operate under a capitalist market and follow its dictates, for example, is to unintentionally reproduce the property rights system. To join a socialist movement, on the other hand, is to attempt to transform structures as a result of an intentional human effort.

The relation between structure and action is therefore historically contingent. Historical work attempts to discover the importance of structures and hence the limits of what the deliberate actions of individuals could accomplish. Bendix suggests that "the scope of free action which was once available to historical actors, and which remains open to contemporary conduct, should be discovered" (1984, xvi).

17. Giddens argues that research programs in social science are either "strong on action, weak on structure; or strong on structure, weak on action." He also maintains that the difference between structural and action theories "is a difference of emphasis, there is no clear-cut line that can be drawn between these, and each, crucially, has to be in principle rounded out by a concentration upon the duality of structure" (1984, 288). His own approach, "structuration," attempts to mix the two.

18. Alexander indicates that "one sidedness has created debilitating contradictions within both the micro and macro traditions" and hence that analysts should mix structure and action (1988, 77).

19. Lloyd writes of "the duality of structure—i.e., structure as both the *condition* for action and the *consequence* of action" (1986, 171, emphasis in original). He raises the following questions.

> How is it that an entity such as society, which neither is constituted by individuals nor has holistic powers, can develop some emergent properties and powers of its own? How do those properties and powers relate to the properties and powers of persons? Is constant individual and collective consciousness and action necessary to their continuance? Will society disintegrate if people stop acting in the required ways? (17)

A resolution is "methodological structurism," in which "persons have agential power, structures have conditioning power" (1993, 7, 46).

20. Turner writes:

> the individual-society, subject-object, and micro-macro dichotomies do not constitute a dualism, but a "duality." That is, people in interaction use the rules and resources that constitute social structure in their day-to-day routines in contexts of co-presence, and in so doing, they reproduce these rules and resources of structure. . . . One cannot understand action and interactions without reference to the rules and resources of social structures, whereas one cannot fully understand large-scale, long-term institutional structures without knowledge of how actors use the rules and resources of these institutional structures in concrete interaction. (1986, 458)

21. Taylor writes: "But the fact that individual actions, attitudes and beliefs are caused by structures or by anything else does not make them explanatorily irrelevant, any more than the fact that structures are in part the product of individual acts makes structures explanatorily irrelevant. We need, then, both individualist explanations of structures and other macrophenomena *and* structuralist explanations (amongst other kinds of explanation) of individual attitudes and beliefs. To deny either side of this supposition is to deny any causal force to structure or to individuals, to attach all the explanatory power to one or the other" (1988b, 94).

22. Wendt suggests that "in both a causal and constitutive sense, therefore,

structure is an ongoing effect of process . . . social processes are always struc-tured, and social structures are always in process" (1999, 186).

23. Snidal (1985) refers to a (game) model embedded in a (international relations) theory.

24. Huckfeldt and Sprague (1993) suggest that laws vary across contexts and hence that one make cross-level inferences with respect to the contexts within which a process occurs.

25. Contemporary network theorists (Knoke 1990) view structure and action as mutually constitutive.

26. Since Przeworski and Teune's (1970) work is so important to compara-tivists but yet not thought of in terms of social theory, it bears elaboration here. Przeworski and Teune argue that comparativists typically compare social phenomena that are observed in different social systems. They argue that this macro-cross-national work is usually too holistic because whole sys-tems are complex units of interrelated components. Particular systems, more-over, are residues of these theoretical variables. Comparativists can thus gen-eralize beyond the limits of any particular historical system by replacing proper names of social systems by relevant variables. The assumption here is that the social system is a set of spatiotemporal parameters that are reducible to variables: names of social systems are residues of variables. System-level differences are variables and not typological configurations.

Przeworski and Teune thus advocate the alternative of cross-level infer-ence. Their point of departure is a population of units (probably individuals) at the level observed. They thus argue that "in order to develop theories about social systems—that is, to study them generally or comparatively—it is neces-sary to observe phenomena within systems." Hence we "observe relations among data with a particular system" (132, 133).

The initial assumption is that all within-system cases (e.g., individuals) were drawn from the same population; in other words, that systemic factors do not play any role in explaining the observed factor. Further investigation consists of tweaking this assumption. As long as this assumption is not rejected, the analysis remains at the *intrasystemic* level; whenever the assumption is rejected, systemic factors must be considered. Przeworski and Teune therefore argue that there are relations between observations within a system that are structured by the system. Comparativists might eventually have to explain within-system processes and relations with system-level conditions. Prze-worski and Teune thus suggest that "comparative research should focus on *within-system relationships* rather than *attributes of systems*," that "the inter-action of various characteristics within each social system creates *unique* or *varying* patterns of determination in relation to each system," and that "the same theories must be evaluated in different system settings" (72, 134, empha-sis in original). This procedure does not apply only to countries. The sample could consist of revolutions, civil wars, insurrections, or protest campaigns. The question is how internal processes differ across structures.

27. This is referred to as methodological situationalism: the individual actor's environment, context, or setting (Popper 1965; Farr 1987; Weber [1924] 1968)—the political, economic, social, and cultural structure—provides opportunities and constraints, presents goals and means, and affects costs and benefits. Institutions thus define, transform, mobilize, organize, and activate preferences, beliefs, endowments, and technologies.

Social-situation rationalists (sect. 3.1) recognize these points. Bates indicates that "because the collective-choice approach is sensitive to the determining power of cultural and institutional settings, it is highly resistant to any effort to artificially 'homogenize' human behavior. . . . [T]he approach *requires* the use of a precise and detailed knowledge of cultures, structures and institutional environments. It requires a far more complex vision of man" (1983, 140, emphasis in original). Elster argues that "a simple scheme for explaining an action is to see it as the end result of two filtering operations. We begin with a large set of all abstractly possible actions that an individual might undertake. The first filter is made up of all the physical, economic, legal, and psychological *constraints* that the individual faces. The actions consistent with these constraints form his *opportunity set.* The second filter is a mechanism that determines which action within the opportunity set will actually be carried out" (1989b, 13). The latter mechanism could involve rational choice. Hence, rationalists should not focus only on strategic action, oblivious to the situation. They must analyze action in concrete situations, and for this they need both general models and detailed case studies.

28. Bates (1989) studies how the impact of an exogenous shock is filtered through social structures and institutions.

29. Becker (1976) maintains that general equilibrium models are never used in practice. Economists use partial equilibrium models with specific institutions.

30. It is widely recognized that one must place a game within a well-defined context. Wildavsky thus argues that "the rationality of prisoners, like rationality in general, is context dependent" (1992, 10). Hechter points to "the insufficiency of game theory for the resolution of real-world collective action problems" because one must figure out how to link the model with reality, the abstract categories with actual social structures (1992, 33). Friedman in effect agrees.

No one game is *the correct game* independent of context. As social scientists we must tailor the games we use so that they are descriptive of the situations we wish to analyze. My own experience has been that "off the shelf" game-theoretic models have not been useful for my work in oligopoly. There is an approach which has been useful that a person trained in game theory brings to a situation. There are also basic concepts such as *move, strategy, game,* and *noncooperative equilibrium* that have also been useful. But new models have had to be forged to suit the economic circumstances that were under analysis. (1992, 48, emphasis in original)

Game theory thus examines how politics—strategizing processes—take place within contexts and institutions that structure outcomes.

31. Mechanisms are processes of human interaction. Environments (contexts, backgrounds, situations, institutions) endow the preferences and beliefs that allow mechanisms to work. Since some mechanisms work only in certain environments, the comparative study of environments or the comparative statics of mechanisms is an important part of social science. For example, one may begin with a mechanism to solve a collective action problem and then look for environments in which it will produce Pareto-optimal results.

32. Structures are the constants—the long-term rules (norms) and relationships (institutions) among actors—that contain processes, or the variables. Examples of these short-term transactions among actors include discrete interactions and events such as collective action and coalition formation. Processes are embedded in structures and produce new outcomes or structures. The basic idea is that the relations and rules of a social order structure the transactions among individuals. Hence, by *processes within structures* I mean transactional processes among the parts (individuals) of material and ideal structures. In short, structures condition processes that recondition (reproduce and transform) the structures.

33. Students of the new institutional economics (North 1990; Bates 1989) argue that one must place processes within institutions to study outcomes. Micro-macro or cross-level theorizing is consistent with Shepsle's (1979) view of social choice and the Boudon-Coleman diagram cited earlier. Three examples are illustrative.

North supplements neoclassical assumptions with "(1) a theory of ideology and morality to help explain behavior; (2) a theory of property rights to help explain incentives for economic behavior; (3) a theory of the state as the enforcer of property rights and setter of rules of exchange and cooperation; (4) a theory of the structure of the economy in terms of these constitutional rules; (5) a theory of the population/resource relationship" (1981, 46–47, see Lloyd 1986, 234–35).

Levi argues that one must bridge the macro-micro gap and speaks about "Bringing People Back into the State" (1988, 185). She writes that "a process of collective action underlies the acquisition and maintenance of rule. To become ruler requires first coordinating a group of individuals who face a common enemy or problem, but rule ultimately rests on control of resources necessary to enforce participation in the dominant group by the individuals who agreed to become its members. Successful rulers are those able to maintain the group, able to maintain its relative dominance over the opposition, and able to build sufficient coercive power to block rivals." Hence, "rulers are always predatory, but they cannot always do as they please" (1988, 46–47).

Lichbach's (1995) study of protest and rebellion urges that one look for the structures (preexisting organizations, political opportunities, labor markets, etc.) that produce collective dissent by helping or hindering collective action solutions. The goal is to mix Olson's social choice with Mill's sociological imagination and examine collective action in comparative and historical perspective.

34. Riker and Weimer suggest that

social science consists of generalizations about two kinds of objects: transactions and institutions. By transactions we mean such things as exchanges of goods in a market, decisions on expenditures in a legislature, parental division of child care tasks, or, in short, all kinds of choices made jointly by two or more people. By institutions, on the other hand, we mean more or less agreed upon and relatively stable rules that guide people in carrying out their transactions. They can be thought of as sets of widely shared expectations . . . about how people will behave in particular social, economic, or political circumstances.

In generalizing about transactions we take some particular governing institutions, or set of related institutions, as given and then describe the outcomes that result from the governed transactions. For a particular kind of transaction under a particular institution, we can describe some specific equilibrium outcome such as the equilibrium price for a certain good in an auction market, or the equilibrium sum of public expenditures under majority rule, or the equilibrium division of parental tasks in a particular culture.

In generalizing about institutions, on the other hand, we seek to explain theoretically why it is that some form of institution leads to a characteristic type of outcome and why it appears in some societies and not others. For markets we seek to explain why equilibrium price is at the point that demand exhausts supply and why some goods are traded in markets and others are not; for legislatures we seek to explain why and when choices end up close to the preferences of the median voter and why legislatures take different forms in different countries; and for partners we seek to explain how linkage affects the roles of fathers and uncles and mothers and aunts and how the norms covering these roles evolved. (1995, 82)

35. Arguments about methodological individualism are advanced by Boudon (1987) and Coleman (1987).

36. Geertz (see the review in Lloyd 1986, 274) explores how macrochanges in employment, investment, economic growth, and so on set the context for microcultural changes at the individual and group levels in villages and hence how capitalist entrepreneurship emerged. Gurr (1970) studies how the balance of coercion and the balance of institutional support affect individual involvement in protest and rebellion. Efforts by survey researchers include Campbell et al.'s (1960) funnel of causality, Barnes, Kaase, et al.'s (1979) state-organiza-

tions-behavior model, and Verba and Nie's (1972) model of participation.

37. Even Skocpol eventually softened her structuralism and recognized the importance of both structure and action. She writes that

> few aspects of *States and Social Revolutions* have been more misunderstood than its call for a "nonvoluntarist," "structuralist" approach to explaining social revolutions. "Nonintentionalist at the macroscopic level" might have been a better way to label my approach. For the point is simply that no single acting group, whether a class or ideological vanguard, deliberately shapes the complex and multiply determined conflicts that bring about revolutionary crises and outcomes. The French Revolution was not made by a rising capitalist or bourgeois class or by the Jacobins; the Russian Revolution was not made by the industrial proletariat or even the Bolshevik party. If the purpose is to explain in cross-nationally relevant terms why revolutions break out in some times and places and not others, and why they accomplish some changes and not others, we cannot achieve this by theorizing as if some grand intentionality governs revolutionary processes. . . . Since the historical case studies of *States and Social Revolutions* are replete with groups acting for material, ideal and power goals, it should be apparent that I never meant to read intentional group action out of revolutions—only to situate it theoretically for the explanatory purposes at hand. (1985)

Skocpol thus writes of "the dialectic of meaningful actions and structural determinants" and acknowledges that historical analysis requires both (1984, 4). This modification brings Skocpol's basic approach to revolution, as "a complex unfolding of multiple conflicts that ultimately give rise to outcomes not originally foreseen or intended by any of the particular groups involved," close to rationalist thinking (1976, 169). She thus claims that "social-scientific analysts of revolutions almost never . . . give sufficient analytic weight to the conjunctural, unfolding interactions of originally separately determined processes" (1979, 320).

38. Tilly (1984) is concerned with how the development of capitalism and the nation-state affects collective action.

39. Skocpol's comments: "Moore has made it evident through his practice over several decades that our explanations of social order and social change can only benefit from systematically taking account of not only structural constraints but also the motivations, perceptions, and choices of human beings. His work provides a convincing demonstration of the proposition that the social processes that are most worth examining in detail and seeking to understand are those that have not only helped to shape the aspirations and values to which we are attached, but have also circumscribed the means and the opportunities that we have to pursue them" (1984, 335). But Moore never tied structure and culture together: *Social Origins* is strong on structure and weak on culture; *Injustice* is strong on culture and weak on structure.

40. Marxists appreciate the micro-macro gap, or the problem of linking

economic crises to political action. Marx wrote in the "18th Brumaire" that "men make their own history, but they do not make it just as they please; they do not make it under circumstances chosen by themselves, but under circumstances directly encountered, given and transmitted from the past. The tradition of all the dead generations weighs like a nightmare on the brain of the living" (1962, i, 252, in Abrams 1982, 34).

41. Rational choice Marxists (Przeworski 1985a, 1985b; Savia 1988; Roemer 1982; Elster 1985) recognize that one must situate general social processes of action within the specific institutions of society. Nordlinger (1988, 880) and Evans and Stephens (1988, 761) thus argue that statist and historical political economy approaches are compatible with rational choice approaches and that a combination would be useful.

42. In order to study outcomes, one must place specific institutions within their historical context. Without microfoundations, this may be seen as:

shock + historical context → institution → outcome

With microfoundations this may be seen as:

shock + historical context → institution → outcome
$\downarrow$ $\uparrow$
individual situation → individual act

43. This version of realism leads to a "processes within structures" perspective. Little argues that

> social entities possess causal powers only in a weak and derivative sense: they possess characters that affect individuals' behavior in simple, widespread ways. Given features of the common constitution and circumstances of individuals, such alternations at the social level produce regularities of behavior at the individual level that eventuate in new social circumstances. . . . [In] Skocpol's causal analysis of the state and revolution . . . causal powers derive entirely from the ways in which the institutions of the state assign incentives, powers, and opportunities to various individuals. (1993, 190)

Lloyd argues similarly.

> Actions always take place within structures of relations, rules, roles, and classes. But structures are not agents in the way that some functionalists and holists seem to believe. They do have powers of a *conditioning* kind, which set parameters for the exercising of human agential action, but they cannot cause themselves to change. This means that humans are not pure agents because their power is limited and constrained both internally and externally and it always means that individual and collective human action is the fundamental agent of history. Thus methodological structuralism is not reductionist, holding that explanations of

mechanism have to be given on both the micro and macro levels. (1986, 37, emphasis in original)

Causal realism thus mixes structure and action. Little thus writes that

social causality depends on regularities; but these are not generally social regularities, but rather lawlike characteristics of agents (e.g., the central axioms of rational choice theory). I would assert, then that the rock-bottom causal stories—the governing regularities for the social sciences—are stories about the characteristics of typical human agents. The causal powers of a particular social institution—a conscription system, a revenue system, a system of democratic legislation—derive from the incentives, powers, and knowledge that these institutions provide for participants. (1993, 195–96)

44. For a nice discussion of how Weber integrates interpretive and causal thinking, or motives and Humean-type statistical generalizations, see Zuckerman 1991, 75–76.

45. I therefore do not advocate such a grand synthesis—that is, a multidimensional conceptual scheme transcending all antinomies—in the manner of Parsons 1937, Habermas 1984, Bourdieu 1977, Giddens 1984, and Alexander 1982. Rather than developing a grand synthesis at a paradigmatic level, I advocate the use of mechanisms as an approach to social theory. These mechanisms derive from the rationalist, culturalist, and structuralist research programs. These points are illustrated in Lichbach 1995 and 1996 and elaborated in the final chapter.

Chapter 8

1. Weber argues that since "perception of [reality's] meaningfulness to us is the presupposition of its becoming an *object* of investigation," knowledge of reality is always knowledge from particular points of view ([1903–17] 1949, 76). Parsons maintains that "observation is always in terms of a conceptual scheme" (1937, 597). Parkin writes that "it is illusory to imagine that we can somehow capture the 'real essence' of social reality. Social reality does not possess a real essence because it is always capable of being constructed or represented in various different ways. What counts as social reality depends pretty much upon the conceptual apparatus through which we view it in the first place" (1982, 28). Simmel puts it well.

We cannot describe the individual phenomenon as it really was, because we cannot describe the whole. A science of everything that happens is impossible not only for reasons of unmanageable quantity; it is also impossible because it would lack a point of view—a requirement for producing a construct that would satisfy our criteria for knowledge. There is no knowledge per se. Knowledge is possible only insofar as it is produced and structured by concepts that are qualitatively determined and inevitably partial and biased. If the criterion for knowledge is that it be perfectly general it would be impossible to identify or distinguish any element of reality. This is the deeper reason why there are only histories, but no History per se. What we call general or world history can at best be the simultaneous application of a variety of those diverse viewpoints or it may be the sort of history that throws into relief the aspects of the event that are most significant from the perspective of our sense of values. (Cited in Schluchter 1981, 176)

2. Three Jewish sayings are relevant here: "A fool can ask more questions than nine wise men can answer"; "If you spend your life trying to answer foolish questions, all your answers will also be foolish" (Telushkin 1992, 49); and "When you grasp for everything, you end up grasping nothing" (Schneerson 1995, 149).

3. Nietzsche complains about

knowledge of the past [that] is foundationless, unlimited striving, an infinite quest in which "memory opens all its gates," in which "we moderns have nothing whatever of our own; only by replenishing and cramming ourselves with the ages, customs, arts, philosophies, religions, and discoveries of others do we become anything worthy of notice, that is to say, walking encyclopedias." The ultimate effect of this is a form of indigestion in which the individual, far from being cultivated through history, is weakened by it. (Cited in C. Turner 1992, 63)

Kitcher agrees.

Truth is very easy to get. Careful observation and judicious reporting will enable you to explain the number of truths you believe. Once you have some truths, simple logical, mathematical and statistical exercises will enable you to acquire lots more. Tacking truths together is something any hack can do. . . . [T]he trouble is that most of the truths that can be acquired in these ways are boring. Nobody is interested in the minutiae of the shapes and colors of the objects in your vicinity, the temperature fluctuation in your microenvironment, the infinite number of disjunctions you can generate with your favorite true statement as one disjunct, or the probability of the events in which chance setups you contrive with objects in your vicinity. What we want is significant truth. (1993, 94)

4. Parkin writes that "the selection of elements that go to make up ideal-types is a somewhat arbitrary affair. What is picked out and accented and what is played down will to some extent be influenced by the kinds of problems being investigated and the question being posed. It would thus not make much sense to speak of an ideal-type being correct or incorrect. For one type of enquiry it might be best to select one constellation of elements, for another type of enquiry a quite different set of elements might be appropriate" (1982,

28). Oakes suggests that "given the irrationality of reality, knowledge is possible only by means of concepts that simplify, recast, and transform reality on the basis of the interests these concepts are intended to meet" (1988, 61). Weber argues that "all the analysis of infinite reality which the finite mind can conduct rests on the tacit assumption that only a finite portion of this reality consists of the object of scientific investigation and that only it is 'essential' in the sense of being 'worth knowing' " ([1903–17] 1949, 72). Aron thus writes that

> Max Weber combined a vast and profound knowledge of history with a curious concern in what is essential. We all agree that the depth of an interpretation of the past depends on the depth of the questions asked. Max Weber asked the most important questions. What is the meaning men have given their existence? What is the relation between the meaning men have given their existence and the way they have organized their societies? What is the relation of men's attitudes toward profane activities and their conception of the sacred life? (1970, 295)

5. Parkin writes that

> patterns of behavior and institutional forms like capitalism, or Protestantism, or bureaucracy, are each composed of a large number of interconnected elements, both normative and structural. In order to comprehend such an institution or social formation it is necessary to reduce it to its core components. We do this by singling out and accentuating the central or basic features of the institution in question and suppressing or downgrading those features that could be considered marginal to it. This means that our ideal-type of capitalism, or the bourgeois revolution, or whatever, is unlikely to be an accurate representation of the real thing. It is almost bound to be a somewhat slanted or exaggerated version, rather in the way that a cartoonist's caricature is an exaggerated version of a still recognizable face. Thus, an ideal type of the bourgeois revolution will not conform exactly to the features of any one particular bourgeois revolution; rather, it will be a kind of distillation of the principal features that are characteristic of these revolutions in general. (1982, 28)

6. In Descartes's method of doubt, every belief is considered false until proven true. In Popper's (1968) method of falsification, science continually eliminates untrue hypotheses.

7. Miller refers to "the classical positivist assumption that confirmation is a logical relation between the confirmed hypothesis and the confirming data, unaffected by further historical variations in the state of scientific controversy" (1987, 170). He stresses that "in classical positivism, comparison is neither sufficient nor necessary for confirmation. A hypothesis is confirmed by data just in case it entails data in appropriate ways, when appropriately supplemented. Confirmation is a lonely encounter of hypothesis with evidence"

(1987, 173). Parsons counters that social scientists should be concerned "on the theoretical plane, with relatively simple bold outlines and clear-cut alternatives" (1937, 501). Each hypothesis must defend itself against its plausible rivals rather than only against data. The classic positivist position is indeed now universally rejected. Newton-Smith suggests that "no theory is free of anomalies and it would not be very shrewd to abandon a theory just because it faces no anomaly. The man who has no friends except those without fault has few, if any friends. The man who rejects any theory which has an anomaly has no theory whatsoever" (1981, 137). Laudan argues that "assessment in science is invariably comparative" (1990, 143). He maintains that "the only reliable guide to the problems relevant to a particular theory is an examination of the problems which predecessor—and competing—theories in that domain (including the theory itself) have already solved" (1977, 21). Laudan further suggests that all scientists engage in pragmatic comparison among existing theories: "What scientists are trying to decide . . . is not whether their theories will last for all time, or whether they will always stack up favorably against all conceivable rivals; rather they are trying to decide which of the theories presently contending in the science market place is best supported by the evidence. Scientists, in the view I am advocating, should be seen, not as looking for simply the best theory, but for the best theory they can find" (1984, 27). Blaug suggests that science cannot be conducted in terms of a single theory: "Scientific theories can only be meaningfully assessed in terms of competing hypotheses for the simple reason that methodology provides no absolute standards to which all theories must conform: what it does provide are criteria in terms of which theories may be ranked as more or less promising. Thus, the appraisal of economic theories is essentially a matter of asking: which of the competing theories is the one best fitted to survive?" (1992, 137).

8. On the other hand, crucial experiments or crucial tests among theories have their limitations. Incompatible theories are often compatible with "the" evidence. Since competing theories ask different questions and determine different data, evidence often cannot arbitrate among them. Tests thus radically underdetermine the choice between rival theories. There might not be compelling reasons to accept one theory over another, and all rivals could be equally well supported. Chapter 10 addresses the indeterminacy of theory and evidence.

9. MacIntyre thus suggests that "instead of interpreting rival traditions as mutually exclusive and incompatible ways of understanding one and the same world, one and the same subject matter, let us understand them instead as providing very different, complementary perspectives for envisaging the realities about which they speak to us" (1988, 352). Little agrees: "A plurality of theoretical frameworks is neither an inconsistency nor a sign of conceptual indecisiveness; instead, it is a recognition of the multiple causation at work in most complex social processes. . . . [O]nly a mistaken desire for theoretical purity would lead us to demand that just one of the theories may be true. The inves-

tigator must recognize that the phenomena are complex, embodying a variety of social processes; a plurality of theories may well be needed to identify the causal properties of the processes" (1989, 25). Katznelson refers to "strategies of oscillation" that bring together in dialectical fashion competing perspectives. Each perspective has its "moment of truth" or "place of relevance" (1997, 100).

10. The use of models and foils is consistent with Popper's (1965, 1968) critical rationalism. He stresses the need for rational discussion and critical examination of proposals, and suggests that scientists should be open to criticism and ready to argue with their opponents. Agreement is thus unhealthy for science because disagreement leads to the trial-and-error methodology that advances science. Popper thus emphasizes criticism of theories and not their justification or verification.

11. There might be a chicken-and-egg problem here.

12. Since structuralists maintain that causes are opaque, and rationalists, that consequences are unintended, can one blame interpretivists for their skepticism about nomothetic modes of reasoning?

13. MacIntyre refers to liberalism and "the internationalized languages of modernity, the languages of everywhere and of nowhere" (1988, 395, 346). Liberalism is thus not tradition-neutral but is itself a tradition that hides choices.

14. Rosen thus writes of "a kind of Gödel's Theorem in human affairs: Every attempt to systematize life or to govern it by a set of axioms rich enough to encompass the totality of experience leads to a contradiction" (1989, 17).

15. The sources of these quotations are Schmitt 1995, 69; Nietzsche 1989, 232; and Nehamas 1996, 234.

Chapter 9

1. Each research program has its pretenders to science—Smith hopes for a science of interests, Durkheim for a science of norms, and Marx for a science of structures—though by "science" each means something different.

2. In Przeworski and Teune's words, they wish to "substitute names of variables for names of social systems" (1970, 8).

3. One strategy for discovering the presocial, a priori, and natural is to collect as many accurate accounts as possible of as many different countries and histories as possible; cancel out what is peculiar to any particular society; and distill what is left. The results are the universal and uniform laws of humans and societies. Examples, extending beyond the rationalists, include Smith (supply-demand), Freud (repression), Lévi-Strauss (binary opposition), Bordieu (power and inequality), Habermas (validation claims of ideal speech), Kant (mental processes), Hobbes (anarchy), Locke (property), Rousseau (order), and Rawls (social justice).

4. Variations are possible: some scientific laws are statistical, and explananda also include scientific laws.

5. As Popper indicates:

History is characterized by its interest in actual, singular or specific events, rather than in laws or generalizations. This view is perfectly compatible with the analysis of scientific method, and especially of causal explanation. . . . The situation is simply this: while the theoretical sciences are mainly interested in finding and testing universal laws, the historical sciences take all kinds of universal laws for granted and are mainly interested in finding and testing singular statements. . . . All causal explanations of a singular event can be said to be historical insofar as the "cause" is always described by singular initial conditions. And this agrees entirely with the popular idea that to explain a thing causally is to explain it and why it happened, that is to say, to tell its "story." But it is only in history that we are really interested in the causal explanation of a singular event. In the theoretical sciences, such causal explanations are mainly a means to a different end—the testing of universal laws. (1957, cited in Hechter 1995, 1525)

6. As Kincaid suggests, this perspective "prevents laws only if no science produces laws. When gases become fluids, the gas laws no longer apply and we need different laws for the new situation. Thus the gas laws are specific to context. So are innumerable other generalizations in the natural sciences. If appeal to context prevents laws, then the natural sciences have few or no laws either. Thus reference to contexts does not rule out laws" (1996, 62).

7. While subjective culturalists like Inglehart are positivists looking for universal truths, recall that this book focuses on intersubjective culturalists like Geertz (sect. 5.1).

8. While some thick structuralists want general propositions that are valid across time and space, recall that this book focuses on thin structuralists like Skocpol who eschew such generalizations (sect. 6.1).

9. Bloom writes that "the method of science is designed to see only what is everywhere and always, whereas what is particular and emergent is all that counts historically and culturally. Homer is not merely one example of an epic, or the Bible of a revealed text, but that is what science sees them as, and the only reasons it is interested in them. The scholar turns away from them to comparative religion or comparative literature, i.e., either to indifference or to flabby ecumenism compounded out of the lowest, common denominator of a variety of old and incompatible creations" (1987, 308).

Bloom continues: "Producing theories is not theorizing, or a sign of theoretical life. Concreteness, not abstractness, is the hallmark of philosophy. All interesting generalizations must proceed from the rich awareness of what is to be explained, but the tendency to abstractness leads to simplifying the phenomena in order more easily to deal with them." He also observes that Tocqueville warned against democracy's tendency toward abstractness: "Because there is no tradition and men need guidance, general theories that are produced in a day and not properly grounded in experience, but seem to explain things and are useful crutches for finding one's way in a complicated

world, have currency. . . . [T]he very universality of democracy and the same-
ness of man presupposed by it encourage this tendency and make the mind's
eye less sensitive to differences" (255, 254)

Bloom summarizes his critique against the rationalists-cum-universalists by
recounting the theme of Swift's *Gulliver's Travels:* "On the flying island the
men have one eye turned inward, the other toward the zenith. They are perfect
Cartesians—one egoistical eye contemplating the self, one cosmopological eye
surveying the most distant things. The intermediate range, which previously
was the center of concentration and defined both the ego and the pattern for
the study of the stars, is not within the Laputan purview" (294).

10. Colburn argues that "the pungency of theory is best demonstrated in
the specificity of analysis" (1986, 4). Bloch writes that "it requires years of
analysis before there is material for one day's synthesis" (1967, 72). Polya
writes that "examples are better than precepts—the mere statement of the pattern cannot do you much good. The pattern will grow in color and interest and
value with each example to which you apply it successfully" (1962, 5).

11. This was one of Weber's principal methodological themes (Lichbach
1995, 290–91).

12. But not necessarily. Among philosophers Nietzsche, for example, is a
case-thinker who does lots of small-scale case studies. His cases raise problems
in particularly revealing and vivid ways. While he shifts back and forth
between quite particular cases and general reflections, he always has a theme
or point to advance. Schact writes that Nietzsche's

> most common strategy in those works is to invoke a case to raise a prob-
> lem, and then to examine it and employ it and other related cases to
> address the problem. The cases are (as it were) the witnesses he calls to
> the stand, the interrogation and interpretation of which serve to shed
> light upon the larger problems they exemplify or broach. They also serve
> the important function of keeping his treatments of problems from
> becoming lost in abstract reflections, and of keeping him (and us) mind-
> ful that these problems have real relevance to human life and experience.
> (1996, 157)

13. This is the nub of the problem with such generalizations. As Moore
writes: "Marx saw the general features of mid-nineteenth-century capitalism,
as it had developed out of earlier social forms, in the single case of nineteenth-
century England. England was at the time the most advanced form of a capitalist economy. On the basis of an understanding of the inherent dynamic
characteristics of competitive capitalism, he tried to predict the form it might
take in the future" (1966, 149).

14. MacIntyre sums up the argument with this widely cited tale.

> There once as a man who aspired to be the author of the general theory
> of holes. When asked, "what kind of holes—holes dug by children for
> amusement, holes dug by gardeners to plant lettuce seedlings, tank

traps, holes made by roadmakers?" he would reply indignantly that he wished for a *general* theory that would explain all of them. He rejected *ab initio*—as he saw it—the pathetically common sense view that of the digging of different kinds of holes there are quite different explanations to be given; why then he would ask do we have the concept of a hole?
. . . Had he . . . concerned himself not with holes, but with modernization, suburbanization or violence, I find it difficult to believe that he might not have achieved high office in the APSA. (1971, cited in Rule 1988, 255)

He also tells the following story: "Charles II once invited the members of the Royal Society to explain to him why a dead fish weighed more than the same fish alive; a number of subtle explanations were offered to him. He then pointed out that it does not" (MacIntyre 1984, 82).

15. Moore rejects nomothetic research conducted on random samples of the world's population in order to develop generalizations that hold independently of space, time, and context. Moore describes such comparativists as follows: "For them, history, if it is used at all, becomes merely a storehouse of examples. Using historical data, one can supposedly discover the social correlates of democracy, tyranny, class struggle or class peace, and the like. The existing body of theory should, from this standpoint, indicate the likelihood or unlikelihood of finding a particular combination of traits. Historical and social facts are then drawn upon as if they were colored balls from an urn, and the results subjected to tests for statistical significance in order to disprove the hypothesis or derive additional support for it" (1958, 131–32). He rejects such a procedure because it "starts with the assumption that the facts of history are separate and discrete units. . . . The modern social scientist searches for invariant laws that govern the relationship among these atomized observations reflected in statistics. Such laws are implicitly or explicitly thought to apply to masses of single facts of equal importance which are expected to display at least the statistical regularity that molecules do in a gas under specified conditions." Moore sees fundamental limits to such ahistorical generalizations: "To abstract from all historical situations in the hope of discovering some pan-human or universal kind of social necessity does not seem to me a very promising procedure. Can we really make any worthwhile generalizations that apply equally well to the Stone Age and twentieth-century America? Perhaps one cannot answer this question with a flat negative in advance, though I remain most skeptical. One certainly has the right to object vehemently to any science that eliminates from its vision all change that has take place between the Stone Age and the twentieth century merely for the sake of formulating universal propositions like those in the natural sciences" (131). In other words, Moore argues that one cannot study transhistorical phenomena in order to develop theories that hold at all times and for all places; historically concrete and specific phenomena cannot be understood statically and ahistorically in terms of general laws; and comparativists can not pluck events out of complex historical contexts and use them illustratively to build and test theories.

16. Skocpol thus asks: "Can [these findings] be applied beyond the French, Russian, and Chinese cases? In a sense, the answer is unequivocally 'no': one cannot mechanically extend the specific causal arguments that have been developed for France, Russia, and China into a 'general theory of revolutions' applicable to all other modern social revolutions. There are two important reasons why such a strategy would be fruitless" (1979, 288). First, new cases might have new causes: "The causes of revolutions (whether of individual cases, or sets of similar cases) necessarily vary according to the historical and international circumstances of the countries involved" (288). Second, new cases might interact with old causes: "Patterns of revolutionary causation and outcomes are affected by world-historical changes in the fundamental structures and bases of state power as such" (288). Skocpol concludes that "other revolutions require analyses in their own right" because they occur in different types of structures (e.g., different states and different world-historical circumstances) (290).

17. Scientists are basically classifiers and typologizers: this is the sense in which most sciences, such as chemistry, physics, and mathematics, study structures (Grossmann 1992, 1). Hayakawa adds an interesting example from a different field of inquiry: "How are dictionaries written? For each word or word group encountered in the sources, make a report of the sentence in which the word is used is made, often on 5 × 8 cards. When all the sources are read, the cards are alphabetized, and each word and word group has several hundred reports. These are then classified into groups of common meanings and definitions are then written" (1990).

18. Examples include Brenner 1976, 1982, and Katzenstein 1978.

19. Examples include Moore 1966 and Skocpol 1979.

20. Moore stresses the importance of understanding the world-historical development of structures. "The important regularities in human behavior, as well as some of the trivial ones, are found within the context of historical change. For example, we can observe recurring patterns in the behavior of a slave-holder and still other patterns in those of a feudal lord. There may even be some common features in all the major historical forms of domination. To find them would be a worthwhile task. . . . But we cannot stop there, even if we arrive at such a point. Accurate knowledge requires that we understand each slave type, slave-holder, feudal lord, capitalist entrepreneur, and socialist bureaucrat, within its proper historical context, that is, in relation to previous forms and possible subsequent ones" (1958, 130–31).

21. Katznelson's summary of Tocqueville's *Democracy in America* is a good characterization of this style of analysis.

America is treated simultaneously as a highly distinctive, even exceptional constellation of elements, yet also as a harbinger of things to come. Though the United States is Tocqueville's only case, it always is constructed against empirical (especially French) and conceptual counterfactuals. Further, the United States is situated in place and time not as a hermetically sealed "case" but as a relationally inscribed instance in three senses: First, its own history and special qualities of institutions, values, and demography are composed in relationship to the experiences of other countries and to global flows of information, ideology, and people. Second, its development is situated in relation to larger trends and processes that affect the modern, western world more generally, especially those of social and political equalization. Third, America, as the first egalitarian regime for white males, is presented as the most important cause shaping the prospects, choices, and trajectories of other countries by way of the effects of a visible demonstration.

Though *Democracy in America* contains a strong causal story about liberal and egalitarian political culture and the construction of particular kinds of agents and their association ties under determinate structural conditions, it also underscores variation and complexity, especially with respect to questions of race and the confrontation of civilizations. The text carefully distinguishes levels of causation—those specific and limited to the American milieu; those shared broadly by the larger thrust toward social equality and the movement of masses into politics; and those of political culture deeply implicated with the patterning of institutions like the law, religion, the press, and secular voluntary associations. Throughout, individual and group dispositions and collective actions are shaped by and reshape large-scale structural and ideological arrangements and trends. Human nature is not fixed either as benevolent or as interest-seeking; rather, human behavior is conditioned on the structural and institutional shaping of values and mores which, in turn, remake contextual conditions for action. Structures and actors make democracy and democracy remakes structures and actors. Motivated by broadly liberal values and fears in a revolutionary world, Tocqueville combined classification and typological thinking with the dense historical, sociological, and political depiction of a single, complicated, dense case. He understood that out of context the factors deployed in his analysis would lose their relational quality; yet he insisted that a configurative study of the United States contained deeply comparative lessons. (1997, 97)

America is thus a complex configuration of elements: situated in place and time, it has its own history, special qualities, and particular institutions and values. America is also an archetype of equality: as the dominant model for the future, it represents larger trends faced by all of the Western world. Yet there are relevant empirical counterfactuals: France. And as the first case in a larger pattern of development, it has demonstration effects on other cases.

22. Ruggie (1998, 31) thus indicates that Weber followed a three-step procedure: understand a particular actor, understand the group within which the actor functioned, use ideal types to place the group in comparative and world-historical context.

23. Bendix adopts a similar strategy of emphasizing "polar concepts. Tradition *and* modernity, formal *and* substantive criteria of law, bureaucratic *and* substantive criteria of law, bureaucratic *and* traditional authority patterns, charismatic *and* routinized leadership, individuation *and* socialization as consequences of the impact of social life on the individual—all signify dual tendencies that always coexist, though in different balances that are dependent on the interests of dominant and subordinate groups in changing historical circumstances. While one of these paired concepts may be most useful in analyzing a given phenomenon, keeping its opposite in view will elucidate the analysis and make it more adequate" (Rueschemeyer 1984, 134–35, emphasis in original).

24. Parkin comments:

Seen from Weber's angle, even if it were possible to pinpoint some quintessential substance of religion or morality or law, this would still leave all the interesting questions unanswered. In the case of religion for example, it would still be necessary to show how the doctrinal expressions of the sacred varied from one religion to another. For Durkheim, "the details of dogmas and rites are secondary." For Weber, they are of the utmost importance, since different dogmas motivate very different types of social action. Forget the essence of religion, he implies; let us examine instead the ways in which religions differ in their consequences for social conduct. And the same goes for other complex institutions. Sociological enquiry is more fruitfully directed to the factors that are found within and between institutional forms, rather than to the search for some metaphysical entity they supposedly share in common. (1982, 29)

25. Kuran points out that "the study of particularities [is compatible] with the search for underlying common processes. In fact, universal social processes may be responsible for the emergence and persistence of observed differences. Where differences fascinate, says Stephen Jay Gould, generalities instruct. Anyone who has seen a tiger and a leopard knows that one is striped and the other spotted. It is a general theory, the theory of natural evolution, that accounts for the origins and stability of this intriguing difference" (1995, preface, 6).

26. Mathematics is often developed with respect to a representative element from a particular class of cases. While there is an infinity of t-distributions, for example, each may be characterized by three parameters (mean, standard deviation, degrees of freedom). For particular degrees of freedom, all such t-distributions may be examined using the standard case where the mean = 0 and the standard deviation = 1. Mathematics is also developed with respect to characteristic special cases, as Von Neumann and Morgenstern argue: "We wish to find the mathematically complete principles which define 'rational behavior' for the participants in a social economy, and to derive from them

several characteristics of that behavior. And while the principles ought to be perfectly general—i.e., valid in all situations—we may be satisfied if we can find solutions, for the moment, only in more characteristic special cases" (1953, 31).

Chapter 10

1. Merton's problem-oriented "middle range" theorizing, for example, clarifies and rethinks existing theoretical puzzles by providing a small number of heuristic tools or concepts that further empirical investigations (1959; 1968, chap. 2). See Elster 1989b; 1999, chap. 1.

2. Snidal suggests that models are embedded in rich interpretive frameworks called *theories* and are carefully tailored to important contexts.

> Since the same representation can be a model for different theories [e.g., differential equations model problems in physics and in arms races], interpretations of a model depend on the theory in which it is embedded. The theory contains a deductive structure plus an interpretation of fundamental assumptions and theoretical constructs. This richer interpretive structure (as compared to the tighter correspondences in the model) provide[s] for greater richness of explanation. Through it, the theory maintains a greater open-endedness and a surplus meaning which guides revision and extension of the model. A further source of theoretical richness lies in the multiple models that may be compared within a theory and that emerge according to specific parametric conditions. Through these models, seemingly different phenomena—perhaps varying due to contextual factors—can be understood within the same theoretical framework. (1985, 34–35)

He uses the example of "the" game theory of international relations in which the study of the power-maximizing behavior of states, in the absence of centralized and authoritative institutions, illuminates questions of international anarchy. Different specifications of actors' policy preferences and contexts lead to the different games (e.g., Chicken, Prisoner's Dilemma) that can arise from one fundamental theory of international relations.

3. Lave and March (1975) fail to recognize that stylized observations and formal models are embedded in research programs that come from research traditions Parsons's (1937, 627) hope for "cautious advance from well-known and clearly formulable 'islands' of theoretical knowledge" and Guetzkow's (1950) advocacy of "islands of theory," are similarly flawed: for island hopping between puzzles, problems, and questions to be cumulative, island hoppers need to take account of larger research traditions.

4. While I argue that perspectives help overcome a chaotic world that is infinitely prolific, postmodernists counter that perspectives are never comprehensive and enduring representations of what is "out there." There is no final ground to judge rival representations and the attempt to choose simply

leads to more representations. By forming and transforming their subject matters, metanarratives thus ultimately proliferate rather than reduce representations.

5. Since nuts and bolts or causal mechanisms can come from all three traditions, they need not be based on methodological individualism. Macrolevel mechanisms exist, contra Hedström and Swedberg (1998, 11–13, 24).

6. As Kant put it: "It is obvious that no matter how complete the theory may be, a middle term is required between theory and practice, providing a link and a transition from one to the other. For a concept . . . which contains a general rule, must be supplemented by an act of judgment whereby the practitioner distinguishes instances where the rule applies from those where it does not" (cited in Rae et al. 1981, 15).

7. Mill suggests that there are two procedures to fashion a scientific explanation of a phenomenon.

Suppose W is sick, and we would like to know whether penicillin will help cure W. . . . The empirical a posteriori method, or, as Mill calls it, the method of specific experience, would have us inquire whether others with symptoms resembling W's recovered more often or more rapidly when given penicillin. The method of a priori in contrast would have us draw upon our knowledge of the causes of W's symptoms and upon our knowledge of the operation of penicillin to decide whether penicillin will help cure W. Both methods are "empirical" and involve testing. The difference is that the former attempts to use experiment or observation to learn about the complex phenomena directly, while the latter employs observation or experiment to study the relevant component's causal factors. Similarly, one could determine empirically the range of an artillery piece directed at different angles with different charges, wind conditions, and atmospheric pressure. Or one could make use of the law of inertia, Galileo's law of falling bodies, and experimentally determined laws of air resistance and explosive force to calculate the range. The latter deductive method is, in Mill's view, the method of all advanced sciences. But deductive conclusions should be checked by the method of specific experience, whose results can also be useful in themselves. (Hausman 1992, 144)

8. Hacking writes that

God did not write a Book of Nature of the sort that the old Europeans imagined. He wrote a Borgesian library, each book of which is as brief as possible, yet each book of which is inconsistent with every other. No book is redundant. For every book, there is some humanly accessible bit of Nature such that that book, and no other, makes possible the comprehensive, prediction, and influencing of what is going on. Far from being untidy, this is New World Leibnizianism. Leibniz said that God chose a world which maximized the variety of phenomena while choosing the simplest laws. Exactly so: but the best way to maximize phenomena and have simplest laws is to have the laws inconsistent with each other, each applying to this or that but none applying to all. (1983, 219)

9. Cartwright writes that

the French mind sees things in an elegant, unified, way. It takes Newton's three laws of motion and the law of gravitation and turns them into the beautiful abstract mathematics of Lagrangian mathematics. The English mind, says Duhem, is an exact contrast. It engineers bits of gears, and pulleys, and keeps the strings from tangling up. It holds a thousand different details all at once, without imposing much abstract order or organization. The difference between the realist and me is almost theological. The realist thinks that the creator of the universe worked like a French mathematician. But I think that God has the untidy mind of the English. (Cited in Hacking 1983, 219)

10. Recall that from a realist point of view nuts and bolts are causal mechanisms. Miller thus writes that "a theory is a description of underlying causal facts which, in actual circumstances, are sufficient to bring about more directly observable phenomena of the kind studied by the field in question. A theoretical explanation is an explanation describing a factor which is an instance of a relatively unobservable factor described in the corresponding theory. An underlying, relatively unobservable factor responsible for a relatively observable fact might be called a causal mechanism. Thus, one might say that a theory is a description of a repertoire of causal mechanisms, a theoretical explanation, an explanation appealing to instances of such a repertoire" (1987, 139).

11. Recall that positivists argue similarly. The assumptions behind a theory are connected to its implications only in the absence of auxiliary hypotheses about disturbing factors or only in the absence of complicated interactions and admixtures of causes among a priori truths. Predictions are therefore always inexact because other conditions are counteracting, as extraneous factors offset the action of the independent variable under consideration. In other words, a theory might say that x will cause y to occur, but in the presence of x not-y occurs because of the overwhelming power of other variables, z. "Only a unified and true theory of everything, encompassing all the more limited theories human beings can understand, would apply with precision at all times and in all places" (Friedman 1996, 14). Mill thus argued that there were few regularities in science (Cartwright 1999a, 141). Positivists, as indicated above, see universal theory as primary and auxiliary assumptions as secondary. The postpositivist position advocated here reverses this emphasis and suggests that social science seeks to discover how the models of a theory—a general set of nuts and bolts—work in a specific problem domain.

12. This first step can be given a falsificationist twist, as stated by Nobel Prize–winning physicist Feynman: "If you can find any other view of the world which agrees over the entire range where things have already been observed,

but disagrees somewhere else, you have made a great discovery" (1965, 171). Feynman thus suggests that "every theory that you make up has to be analyzed against *all* possible consequences, to see if it predicts anything else" (39, emphasis in original). Feynman also suggests that to find a new law, discover trouble with an old one. And to discover trouble with an old one, extend the law to a domain beyond previous tests.

> One of the ways of stopping science would be only to do experiments in the region where you know the law. But experimenters search most diligently, and with the greatest effort, in exactly those places where it seems most likely that we can prove our theories wrong. In other words we are trying to prove ourselves wrong as quickly as possible, because only in that way can we find progress. (158)

Feynman's ideas are consistent with Eckstein's (1975) perspective on case studies. Eckstein urges that we look most diligently for tests that are either *most* likely to prove our ideas wrong (i.e., lead to confirmation of theories) or *least* likely to do so (i.e., lead to rejection of theories). Popper thus got it wrong: (normal) science is not conjecture and refutation but rather refutation and conjecture. When an off-the-shelf model of a theory does not fit an interesting new problem domain (refutation), scientists who believe in the theory adjust the model accordingly (conjecture).

13. The logical positivists believed that the context of discovery is shrouded in mystery. There is no logic, method, rationale, heuristic, or rule, in other words, for generating scientific ideas. "Anything goes," as in Feyerabend's (1988) anarchist approach to science. "Problemation" (Eckstein 1964) is an art or craft that is indeed difficult to teach. While Popper's (1965) discussion of the "problem situation" was incomplete, Kuhn (1970) and his followers focused on larger structures of knowledge, for example, on the anomalies that come from paradigms.

14. This important point of view buttresses the search for modest rational choice theory. Giere thus advocates a "generalized model-based understanding of scientific theories which makes no commitments to any particular formalism" (e.g., types of mathematics) and hence takes models and not statements as fundamental to science (2000, 522). "This makes it possible to interpret much of scientists' theoretical discourse as being about theoretical models rather than directly about the world. What have traditionally been interpreted as laws of nature thus turn out to be merely statements describing the behavior of theoretical models" (523). Hence, "it is the possession of such mental models [e.g., harmonic oscillators] that makes it possible for them to recognize a new situation as one for which a particular sort of theoretical model is appropriate" (523). Since "theoretical models are the means by which scientists represent the world—both to themselves and for others" (Giere 1988, 80), high-level theories (e.g., evolutionary theory, quantum mechanics) should be seen "not so much as a unitary formal system, but as a family or families of

models," "together with claims about the sort of thing to which the models apply." "When viewing the content of a science, we find the models occupying center stage," and thus "the main general lesson is: when approaching a theory, look first for the models and then for the hypotheses employing those models. Don't look for general principles, axioms, or the like" (91, 20, 79, 90).

15. Consider Newton's second law of motion, $F = ma$: "The various families [of models] are constructed by combining Newton's laws of motion, particularly the second law, with various force functions—linear functions, inverse square functions, and so on. The models thus defined are then multiplied by adding other force functions to the definition. These define still further families of models. And so on" (Giere 1988, 82). Hence, these physical laws are "part of the characterization of theoretical models, which in turn may represent various real systems. But only part of the characterization. [By itself $F = ma$ in no way] defines a model of anything. One always needs more details, specific force functions, approximations, boundary conditions, and so on. Only then does one have a model that can be compared with a real system" (Giere 1988, 90). Cartwright agrees.

> In mechanics we do get this kind [$F = ma$] of exact relation, but at the cost of introducing abstract concepts like *force,* concepts whose relation to the world must be mediated by more concrete ones. These more concrete concepts, it turns out, are very specific in their form: the forms are given by the *interpretive models* of the theory, for example, two compact masses separated by a distance r, the linear harmonic oscillator, or the model for a charge moving in a uniform magnetic field. This ensures that "force" has a very precise content. But it also means that it is severely limited in its range of applications. For it can be attached to only those situations that can be represented by these highly specialized models. (1999a, 3, emphasis in original)

Cartwright thus indicates that the relation $F = ma$ is specified in "stereotypical situations . . . in which various functional forms of the force are exhibited. That is what the working physicist has to figure out, and what the aspiring physicist has to learn. . . . [The purpose of a typical mechanics text is to teach students] which abstract force functions are exhibited in which stereotypical situations" (1999a, 43).

16. Some of these derive from Rogowski 1995. Blaug (1992, xv, 138) creates a similar list for economics, and Bunge (1999, 9), for social science.

17. Some claim that general laws have never been discovered in the social sciences. The critics suggest that exceptions are the rule in social science; generalizations coexist with recognized counterexamples; laws fail in very important circumstances; laws are highly qualified; and social scientists cannot establish scope conditions and qualifiers that remove the counterexamples and restore the generalizations. MacIntyre thus argues that "the social sciences are almost or perhaps completely devoid of achievements. For the salient fact

about those sciences is the absence of the discovery of any law-like generalizations, whatsoever" (1984, 88). The alleged laws are either false or trivial: "We
do not know how to apply them systematically beyond the limits of observation to unobserved or hypothetical instances" (91). In a backhanded compli-
ment, MacIntyre argues that "the generalizations and maxims of the best
social science share certain characteristics of their predecessors—the proverbs
of folk societies, the generalizations of jurists, the maxims of Machiavelli"
(1984, 105). It therefore must be, as Burnham puts it, that "history is to all
intents and purposes one damned thing after another" (1994, 60). Even a social
scientist like Verba laments, "Where are the general laws? Generalizations
fade when we look at the particular cases. We add intervening variables after
intervening variables. Since the cases are few in number, we end with an explanation tailed to each case. The result begins to sound quite idiographic or
configurative" (1967, 113). Such criticisms and laments, as indicated in the text,
result from the positivists' inflated understanding of the generalizability of
laws in physics and chemistry. A postpositivist understanding of theory leads
to a more modest physics and a more modest rational choice theory that dis-
arms critics and soothes partisans.

18. Similarly, the rational choice theory of protest is saved by shortening
the time span: almost no one is rebelling *now*.

19. Blaug writes that "storytelling makes use of the method of what historians call colligation, the binding together of facts, low-level generalizations,
high-level theories, and value judgments in a coherent narrative, held together
by a glue of an implicit set of beliefs and attitudes that the author shares with
his readers. In able hands, it can be extremely persuasive, and yet it is never
easy to explain afterwards why it has persuaded" (1992, 110). Blaug thus wonders how

> one validate[s] a particular piece of storytelling. One asks, of course, if
> the facts are correctly stated; if other facts are omitted; if the lower-level
> generalizations are subject to counterexamples; and if we can find com-
> peting stories that will fit the facts. In short, we go through a process that
> is identical to the one that we regularly employ to validate the hypo-
> thetico-deductive explanations of orthodox economics. However,
> because storytelling lacks rigor, lacks a definite logical structure, it is all
> too easy to verify and virtually impossible to falsify. It is or can be per-
> suasive precisely because it never runs the risk of being wrong. (110)

20. Related problems in logic are that one can deduce identical conclusions
from different assumptions and that one can deduce true sentences from false
premises.

21. I do not have the space to discuss the problems with falsification. See,
for example, Lakatos's (1970) critique. Since many rational choice hegemons
see it as a panacea for empirical work, I will, however, mention three interrelated difficulties. First, Laudan writes that "it leaves ambiguous the scientific

status of virtually every singular existential statement, however well supported (e.g., the claim that there are atoms, that there is a planet closer to the Sun than the Earth, that there is a missing link" (1996, 218–19). Second, "it has the untoward consequence of counting as scientific every crank claim which makes ascertainably false assertions. Thus flat Earthers, biblical creationists, proponents of laetrile or orgone boxes, Uri Geller devotees, Bermuda Triangulators, circle squarers, Lysenkoists, charioteers of the gods, perpetual motion builders, Big Foot searchers, Loch Nessians, faith healers, polywater dabblers, Rosicrucians, the world-is-about-to-enders, primal screamers, water diviners, magicians, and astrologers all turn out to be scientific on Popper's criterion—just as long as they are prepared to indicate some observation, however improbable, which (if it came to pass) would cause them to change their minds." Third, falsifications can be endless whereas we must ultimately believe in the truth of our theories: "In the old story, the peasant goes to the priest for advice on saving his dying chickens. The priest recommends prayer, but the chicks continue to die. The priest then recommends music for the chicken coop, but the deaths continue unabated. Pondering again, the priest recommends repainting the chicken coop in bright colors. Finally, all the chickens die. 'What a shame,' the priest tells the peasant. 'I had so many more good ideas'" (*Economist,* June 29, 1996, 19–21).

22. Indeed, "judgment" with respect to "truth" can be enhanced. Research methodologists accept the trade-off of Type I and Type II errors, recognize that neither error can be reduced to zero, and try to develop valid research designs that move the curve closer to the origin. Campbell and Stanley (1963) and Cook and Campbell (1979) thus develop checklists of challenges to internal and external validity in experimental designs, and King, Keohane, and Verba (1994) propose valuable methods for small-n studies. While these research design issues are an essential part of the evaluation to follow (one element in Lakatos's approach is that theories resist falsification, and one element of Popper's approach is that a theory provides a better fit to evidence than another theory), questions of research design are not explored here.

23. For example, a sufficient condition for the collective action research program to be progressive in Lakatos's sense is that it meet the preceding tests for, say, collective dissent. Such tests, however, are not necessary. There are many substantive areas, such as interest-group activity and voting behavior, where the collective action research program may yield insights. Whether the program is valuable for protest and rebellion says nothing about whether or not it is valuable for these other fields. A Lakatosian analysis of the collective action research program therefore cannot be limited to a single domain of study because limiting the empirical focus deprives the analyst of the most novel implications of the program. Focusing on a single field does not yield the full picture of the progressivity of a research program. A Lakatosian evaluation would, on the contrary, determine the impact of the program on a number of different fields: collective action theories are thus progressive if they yield diverse implications in different and new substantive domains. The ques-

tion "Is the collective action research program progressive or degenerative?" cannot be addressed with respect to a single substantive domain like collective dissent.

24. Conciliation with old facts (sect. 4.2.2) is even more suspect: "Why should an ideology be constrained by older problems which, at any rate, make sense only in the abandoned context and which look silly and unnatural now? Why should it even consider the 'facts' that give rise to problems of this kind or played a role in their solutions? Why should it not rather proceed in its own way, devising its own task and assembling its own domain of 'facts'? A comprehensive theory, after all, is supposed to contain also an ontology that determines what exists and thus delimits the domain of possible facts and possible questions. . . . New views soon strike out in new directions and from upon the older problems" (Feyerabend 1988).

25. Given that theories are underdetermined by facts, no amount of accumulated facts can lead to acceptance or rejection of a theory (Giddens 1979, 243). Only a better theory beats a theory. Feyerabend thus advises scientists to "proliferate" inconsistent theories rather than eliminate rivals (1988, 24). He counsels pluralism and competition rather than authoritarianism and monopoly. Miller offers the most extensive arguments here: "A theory is tested by comparing it with relevant current rivals. Very abstractly put, the question is which theory is a better basis for explaining phenomena. . . . One confirms a theory by showing the best explanations of relevant phenomena appeal to instances of mechanisms in the repertoire of the theory rather than relying on rival theories" (1987, 140). In other words, Miller stresses that each competing theory has a repertoire of causal mechanisms that can be applied to the relevant phenomena or subject domains it purports to cover. For each phenomenon or domain under investigation, the question is to find the theory that supplies the best causal mechanisms. And Most (1990) draws on Platt (1966) and offers a positivist research-design to address the question of competing theories:

1. consider a phenomenon or an existing result
2. devise as many alternative hypotheses as possible that might be capable of explaining it
3. for each hypothesis, specify additional predictive expectations that should hold if it is valid
4. devise a crucial experiment (or several of them) that will as nearly as possible exclude one or more of the hypotheses
5. move quickly to carry out the experiment to get a clear result
6. exclude the falsified hypotheses
7. recycle the procedure, making subhypotheses or sequential hypotheses to refine the possibilities, and so on.

26. Rule argues that "rational choice models only move from the provocative and intriguing to the convincing by identifying sets of data for which the models provide better accounts than do alternative possibilities. We need

more serious efforts to confront the models with such pertinent evidence" (1988, 43). Mueller maintains that "unless public choice–derived models can outperform the 'traditional, ad hoc' models against which they compete, the practical relevance of public choice theories must remain somewhat in doubt" (1989, 193). Eckstein (1980) offers a classic test of rational actor versus deprived actor theories of protest and rebellion. Arrow's comments about competition and authority systems also apply to competition and research programs: "The owl of Minerva flies not in the dusk but in the storm" (1974, 65). Hence, social scientists should test their pet predictions of empirical regularities to see whether they are different from our existing understanding (i.e., preexisting theory) of the phenomena in question: "This conformity with preexisting theories is important because in the realist view, all observation is theory-laden to a degree. Scientists compare theories not with 'the evidence' as empiricists claim but with alternative theories and background understandings of how the world works. Confirmation of a theory with those understandings is never a sufficient reason to accept it, but theory wildly at odds with them will inevitably bear a heavier burden of proof" (Shapiro and Wendt 1992, 217).

27. For examples of this approach in the field of domestic political conflict, see Lichbach 1997b, 1998a, and 1998b.

28. Pascal expressed this relativism or perspectivism in a way that is deceptively appealing to comparativists: "Truth is different on the other side of the Pyrenees." Or, as Norman, citing Protagoras, the most famous of the Sophists, put it: "Man is the measure of all things, of what is, that it is, and of what is not, that it is not.' Whatever seems to me to be the case, is true for me, and whatever seems to you to be the case, is true for you. No belief can be said to be true or false in itself, for there is no objective truth" (1983, 9).

29. Kincaid thus argues that Kuhn's (1970) relativism is self-defeating and self-referentially incoherent.

> If paradigms speak in entirely different languages, then they really never disagree. Since they share no meanings, they cannot assert what the other denies. Moreover, if meaning depends entirely on the overarching theory, then every difference in theory produces differences in meaning. So when any two individuals have different beliefs about the world, meanings will differ as well. According to Kuhn, however, differences in meaning preclude successful translation. Those who did not share Kuhn's theory of science should be unable to understand him. (1996, 30–31)

The problem with pure relativism, the position that truth is bound in space and time (i.e., to cultures), is indeed self-referential incoherence: the only social scientific law is that there are no social scientific laws. This historicist doctrine has the same universalist pretensions as the social scientific doctrine. It is, however, self-contradictory and thrives only by exempting itself from its own conclusions. As Quine puts it: "But if it were, then he, within his own culture, ought to see his own culture-bound truth as absolute. He cannot proclaim cultural relativism without rising above it, and he cannot rise above it without giving it up" (1975, 238). One therefore cannot argue that all beliefs are unfounded, except this belief itself, or that all statements are biased, except this statement itself. Nihilism, relativism, and perspectivism, goes the counterargument, are illusory and only lead to sophistry, casuistry, and historicism.

30. Since scientists face incentives to strategically reveal their results and the collective action problem of monitoring their actions, Moore's "immunizing stratagem" is to be judicious: "As one tries to grapple with the details of contradictory and fragmentary evidence, either of two things may happen. The certainty may evaporate into a chaos of ill-assorted facts, or else the evidence may be selected to produce an argument that runs too smoothly to be true" (1966, 356). Moore thus promises:

> I had no intention of forcing the facts of German history though a conceptual sieve in order to "test" hypotheses. Historical facts have a certain patterned relationship to each other that such a procedure would obliterate and destroy. It is the task of the investigator to elicit this pattern through careful and critical attention to the evidence. It is necessary to proceed dialectically, patiently, listening for contradictory clues and signals, much as a skilled diagnostician tries to understand the set of organs and tissues in a live human patient while searching for patterns that will reveal a state of health or a specific disease. Dissection and hypotheses are necessary in both forms of inquiry at certain points. But they are nowhere near enough. (1978, xvi)

Moore thus rejects relativism, or the idea that we are trapped in our own research communities.

31. Bacon argues that "the men of experiment are like the ant; they only collect and use; the reasoners resemble spiders who make cobwebs out of their own substance. But the bee takes a middle course; it gathers material from the flowers of the garden and the field, but transforms and digests it by a power of its own. Not unlike this is the true business of philosophy for it neither relies solely or chiefly on the powers of the mind, nor does it take the matter which it gathers from natural history and mechanical experiments and lay it up in the memory whole, as it finds it; but lays it up in the understanding altered and digested" (cited in Hacking 1983, 247).

32. Kuhn (1970) challenges the traditional view of theory as a formal and unified nomological deductive system that can be used to explain particular cases. He maintains that the fruitfulness of a theory is demonstrated in model treatments of specific problems. A paradigm is therefore a collection of models with an unspecified range of application. The effectiveness of the models within the range varies considerably. The paradigm develops by adjusting ceteris paribus conditions to take account of local variations.

33. Lakatos offers a classic reflection on this problem (1970, 151–52). He indicates several potentially productive sequences of inquiry: data-theory-data-theory (Hempel), theory-data-theory-data (Popper), theory-theory-data-data, and data-data-theory-theory. Given the problem of observational equivalence of these four sequences and given that fields develop by the autonomous development of ideas (theory-theory-data-data) and the autonomous development of experiment (data-data-theory-theory), why privilege the specific alternation of theory and evidence (data-theory-data-theory or theory-data-theory-data) favored by positivists like Hempel or Popper? Where is the evidence that this is the best way to make progress in a field? More practically, why should scientific reports involve tortuous reconstructed logics (even if skeptics believed that they were more than post hoc reconstructions anyway)?

34. Hacking argues:

> Suppose we say that there are theories, models, and phenomena. A natural idea would be that the models are doubly models. They are models of the phenomena, and they are models of the theory. That is, theories are always too complex for us to discern their consequences, so we simplify them in mathematically tractable models. At the same time these models are approximate representations of the universe. In this picture, what Kuhn calls articulation becomes partly a matter of constructing models that human minds and known computational techniques can operate. That leads to the following conception.
>
> 1. The phenomena are real, we saw them happen.
> 2. The theories are true, or at any rate aim at the truth.
> 3. The models are intermediaries, siphoning off some aspects of real phenomena and connecting them, by simplifying mathematical structures, to the theories that govern the phenomena. (1983, 216–17)

35. Cartwright refers to a patchwork of laws, a set of local and inconsistent models. She is antirealist about theories in that she believes that theories can have heuristic value in particular domains.

> Metaphysical nomological pluralism is the doctrine that nature is governed in different domains by different systems of laws not necessarily related to each other in any systematic or uniform way: by a patchwork of laws. Nomological pluralism opposes any kind of fundamentalism. We are here concerned especially with the attempts of physics to gather all phenomena into its own abstract theories. In *How the Laws of Physics Lie* I argue that most situations are brought under a law of physics only by distortion, whereas they can often be described fairly correctly by concepts from more phenomenological laws (p. 289). (1994, 279)

She argues that models are not deducible from the theory in which they are embedded. She also suggests that because of practical needs, physics can employ a number of mutually inconsistent models within the same theory. These models, moreover, are robust under theory change: often physicists keep the model and dump the theory. Local truth in these inconsistent models may therefore not be captured by the global theories.

36. Weber stresses the need for empirical investigation of the applicability of ideal-type laws. He uses the example of the generalization called Gresham's Law, which is but "a rationally evident anticipation of human action under given conditions and under the ideal-typical assumption of purely rational action." According to Weber, only experience "can teach us how far action really does take place in accordance with it. This experience does in fact demonstrate that the proposition has a very far-reaching validity" (1978, 10).

37. Stinchcombe suggests that "mechanisms . . . are a subtype of 'model,' or in the more informative phrase of James S. Coleman (1964), sometimes-true theories. In the clearest of models, there will be included a statement of empirical conditions which are assumed for the model to hold. . . . A statement of a model that is sometimes true . . . together with the relevant statements which give necessary and sufficient empirical conditions for the model to hold, constitute a theory" (1991, 375). Mechanisms thus have "boundary conditions, conditions beyond which the mechanism is known not to hold" (376). Variations in the boundary conditions enable scientists to predict how closely the predictions of model match reality.

Stinchcombe (1978) also advocates an a posteriori rather than an a priori approach to comparative analysis. Rather than using Trotsky's and Tocqueville's grand theories, he recommends that social scientists focus on these scholars' historical narratives, especially the causal reasons they use to chain together sequences of events, that break down big events into causally connected sequences. In other words, he argues that "one does not apply theory to history; rather one uses history to develop theory" (in Goldstone 1991, 39). He also advocates that social scientists build "as a carpenter builds, adjusting the measurements as he goes along, rather than as an architect builds, drawing first and building later" (in Skocpol 1985, 385).

38. Boudon refers to the Cournot effect, "the convergence of two independent causal series" (1986, 175). Scharpf argues similarly: "I find it useful to conceptualize real-world events as 'intersections' of processes and facts whose separate 'logics' may be captured by explanatory theories, but whose interaction may only be accessible to historical description" (1987, 9).

39. Hechter argues that

transhistorical regularities in political life . . . do not operate in the form of recurrent structures and processes on a large scale. Whereas students of revolution have assumed they were studying phenomena like tides or celestial appearances, in reality they are studying phenomena like floods. Although floods are natural phenomena that are consistent with general principles like the physics of incompressible fluids in open channels, they cannot be precisely predicted because every instance is different. Time, place, and sequence strongly influence how the relevant processes unfold. (1995, 1524)

40. Shubik suggests that the "compatibility between different models in the same subject area is desirable, perhaps, but it is a luxury not a necessity. A rigorously consistent superstructure, into which the separate models all nicely fit, is too much to expect even in principle. A patchwork theory is to be expected, even welcomed, when one is committed as in the social sciences to working with mathematical approximations to a nonmathematical reality" (1982, 1–2).

41. George (1979) suggests that case studies emphasize process tracing of presumably general mechanisms.

42. Burnham argues that "there is a cardinal distinction between laws in the background and contingency in the (often vitally important) details. The universe runs by law, in this formulation, with details whether good or bad, left to the working out of what we may call chance. . . . Both regularity and contingency exist in history. The historian's task, ideally, is to provide an account of causalities and sequences of events that strikes the most accurate possible balance between the two" (1994, 60, 80).

43. Verba refers to the "disciplined configurative approach." He argues that case studies are "based on general rules, but on complicated combinations of them" (1967, 115). Hence, "explanation[s] may be tailored to the specific case, but they must be made of the same material and follow the same rules of tailoring" (115). Thus, "the uniqueness of the explanation for any particular case arises from the fact that the combination of relevant factors that accounts for a nation's pattern of politics will be different from the combination in another case, and the relative importance of various actors will differ from case to case" (114). However, the unique explanation of one particular case can be based on a set of general hypotheses.

44. Goldstone offers the idea of robust processes. Whereas a law is invariant with respect to initial conditions, a robust process is not. Since robust processes work out differently depending upon the initial conditions, the combination of characteristic initial conditions and laws produce outcomes. In other words, initial conditions and boundary conditions join with robust processes in complex ways and produce interaction effects. Alternatively, one can say that since the causes of a robust process vary from case to case, the outcome also varies. A robust process is therefore a sequence of events that unfolds in similar (but not necessarily identical) fashion in a variety of different historical contexts. As Goldstone puts it, "To identify the process, one must perform the difficult cognitive feat of figuring *which aspects* of the initial conditions observed, in conjunction with *which simple principles* of the many that may be at work, could have *combined* to generate the observed sequence of events" (1991, 59, emphasis in original).

Goldstone, for example, suggests that states failed to cope with external pressure either because of inadequate economic development (Russia) or because powerful elites blocked changes necessary to improve state efficiency (China, France). These variations in initial conditions produce variations in the process of state breakdown that ultimately culminated in the same outcome of social revolution. For another example, in France and Russia, villages with local autonomy reacted spontaneously to the opportunity of state paralysis while in China villages that lacked autonomy from local elites could not react until the Japanese invasion and mobilization by CCP created village-level organizations that were autonomous of local officials.

45. Tilly argues that one cannot "explain" revolutions: "It is impossible to state the invariant necessary and sufficient conditions of revolution for all times and places" (1993, 8). The reason we cannot develop universal models of revolution is that there are no macroscopic structural causes that are recurrent. Tilly thus indicates that "the attempt to build transhistorical models of revolution is doomed to eternal failure" because causal regularities "do not operate in the form of recurrent structures and processes at a large scale" (1995, 1600, 1601). As he indicates, "The conditions for revolution are not uniform, but vary from region to region and period to period. The conditions vary as politics in general varies" (1600).

There are nevertheless transhistorical regularities in the study of revolution. Tilly indicates that "general propositions consist of principles of variation for analytically separable aspects of the phenomena under examination" (1995, 1605–6). In other words, repeatable causal mechanisms are the parts of revolutions: "It is nevertheless quite possible to show that similar causal mechanisms come into play within a broad range of revolutionary situations, such mechanisms as the dramatic demonstration that a previously formidable state is vulnerable and the partial dissolution of existing state powers that commonly occurs in post-war demobilizations. I am wagering, and hoping to show, that the same sorts of mechanisms underlay the broad range of events I will call revolutions, indeed a wide variety of conflicts that do not issue in revolution" (1993, 8). Social scientists can then use these regularities to "explain" revolutions: "I also hope to show that variation in the character and incidence of revolutions results from variation in those recurrent mechanisms" (8).

The social scientist's problem, however, is that the same processes operate in variable combinations and circumstances. As Tilly puts it, these regularities "in different circumstances and sequences compound into highly variable but nonetheless explicable effects" (1995, 1601). Revolutionary "sequences and outcomes turn out to be path, time, and situation dependent, not constant from one revolution to the next." He thus suggests that "time, place, and sequence strongly influence how the relevant processes unfold; in that sense, they have an inescapably historical character" (1605, 1601).

The same general processes therefore interact with one another and with concrete historical circumstances to produce different outcomes—with the consequence that "revolutions" differ widely. Tilly thus argues that "every instance of the phenomenon . . . differs from every other one; the test of a good theory is therefore not so much to identify similarities among instances as to account systematically and parsimoniously for their variation" (1995, 1601). Consequently, as Lichbach (1995) argues, while the regularities of protest and rebellion spring from the uniformities of collective action processes, variations in the outbreaks and character of collective dissent result from combining the recurrent mechanisms of collective action. Revolution is thus continuous with a variety of adjacent phenomena. These include revolutionary politics—coups d'état and guerrilla warfare—and nonrevolutionary politics—interest groups and elections. As Tilly puts it, "In studies of revolution the work entails explaining why and how different sorts of social settings produce different varieties of forcible seizure of power over states" (1995, 1603). Another implication is that revolution is not self-contained and self-motivated. As Tilly indicates: "The events in question are far from self-motivating experience[s] of self-contained structures; they are local manifestations of fluxes extending far beyond their own perimeters. Floods and revolutions have no natural boundaries; observers draw lines around them for their own analytic convenience" (1601).

Tilly offers two analogies. The first is a traffic jam: one cannot predict when a traffic jam will occur, but once it does occur a traffic jam displays recurring patterns that can be understood. The second analogy is floods: "Students of revolution have imagined they were dealing with phenomena like ocean tides, whose regularities they could deduce from sufficient knowledge of celestial motion, when they were actually confronting phenomena like great floods, equally coherent occurrences from a causal perspective, but enormously variable in structure, sequence, and consequences as a function of terrain, previous precipitation, built environment, and human response" (1995, 1601). He continues: "For hydrologists, a flood is a wave of water that passes through a basin; a severe flood is one in which a considerable share of the water overflows the basin's perimeter. For our purposes, the equations hydrologists use to compute water flow in floods have three revealing characteristics: they reduce floods to special cases of water flow within basins rather than making them sui generis, their results depend heavily on the hydrologist's delimitation of the basin, while estimation of the flood's perimeters requires extensive empirical knowledge of that basin. Yet the equations embody very general principles, the physics of incompressible fluids in open channels."

In sum, individual features but not the totality of revolution can be explained by general theories. Tilly thus suggests that "revolution turns out to be a coherent phenomenon, but coherent in its variation and in its continuity with nonrevolutionary politics, not in any repetitious uniformity" (1995, 1605).

46. King, Keohane, and Verba (1994) suggest that social scientists put together causal processes to explain outcomes. While any concrete social phenomenon is describable in terms of particular combinations of general properties, there are few rules of combination and interaction.

47. Another interesting application (the analytical narrative version of Chong 1991) would be to civil rights. One can show how the civil rights movement navigated a series of crises from Montgomery, to the freedom rides, to the March on Washington, to the urban riots, and finally to the Poor People's Campaign.

References

Abelson, Robert P. 1996. "The Secret Existence of Expressive Behavior." In *The Rational Choice Controversy,* ed. Jeffrey Friedman, 25–36. New Haven: Yale University Press.

Abraham, David. 1986. *The Collapse of the Weimar Republic: Political Economy and Crisis.* 2d ed. New York: Holmes and Meier.

Abrams, Philip. 1982. *Historical Sociology.* Ithaca: Cornell University Press.

Akerlof, George A. 1984. *An Economic Theorist's Book of Tales: Essays That Entertain the Consequences of New Assumptions in Economic Theory.* Cambridge: Cambridge University Press.

Aldrich, John H. 1995. *Why Parties? The Origin and Transformation of Party Politics in America.* Chicago: University of Chicago Press.

Alexander, Jeffrey C. 1982. *Theoretical Logic in Sociology.* Vol. 1, *Positivism, Presuppositions, and Current Controversies.* Berkeley: University of California Press.

———. 1987. *Twenty Lectures: Sociological Theory since World War II.* New York: Columbia University Press.

———. 1988. "The New Theoretical Movement." In *Handbook of Sociology,* ed. Neil J. Smelser, 77–101. Beverly Hills: Sage.

———. 1990. "Analytic Debates: Understanding the Relative Autonomy of Culture." In *Culture and Society: Contemporary Debates,* ed. Jeffrey C. Alexander, 1–27. Cambridge: Cambridge University Press.

Alexander, Jeffrey C., et al., eds. 1987. *The Micro-Macro Link.* Berkeley: University of California Press.

Alexander, Jeffrey C., and Steven Seidman, eds. 1990. *Culture and Society: Contemporary Debates.* Cambridge: Cambridge University Press.

Almond, Gabriel A. 1990. *A Discipline Divided: Schools and Sects in Political Science.* Newbury Park, Calif.: Sage.

Almond, Gabriel A., Scott C. Flanagan, and Robert J. Mundt., eds. 1973. *Crisis, Choice, and Change: Historical Studies of Political Development.* Boston: Little, Brown.

Almond, Gabriel A., and Sidney Verba. 1963. *The Civic Culture: Political Attitudes and Democracy in Five Nations.* Boston: Little, Brown.

———, eds. 1980. *The Civic Culture Revisited.* Newbury Park, Calif.: Sage.

Ames, Barry. 1987. *Political Survival: Politicians and Public Policy in Latin America.* Berkeley: University of California Press.

Aminzade, Ronald. 1992. "Historical Sociology and Time." *Sociological Methods and Research* 20 (May): 456–80.

Antonio, Robert J. 1985. "Values, History, and Science: The Metatheoretic Foundations of the Weber-Marx Dialogue." In *A Weber-Marx Dialogue,* ed. Robert J. Antonio and Ronald M. Glassman. Lawrence: University Press of Kansas.

Aranson, Peter H., and Peter C. Ordeshook. 1985. "Public Interest, Private Interest, and the Democratic Polity." In *The Democratic State,* ed. Roger Benjamin and Stephen L. Elkin. Lawrence: University Press of Kansas.

Archer, Margaret S. 1988. *Culture and Agency: The Place of Culture in Social Theory.* Cambridge: Cambridge University Press.

Archibald, G. C. 1965. "The Qualitative Content of Maximizing Models." *Journal of Political Economy* 73 (February): 27–36.

Aron, Raymond. 1970. *Main Currents in Sociological Thought II: Durkheim, Pareto, Weber.* New York: Anchor Books.

Arrow, Kenneth J. 1963. *Social Choice and Individual Values.* 2d ed. New Haven: Yale University Press.

———. 1974. *The Limits of Organization.* New York: W. W. Norton.

———. 1987. "Oral History I: An Interview." In *Arrow and the Ascent of Modern Economic Theory,* ed. George R. Feiwel, 191–242. Washington Square: New York University Press.

Axelrod, Robert. 1984. *The Evolution of Cooperation.* New York: Basic Books.

———. 1986. "An Evolutionary Approach to Norms." *American Political Science Review* 80 (December): 1095–1111.

Balbus, Issac D. 1971. "The Concept of Interest in Pluralist and Marxian Analysis." *Politics and Society* 1 (2): 151–77.

Baldwin, David A., ed. 1993. *Neorealism and Neoliberalism: The Contemporary Debate.* New York: Columbia University Press.

Ball, Terence. 1987. "Is There Progress in Political Science?" In *Idioms of Inquiry: Critique and Renewal in Political Science,* ed. Terrence Ball, 13–44. Albany: State University of New York Press.

Banfield, Edward C. 1958. *The Moral Basis of a Backward Society.* Glencoe, Ill.: Free Press.

Barnes, Samuel H. 1997. "Electoral Behavior and Comparative Politics." In *Comparative Politics: Rationality, Culture, and Structure,* ed. Mark Irving Lichbach and Alan S. Zuckerman, 115–41. Cambridge: Cambridge University Press.

Barnes, Samuel, Max Kaase, et al. 1979. *Political Action: Mass Participation in Five Western Democracies.* Beverly Hills, Calif.: Sage.

Barnett, Vic. 1999. *Comparative Statistical Inference.* 3d ed. New York: Wiley.

Barry, Brian. 1965. *Political Argument.* London: Routledge and Kegan Paul.

———. 1978. *Economists and Democracy.* Chicago: University of Chicago Press.

Barry, Brian, and Russell Hardin, eds. 1982. *Rational Man and Irrational Society?* Beverly Hills, Calif.: Sage.

Bartels, Larry. 1995."Symposium on *Designing Social Inquiry.*" *Political Methodologist* 6:8–11.

Bates, Robert H. 1981. *Markets and States in Tropical Africa: The Political Basis of Agricultural Policies.* Berkeley: University of California Press.

———. 1983. *Essays on the Political Economy of Rural Africa.* Cambridge: Cambridge University Press.

———, ed. 1988. *Toward a Political Economy of Development.* Berkeley: University of California Press.

———. 1989. *Beyond the Miracle of the Market: The Political Economy of Agrarian Development in Kenya.* Cambridge: Cambridge University Press.

———. 1996. "Letter from the President: Area Studies and the Discipline." *APSA-CP: Newsletter of the APSA Organized Section on Comparative Politics* 7 (winter): 1–2.

———. 1997a. "Area Studies and the Discipline: A Useful Controversy." *PS: Political Science and Politics* 30 (June): 166–69.

———. 1997b. *Open-Economy Politics: The Political Economy of the World Coffee Trade.* Princeton: Princeton University Press.

———. 1998. "The International Coffee Organization: An International Institution." In *Analytic Narratives,* ed. Robert H. Bates, Avner Greif, Margaret Levi, Jean-Laurent Rosenthal, and Barry R. Weingast, 194–230. Princeton: Princeton University Press.

Bates, Robert H., and William T. Bianco. 1990. "Applying Rational Choice Theory: The Role of Leadership in Team Production." In *The Limits of Rationality,* ed. Karen Schweers Cook and Margaret Levi, 349–57. Chicago: University of Chicago Press.

Bates, Robert H., Rui J. P. de Figueiredo Jr., and Barry R. Weingast. 1998. "The Politics of Interpretation: Rationality, Culture, and Transition." *Politics and Society* 26 (December): 603–42.

Bates, Robert H., Avner Greif, Margaret Levi, Jean-Laurent Rosenthal, and Barry R. Weingast. 1998. *Analytic Narratives.* Princeton: Princeton University Press.

———. 2000. "The Analytic Narrative Project." *American Political Science Review* 94 (September): 696–702.

Becker, Gary S. 1976. *The Economic Approach to Behavior.* Chicago: University of Chicago Press.

Becker, Gary, and George Stigler. 1977. "De Gustibus Non Est Disputandum." *American Economic Review* 67:76–90.

Bell, Daniel. 1973. *The Coming of Post-Industrial Society: A Venture in Social Forecasting.* New York: Basic Books.

Bendix, Reinhard. 1962. *Max Weber: An Intellectual Portrait.* Garden City, N.Y.: Doubleday.

———. 1965. "Max Weber and Jakob Burckhardt." *American Sociological Review* 30 (April): 176–84.

———. 1984. *Force, Fate, and Freedom: On Historical Sociology.* Berkeley: University of California Press.

Berger, Bennett M. 1995. *An Essay on Culture: Symbolic Structure and Social Structure.* Berkeley: University of California Press.

Berger, Peter L., and Thomas Luckman. 1966. *The Social Construction of Reality: A Treatise in the Sociology of Knowledge.* New York: Doubleday.

Bernstein, Richard J. 1992. *The New Constellation: The Ethical-Political Horizons of Modernity/Postmodernity.* Cambridge: MIT Press.

―――. 1996. *Hannah Arendt and the Jewish Question.* Cambridge: MIT Press.

Bhaskar, Roy. 1997. *A Realist Theory of Science.* 2d ed. London: Verso.

Bill, James A., and Robert L. Hardgrave. 1973. *Comparative Politics: The Quest for Theory.* Columbus, Ohio: Charles E. Merrill.

Blake, Judith, and Kingsley Davis. 1964. "Norms, Values, and Sanctions." In *Handbook of Modern Sociology,* ed. Robert E. L. Faris. Chicago: Rand McNally.

Blaug, Mark. 1992. *The Methodology of Economics: Or How Economists Explain.* 2d ed. Cambridge: Cambridge University Press.

Bloch, Marc. 1967. "A Contribution towards a Comparative History of European Societies." In *Land and Work in Medieval Europe,* Marc Bloch. Berkeley: University of California Press.

Bloom, Allan. 1987. *The Closing of the American Mind.* New York: Touchstone.

Bohman, James. 1993. *New Philosophy of Social Science: Problems of Indeterminacy.* Cambridge: MIT Press.

Boudon, Raymond. 1986. *Theories of Social Change: A Critical Appraisal.* Berkeley: University of California Press.

―――. 1987. "The Individualistic Tradition in Sociology." In *The Micro-Macro Link,* ed. Jeffrey C. Alexander, Bernhard Giesen, Richard Münch, and Neil J. Smelser, 45–70. Berkeley: University of California Press.

Boumans, Marcel. 1999. "Built-in Justifications." In *Models As Mediators: Perspectives on Natural and Social Science,*ed. Mary S. Morgan and Margaret Morrison, 66–96. Cambridge: Cambridge University Press.

Bourdieu, Pierre. 1977. *Outline of a Theory of Practice.* Cambridge: Cambridge University Press.

Boylan, Thomas A., and Paschal F. O'Gorman. 1995. *Beyond Rhetoric and Realism in Economics: Towards a Reformulation of Economic Methodology.* London: Routledge.

Brady, Henry E. 1995. "Symposium on *Designing Social Inquiry.*" *Political Methodologist* 6:11–14.

Braudel, Fernand. 1980. *On History,* trans. Sarah Matthews. Chicago: University of Chicago Press.

Brenner, Robert. 1976. "Agrarian Class Structure and Economic Development in Preindustrial Europe." *Past and Present* 70:30–75.

―――. 1982. "The Agrarian Roots of European Capitalism." *Past and Present* 97:16–113.

Brink, Chris. 2000. "Verisimilitude." In *A Companion to the Philosophy of Science,* ed. W. H. Newton-Smith, 561–63. Oxford: Blackwell.

Brown, Courtney. 1995. *Chaos and Catastrophe Theories*. Thousand Oaks, Calif.: Sage.

Brown, Michael E., Owen R. Coté Jr., Sean M. Lynn-Jones, and Steven E. Miller, eds. 2000. *Rational Choice and Security Studies: Stephen Walt and His Critics*. Cambridge: MIT Press.

Brustein, William. 1996. *The Social Origins of the Nazi Party, 1925–1933*. New Haven: Yale University Press.

Buchanan, James M., and Gordon Tullock. 1965. *The Calculus of Consent: Logical Foundations of Constitutional Democracy*. Ann Arbor: University of Michigan Press.

Bueno de Mesquita, Bruce. 1981. *The War Trap*. New Haven: Yale University Press.

Bunge, Mario. 1999. *The Sociology-Philosophy Connection*. New Brunswick, N.J.: Transaction Publishers.

Burger, Thomas. 1987. *Max Weber's Theory of Concept Formation: History, Laws, and Ideal Types*. Durham, N.C.: Duke University Press.

Burnham, Walter Dean. 1994. "Pattern Recognition and 'Doing' Political History: Art, Science, or Bootless Enterprise." In *The Dynamics of American Politics: Approaches and Interpretations*, ed. Lawrence C. Dodd and Calvin Jillson, 59–98. Washington, D.C.: Congressional Quarterly Press.

Calhoun, Craig, ed. 1994. *Social Theory and the Politics of Identity*. Oxford: Blackwell.

———. 1995. *Critical Social Theory: Culture, History, and the Challenge of Difference*. Oxford: Basil Blackwell.

Callinicos, Alex. 1988. *Making History: Agency, Structure and Change in Social Theory*. Ithaca: Cornell University Press.

Camic, Charles. 1989. "Structure after 50 Years: The Anatomy of a Charter." *American Journal of Sociology* 95:38–107.

Campbell, Angus, Philip E. Converse, Warren E. Miller, and Donald E. Stokes. 1960. *The American Voter*. New York: Wiley.

Campbell, D. T., and J. C. Stanley. 1963. *Experimental and Quasi-Experimental Designs for Research*. Skokie, Ill.: Rand McNally.

Caporaso, James. 1995. "Research Design, Falsification, and the Qualitative-Quantitative Divide." *American Political Science Review* 89:457–60.

Cartwright, Nancy. 1983. *How the Laws of Physics Lie*. Oxford: Clarendon.

———. 1989. *Nature's Capacities and Their Measurement*. Oxford: Oxford University Press.

———. 1994. "Fundamentalism vs. The Patchwork of Laws." *Proceedings of the Aristotelian Society* 94:279–92.

———. 1999a. *The Dappled World: A Study of the Boundaries of Science*. Cambridge: Cambridge University Press.

———. 1999b. "Models and the Limits of Theory: Quantum Hamiltonians and the BCS Model of Superconductivity." In *Models As Mediators: Perspectives on Natural and Social Science*, ed. Mary S. Morgan and Margaret Morrison, 241–81. Cambridge: Cambridge University Press.

Carver, Terrell, and Paul Thomas, eds. 1995. *Rational Choice Marxism.* University Park: Penn State University Press.

Chilcote, Ronald H. 1994. *Theories of Comparative Politics: The Search for a Paradigm Reconsidered.* 2d ed. Boulder: Westview.

Chilton, Stephen. 1988. "Defining Political Culture." *Western Political Quarterly* 41 (September): 420–45.

Chong, Dennis. 1991. *Collective Action and the Civil Rights Movement.* Chicago: University of Chicago Press.

Cohen, Youssef. 1994. *Radicals, Reformers, and Reactionaries: The Prisoner's Dilemma and the Collapse of Democracy in Latin America.* Chicago: University of Chicago Press.

Colburn, Forrest D. 1986. *Post-Revolutionary Nicaragua: State, Class, and the Dilemmas of Agrarian Policy.* Berkeley: University of California Press.

Coleman, James S. 1987. "Microfoundations and Macrosocial Behavior." In *The Micro-Macro Link,* ed. Jeffrey C. Alexander, Bernhard Giesen, Richard Münch, and Neil J. Smelser. Berkeley: University of California Press.

———. 1990. *Foundations of Social Theory.* Cambridge, Mass.: Belknap.

Collier, David. 1993. "The Comparative Method." In *Political Science: The State of the Discipline II,* ed. Ada W. Finifter. Washington: American Political Science Association.

———. 1995. "Translating Quantitative Methods for Qualitative Researchers: The Case of Selection Bias." *American Political Science Review* 89:461–66.

Collier, David, and James Mahon. 1993. "Conceptual 'Stretching' Revisited: Adapting Categories in Comparative Analysis." *American Political Science Review* 87:845–55.

Collins, Randall. 1986. *Max Weber: A Skeleton Key.* Beverly Hills: Sage.

———. 1996. "Can Rational Action Theory Unify Future Social Science?" In *James S. Coleman,* ed. Jon Clark. London: Falmer Press.

Cook, Thomas D., and Donald T. Campbell. 1979. *Quasi-Experimentation: Design and Analysis Issues for Field Settings.* Boston: Houghton Mifflin.

Cox, Gary W. 1987. *The Efficient Secret: The Cabinet and the Development of Political Parties in Victorian England.* Cambridge: Cambridge University Press.

———. 1997. *Making Votes Count: Strategic Coordination in the World's Electoral Systems.* Cambridge: Cambridge University Press.

Crespi, Franco. 1989. *Social Action and Power.* Oxford: Basil Blackwell.

Dahl, Robert A. 1966. "Some Explanations." In *Political Oppositions in Western Democracies,* ed. Robert A. Dahl, 348–86. New Haven: Yale University Press.

Dahrendorf, Ralf. 1958. "Out of Utopia: Toward a Re-Orientation of Sociological Analysis." *American Journal of Sociology* 64 (September): 115–27.

Davidson, Donald. 1973–74. "On the Very Idea of a Conceptual Scheme." *Proceedings and Addresses of the American Philosophical Association* 47:5–20.

———. 1980. *Essays on Actions and Events.* Oxford: Oxford University Press.

Davis, Philip J., and Reuben Hersh. 1981. *The Mathematical Experience.* Boston: Houghton Mifflin.

Derry, T. K. 1981. "Norway." In *Fascism in Europe,* ed. S. J. Woolf, 223–36. London: Methuen.

Deutsch, Karl W. 1963. *The Nerves of Government: Models of Politial Communication and Control.* New York: Free Press.

Diermeier, Daniel. 1996. "Rational Choice and the Role of Theory in Science." In *The Rational Choice Controversy,* ed. Jeffrey Friedman, 59–84. New Haven: Yale University Press.

Dixit, Avinash K. 1996. *The Making of Economic Policy: A Transaction-Cost Politics Perspective.* Cambridge: MIT Press.

Downs, Anthony. 1957. *An Economic Theory of Democracy.* New York: Harper and Row.

Dreyfus, Hubert L., and Paul Rabinow. 1983. *Michel Foucault: Beyond Structuralism and Hermeneutics.* 2d ed. Chicago: University of Chicago Press.

Durkheim, Emile. [1893] 1933. *The Division of Labor in Society,* trans. George Simpson. New York: Free Press.

———. [1897] 1951. *Suicide: A Study in Sociology,* trans. John A. Spauling and George Simpson. New York: Free Press.

Easton, David. 1965. *A Framework for Political Analysis.* Englewood Cliffs, N.J.: Prentice-Hall.

Eckstein, Harry. 1963. "A Perspective on Comparative Politics, Past and Present." In *Comparative Politics: A Reader,* ed. Harry Eckstein and David E. Apter, 3–32. New York: Free Press.

———. 1964. "Introduction: Toward the Theoretical Study of Internal War." In *Internal War: Problems and Approaches,* ed. Harry Eckstein, 1–32. New York: Free Press.

———. 1965. "On the Etiology of Internal Wars." *History and Theory* 4 (2): 133–65.

———. 1966. *Division and Cohesion in Democracy: A Study of Norway.* Princeton: Princeton University Press.

———. 1968. "Political Parties: Party Systems." In *International Encyclopedia of the Social Sciences,* ed. David L. Sills, vol. 11, 436–53. New York: Macmillan.

———. 1975. "Case Study and Theory in Political Science." In *Handbook of Political Science.* Vol. 7, *Strategies of Inquiry,* ed. Fred I. Greenstein and Nelson W. Polsby, 79–137. Reading, Mass.: Addison-Wesley.

———. 1980. "Theoretical Approaches to Explaining Collective Political Violence." In *Handbook of Political Conflict: Theory and Research,* ed. Ted Robert Gurr, 135–66. New York: Free Press.

———. 1988. "A Culturalist Theory of Political Change." *American Political Science Review* 82 (September): 789–804.

Eckstein, Harry, and Ted Robert Gurr. 1975. *Patterns of Authority: A Structural Basis for Political Inquiry.* New York: Wiley.

Econometric Theory. 1990. Vol. 6.

Economic Record. 1988. Vol. 10.

Edgerton, Robert B. 1985. *Rules, Exceptions, and Social Order.* Berkeley: University of California Press.

Eisenstadt, S. N., ed. 1968. *Max Weber on Charisma and Institution Building.* Chicago: University of Chicago Press.

Elias, Norbert. 1982. *State Formation and Civilization.* Oxford: Basil Blackwell.

Elkins, David, and Richard Simeon. 1979. "A Cause of Its Effect, or What Does Political Culture Explain?" *Comparative Politics* 11 (January): 127–43.

Elster, Jon. 1983a. *Sour Grapes: Studies in the Subversion of Rationality.* Cambridge: Cambridge University Press.

————. 1983b. *Explaining Technical Change: A Case Study in the Philosophy of Science.* Cambridge: Cambridge University Press.

————. 1984. *Ulysses and the Sirens: Studies in Rationality and Irrationality.* Cambridge: Cambridge University Press.

————. 1985. *Making Sense of Marx.* Cambridge: Cambridge University Press.

————. 1989a. *The Cement of Society: A Study of Social Order.* Cambridge: Cambridge University Press.

————. 1989b. *Nuts and Bolts for the Social Sciences.* Cambridge: Cambridge University Press.

————. 1989c. *Solomonic Judgements: Studies in the Limitations of Rationality.* Cambridge: Cambridge University Press.

————. 1999. *Alchemies of the Mind: Rationality and the Emotions.* Cambridge: Cambridge University Press.

————. 2000. "Rational Choice History: A Case of Excessive Ambition." *American Political Science Review* 94 (September): 685–95.

Ensminger, Jean. 1992. *Making a Market: The Institutional Transformation of an African Society.* Cambridge: Cambridge University Press.

Evans, Peter B., and John D. Stephens. 1988. "Development and the World Economy." In *Handbook of Sociology,* ed. Neil Smelser, 739–73. Beverly Hills, Calif.: Sage.

Fahey, Tony. 1982. "Max Weber's Ancient Judaism." *American Journal of Sociology* 88 (July): 62–87.

Farr, James. 1987. "Resituating Explanation." In *Idioms of Inquiry: Critique and Renewal in Political Science,* ed. Terrence Ball, 45–66. Albany: State University of New York Press.

Ferejohn, John. 1993. "Structure and Ideology: Change in Parliament in Early Stuart England." In *Ideas and Foreign Policy: Beliefs, Institutions, and Political Change,* ed. Judith Goldstein and Robert O. Keohane. Ithaca: Cornell University Press.

Feyerabend, Paul. 1988. *Against Method.* Rev. ed. London: Verso.

Feynman, Richard. 1965. *The Character of Physical Law.* Cambridge: MIT Press.

Fiorina, Morris P. 1996. "Rational Choice, Empirical Contributions, and the

Scientfic Enterprise." In *The Rational Choice Controversy,* ed. Jeffrey Friedman, 285–94. New Haven: Yale University Press.

Firmin-Sellers, Kathryn. 1996. *The Transformation of Property Rights in the Gold Coast: An Empirical Analysis Applying Rational Choice Theory.* Cambridge: Cambridge University Press.

Freud, Sigmund. 1938. *A General Introduction to Psychoanalysis.* New York: Garden City.

Frieden, Jeffry A. 1991. *Debt, Development, and Democracy: Modern Political Economy and Latin America, 1965–1985.* Princeton: Princeton University Press.

Friedman, James W. 1992. "Views on the Relevance of Game Theory." *Rationality and Society* 4 (January): 41–50.

Friedman, Jeffrey. 1996. "Introduction: Economic Approaches to Politics." In *The Rational Choice Controversy,* ed. Jeffrey Friedman, 1–24. New Haven: Yale University Press.

Friedman, Milton, and Anna Jacobson Schwartz. 1963. *A Monetary History of the United States, 1867–1960.* Princeton: Princeton University Press.

———. 1982. *Monetary Trends in the United States and the United Kingdom: Their Relation to Income, Prices, and Interest Rates, 1867–1975.* Chicago: University of Chicago Press.

———. 1991. "Alternative Approcahes to Analyzing Economic Data." *American Economic Review* 81 (March): 39–49.

Gambetta, Diego. 1993. *The Sicilian Mafia: The Business of Private Protection.* Cambridge: Harvard University Press.

Gamson, William. 1990. *The Strategy of Social Protest.* 2d ed. Belmont, Calif.: Wadsworth.

Garrett, Geoffrey, and Barry R. Weingast. 1993. "Ideas, Interests, and Institutions: Constructing the European Community's Internal Market." In *Ideas and Foreign Policy: Beliefs, Institutions, and Political Change,* ed. Judith Goldstein and Robert O. Keohane. Ithaca: Cornell University Press.

Geddes, Barbara. 1994. *Politician's Dilemma: Building State Capacity in Latin America.* Berkeley: University of California Press.

Geertz, Clifford. 1973. "Thick Description: Toward an Interpretive Theory of Culture." In *The Interpretation of Cultures,* ed. Clifford Geertz. New York: Basic Books.

Gellner, Ernest. [1962] 1970. "Concepts and Society." Reprinted in *Sociological Theory and Philosophical Analysis,* ed. D. Emmet and A. MacIntyre. London: Macmillan.

———. 1992. *Postmodernism, Reason, and Religion.* London: Routledge.

———. 1998. *Language and Solitude: Wittgenstein, Malinowski and the Habsburg Dilemma.* Cambridge: Cambridge University Press.

George, Alexander. 1979. "Case Studies and Theory Development." In *Diplomacy,* ed. P. Lauren, 43–68. New York: Free Press.

Gibbard, Allan. 1973. "Manipulation of Voting Schemes: A General Result." *Econometrica* 41 (July): 587–601.

Gibbard, Allan, and Hal Varian. 1978. "Economic Models." *Journal of Philosophy* 75 (November): 664–77.

Giddens, Anthony. 1976. *New Rules of Sociological Method.* London: Hutchinson.

———. 1979. *Central Problems in Social Theory: Action, Structure and Contradiction in Social Analysis.* Berkeley: University of California Press.

———. 1981. *A Contemporary Critique of Historical Materialism.* Vol. 1, *Power, Property, and the State.* Berkeley: University of California Press.

———. 1982. *Profiles and Critiques in Social Theory.* Berkeley: University of California Press.

———. 1984. *The Constitution of Society: Outline of the Theory of Structuration.* Berkeley: University of California Press.

Giere, Ronald N. 1988. *Explaining Science: A Cognitive Approach.* Chicago: University of Chicago Press.

———. 2000. In *A Companion to the Philosophy of Science,* ed. W. H. Newton-Smith, 515–24. Oxford: Blackwell.

Golden, Miriam A. 1997. *Heroic Defeats: The Politics of Job Loss.* Cambridge: Cambridge University Press.

Goldstein, Judith, and Robert O. Keohane. 1993. "Ideas and Foreign Policy: An Analytical Framework." In *Ideas and Foreign Policy: Beliefs, Institutions, and Political Change,* ed. Judith Goldstein and Robert O. Keohane. Ithaca: Cornell University Press.

Goldstone, Jack A. 1991. *Revolution and Rebellion in the Early Modern World.* Berkeley: University of California Press.

Green, Donald P., and Ian Shapiro. 1994. *Pathologies of Rational Choice Theory: A Critique of Applications in Poliical Science.* New Haven: Yale University Press.

———. 1996. "Pathologies Revisited: Reflections on Our Critics." In *The Rational Choice Controversy,* ed. Jeffrey Friedman, 235–76. New Haven: Yale University Press.

Greif, Avner. 1998. "Self-Enforcing Political Systems and Economic Growth: Late Medieval Genoa." In *Analytic Narratives,* ed. Robert H. Bates, Avner Greif, Margaret Levi, Jean-Laurent Rosenthal, and Barry R. Weingast, 23–63. Princeton: Princeton University Press.

Griffin, Larry J. 1992. "Temporality, Events, and Explanation in Historical Sociology: An Introduction." *Sociological Methods and Research* 20 (May): 403–27.

Grossmann, Reinhardt. 1992. *The Existence of the World: An Introduction to Ontology.* London: Routledge.

Guetzkow, Harold. 1950. "Long Range Research in International Relations." *American Perspective* 4 (fall): 421–40.

Gurr, Ted Robert. 1970. *Why Men Rebel.* Princeton: Princeton University Press.

Haas, Peter M. 1992. "Introduction: Epistemic Communities and International Policy Coordination." *International Organization* 46 (winter): 1–35.

Habermas, Jürgen. 1984. *The Theory of Communicative Action.* Vol. 1, *Reason and the Rationalization of Society,* trans. Thomas McCarthy. Boston: Beacon.

Hacking, Ian. 1983. *Representing and Intervening: Introductory Topics in the Philosophy of Natural Science.* Cambridge: Cambridge University Press.

Hall, John A. 1986. *Powers and Liberties: The Causes and Consequences of the Rise of the West.* Berkeley: University of California Press.

———. 1993. "Ideas and the Social Sciences." In *Ideas and Foreign Policy: Beliefs, Institutions, and Political Change,* ed. Judith Goldstein and Robert O. Keohane. Ithaca: Cornell University Press.

Hall, Peter A., ed. 1989. *The Political Power of Economic Ideas.* Princeton: Princeton University Press.

———. 1997. "The Role of Interests, Institutions, and Ideas in the Comparative Political Economy of the Industrialized Nations." In *Comparative Politics: Rationality, Culture, and Structure,* ed. Mark Irving Lichbach and Alan S. Zuckerman, 174–207. Cambridge: Cambridge University Press.

Hamilton, Richard F. 1996. *The Social Misconstruction of Reality: Validity and Verification in the Scholarly Community.* New Haven: Yale University Press.

Hamlyn, D. W. 1987. *The Penguin History of Western Philosophy.* New York: London.

Hannan, Michael T., and John Freeman. 1989. *Organizational Ecology.* Cambridge: Harvard University Press.

Hardin, Russell. 1982. *Collective Action.* Baltimore: Johns Hopkins University Press.

———. 1995. *One for All: The Logic of Group Conflict.* Princeton: Princeton University Press.

Harris, James F. 1992. *Against Relativism: A Philosophical Defense of Method.* LaSalle, Ill.: Open Court.

Harsanyi, John. 1969. "Rational-Choice Models of Political Behavior vs. Functionalist and Conformist Theories." *World Politics* 21 (July): 513–38.

Hartmann, Stephan. 1999. "Models and Stories in Hadron Physics." In *Models As Mediators: Perspectives on Natural and Social Science,* ed. Mary S. Morgan and Margaret Morrison, 326–46. Cambridge: Cambridge University Press.

Hausman, Daniel M. 1992. *The Inexact and Separate Science of Economics.* Cambridge: Cambridge University Press.

———. 1994. "Kuhn, Lakatos and the Character of Economics." In *New Directions in Economic Methodology,* ed. Roger E. Blackhouse, 195–215. London: Routledge.

Hayakawa, S. I. 1990. *Language in Thought and Action.* 5th ed. San Diego: Harcourt Brace Jovanovich.

Hayek, F. A. 1979. *The Counter-Revolution of Science.* 2d ed. Indianapolis: Liberty Press.

Heap, Shaun Hargreaves, Martin Hollis, Bruce Lyons, Robert Sugden, and

Albert Weale. 1992. *The Theory of Choice: A Critical Guide.* Oxford: Basil Blackwell.

Hechter, Michael. 1990. "On the Inadequacy of Game Theory for the Solution of Real-World Collective Action Problems." In *The Limits of Rationality,* ed. Karen Schweers Cook and Margaret Levi, 240–49. Chicago: University of Chicago Press.

———. 1992. "The Insufficiency of Game Theory for the Resolution of Real-World Collective Action Problems." *Rationality and Society* 4 (January): 33–40.

———. 1995. "Reflections on Historical Prophecy in the Social Sciences." *American Journal of Sociology* 100 (May): 1520–27.

Heclo, Hugh. 1994. "Ideas, Interests, and Institutions." In *The Dynamics of American Politics: Approaches and Interpretations,* ed. Lawrence C. Dodd and Calvin Jillson. Boulder: Westview.

Hedström, Peter, and Richard Swedberg. 1998. "Social Mechanisms: An Introductory Essay." In *Social Mechanisms: An Analyical Approach to Social Theory,* ed. Peter Hedström and Richard Swedberg, 1–31. Cambridge: Cambridge University Press.

Hegel, G. W. F. 1975. *Hegel's Logic.* Part I of the *Encyclopedia of the Philosophical Sciences,* trans. W. Wallace. Oxford University Press.

Heineke, J. M. 1978. "Economic Models of Criminal Behavior: An Overview." In *Economic Models of Criminal Behavior,* ed. J. M. Heineke. Amsterdam: North-Holland Publishing Co.

Hempel, Carl. 1966. *The Philosophy of Natural Science.* Englewood Cliffs: Prentice-Hall.

Hendry, David F. 1993. *Econometrics: Alchemy or Science? Essays in Econometric Methodology.* Oxford: Blackwell.

Hennis, Wilhelm. 1983. "Max Weber's 'Central Question.' " *Economy and Society* 12 (May): 135–80.

Heschel, Abraham Joshua. 1995. *A Passion for Truth.* Woodstock, Vt.: Jewish Lights Publishing.

Hesse, Mary. 2000. "Models and Analogies." In *A Companion to the Philosophy of Science,* ed. W. H. Newton-Smith, 299–307. Oxford: Blackwell.

Hirschman, Albert O. 1970. "The Search for Paradigms as a Hindrance to Understanding." *World Politics* 22 (April): 329–43.

———. 1977. *The Passions and the Interests: Political Arguments for Capitalism before Its Triumph.* Princeton: Princeton University Press.

Hobbes, Thomas. [1651] 1988. *Leviathan.* London: Penguin.

Holland, John H. 1995. *Hidden Order: How Adaptation Builds Complexity.* Reading, Mass.: Addison-Wesley.

Hollis, Martin. 1994. *The Philosophy of Social Science: An Introduction.* Cambridge: Cambridge University Press.

Holt, Robert T., and John E. Turner, eds. 1970. *The Methodology of Comparative Research.* New York: Free Press.

Howson, Colin. 2000. "Evidence and Confirmation." In *A Companion to the Philosophy of Science,* ed. W. H. Newton-Smith, 108–16. Oxford: Blackwell.

Huber, John D. 1996. *Rationalizing Parliament: Legislative Institutions and Party Politics in France.* Cambridge: Cambridge University Press.

Huckfeldt, Robert, and John Sprague. 1993. "Citizens, Contexts, and Politics." In *Political Science: The State of the Discipline, II,* ed. Ada W. Finifter, 281–303. Washington, D.C.: APSA.

Huff, Tobey E. 1984. *Max Weber and the Methodology of the Social Sciences.* New Brunswick: Transaction Books.

Hume, David. [1739] 1984. *A Treatise of Human Nature,* ed. Ernest C. Mossner. London: Penguin Books.

Hunter, Wendy. 1997. *Eroding Military Influence in Brazil: Politicians against Soldiers.* Chapel Hill: University of North Carolina Press.

Huntington, Samuel P. 1968. *Political Order in Changing Societies.* New Haven: Yale University Press.

———. 1996. *The Clash of Civilizations and the Remaking of World Order.* New York: Simon and Schuster.

Inglehart, Ronald. 1977. *The Silent Revolution: Changing Values and Political Styles among Western Publics.* Princeton: Princeton University Press.

———. 1988. "The Renaissance of Political Culture." *American Political Science Review* 82 (December): 1203–30.

———. 1990. *Culture Shift in Advanced Industrial Society.* Princeton: Princeton University Press.

———. 1997. *Modernization and Postmodernization: Cultural, Economic, and Political Change in Forty-three Societies.* Princeton: Princeton University Press.

Jackson, Frank, and Philip Pettit. 1992. "In Defense of Explanatory Ecumenism." *Economics and Philosophy* 8:1–21.

———. 1993. "Structural Explanation in Social Theory." In *Reduction, Explanation, and Realism,* ed. D. Charles and K. Lennon, 97–131. Oxford: Oxford University Press.

Jackson, Robert H. 1993. "The Weight of Ideas in Decolonization: Normative Change in International Relations." In *Ideas and Foreign Policy: Beliefs, Institutions, and Political Change,* ed. Judith Goldstein and Robert O. Keohane. Ithaca: Cornell University Press.

Jasay, Anthony de. 1989. *Social Contract, Free Ride: A Study of the Public Goods Problem.* Oxford: Clarendon.

Jervis, Robert. 1997. *System Effects: Complexity in Political and Social Life.* Princeton: Princeton University Press.

Johnson, Chalmers. 1997. "Preconception vs. Observation, or the Contributions of Rational Choice Theory and Area Studies to Contemporary Political Science." *PS: Political Science and Politics* 30 (June): 170–74.

Johnson, Chalmers, and E. B. Keehn. 1994. "A Disaster in the Making: Rational Choice and Asian Studies." *National Interest* 36 (summer): 14–22.

Jones, Larry Eugene. 1988. *German Liberalism and the Dissolution of the*

Weimar Party System, 1918–1933. Chapel Hill: University of North Carolina Press.

Journal of Econometrics. 1988. Vol. 39.

Kant, Immanuel. [1781] 1964. *Critique of Pure Reason.* New York: St. Martin's.

Kato, Junko. 1994. *The Problem of Bureaucratic Rationality: Tax Politics in Japan.* Princeton: Princeton University Press.

Katzenstein, Peter, ed. 1978. *Between Power and Plenty.* Madison: University of Wisconsin Press.

Katznelson, Ira. 1997. "Structure and Configuration in Comparative Politics." In *Comparative Politics: Rationality, Culture, and Structure,* ed. Mark Irving Lichbach and Alan S. Zuckerman, 81–112. Cambridge: Cambridge University Press.

Katznelson, Ira, and Aristide R. Zolberg, eds. 1986. *Working-Class Formation: Nineteenth-Century Patterns in Western Europe and the United States.* Princeton: Princeton University Press.

Kaufman, William E. 1992. *Contemporary Jewish Philosophies.* Detroit: Wayne State University Press.

Kaye, Harvey J. 1984. *The British Marxist Historians.* Oxford: Polity Press.

Keech, William R., Robert H. Bates, and Peter Lang. 1991. "Political Economy within Nations." In *Political Science: Looking to the Future: Comparative Politics, Policy, and International Relations,* vol. 2, ed. William Crotty. Evanston, Ill.: Northwestern University Press.

Kegley, Charles W., Jr., ed. 1995. *Controversies in International Relations Theory: Realism and the Neoliberal Challenge.* New York: St. Martin's.

Keohane, Robert O. 1984. *After Hegemony.* Princeton: Princeton University Press.

———, ed. 1986. *Neorealism and Its Critics.* New York: Columbia University Press.

Keohane, Robert O., and Helen V. Milner, eds. 1996. *Internationalization and Domestic Politics.* Cambridge: Cambridge University Press.

Kim, Young C. 1964. "The Concept of Political Culture in Comparative Politics." *Journal of Politics* 26 (May): 313–36.

Kincaid, Harold. 1988. "Supervenience: An Explanation." *Synthese* 77: 251–81.

———. 1996. *Philosophical Foundations of the Social Sciences: Analyzing Controversies in Social Research.* Cambridge: Cambridge University Press.

King, Gary. 1989. *Unifying Political Methodology: The Likelihood Theory of Statistical Inference.* New York: Cambridge.

King, Gary, Robert O. Keohane, and Sidney Verba. 1994. *Designing Social Inquiry: Scientific Inference in Qualitative Research.* Princeton: Princeton University Press.

Kiser, Edgar. 1994. "Markets and Hierarchies in Early Modern Tax Systems: A Principal-Agent Analysis." *Politics and Society* 22 (3): 284–315.

Kiser, Edgar, and Yoram Barzel. 1991. "The Origins of Democracy in England." *Rationality and Society* 3 (4): 396–422.

Kitcher, Philip. 1993. *The Advancement of Science: Science without Legend, Objectivity without Illusions.* Oxford: Oxford University Press.

Kitschelt, Herbert. 1985. "New Social Movements in West Germany and the United States." In *Political Power and Social Theory,* ed. Maurice Zeitlin, vol. 5, 273–324. Greenwich, Conn.: JAI.

———. 1989. *The Logics of Party Formation: Ecological Politics in Belgium and West Germany.* Ithaca: Cornell University Press.

———. 1994. *The Transformation of European Social Democracy.* Cambridge: Cambridge University Press.

———. 1995. *The Radical Right in Western Europe: A Comparative Analysis.* Ann Arbor: University of Michigan Press.

Knoke, David. 1990. *Political Networks: The Structural Perspective.* Cambridge: Cambridge University Press.

Kontopoulos, Kyriakos M. 1993. *The Logics of Social Structure.* Cambridge: Cambridge University Press.

Kuhn, Thomas S. 1970. *The Structure of Scientific Revolutions.* 2d ed., enlarged. Chicago: University of Chicago Press.

Kuran, Timur. 1995. *Private Truths, Public Lies: The Social Consequences of Preference Falsification.* Cambridge: Harvard University Press.

Laitin, David. 1986. *Hegemony and Culture: Politics and Religious Change among the Yoruba.* Chicago: University of Chicago Press.

———. 1992. *Language Repertoires and State Construction in Africa.* Cambridge: Cambridge University Press.

———. 1995. "Disciplining Political Science." *American Political Science Review* 89:454–56.

Laitin, David, and Aaron Wildavsky. 1988. "Political Culture and Political Preferences." *American Political Science Review* 82 (June): 589–96.

Lakatos, Imre. 1970. "Falsification and the Methodology of Scientific Research Programs." In *Criticism and the Growth of Knowledge,* ed. Imre Lakatos and Alan Musgrave, 91–196. Cambridge: Cambridge University Press.

Lamont, Michèle, and Robert Wuthnow. 1990. "Betwixt and Between: Recent Cultural Sociology in Europe and the United States." In *Frontiers of Social Theory: The New Syntheses,* ed. George Ritzer. New York: Columbia University Press.

Langlois, Richard N. 1986. "Rationality, Institutions, and Explanation." In *Economics as a Process: Essays in the New Institutional Economics,* ed. Richard N. Langlois, 225–55. Cambridge: Cambridge University Press.

Laudan, Larry. 1977. *Progress and Its Problems: Towards a Theory of Scientific Growth.* Berkeley: University of California Press.

———. 1984. *Science and Values: The Aims of Science and Their Role in Scientific Debate.* Berkeley: University of California Press.

————. 1990. *Science and Relativism: Some Key Controversies in the Philosophy of Science.* Chicago: University of Chicago Press.

————. 1996. *Beyond Positivism and Relativism: Theory, Method, and Evidence.* Boulder: Westview.

Lave, Charles A., and James G. March. 1975. *An Introduction to Models in the Social Sciences.* New York: Harper and Row.

Laver, Michael, and W. Ben Hunt. 1992. *Policy and Party Competition.* New York: Routledge.

Laver, Michael, and Norman Schofield. 1990. *Multiparty Government: The Politics of Coalition in Europe.* Oxford: Oxford University Press.

Laver, Michael, and Kenneth A. Shepsle, eds. 1994. *Cabinet Ministers and Parliamentary Government.* Cambridge: Cambridge University Press.

————. 1996. *Making and Breaking Governments: Cabinets and Legislatures in Parliamentary Democracies.* Cambridge: Cambridge University Press.

Lawson, Tony. 1994. "A Realist Theory for Economics." In *New Directions in Economic Methodology,* ed. Roger E. Blackhouse, 257–85. London: Routledge.

Levi, Margaret. 1988. *Of Rule and Revenue.* Berkeley: University of California Press.

————. 1997. *Consent, Dissent, and Patriotism.* Chicago: University of Chicago Press.

————. 1998. "Conscription: The Price of Citizenship." In *Analytic Narratives,* ed. Robert H. Bates, Avner Greif, Margaret Levi, Jean-Laurent Rosenthal, and Barry R. Weingast, 109–47. Princeton: Princeton University Press.

Levi, Margaret, Karen S. Cook, Jodi A. O'Brien, and Howard Faye. 1990. "Introduction: The Limits of Rationality." In *The Limits of Rationality,* ed. Karen Schweers Cook and Margaret Levi, 1–16. Chicago: University of Chicago Press.

Levi, Margaret, Elinor Ostrom, and James E. Alt. 1999. "Conclusion." In *Competition and Cooperation: Conversations with Nobelists about Economics and Political Science,* ed. James E. Alt, Margaret Levi, and Elinor Ostrom. New York: Russell Sage Foundation.

Lévi-Strauss, Claude. 1966. *The Savage Mind.* London: Weidenfeld and Nicholson.

Levine, Donald N. 1995. *Visions of the Sociological Tradition.* Chicago: University of Chicago Press.

Levine, Lawrence W. 1996. *The Opening of the American Mind: Canons, Culture, and History.* Boston: Beacon.

Lewin, Leif. 1988. *Ideology and Strategy: A Century of Swedish Politics.* Cambridge: Cambridge University Press.

Libecap, Gary D. 1996. "Economic Variables and the Development of the Law: The Case of Western Mineral Rights." In Lee J. Alston, Thráinn Eggertsson, and Douglass C. North. *Empirical Studies in Institutional Change.* Cambridge: Cambridge University Press.

Lichbach, Mark Irving. 1989. "Stability in Richardson's Arms Races and Cooperation in Prisoner's Dilemma Arms Rivalries." *American Journal of Political Science* 33 (November): 1016–47.

———. 1990. "Will Rational People Rebel against Inequality? Samson's Choice." *American Journal of Political Science* 34 (November): 1049–75.

———. 1992. "Nobody Cites Nobody Else: Mathematical Models of Domestic Political Conflict." *Defence Economics* 3 (4): 341–57.

———. 1995. *The Rebel's Dilemma.* Ann Arbor: University of Michigan Press.

———. 1996. *The Cooperator's Dilemma.* Ann Arbor: University of Michigan Press.

———. 1997a. "Social Theory and Comparative Politics." In *Comparative Politics: Rationality, Culture, and Structure,* ed. Mark Irving Lichbach and Alan S. Zuckerman, 239–76. Cambridge: Cambridge University Press.

———. 1997b. "Contentious Maps of Contentious Politics." *Mobilization* 2 (March): 87–98.

———. 1998a. "Contending Theories of Contentious Politics and the Structure-Action Problem of Social Order." *Annual Review of Political Science* 1 (1998): 401–24.

———. 1998b. "Competing Theories of Contentious Politics: The Case of the Civil Rights Movement." In *Social Movements and American Political Institutions,* ed. Anne Costain and Andrew McFarland, 268–84. Boston: Rowman and Littlefield.

Lichbach, Mark Irving, and Adam Seligman. 2000. *Market and Community: Social Order, Revolution, and Relegitimation.* University Park: Penn State University Press.

Lichbach, Mark Irving, and Alan S. Zuckerman, eds. 1997. *Comparative Politics: Rationality, Culture, and Structure.* Cambridge: Cambridge University Press.

Lijphart, Arend. 1971. "Comparative Politics and Comparative Method." *American Political Science Review* 65:682–93.

Lipset, Seymour Martin, and Stein Rokkan. 1967. "Cleavage Structures, Party Systems, and Voter Alignments: An Introduction." In *Party Systems and Voter Alignments,* ed. Seymour Martin Lipset and Stein Rokkan, 1–64. New York: Free Press.

Little, Daniel. 1989. *Understanding Peasant China: Case Studies in the Philosophy of Social Science.* New Haven: Yale University Press.

———. 1991. *Varieties of Social Explanation: An Introduction to the Philosophy of Science.* Boulder: Westview.

———. 1993. "On the Scope and Limits of Generalizations in the Social Sciences." *Synthese* 97 (November): 183–207.

Lloyd, Christopher. 1986. *Explanation in Social History.* Oxford: Basil Blackwell.

———. 1993. *The Structures of History.* Oxford: Basil Blackwell.

Löwith, Karl. 1991. *From Hegel to Nietzsche: The Revolution in Nineteenth-Century Thought.* New York: Columbia University Press.

Luce, R. Duncan, and Howard Raiffa. 1957. *Games and Decisions: Introduction and Critical Survey.* New York: Wiley.

Luckmann, Thomas. 1975. "On the Rationality of Institutions in Modern Life." *Archiv Europe Sociology* 16:3–15.

Luebbert, Gregory M. 1991. *Liberalism, Fascism, or Social Democracy: Social Classes and the Political Origins of Regimes in Interwar Europe.* New York: Oxford University Press.

Lukes, Steven. 1974. *Power: A Radical View.* London: Macmillan.

———. 1985. *Emile Durkheim: His Life and Work. A Historical and Critical Study.* Stanford: Stanford University Press.

MacIntyre, Alasdair. 1984. *After Virtue.* 2d ed. Notre Dame, Ind.: University of Notre Dame Press.

———. 1988. *Whose Justice? Which Rationality?* Notre Dame, Ind.: University of Notre Dame Press.

———. 1990. *Three Rival Versions of Moral Enquiry: Encyclopaedia, Genealogy, and Tradition.* Notre Dame, Ind.: University of Notre Dame Press.

Maher, Patrick. 1993. *Betting on Theories.* Cambridge: Cambridge University Press.

Maier, Charles S. 1975. *Recasting Bourgeois Europe: Stabilization in France, Germany, and Italy in the Decade after World War I.* Princeton: Princeton University Press.

Mann, Michael. 1993. *The Sources of Social Power.* Vol. 2, *The Rise of Classes and Nation-States, 1760–1914.* Cambridge: Cambridge University Press.

Mansbridge, Jane J. 1990. "Preface." In *Beyond Self-Interest,* ed. Jane J. Mansbridge, ix–xiii. Chicago: University of Chicago Press.

Marx, Karl. 1906. *Capital: A Critique of Political Economy.* New York: Modern Library.

———. [1895] 1964. *Class Struggles in France, 1848–1850.* New York: International.

Mayer, Lawrence C. 1972. *Comparative Political Inquiry: A Methodological Survey.* Homewood, Ill.: Dorsey.

Mayer, Thomas. 1993. *Truth versus Precision in Economics.* England: Edward Elgar.

Mayo, Deborah G. 1996. *Error and the Growth of Experimental Knowledge.* Chicago: University of Chicago Press.

McAdam, Doug. 1982. *Political Process and the Development of Black Insurgency, 1930–1970.* Chicago: University of Chicago Press.

McAdam, Doug, Sidney Tarrow, and Charles Tilly. 1997. In *Comparative Politics: Rationality, Culture, and Structure,* ed. Mark Irving Lichbach and Alan S. Zuckerman, 142–73. Cambridge: Cambridge University Press.

McKelvey, Richard D. 1976. "Intransitivities in Multi-dimensional Voting Models and Some Implications for Agenda Control." *Journal of Economic Theory* 12 (June): 472–82.

Merkl, Peter H. 1970. *Modern Comparative Politics.* New York: Holt, Rinehart and Winston.

Merritt, Richard L. 1971. *Systematic Approaches to Comparative Politics*. Chicago: Rand-McNally.

Merton, Robert K. 1936. "The Unanticipated Consequences of Purposive Social Action." *American Sociological Review* 1 (December): 894–904.

———. 1959. "Notes on Problem-Finding in Sociology." In *Sociology Today: Problems and Prospects*, ed. Robert K. Merton, Leonard Broom, and Leonard S. Cottrell Jr., vol. 1, ix–xxxiv. New York: Harper Torchbooks.

———. 1968. *Social Theory and Social Structure*. New York: Free Press.

Michels, Robert. [1919] 1962. *Political Parties: A Sociological Study of the Oligarchical Tendencies of Modern Democracy*. New York: Free Press.

Migdal, Joel S. 1997. "Studying the State." In *Comparative Politics: Rationality, Culture, and Structure*, ed. Mark Irving Lichbach and Alan S. Zuckerman, 208–35. Cambridge: Cambridge University Press.

Miller, Gary J. 1990. "Managerial Dilemmas: Political Leadership in Hierarchies." In *The Limits of Rationality*, ed. Karen Schweers Cook and Margaret Levi, 324–48. Chicago: University of Chicago Press.

Miller, Richard W. 1987. *Fact and Method: Explanation, Confirmation, and Reality in the Natural and Social Sciences*. Princeton: Princeton University Press.

Miller, Roger Leroy, Daniel K. Benjamin, and Douglass Cecil North. 1998. *The Economics of Public Issues*. 11th ed. New York: Addison-Wesley.

Milner, Henry. 1994. *Social Democracy and Rational Choice: The Scandinavian Experience and Beyond*. London: Routledge

Mitchell, William C. 1983. "Fiscal Behavior of the Modern Democratic State: Public Choice Perspectives and Contributions." In *Political Economy: Recent Views*, ed. Larry L. Wade. Boston: Kluwer-Nijhoff.

Moe, Terry M. 1979. "On the Scientific Status of Rational Models." *American Journal of Political Science* 23 (February): 215–43.

Mohr, Lawrence. 1996. *The Causes of Human Behavior: Implications for Theory and Method in the Social Sciences*. Ann Arbor: University of Michigan Press.

Moon, J. Donald. 1975. "The Logic of Political Inquiry: A Synthesis of Opposed Perspectives." In *Handbook of Political Science*. Vol. 1, *Political Science Scope and Theory*, ed. Fred I. Greenstein and Nelson W. Polsby. Reading, Mass.: Addison-Wesley.

Moore, Barrington. 1958. *Political Power and Social Theory: Six Studies*. Cambridge: Harvard University Press.

———. 1966. *Social Origins of Dictatorship and Democracy: Lord and Peasant in the Making of the Modern World*. Boston: Beacon.

———. 1978. *Injustice: The Social Bases of Obedience and Revolt*. White Plains, N.Y.: M. E. Sharpe.

Morrison, Margaret. 1999. "Models as Autonomous Agents." In *Models As Mediators: Perspectives on Natural and Social Science*, ed. Mary S. Morgan and Margaret Morrison, 38–65. Cambridge: Cambridge University Press.

Morrison, Margaret, and Mary S. Morgan. 1999a. "Introduction." In *Models*

As Mediators: Perspectives on Natural and Social Science, ed. Mary S. Morgan and Margaret Morrison, 1–9. Cambridge: Cambridge University Press.

——. 1999b. "Models As Mediating Instruments." In *Models As Mediators: Perspectives on Natural and Social Science,* ed. Mary S. Morgan and Margaret Morrison, 10–37. Cambridge: Cambridge University Press.

Morton, Rebecca B. 1999. *Methods and Models: A Guide to the Empirical Analysis of Formal Models in Political Science.* Cambridge: Cambridge University Press.

Mosca, Gaetano. 1939. *The Ruling Class,* trans. Arthur Livingston. New York: McGraw-Hill.

Most, Benjamin A. 1990. "Getting Started on Political Research." *Political Science* 23 (December): 592–96.

Mueller, Dennis C. 1989. *Public Choice II.* Cambridge: Cambridge University Press.

——. 1996. *Constitutional Democracy.* New York: Oxford University Press.

Münch, Richard. 1981. "Talcott Parsons and the Theory of Action. I. The Structure of the Kantian Core." *American Journal of Sociology* 86 (4): 709–39.

——. 1987. *Theory of Action: Towards a New Synthesis Going beyond Parsons.* London: Routledge and Kegan Paul.

Münch, Richard, and Neil J. Smelser, eds. 1992. *Theory of Culture.* Berkeley: University of California Press.

Munck, Gerardo L. 2001. "Game Theory and Comparative Politics: New Perspectives and Old Concerns." *World Politics* 53 (January): 173–204.

Murphey, Murray G. 1994. *Philosophical Foundations of Historical Knowledge.* Albany: State University of New York Press.

Nagel, Ernest. 1953. "The Logic of Historical Analysis." In *Readings in the Philosophy of Science,* ed. H. Feigl and M. Broadbeck, 688–700. New York: Appleton-Century-Crafts.

Nehamas, Alexander. 1996. "Nietzsche, Modernity, and Aestheticism." In *The Cambridge Companion to Nietzsche,* ed. Bernd Magnus and Kathleen M. Higgins, 223–51.

Newton-Smith, W. H. 1981. *The Rationality of Science.* London: Routledge.

——. 2000. "Introduction." In *A Companion to the Philosophy of Science,* ed. W. H. Newton-Smith, 1–8. Oxford: Blackwell.

Nietzsche, Friedrich. 1954. *Thus Spoke Zarathustra: A Book for None and All,* trans. Walter Kaufmann. New York: Penguin.

——. 1982. *The Portable Nietzsche,* ed. and trans. Walter Kaufmann. New York: Penguin.

——. 1989. *On the Genealogy of Morals; Ecce Homo,* trans. Walter Kaufmann and R. J. Hollingdale. New York: Vintage Books.

Nolte, Ernst. 1965. *Three Faces of Fascism,* trans. Leila Vennewitz. New York: Mentor.

Nordlinger, Eric. 1988. "The Return to the State: Critiques." *American Political Science Review* 82 (September): 875–85.

Norman, Richard. 1983. *The Moral Philosophers: An Introduction to Ethics.* Oxford: Clarendon.

North, Douglass C. 1981. *Structure and Change in Economic History.* New York: W. W. Norton.

———. 1990. *Institutions, Institutional Change and Economic Performance.* Cambridge: Cambridge University Press.

North, Douglass C., and Barry R. Weingast. 1989. "Constitutions and Commitment: The Evolution of Institutions Governing Public Choice in Seventeenth-Century England." *Journal of Economic History* 49 (4): 802–32.

Nozick, Robert. 1974. *Anarchy, State, and Utopia.* New York: Basic Books.

Oakes, Guy. 1988. *Weber and Rickert: Concept Formation in the Cultural Sciences.* Cambridge: MIT Press.

Olson, Mancur, Jr. 1971. *The Logic of Collective Action: Public Goods and the Theory of Groups.* Cambridge: Harvard University Press.

———. 1982. *The Rise and Decline of Nations: Economic Growth, Stagflation, and Social Rigidities.* New Haven: Yale University Press.

Opp, Karl-Dieter, Peter Voss, and Christiane Gern. 1995. *Origins of a Spontaneous Revolution: East Germany, 1989.* Ann Arbor: University of Michigan Press.

Ordeshook, Peter C. 1986. *Game Theory and Political Theory: An Introduction.* Cambridge: Cambridge University Press.

Ouaknin, Marc-Alain. 1995. *The Burnt Book: Reading the Talmud,* trans. Llewellyn Brown. Princeton: Princeton University Press.

Parfit, Derek. 1984. *Reasons and Persons.* Oxford: Clarendon.

Pareto, Vilfredo. [1920] 1980. *Compendium of General Sociology.* Abridged by Giulio Farina, edited by Elsabeth Abbott. Minneapolis: University of Minnesota Press.

Parkin, Frank. 1982. *Max Weber.* London: Routledge.

Parsons, Talcott. 1937. *The Structure of Social Action.* New York: Free Press.

Payne, Stanley G. 1995. *A History of Fascism, 1914–1945.* Madison: University of Wisconsin Press.

Pheby, John. 1988. *Methodology and Economics: A Critical Introduction.* Armonk, N.Y.: M. E. Sharpe.

Pierson, Paul. 1994. *Dismantling the Welfare State? Reagan, Thatcher, and the Politics of Retrenchment.* Cambridge: Cambridge University Press.

Platt, John Rader. 1966. *The Step to Man.* New York: Wiley.

Plott, Charles R. 1990. "Rational Choice in Experimental Markets." In *The Limits of Rationality,* ed. Karen Schweers Cook and Margaret Levi, 146–75. Chicago: University of Chicago Press.

Polya, George. 1957. *How to Solve It: A New Aspect of Mathematical Method.* 2d ed. Princeton: Princeton University Press.

———. 1962. *Mathematical Discovery: On Understanding, Learning, and Teaching Problem Solving.* Combined ed. New York: Wiley.

Popkin, Samuel L. 1979. *The Rational Peasant: The Political Economy of Rural Society in Vietnam.* Berkeley: University of California Press.

Popper, Karl J. 1965. *Conjectures and Refutations: The Growth of Scientific Knowledge.* New York: Harper Torchbooks.

———. 1968. *The Logic of Scientific Discovery.* New York: Harper and Row.

Posner, Richard A. 1980. "A Theory of Primitive Society, with Special Reference to Law." *Journal of Law and Economics* 23:1–53.

Powell, G. Bingham, Jr. 1982. *Contemporary Democracies: Participation, Stability, and Violence.* Cambridge: Harvard University Press.

Przeworski, Adam. 1985a. *Capitalism and Social Democracy.* Cambridge: Cambridge University Press.

———. 1985b. "Marxism and Rational Choice." *Politics and Society* 14 (4): 379–409.

———. 1991. *Democracy and the Market: Political and Economic Reforms in Eastern Europe and Latin America.* Cambridge: Cambridge University Press.

Przeworski, Adam, and Henry Teune. 1970. *The Logic of Comparative Social Inquiry.* New York: Wiley.

Quine, W. v. O. 1975. "On Empirically Equivalent Systems of the World." *Erkenntnis* 9 (Nov.): 313–28.

Rae, Douglas W. 1971. *The Political Consequences of Electoral Laws.* Rev. ed. New Haven: Yale University Press.

Rae, Douglas, Douglas Yates, Jennifer Hochschild, Joseph Morone, and Carol Fessler. 1981. *Equalities.* Cambridge: Harvard University Press.

Ragin, Charles C. 1987. *The Comparative Method: Moving beyond Qualitative and Quantitative Strategies.* Berkeley: University of California Press.

Ramseyer, J. Mark. 1996. *Odd Markets in Japanese History: Law and Economic Growth.* Cambridge: Cambridge University Press.

Ramseyer, J. Mark, and Frances M. Rosenbluth. 1995. *The Politics of Oligarchy: Institutional Choice in Imperial Japan.* Cambridge: Cambridge University Press.

Rapoport, Anatol. 1970. *N-Person Game Theory: Concepts and Applications.* Ann Arbor: University of Michigan Press.

Rawls, John. 1971. *A Theory of Justice.* Cambridge, Mass.: Belknap.

Redman, Deborah A. 1993. *Economics and the Philosophy of Science.* Oxford: Oxford University Press.

Reuten, Geert. 1999. "Knife-edge Caricature Modelling." In *Models As Mediators: Perspectives on Natural and Social Science,* ed. Mary S. Morgan and Margaret Morrison, 197–240. Cambridge: Cambridge University Press.

Riker, William H. 1980. "Implications from the Disequilibrium of Majority Rule for the Study of Institutions." *American Political Science Review* 76:753–66.

———. 1982a. *Liberalism Against Populism: A Confrontation between the Theory of Democracy and the Theory of Social Choice.* San Francisco: W. H. Freeman.

———. 1982b. "The Two-Party System and Duverger's Law: An Essay on the History of Political Science." *American Political Science Review* 76:753–66.

————. 1987. *The Development of American Federalism.* Boston: Kluwer Academic.

————. 1990. "Political Science and Rational Choice." In *Perspectives on Positive Political Theory,* ed. James E. Alt and Kenneth A. Shepsle, 163–81. Cambridge: Cambridge University Press.

————. 1996. *The Strategy of Rhetoric: Campaigning for the American Constitution,* ed. Randall L. Calvert, John Mueller, and Rick K. Wilson. New Haven: Yale University Press.

Riker, William H., and David L. Weimer. 1995. "The Political Economy of Transformation: Liberalization and Property Rights." In *Modern Political Economy: Old Topics, New Directions,* ed. Jeffrey S. Banks and Eric A. Hanushek, 80–107. Cambridge: Cambridge University Press.

Robinson, Joan. 1933. *Economics of Imperfect Competition.* London: Macmillan.

Roemer, John E. 1982. *A General Theory of Exploitation and Class.* Cambridge: Harvard University Press.

Rogowski, Ronald. 1974. *Rational Legitimacy: A Theory of Political Support.* Princeton: Princeton University Press.

————. 1989. *Commerce and Coalitions: How Trade Affects Domestic Political Alignments.* Princeton: Princeton University Press.

————. 1995. "The Role of Theory and Anomaly in Social-Scientific Inference." *American Political Science Review* 89 (June): 467–70.

Root, Hilton. 1987. *Peasants and King in Burgundy: Agrarian Foundations of French Absolutism.* Berkeley: University of California Press.

————. 1994. *The Fountain of Privilege: Political Foundations of Markets in Old Regime France and England.* Berkeley: University of California Press.

Rorty, Richard. 1989. *Contingency, Irony, and Solidarity.* Cambridge: Cambridge University Press.

Rosen, Stanley. 1989. *The Ancients and the Moderns: Rethinking Modernity.* New Haven: Yale University Press.

Rosenberg, Alexander. 1992. *Economics—Mathematical Politics or the Science of Diminishing Returns.* Cambridge: Cambridge University Press.

Rosenthal, Jean-Laurent. 1992. *The Fruits of Revolution: Property Rights, Litigation, and French Agriculture, 1700–1860.* Cambridge: Cambridge University Press.

————. 1998. "The Political Economy of Absolutism Reconsidered." In *Analytic Narratives,* ed. Robert H. Bates, Avner Greif, Margaret Levi, Jean-Laurent Rosenthal, and Barry R. Weingast, 64–108. Princeton: Princeton University Press.

Ross, Marc Howard. 1993. *The Culture of Conflict: Interpretations and Interests in Comparative Perspective.* New Haven: Yale University Press.

————. 1997. "Culture and Identity in Comparative Political Analysis." In *Comparative Politics: Rationality, Culture, and Structure,* ed. Mark Irving Lichbach and Alan S. Zuckerman, 42–80. Cambridge: Cambridge University Press.

Roth, Guenther. 1971. "The Genesis of the Typological Approach." In *Scholarship and Partnership: Essays on Max Weber,* ed. Reinhard Bendix and Guenther Roth. Berkeley: University of California Press.

Rouse, Joseph. 1987. *Knowledge and Power: Toward a Political Philosophy of Science.* Ithaca: Cornell University Press.

———. 1996. *Engaging Science: How to Understand Its Practices Philosophically.* Ithaca: Cornell University Press.

Rueschemeyer, Dietrich. 1984. "Historical Particularity: Reinhard Bendix." In *Vision and Method in Historical Sociology,* ed. Theda Skocpol, 129–69. Cambridge: Cambridge University Press.

Ruggie, John Gerard. 1998. *Constructing the World Polity: Essays on International Institutionalization.* London: Routledge.

Rule, James B. 1988. *Theories of Civil Violence.* Berkeley: University of California Press.

Runciman, W. G. 1989. *A Treatise on Social Theory.* Vol. 2, *Substantive Social Theory.* Cambridge: Cambridge University Press.

Sahlins, Marshall. 1976. *Culture and Practical Reason.* Chicago: University of Chicago Press.

Salmon, Merrilee H., et al. 1992. *Introduction to the Philosophy of Science.* Englewood Cliffs, N.J.: Prentice-Hall.

Samuelson, Paul. 1947. *Foundations of Economic Analysis.* Enlarged ed. Cambridge: Harvard University Press.

———. 1954. "The Pure Theory of Public Expenditure." *Review of Economics and Statistics* 36:387–89.

Sartori, Giovanni. 1970. "Concept Misformation in Comparative Politics." *American Political Science Review* 64:1033–53.

———. 1994a. "Compare Why and How: Comparing, Miscomparing, and the Comparative Method." In *Comparing Nations: Concepts, Strategies, Substance,* ed. Mattei Dogan and Ali Kazancigil. Oxford: Blackwell.

———. 1994b. *Comparative Constitutional Engineering: An Inquiry into Structures, Incentives and Outcomes.* New York: New York University Press.

Satterthwaite, Mark. 1975. "Strategy Proofness and Arrow's Conditions." *Journal of Economic Theory* 10 (October): 187–217.

Savia, Daniel R., Jr. 1988. "Rationality, Collective Action, and Karl Marx." *American Journal of Political Science* 32 (February): 50–71.

Scaff, Lawrence A. 1989. *Fleeing the Iron Cage: Culture, Politics, and Modernity in the Thought of Max Weber.* Berkeley: University of California Press.

Scandinavian Journal of Economics. 1991. Vol. 93.

Schacht, Richard. 1996. "Nietzsche's Kind of Philosophy." In *The Cambridge Companion to Nietzsche,* ed. Bernd Magnus and Kathleen M. Higgins, 151–79. Cambridge: Cambridge University Press.

Scharpf, Fritz W. 1987. "A Game-Theoretical Interpretation of Inflation and Unemployment in Western Europe." *Journal of Public Policy* 7:227–57.

———. 1997. *Games Real Actors Play: Actor-Centered Institutionalism in Policy Research.* Boulder: Westview.

Schelling, Thomas C. 1978. *Micromotives and Macrobehavior.* New York: Norton.

Schluchter, Wolfgang. 1981. *The Rise of Western Rationalism: Max Weber's Developmental History.* Berkeley: University of California Press.

Schmid, Michael. 1992. "The Concept of Culture and Its Place within a Theory of Social Action: A Critique of Talcott Parsons's Theory of Culture." In *Theory of Culture,* ed. Richard Münch and Neil J. Smelser. Berkeley: University of California Press.

Schmitt, Richard. 1995. *Beyond Separateness: The Social Nature of Human Beings—Their Autonomy, Knowledge, and Power.* Boulder: Westview.

Schmitter, Philippe C. 1977. "Modes of Interest Intermediation and Models of Societal Change in Western Europe." *Comparative Political Studies* 10 (April): 7–38.

Schneerson, Menachem Mendel. 1995. *Toward a Meaningful Life: The Wisdom of the Rebbe.* New York: William Morrow

Scholem, Gershom. 1995. *Major Trends in Jewish Mysticism.* New York: Schocken Books.

Schotter, Andrew. 1981. *The Economic Theory of Social Institutions.* Cambridge: Cambridge University Press.

Schumpeter, Joseph A. 1954. *History of Economic Analysis.* New York: Oxford University Press.

Schwartz, Thomas. 1987. "Votes, Strategies, and Institutions: An Introduction to the Theory of Collective Choice." In *Congress: Structure and Policy,* ed. Matthew D. McCubbins and Terry Sullivan. Cambridge: Cambridge University Press.

Scott, James C. 1976. *The Moral Economy of the Peasant: Rebellion and Subsistence in Southeast Asia.* New Haven: Yale University Press.

———. 1985. *Weapons of the Weak: Everyday Forms of Peasant Resistance.* New Haven: Yale University Press.

Sculli, David, and Dean Gerstein. 1985. "Social Theory and Talcott Parsons in the 1980s." *Annual Review of Sociology* 11:369–87.

Searle, John R. 1995. *The Construction of Social Reality.* New York: Free Press.

Seidman, Steven. 1983. *Liberalism and the Origins of European Social Theory.* Berkeley: University of California Press.

Seligman, Adam B. 1992. *The Idea of Civil Society.* New York: Free Press.

Selznick, Philip. 1992. *The Moral Commonwealth: Social Theory and the Promise of Community.* Berkeley: University of California Press.

Shafer, D. Michael. 1994. *Winners and Losers: How Sectors Shape the Developmental Prospects of States.* Ithaca: Cornell University Press.

Shand, John. 1994. *Philosophy and Philosophers: An Introduction to Western Philosophy.* London: Penguin.

Shapiro, Ian, and Alexander Wendt. 1992. "The Difference That Realism Makes: Social Science and the Politics of Consent." *Politics and Society* 20:197–223.

Shepsle, Kenneth. 1979. "Institutional Arrangements and Equilibrium in Multidimensional Voting Models." *American Journal of Political Science* 23 (February): 27–59.

Shubik, Martin. 1982. *Game Theory in the Social Sciences: Concepts and Solutions.* Cambridge: MIT Press.

Shugart, Matthew Soberg, and John M. Carey. 1992. *Presidents and Assemblies: Constitutional Design and Electoral Dynamics.* Cambridge: Cambridge University Press.

Silberberg, Eugene. 1978. *The Structure of Economics: A Mathematical Analysis.* New York: McGraw-Hill.

Simkin, Colin 1993. *Popper's Views on Natural and Social Science.* Leiden: E. J. Brill.

Simmons, Beth A. 1994. *Who Adjusts? Domestic Sources of Foreign Economic Policy during the Interwar Years.* Princeton: Princeton University Press.

Simon, Herbert A. 1985. "Human Nature in Politics: The Dialogue of Psychology and Political Science." *American Political Science Review* 79: 293–304.

———. 1987. "Rationality in Psychology and Economics." In *Rational Choice: The Contrast between Economics and Psychology,* ed. Robin M. Hogarth and Melvin W. Reder, 25–40. Chicago: University of Chicago Press.

Skocpol, Theda. 1976. "France, Russia, and China: A Structural Analysis of Social Revolutions." *Comparative Studies in Society and History* 18 (April): 175–210.

———. 1979. *States and Social Revolutions: A Comparative Analysis of France, Russia and China.* Cambridge: Cambridge University Press.

———. 1984. "Sociology's Historical Imagination." In *Vision and Method in Historical Sociology,* ed. Theda Skocpol, 1–21. Cambridge: Cambridge University Press.

———. 1985. "Bringing the State Back In: Strategies of Analysis in Current Research." In *Bringing the State Back In,* ed. Peter B. Evans, Dietrich Rueschemeyer, and Theda Skocpol, 3–37. Cambridge: Cambridge University Press.

———. 1995. Contribution to "The Role of Theory in Comparative Politics: A Symposium." *World Politics* 48 (October): 37–46.

Smelser, Neil J. 1992. "Culture: Coherent or Incoherent." In *Theory of Culture,* ed. Richard Münch and Neil J. Smelser, 3–28. Berkeley: University of California Press.

Smith, Adam. [1776] 1976. *An Inquiry into the Nature and Causes of the Wealth of Nations.* Chicago: University of Chicago Press.

Snidal, Duncan. 1985. "The Game *Theory* of International Politics." *World Politics* 25 (October): 25–57.

Solomon, Robert C., and Kathleen M. Higgins. 1996. *A Short History of Philosophy.* Oxford: Oxford University Press.

Steinmo, Sven, Kathleen Thelen, and Frank Longstreth, eds. 1992. *Structuring*

Politics: Historical Institutionalism in Comparative Perspective. Cambridge: Cambridge University Press.

Stigler, G. J., and G. S. Becker. 1977. "De gustibus non est disputandum." *American Economic Review* 67:76–90.

Stinchcombe, Arthur L. 1978. *Theoretical Methods in Social History.* New York: Academic Press.

———. 1980. "Is the Prisoners' Dilemma All of Sociology?" *Inquiry* 23 (June): 187–92.

———. 1991. "The Conditions of Fruitfulnes of Theorizing about Mechanisms in Social Science." *Philosophy of the Social Sciences* 21 (September): 367–88.

Strauss, Leo. 1989. *The Rebirth of Classical Political Rationalism: An Introduction to the Thought of Leo Strauss.* Chicago: University of Chicago Press.

———. 1997. *Spinoza's Critique of Religion,* trans. E. M. Sinclair. Chicago: University of Chicago Press.

Strøm, Kaare. 1990. *Minority Government and Majority Rule.* Cambridge: Cambridge University Press.

Suárez, Mauricio. 1999. "The Role of Models in the Application of Scientific Theories: Epistemological Implications." In *Models As Mediators: Perspectives on Natural and Social Science,* ed. Mary S. Morgan and Margaret Morrison, 168–96. Cambridge: Cambridge University Press.

Suppe, Frederick. 1977. "The Search for Philosophic Understanding of Scientific Theories." In *The Structure of Scientific Theories,* ed. Frederick Suppe, 3–241. Urbana: University of Illinois Press.

Swidler, Ann. 1973. "The Concept of Rationality in the Work of Max Weber." *Sociological Inquiry* 43 (1): 35–42.

———. 1986. "Culture in Action: Symbols and Strategies." *American Sociological Review* 51 (April): 273–86.

Swingewood, Alan. 1986. "Culture in Action: Symbols and Strategies." *American Sociological Review* 51 (April): 273–86.

———. 1991. *A Short History of Sociological Thought.* 2d ed. New York: St. Martin's.

Taagepera, Rein, and Matthew Soberg Shugart. 1989. *Seats and Votes: The Effects and Determinants of Electoral Systems.* New Haven: Yale University Press.

Tarrow, Sidney. 1994. *Power in Movement: Social Movements, Collective Action and Politics.* Cambridge: Cambridge University Press.

———. 1995. "Bridging the Qualitative-Quantitative Divide in Political Science." *American Political Science Review* 89:471–74.

Taylor, Charles. 1991. *The Ethics of Authenticity.* Harvard: Harvard University Press.

Taylor, Michael. 1976. *Anarchy and Cooperation.* New York: Wiley.

———. 1988a. *Rationality and Revolution.* Ed. Cambridge: Cambridge University Press.

———. 1988b. "Rationality and Revolutionary Collective Action." In *Ratio-*

nality and Revolution, ed. Michael Taylor, 63–97. Cambridge: Cambridge University Press.

―――. 1989. "Structure, Culture and Action in the Explanation of Social Change." *Politics and Society* 17 (2): 115–62.

Telushkin, Joseph. 1992. *Jewish Humor: What the Best Jewish Jokes Say about the Jews.* New York: William Morrow.

Thompson, E. P. 1966. *The Making of the English Working Class.* New York: Vintage Books.

Tilly, Charles. 1971. "Review of *Why Men Rebel.*" *Journal of Social History* 4 (summer): 416–20.

―――. 1978. *From Mobilization to Revolution.* Reading, Mass.: Addison-Wesley.

―――. 1984. *Big Structures, Large Processes, Huge Comparisons.* New York: Russell Sage.

―――. 1993. *European Revolutions, 1492–1992.* Cambridge, Mass.: Blackwell.

―――. 1995. "To Explain Political Processes." *American Journal of Sociology* 100 (May): 1594–1610.

―――. 1997. "Kings in Beggars' Raiment." *Mobilization* 2 (March): 107–11.

―――. 1999. "The Trouble with Stories." In *The Social Worlds of Higher Education,* ed. Bernice A. Pescosolido and Ronald Aminzade. Thousand Oaks, Calif.: Pine Forge.

Tolstoy, Leo. 1968. *War and Peace,* trans. Ann Dunnigan. New York: Signet.

Tong, James W. 1991. *Disorder Under Heaven: Collective Violence in the Ming Dynasty.* Stanford: Stanford University Press.

Toulmin, S. 1967. *The Philosophy of Science: An Introduction.* London: Methuen.

Tsebelis, George. 1990. *Nested Games: Rational Choice in Comparative Politics.* Berkeley: University of California Press.

Tsebelis, George, and Jeannette Money. 1997. *Bicameralism.* Cambridge: Cambridge University Press.

Tullock, Gordon. 1971. "The Paradox of Revolution." *Public Choice* 11 (fall): 89–99.

Turner, Bryan S. 1992. *Max Weber: From History to Modernity.* London: Routledge.

Turner, Charles. 1992. *Modernity and Politics in the Work of Max Weber.* London: Routledge.

Turner, Jonathan H. 1986. *The Structure of Sociological Theory.* 4th ed. Belworth, Calif.: Wadsworth.

―――. 1988. *A Theory of Social Interaction.* Stanford: Stanford University Press.

Van Den Berg, Axel. 1998. "Sociological Theory and Social Mechanisms." In *Social Mechanisms: An Analytical Approach to Social Theory,* ed. Peter Hedström and Richard Swedberg, 204–37. Cambridge: Cambridge University Press.

Van Fraassen, Bas C. 1980. *The Scientific Image.* Oxford: Clarendon.

Verba, Sidney. 1967. "Some Dilemmas in Comparative Research." *World Politics* 20 (Oct.): 111–27.

Verba, Sidney, and Norman H. Nie. 1972. *Participation in America: Political Democracy and Social Equality.* New York: Harper and Row.

Von Neumann, John, and Oskar Morgenstern. 1953. *Theory of Games and Economic Behavior.* 3d ed. Princeton: Princeton University Press.

Wade, Robert. 1994. *Village Republics: Economic Conditions for Collective Action in South India.* San Francisco: Institute for Contemporary Studies.

Wallerstein, Immanuel A. 1974. *The Modern World System, I: Capitalist Agriculture and the Origins of the European World-Economy in the Sixteenth Century.* New York: Academic Press.

Wallerstein, Michael. 2001. "Does Comparative Politics Need a TOE (Theory of Everything)?" APSA-CP: *Newsletter of the APSA Organized Section on Comparative Politics* 12 (winter).

Waltz, Kenneth N. 1979. *Theory of International Politics.* Reading, Mass.: Addison-Wesley.

Waterbury, John. 1993. *Exposed to Innumerable Delusions: Public Enterprise and State Power in Egypt, India, Mexico, and Turkey.* Cambridge: Cambridge University Press.

Waters, Malcolm. 1995. *Globalization.* London: Routledge.

Webb, Eugene T., Donald T. Campbell, Richard D. Schwartz, Lee Sechrest, and Janet Belew Grove. 1981. *Nonreactive Measures in the Social Sciences.* 2d ed. Boston: Houghton Mifflin.

Weber, Max. 1946. *From Max Weber: Essays in Sociology,* trans. and ed. Hans H. Gerth and C. Wright Mills. New York: Oxford University Press.

———. 1947. *The Theory of Social and Economic Organization,* trans. A. M. Henderson and Talcott Parsons. New York: Free Press.

———. [1903–1917] 1949. *The Methodology of the Social Sciences,* trans. and ed. Edward A. Shils and Henry A. Finch. New York: Free Press.

———. 1951. *The Religion of China: Confucianism and Taoism,* trans. Hans H. Gerth. New York: Free Press.

———. [1917–19] 1952. *Ancient Judaism,* trans. and ed. Hans H. Gerth and Don Martindale. New York: Free Press.

———. 1958. *The City,* trans. and ed. Don Martindale and Gertrud Neuwirth. New York: Free Press.

———. [1923] 1961. *General Economic History,* trans. F. H. Knight. New York: Collier.

———. [1924] 1968. *Economy and Society.* 2 vols. Berkeley: University of California Press.

———. [1903–6] 1975. *Roscher and Knies: The Logical Problems of Historical Economics,* trans. G. Oakes. New York: Free Press.

———. [1907] 1977. *Critique of Stammler,* trans. Guy Oakes. New York: Free Press.

———. [1904–5] 1985. *The Protestant Ethic and the Spirit of Capitalism,* trans. Talcott Parsons. London: Unwin.

————. [1896] 1988. *The Agrarian Sociology of Ancient Civilizations,* trans. R. I. Frank. London: Verso.

————. [1922] 1991. *The Sociology of Religion,* trans. Ephraim Fischoff. Boston: Beacon.

————. [1958] 1992. *The Religion of India: The Sociology of Hinduism and Buddhism,* trans. and ed. Hans H. Gerth and Don Martindale. New Delhi: Munshiram Manoharlal Publishers.

Weingast, Barry. 1998. "Political Stability and Civil War: Institutions, Commitment, and American Democracy." In *Analytic Narratives,* ed. Robert H. Bates, Avner Greif, Margaret Levi, Jean-Laurent Rosenthal, and Barry R. Weingast, 148–93. Princeton: Princeton University Press.

Weintraub, E. Roy. 1985. *General Equilibrium Analysis: Studies in Appraisal.* Cambridge: Cambridge University Press.

Welch, Claude E., Jr. 1980. *The Anatomy of Rebellion.* New York: State University Press of New York.

Weldes, Jutta. 1989. "Marxism and Methodological Individualism." *Theory and Society* 18:353–86.

Wendt, Alexander. 1987. "The Agent-Structure Problem in International Relations Theory." *International Organization* 41:335–70.

————. 1999. *Social Theory of International Politics.* Cambridge: Cambridge University Press.

Wildavsky, Aaron. 1987. "Choosing Preferences by Constructing Institutions." *American Political Science Review* 81 (March): 3–21.

————. 1992. "Indispensable Framework or Just Another Ideology? Prisoner's Dilemma as an Antihierarchical Game." *Rationality and Society* 4 (January): 8–23.

Winch, Peter. 1990. *The Idea of a Social Science and Its Relation to Philosophy.* Atlantic Highlands, N.J.: Humanities Press International.

Wittman, Donald. 1995. *The Myth of Democratic Failure: Why Political Institutions Are Efficient.* Chicago: University of Chicago Press.

Woever, Ole. 1996. "The Rise and Fall of the Inter-paradigm Debate." In *International Theory: Positivism and Beyond,* ed. Steve Smith, Ken Book, and Marysia Zalewski. Cambridge: Cambridge University Press.

World Politics. 1995. Symposium, "The Role of Theory in Comparative Politics." *World Politics* (October): 1–49.

Wrong, Dennis H. 1994. *The Problem of Order: What Unites and Divides Society.* New York: Free Press.

Wuthnow, Robert. 1987. *Meaning and Moral Order: Explorations in Cultural Analysis.* Berkeley: University of California Press.

————. 1992. "Infrastructure and Superstructure: Revisions in Marxist Sociology of Culture." In *Theory of Culture,* ed. Richard Münch and Neil J. Smelser. Berkeley: University of California Press.

Wuthnow, Robert, James Davison Hunter, Albert Bergesen, and Edith

Kurzweil. 1984. *Cultural Analysis: The Work of Peter L. Berger, Mary Douglas, Michel Foucault, and Jürgen Habermas.* London: Routledge.

Zagorin, Perez. 1982. *Rebels and Rulers, 1500–1660.* Vol. 1, *Society, States and Early Modern Revolution: Agrarian and Urban Rebellions.* Cambridge: Cambridge University Press.

Zuckerman, Alan. 1991. *Doing Political Science: An Introduction to Political Analysis.* Boulder: Westview.

Index

Alternative baseline models. *See* Models and foils

Baselines, xv, xviii, 9, 56–62
Behavioral (mechanistic or material) view of subjectivity, 41–44, 74–75, 83–84
Boundaries, xv, xviii, 9, 62–64

Causal mechanisms. *See* Nuts and bolts
Causal realism, xvi, 105, 152, 177–78
Causal thinking, 129–31
Coleman-Boudon diagram. *See* Microfoundations
Comparative statics, xvi, 39–40, 42, 66–67, 188, 189
Conjunctures, 240
Constitutive thinking, 81–84, 87, 111, 117, 119–22, 241–42
Covering laws, xvi, 152–55, 173–75
Creative confrontations. *See* Disputationalist
Culturalists, xv, 14–15, 73–98, 156–58, 171
    thin and thick, 73–78

Disputationalist, xiv, 8, 9, 47, 139. *See also* Models and foils
Duhem-Quine thesis, 175–77, 195, 199

Empirical conciliation, 53–55
Equilibrium, 39, 64–65, 229
Explanation

causal-mechanism tradition, 105–6
    unification tradition, 105
Evidence, 173–82

Falsificationism, xvii, 194, 271–72
Fixed preferences, 41–44
Functionalism, 108

gedanken, 38, 40
Generalizations, 151–67

Hermeneutics, 89, 104
Holism, 104–5, 112, 126
Human nature rationalists. *See* Rationalists, thin and thick

Ideal types, 16–18, 67–68, 131, 162–63
Identities, 117–25, 131–32
Individualism, 81–82
Induction and deduction, 188–93
Inference to the best explanation, 240–41
Institutions, 117–18, 121–25, 146
Interests, 118–25
Interpretation, xvii, 13, 88–90, 129–31, 142–43, 152, 156–58. *See also* Hermeneutics
Intertheoretical reduction. *See* Microfoundations
Invisible hand explanations. *See* Microfoundations

Kant-Weber perspectivism, 134–39, 142, 163

313

Lakatos, Imre, xvii, 134, 169, 202–5
Laws, 182–86
Learning, 66

Methodological collectivism. *See*
    Holism
Methodological individualism. *See*
    Microfoundations
Microfoundations, xv, 9, 14, 32–37,
    45–49, 126
Models and foils, xvi, 3–10, 53, 62,
    68, 133–47, 209–10
    competitors, xiii, 4–7, 169, 202
    pragmatists, xiii, 4–7, 170, 202
    synthesizers, xiii, 4–7, 115–16,
        131–32, 170, 202
Models of theories, 180–81, 186–93.
    See also Causal mechanisms;
    Nuts and bolts
Modest rational choice theory, xv,
    xvii–xviii, 69, 210–14

Natural kinds, 107–9, 177–79. *See
    also* Causal realism; Social
    kinds
Nested models, xvii, 9, 207–9
Nominalists, 240
Nuts and bolts, xvii, 13, 67, 170–73,
    178, 180

Paradigm, xiii, 133, 172–73, 215, 250.
    See also Models and foils
    rational reconstruction, 18–19
    transparadigmatic comparisons
        and incommensurability, 207–9
    wars, 7, 115–16
Path dependence, 66
Perestroika, xiii
Plausible rival hypotheses. *See* Models and foils
Pluralism. *See* Models and foils
Popper, Karl J., xvii, 134, 152, 169,
    205–9

Positivism, xvi, xvii. *See also* Covering laws
Preferences
    aggregation, 237
    falsification, 97, 237
    revealed, 237
    theory of, 41–44
Problem domain or situation, 135,
    138–39, 180
Punctuated equilibrium, 66

Rationalists, xiv–xv, 14, 29–69,
    153–56, 170
    hegemony, xiii–xv, 3–4, 170
    narrative, 211
    thin and thick, 29–32, 118–19,
        121
Realism. *See* Causal realism
Research Communities/
    Programs/ Traditions.
    See Paradigm
    thin and thick, xv, 19–23
Ricardian vice, 197

Social kinds, xvii, 109, 179–80. *See
    also* Natural kinds
Socially embedded unit act, 49–53,
    122, 128, 132
Social order, 78–79, 84–87, 118,
    120–22, 124–25, 237
Social situation rationalists.
    See Rationalists, thin
    and thick
Social theory, 9–10, 215–16
Sociologists, 215
Stories, xiv, 11–13, 172, 190–91,
    199
Strategizing, 34
Structure-action, xvi, 9, 46, 47,
    125–29
Structuralists, xv, 15, 99–112, 158–61,
    171
    thin and thick, 99–102

Theory, 170–73, 186–88. *See also*
    Laws
Toolbox. *See* Nuts and bolts
Transparadigmatic testing. *See*
    Models and foils
Typologies, xvii, 109–10, 158–61. *See*
    also Ideal types
    of theories, 23–26

Unintended consequences. *See*
    Microfoundations

Vicarious problem solving, 38

Weber, Max, xvii, 16–18, 24, 109–10,
    131, 156, 161–66, 244. *See also*
    Kant-Weber perspectivism